Successful
Telemarketing

Successful Telemarketing

The Complete Handbook on Managing a Profitable Telemarketing Call Center

Kathy Sisk

McGraw-Hill, Inc.

New York   San Francisco   Washington, D.C.   Auckland   Bogotá
Caracas   Lisbon   London   Madrid   Mexico City   Milan
Montreal   New Delhi   San Juan   Singapore
Sydney   Tokyo   Toronto

Library of Congress Cataloging-in-Publication Data

Sisk, Kathy.
    Successful telemarketing: the complete handbook on managing a
profitable telemarketing call center / Kathy Sisk.
        p.   cm.
    Includes index.
    ISBN 0-07-057704-8
    1. Telemarketing—Management—Handbooks, manuals, etc. I. Title.
HF5415.1265.S55 1995
658.8'4—dc20   94-23637
                                                              CIP

1 2 3 4 5 6 7 8 9 0 DOC/DOC 9 0 0 9 8 7 6 5

ISBN 0-07-057704-8

*The sponsoring editor for this book was Betsy N. Brown, the editing supervisor was Caroline
R. Levine, and the production supervisor was Pamela A. Pelton. This book was set in
Palatino by McGraw-Hill's Professional Book Group composition unit.*

Printed and bound by R. R. Donnelley & Sons Company.

McGraw-Hill books are available at special quantity discounts to use as premiums
and sales promotions, or for use in corporate training programs. For more information, please write to the Director of Special Sales, McGraw-Hill, Inc., 11 West 19th
Street, New York, NY 10011. Or contact your local bookstore.

 This book is printed on recycled, acid-free paper containing a
minimum of 50% recycled, de-inked fiber.

This book is dedicated to my Heavenly Father. I spent many long days and grueling late nights finishing the book, and without the inspiration of Him who gifted me, I could not have done it.

Ask, and it will be given to you; Seek, and you will find; knock, and the door will be opened to you. For everyone who asks, receives. For he who seeks, finds and to him who knocks, the door will be opened.

MATTHEW 7: 7 & 8

Contents

7. From a Human Resource Perspective   143

8. Increase TSRs' Motivation Through Your Compensation Plan   159

9. How to Attract, Interview, and Select Your Telemarketing Staff   173

10. The Manager's Template   203

Foreword

If properly setting up and managing a call center is important to you, you need to read this book. It is full of information that will put you on the road to successful call center management, whether you're in the beginning stages of setting up a call center or upgrading an existing one. This book is simple to read, it's user friendly, and the ideas are easy to apply, no matter what size call center you have or how much or how little a budget you have.

At your fingertips, you have access to advanced information on hardware and software selection, hiring and compensating, and training and managing new and existing telephone sales representatives (TSRs) and customer service representatives (CSRs).

Today, the cost of retaining a professional consultant is up into the thousands, and the cost is continuing to escalate as telemarketing progresses in the marketplace. But you can't afford the cost of making mistakes due to lack of information. Let me share with you some history that will prove this point.

Telemarketing Is Corporate America's Competitive Edge

It all began in the late '70s, when we, as future publishers of *Telemarketing*® magazine, started using the telephone to sell advertising space in one of our publications, *Radiation Curing*®. It was as if an overnight explosion in sales had occurred. Having been disenchanted with the performance of our outside sales reps, I picked up the phone and tried to sell a few pages of advertising for *Radiation Curing*. In just one hour, I was able to sell two pages of advertising, and by the end of the week, while spending no more than one hour on the telephone per day, I was able to sell nearly eight pages of advertising while also getting a great education talking with our customers. Since I knew nothing about telemarketing at the time, I made a great many mistakes—among them, putting outside sales reps on the phone; interviewing TSRs (telephone sales representatives) in person as opposed to on the phone; and being completely ignorant about the fact that product knowledge, ego drive, empathy, phone manner, and communication skills all contribute to the success of selling on the phone.

Eventually, and upon making every mistake in the book, I and my staff discovered a successful telephone selling process. Once we perfected this technique and coupled it synergistically with direct mail and trade show marketing, we were able to increase our advertising sales by a whopping 500 percent. It was a staggering accomplishment indeed, which, like many other major discoveries in the world, took place by accident; namely, being disgruntled by sales efforts of outside reps.

Since the industry was practically nonexistent in 1982 (except for three service agencies that became known to us several years later), we were able to obtain a registered trademark for the word *telemarketing* in the name of our company, Technology Marketing Corporation. And what a thrill it was. We felt we had to share the discovery of this method of selling with corporate America to prevent them from having to reinvent the wheel. Thus, in June 1982, we kicked off *Telemarketing* magazine to share what little we knew with the rest of the world.

Twelve years later, we are witnessing an industry that has grown to nearly $600 billion in annual sales, *excluding* what is sold on Wall Street. Never in our wildest dreams would we have believed that this little industry, that began to reach the forefront of acceptance in America through *Telemarketing* magazine, would reach such high esteem in the world community.

I position telemarketing as the industry that protects jobs and creates new jobs. Here's why. It has been said that nothing happens until someone sells something. To the extent that, today, telemarketing is the most powerful way to sell, it's also the most powerful way to create and protect jobs in America. Every job in America depends on what happens on Wall Street. The sale of every stock and bond on Wall Street transpires by telephone. By definition, when your broker calls you to sell a stock or bond, he or she is conducting outbound telemarketing. By the same token, when you call your broker you're performing inbound telemarketing. The bottom line is that every stock and bond in America is sold through outbound and inbound telemarketing. Considering that nearly 200 million shares change hands on Wall Street in an average day, at an average price of approximately $10 per share, $2 billion of stocks and bonds are sold per business day on Wall Street. As such, $490 billion, conservatively, of sales are generated annually on Wall Street alone. Most important, this amount of sales is protecting millions of jobs in the country. The recent worldwide recession has created a major decline in sales for all corporations, which has resulted in massive layoffs of millions of employees across America. The layoffs are occurring because the products are not selling. Hopefully, this will explain what a vital role telemarketing plays in protecting every job in America and creating additional jobs by generating far more sales.

Over the last decade, the telemarketing industry has grown by leaps and bounds because it has produced prosperity for its users. Today, telemarketing is being used in a variety of humanitarian ways. For example, we're aware that the American Red Cross uses telemarketing to generate hundreds of thousands of pints of blood annually, which subsequently save American lives. In fact, the American Red Cross has coined the phrase, "Telemarketing—A Link to Life." We understand that some of the blood generated through telemarketing was used during Operation Desert Storm to save many American lives. In another application, we understand that a telemarketing service agency generated the entire funding for the building of a church, which the church's congregation rebuilt, once again—through telemarketing. All fundraising organizations depend heavily on telemarketing. In short, practically every business has a phone and thus can benefit from the sophisticated technology and know-how that the telemarketing industry has developed over the last decade.

If you get involved in telemarketing, do it with honesty and integrity because selling by any means—telemarketing, personal visit or otherwise—depends on the elements of trust, credibility, and integrity. It is only common sense to say that no one buys anything from anyone they do not trust. Therefore, as a successful telemarketer, your number one objective should be to establish the element of trust between you and your customer.

Over the last decade, a tremendous amount of new technology has been developed that will significantly enhance your telemarketing/customer service functions. Without this technology, you will not be able to effectively compete; therefore, it is mandatory to thoroughly research products before you invest in new technology for your call center. To the extent that virtually all major technology and service providers to this industry currently exhibit at TBT, The Integrated Marketing Expo, sponsored by *Telemarketing* magazine, it is strongly suggested that you attend the TBT conference and exhibition to compare the available technologies side by side and decide which best serve your needs. In short, do not buy anything until you first inspect the technology and, most important, find out if anyone else in your industry is currently using the same technology with success.

Use the latest technology in your call center to increase productivity, but never lose sight of the fact that the human element is by far the most important ingredient and the key to your success. Telemarketing is defined as a new, powerful, profit-generating managerial tool which draws its strength from *people-to-people interactive communication*. No other form of sales, marketing, advertising, or promotion technique is as interactive as telemarketing. This explains why telemarketing's growth has been very significant and vigorous. It's important to re-emphasize that strength comes from *people-to-people interactive communication* and not from equipment-to-equipment interaction. Technology is extremely important, but human resource development and proper training are far more important.

Rapid advancements in technology, techniques, and applications over the last decade have made it necessary for an organization to gain as much information as possible before it makes the expensive commitment of setting up a telemarketing department.

Telemarketing success does not come quickly. It is achieved through hard work, dedication, and commitment. Above all, *do not get involved in telemarketing if you are not 100% committed to it. Further, do not get involved if you don't have the necessary funds to do the job right*. That is why this handbook is so vital. It provides the same information as a consultant would, but for a fraction of the cost.

Before you even think of getting involved in telemarketing, you need to thoroughly read this book and understand every aspect of it. Kathy Sisk has made a great contribution to the telemarketing industry by including in this book her self-published training programs for both inbound and outbound call centers. Since 1991, Kathy has trained hundreds of professionals with her "12-Step" method for applying inbound and outbound telemarketing, at our trade show conferences held twice a year. Kathy always gets top ratings as one of our best speakers. When attendees at the show take her course, they walk away with new ideas that are designed to meet the current market. No one has ever been disappointed with her training—they keep coming back every year for more. My congratulations to Kathy for helping us all to further streamline our industry and for her dedication to providing quality training, reliable information, and sharing her success with us all!

The best advice I can give you is this: there is no shortcut to success in telemarketing. Indeed, many have tried shortcuts—and have managed to lose millions and *fail in the end*! Don't become one of them. Remember, your best guidelines are education, honesty, integrity, know-how, and, above all—training, training, training!

Good luck, and best wishes for success!

Nadji Tehrani
Publisher & Editor in Chief
Telemarketing *magazine*

Preface

How I Got Started in the Telemarketing Industry

When I began in 1975, telemarketing was not yet an industry. This was the "boiler room" era. What exactly is a "boiler room"? Picture a smoke-filled room, with as few as three and as many, depending upon its size, as a room can contain of telephone solicitors punching the key pads of their desktop single line telephones. These solicitors are using lists from either the white pages of the local telephone book or the criss-cross (street) directory. Solicitors were pressured to dial as many phone numbers as they could each hour and present their long-winded "pitch" *without a breath* to as many people as possible. (Today, we call this pitch a *call guide* or *presentation*.) We didn't concern ourselves with "rejection"; in that day and age, we would just hang up and move on to the next number until after 50–100 repetitions, we finally would get an appointment! For incentive, there was a lot of cash doled out as appointments were made, and as long as we had the date and time, it didn't matter how many cancellations occurred. We got as many appointments as we could and something always came through! No confirmations were ever made on the appointments for fear of last minute cancellations. Instead, the telemarketer/salesperson would just show up, or call minutes prior to the scheduled time and say, "I'm on my way, what is your cross street?" You had to do something really terrible to get fired. In most cases, the only way you could lose your job was if you quit!

Telemarketing was not my chosen career way back then. I got into the telemarketing industry by *accident*. I guess most of us who consider ourselves professionals and have as many candles on their birthday cake as I do can probably testify to same reason as I—*pure accident*!

One day, when scanning through the classifieds in my local newspaper, somehow I looked under the *S* section of the classifieds and saw the job title "solicitors." What really attracted me was … "*no experience necessary, big bucks, paid weekly …* " Now that fit my profile nicely! Of course, today, this job title isn't listed in the *S* section any longer; fortunately our titles have become much more sophisticated!

When I arrived for my interview, I realized quickly that as long as you could speak English and had a way to get to work, you were just the *ideal* candidate these businesses were seeking. After my 15-minute interview, the phone room manager shook my hand and said, "I'll see you tomorrow at 4:00 p.m."

My First Day as a Telemarketer

When I arrived, my manager introduced me to the owner. (I still remember his name. Not too long ago, I called him—amazingly he is still in the same kind of business—and thanked him for hiring me way back when!) After meeting with the boss, I was handed a script and told to "go sick 'em tiger!" That's when rigor mortis set in. Yes, I stared at my lengthy script that offered no clue to the desired interaction with the prospects I was to cold call. I kept staring at it until I got cold hands, my voice was trembling, and I was ready to find a way to *escape* from this torture! My manager, sensing my terror, told me to sit next to one of the other solicitors and listen for awhile. That did not do a whole lot of good since all she was getting were hang ups, screams, and profanity.

Finally, I was *encouraged* (to say the least) to get on the telphone. I made some calls the last hour of the evening but by that time I had already made up my mind that I was not coming back. Well, after some motivating words from my manager and my co-workers, I decided to try it one more time.

The next day I came in and was determined to put my best foot forward and do my very best so when I *did* quit, I could at least say I didn't give up without trying! After an hour, the ice was broken and *I made my first appointment*. It was so invigorating and it lifted me up so high that by the time the evening was through, I had made more appointments than my manager.

How I Became a Phone Room Manager

Within three months of employment, I was promoted to manager. And after I had been a manager for six months the business, which had been in a slump, turned around and my department generated more qualified appointments than ever before. The operation was growing into a *full service center*. During that era no one could foresee the success the industry is enjoying today, and even national headquarters was thoroughly impressed and wanted to know what *I* was doing that they weren't. Just to give you an insight into why my call center was so successful—I was training my telemarketers in the concept of "relationship selling" when it wasn't even recognized. Remember, in the beginning I said the typical boiler room tactic was the "numbers game"—make a lot of calls and contacts and something would eventually stick. I'm not sure I started the new era of telemarketing single-handedly, but I was doing something new and it was working.

How I Used My Telemarketing Experience for Outside Sales

After a few months of this success I needed something more challenging, so I decided to go into outside sales for the same company where I had been working as a telemarketer.

During the first month of selling I missed salesperson of the month by one sale and after that first month, I was top salesperson for four months in a row. Then I decided to become my own recruiter and trainer. What is significant about my experience in outside sales is that today I use the same recruiting method I first developed as a salesperson for many sales organizations, and it is extremely effective. What is my method? I find ideal candidates that first do well at telemarketing; once they achieve their mark in telemarketing, I recruit them into the outside sales force if they qualify and have the interest. The salespeople I recruited and trained in this way became self-sufficient. They could prospect all their own appointments, conduct their own confirmations, reschedule whenever necessary, and were highly effective closers in the outside selling environment. My philosophy was and still is, "If you can sell over the phone (appointment setting is *selling* appointments) then selling face to face becomes *easier*.

How Did I Become a Consultant?

One day out of the clear blue sky, I decided to open a telemarketing service agency. In those days we called them *service bureaus*. I was accustomed to opening up or revamping everyone else's telemarketing operation while recruiting, training, and managing the entire process; so why shouldn't I do this on my own and sell the appointments to others. Making more money, managing my own time, and not having to worry about someone getting the credit for my ideas was very appealing.

After five years of developing a service agency working with small accounts—and by that time service agencies were sweeping the country—I was given a hot tip by someone I highly respected, a vice president of one of the largest service agencies in the country. Because of my success and my ability to train others, he suggested I go into the telemarketing consulting field. After careful research and consideration, I saw the opportunities and followed his advice.

Final Thoughts for You to Ponder

What a difference telemarketing is today compared to when I first started. My purpose in sharing an overview of my background is not just to give the validity of my experience; I also want to say that no matter what your role is in the telemarketing industry—whether you are a telemarketer, manager, supervisor, a business owner, or whatever—with this everchanging market and industry, *all* of you have and will go through many trials and tribulations. When facing certain trials, some people will call it quits and move on. For those of us who are willing to hang in there, we will find that it's much more exciting to deal with trials as "challenges" rather than feel defeated.

Keep your objectives focused, know where you want to go, and always use honest and ethical means to get you there. Whenever you encounter trials, consider them temporary "road blocks." These road blocks should not hurt or discourage you; they are there to prevent you from moving on in the wrong direction. Many times I've tried to *push* those road blocks out of my way, but the danger in doing so is that you may find yourself on the wrong path. Instead, consider those road blocks as a time to "rethink" your position. You may find there is a more effective route. When you find that your road is smooth and you are going in the right direction, then *keep on going* and you will find success.

How does *this* have anything to do with successful telemarketing? Because of my many years of active involvement in the telemarketing and sales industry and all the trials I have been through, I have been able to create and develop methods that are superior to and more successful than those currently on the market. Since 1975, I have designed and set up many telemarketing call centers and trained thousands of professionals. My consulting business provides me with the unique opportunity to see firsthand numerous telemarketing departments and how they are designed and operated. The majority of the departments I've seen have been frozen in time, using outdated concepts and training methods—some with a 20 percent closing ratio which is no longer considered highly productive. A 34 percent cancellation is standard and even a 50 percent telephone sales representative (TSR) turnover factor is considered average and acceptable in these outmoded departments.

I'm very confident this book is the most up-to-date, advanced, thorough training concept and reference guide in the field of telemarketing and customer servicing. I'm not saying that once you've read the ideas in this book your call center will be magically free from TSR turnover, fear of rejection, a poor closing ratio, inconsistency in production, and so forth. Instead, if you have a sincere dedication and a strong determination you *will* be more successful with the ideas and skills provided in this book than if you did not have them at all.

This book has been written with sincerity from the heart to *ensure* you have the most advanced information available in *one resource*. Whatever your current level in your call center, this book is designed to give you proven ideas that *will* work. You will be more motivated to follow ideas that will further professionalize the telemarketing industry, so that together we can continue to make this an industry we all can be proud of. Finally, this is a book that will help you grow and advance your knowledge to higher levels while assisting you in your career path.

Each of us has been given special gifts, and it is up to us to use those gifts in such a way that will benefit not only ourselves but others as well. This is my path in life, to share my God-given gifts with you and help *you* to be more successful. One of my favorite mentors says, "If you first help enough people get what they want, you will get what you want." When I started running my business and treating others with this attitude, I found my true success! *Your* success is important to me and I want to assist you.

Acknowledgments

Thanks to my office staff, who worked hard to cover for me while I was writing this book. You're the most loyal and dedicated staff anyone could ever ask for; you're terrific!

My love and appreciation to my children, Alaine, Sean, and Katie who tried very hard to give me the space I needed to dedicate precious time ordinarily spent with them to write this book.

Last but not least, to my supportive husband Len, who played Mr. Mom with dinner, laundry, and taxiing the kids. Also, I really appreciate him for filling in the gaps and working many long hours into the night to ensure that business doors remained opened.

A special thanks and appreciation to those who contributed their time to share their knowledge and expertise. Without your help this book would not be complete.

Allan Adler, Attorney, Cohen and Marks, 1333 New Hampshire Ave., N.W. Washington, DC 20036-1573

Patrick Lusey, CEO, UPTRENDS Management Software, Inc., 10555 Old Placerville Rd. Sacramento, CA 95827-2503

Melodye DeWine, President, Abstract Records Services, Inc., 20450 Walnut Drive, Walnut, CA 91789

Jeff Multz, President, Emerging Market Technologies, Inc., 1230 Johnson Ferry Rd. Suite D-10 Marietta, GA 30068

Ted Schwartz, President, APAC Teleservices, 1419 Lake Cook Road, Deerfield, IL 60015

Robert Swedo, President, Netcom International, Inc., 741 Boston Post Rd., Guilford, CT 06437

Telemarketing® magazine, published by Technology Marketing Corporation, One Technology Plaza, Norwalk, CT 06854

Steven Walker, President, Walker Direct Marketing L.P., 3535 E. 96th Street Suite 122, Indianapolis, IN 4 6240

Kathy Sisk

1

Introduction

What Telemarketing Has Done for America—the Untold Story*

Telemarketing is an industry very much alive and buzzing with innovations and improvements. Consider the technological advancements, the dynamic improvements in operator training, and the increased emphasis on quality control. These are just the tip of the growing economic success story being written. But imagine, for a moment, what it would be like if writing this story suddenly stopped. Picture these headlines in your morning paper:

- Four Million Jobs Cut
- Tens of Billions in Corporate Profits Slashed
- Millions of Computers Turned Off
- Hundreds of Products and Services Removed from the Market

How would those announcements grab you? I can tell you how they would grab the U.S. economy—right around the throat!

These not-so-impossible headlines have nothing to do with the auto industry, with unfair trading practices, or with anything else the U.S. public has been reading about lately. The headlines have to do with something the U.S. public probably *has not* been reading about. The headlines have to do with the fact that telemarketing in the United States has become a powerful force for economic good; without it, the entire country would be crippled by jobs lost, profits cut, and products and services wiped out.

The telemarketing industry is often regarded in a negative light due to disturbing experiences with poor telemarketers. Ask any telemarketing professionals what type of response is generated when they are asked about their

*The following was presented on June 10, 1992, at the Telemarketing and Business Telecommunications (TBT) conference held in Rosemont, Illinois, by Ted Schwartz, president and CEO of APAC TeleServices.

1

profession. Inevitably, people will relate negative experiences they have had in regards to telemarketing.

Today's savvy telemarketer can deflect these negative feelings by relating the facts and growing number of success stories within the telemarketing industry. As a result, the conversation will end on a positive note and with enthusiastic converts! Why? Because telemarketing is good business when done right and because most of the negative experiences were old and isolated cases. If asked about more recent experiences, those same people will agree that there has been—let's call it—a "purification process" at work. *Market forces are driving out poor performer and unethical practices, while market successes are raising the overall standards.*

Some of the Facts

Ten years ago there were 50 service agencies in America. Today there are over 900, and 60 percent of them employ 50 or more professionals.

Only a decade ago there were approximately ½ million people employed in telemarketing. Today there are almost 4-½ million, and industry experts predict as many as 8 million by the end of this decade. The number of people employed in telemarketing today equals the *entire* population of the state of Minnesota. When you factor in the families of those employed in the telemarketing industry, you can imagine a political force of 12 million potential voters! That should be music to the ears of our politicians, especially in an election year.

Even more significant is the dramatic change in the number of businesses that have integrated telemarketing as a vital element of their marketing mix. In the early 1980s there were fewer than 80,000 telemarketing operations in the United States. In only five years that number nearly tripled, and today there are over 565,000. What other industry can claim this kind of growth?

What about expenditures? U.S. business spends between $80 and $90 billion per year on the telephone for marketing, sales, and service. This represents a *400 percent* increase in the last 15 years. It truly is amazing when you consider the fact that long-distance communication costs, which are a key component of expenditures, have actually dropped 65 percent during that time. Impressive numbers? You bet.

Also consider the business-to-business sector. With the average business-to-business field sales call costing over $300, it's no wonder thousands of corporations that market to businesses are turning to telemarketing, where the average cost per contact is only about $7.

Telemarketing has become a major tool for financial service companies launching new credit cards and services; technology corporations selling and servicing their products; automotive manufacturers ensuring satisfaction; insurance companies cross-selling additional services and upgrades; and telephone companies selling custom calling features.

When you add up the enormous scope and depth of U.S. telemarketing, you can see what a travesty and tragedy it would be if local businesses suddenly were forced to check with Washington, D.C., every time they hoped to implement a new campaign. Along those lines, the FCC should be commended for its insightful analysis and careful study of the issues at hand.

Statistics like these should help remind us that telemarketing is a potent economic force in our national economy. Yet what percentage of the population is aware of this? Associations and friends, including the Direct Marketing Association (DMA), American Telemarketing Association (ATA), and The Alliance Against Fraud in Telemarketing, to mention a few, have been strong advocates of the telemarketing industry and have helped to educate the public on the intensive economic role this industry plays.

Telemarketing and the U.S. Economy

As you are well aware, statistics for statistic's sake don't mean a great deal. But statistics for the economy's sake cannot be ignored. And *that,* you see, is the "untold story" that needs to be told—told more effectively, more convincingly, and more often. Defining the telemarketing industry, in purely economic terms, is a monumental task.

First, the telemarketing industry consistently creates jobs; over 4 million today and double that number by the year 2000 according to *US News and World Report.* In today's tough economic times an industry creating this incredible number of jobs should be considered a national example.

Next, telemarketing helps train the U.S. work force. Telemarketing provides great entry level positions to prepare future managers and leaders due to the development of confidence and the training they receive in communication and computer skills that are so essential to compete in today's growing service sector economy.

Third, telemarketing is a large consumer of goods and services, including a capital expenditure of over $10 billion in computer equipment alone.

The socioeconomic ripple effect on the communities where telemarketing employs a local work force is often overlooked when considering the impact that the telemarketing industry has on the economy. The economic impact multiplier states that for every dollar spent on payroll, $3 is spent in the local economy. Imagine 4 million telemarketers working an average of 30 hours per week. That spending extrapolates to $152 billion per year pumped into local economies through telemarketing wages alone.

Telemarketing gives the U.S. economy a welcome competitive edge in today's global marketplace as it is a uniquely U.S. industry, using a uniquely U.S. invention, the telephone, to help energize the U.S. economy at a time when it really needs it.

In addition, telemarketing is projected to play an important role in marketing U.S. products and services globally, including such new markets as the European Common Market. A weapon like this in the national arsenal must be treasured and protected.

The final, and perhaps most striking statistic, is that the telemarketing industry is now generating over $280 billion in goods and services sold

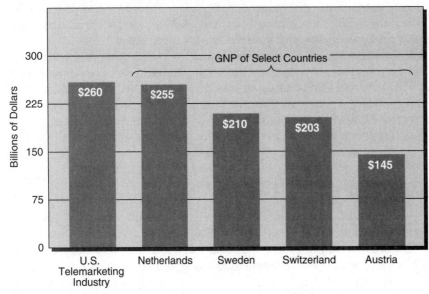

Figure 1-1. Goods and services sold.

according to a study by AT&T. That figure constitutes more than the entire GNP of Sweden, Austria, or the Netherlands. There are only 12 countries in the world with a greater total GNP than the dollar amount generated by telemarketing alone in this country. *Doesn't that make telemarketing an industry worth valuing?*

The numbers in Fig. 1-1 capture the incredible strength of the untold story. Not only do they depict a growing industry, but they also emphasize the growing role that telemarketing plays in the U.S. economy of the 1990s. It's an industry which serves every application from sales to customer care. Today even members of Congress are utilizing telemarketing for surveying and influencing their constituencies.

Are you aware of and do you understand this economic role? Your answer may be yes, but do you help to heighten awareness of that role? There is no better time or more crucial opportunity to tell the untold story than right now! Fortunately there are countless success stories to help make these points.

Telemarketing Past and Present

The very first of these success stories probably goes back more than 100 years to New York City where the original Bell Telephone Company, created by Alexander Graham Bell, connected some of the city's brokers to their customers. This network of instant communication helped launch a revolution in marketing.

This revolution exploded in the 1970s. There may have been some early mistakes made, and misuses of this powerful medium are not unknown. However, history records that mistakes have been made with almost everything—from the first pyramids to the first insurance policies. But mistakes are to be corrected not just regretted, and the telemarketing industry has worked to correct the mistakes made in the past.

Telemarketing today has become a sophisticated medium employed by major multinational corporations such as: AT&T, American Express, GE, and the list goes on. In addition, the 800 number has become a vital communications link for U.S. business.

Try to find a product on your supermarket shelves without an 800 number on the label. Appliances, cars, and investments all have 800 numbers today. It would be difficult to find a *Fortune* 500 company without a toll-free number, and finding one that hasn't implemented an inbound or outbound telemarketing program as part of its marketing mix may be even more difficult.

Roles and Challenges

Telemarketing plays a major role in contributing to a social networking of the world. That may sound a little esoteric, but in an age of increased mechanization and impersonalization, the telephone connects the world by linking the global economy and serving the isolated, physically disabled, and the burgeoning aging population—and that's good, because it provides us a bridge with which to reach one another.

Today is a time for those who know and understand the telemarketing industry (and the impact that it makes on the U.S. economy) to participate in an effort to educate the public. For instance, telemarketing professionals can take part in raising the standards of the industry through the use of better-qualified databases, better-trained personnel, and better-thought-out campaigns.

Those in telemarketing also have a role in helping people understand just how valuable the telemarketing industry is to U.S. business and, yes, to the United States itself. That's not bravado—that's fact! Unfortunately it's been an untold story for far too long, and there is no time to waste in telling it. Make a commitment to relate this untold story every chance you get—at the health club, on the golf course, at a social gathering, and, especially, in your office, whenever you can find an opening.

Local bureaucracies and state and federal legislators should not dictate to those in telemarketing how business should be done, as it is becoming increasingly apparent that today's telemarketers have a clear understanding of what needs to be done.

Recall, if you will, our inalienable right as Americans which pertains to the first amendment and the fact that our industry is protected by that freedom. The future is a time when that right will continue to be tested. Occasional unprofessional behavior in this industry is no more reason to limit telemarketing than some bad editorials should limit a free press! Americans have always believed in a free marketplace—for both goods and ideas. That means that almost anyone has the right to be out there, and market forces, not the government, should decide who will stay and who will desist. The questionable tele-marketers of the past are disappearing because they simply do not have what it takes to survive.

Telemarketing also has an important role in winning over the competition in today's increasingly tough global economy. By offering our expertise in telemarketing, the United States has an additional exportable service as well as a clear-cut edge over every nation on Earth. This advantage pumps added vitality into our economy. Not only do the telemarketers benefit but so does U.S. business and, therefore, the United States itself.

One last role for those in the telemarketing industry is unlike the roles previously mentioned. This particular role has to do with the face that you see in the mirror each morning—the inner you—where your deepest values and convictions lie. The image of the telemarketing industry needs to be transformed and upraised. Much has been done, but the highest standards must be maintained. Accept this challenge: Don't fail that inner you! Believe in your highest standards and then go out there and make them happen—in whatever you do.

Consider these roles and challenges. Expand on them and act upon them with pride in the telemarketing industry—an industry generating more than 4 million jobs, pumping more than $152 billion per year into local economies, selling over $280 billion per year in goods and services. But operate on a short time line. The forces that would undermine this industry are working fast. We need to work faster. Our listeners need to be reminded that when all things are taken into consideration this industry is an *incredible force for good*.

Yes, there is an untold story to tell, but be my guest, and start telling it—now!

What Is This Book About?

The presentation, "What Telemarketing Has Done for America" above, is the best example of why this book is so vital both for those who are just in the beginning stages of setting up a call center and for those who want to update and enhance their existing telemarketing efforts. You've learned that the telemarketing industry is one of the fastest growing industries in the market today. It is predicted that telemarketing will be the number one industry in the world by the year 2000. Legislators are cracking down and toughening the rules regarding telemarketing to control telemarketers who don't really care about the direction the industry is heading. However, those who do care and who have a vested interest in the industry's growth need to take aggressive measures to make a change that will have a positive impact on the industry's future reputation. These measures begin when you set up and run your center.

This book is written precisely for today's telemarketing and customer servicing and will be a viable handbook at least for the next decade. Professionals are desperately searching for ways to improve this industry's image and to conduct quality prospecting and customer servicing. This book enables you to achieve these goals faster and more cost effectively.

Successful telemarketing is an opportunity for telemarketers, managers, supervisors, trainers, and business owners to learn everything they need to know prior to implementation of their telemarketing operations call center. The information contained in this book removes the guesswork pertaining to setting up and designing a telemarketing call center. The book offers a range of information that addresses various topics regarding inbound and outbound applications, including hardware and software selection, prospecting lists, constructing and placing recruitment ads to attract the "true telemarketing professional," and cost-effective compensation plans that will motivate and encourage increased production.

The chapters regarding the 12 steps to successful telemarketing and associated scripts teach you exactly what to say, how to say it, and when to say it each second of a telemarketer's telephone presentation. When the "12-step" concepts are used, scripts are easily created and customized without having to spend hours and even days to test them. It's not unusual for professional script writers to take hours writing their first drafts and then days, even weeks, of testing and redefining a script until they have what they believe will work to its fullest potential. The 12-step procedure for outbound telemarketing has eliminated that guesswork completely. The "roll-out" time factor is quicker, and the telemarketer is more successful in the early stages of the marketing campaign, thereby experiencing results in a shorter period.

When it comes to hiring a telemarketer, many companies feel all they have to do is find someone who is willing to pick up the telephone and talk. Some of the largest companies in Corporate America just place a script in front of the telemarketer and expect them to be productive without any training, even without product training! While others may provide training, they have no real method of hiring the right individual best suited for the telemarketing position. This is why many companies experience a turnover rate of at least 50 percent within the first few months of hiring the telemarketer. That turnover rate is costly to any company's bottom line!

You will learn customer service etiquette, featuring 12 steps to successful customer service. The information provides ideas to enable companies to retain their existing customer base and set themselves apart from their competition by providing "extra" customer service. The book's focus on etiquette creates an awareness of professional language by listing negative words and phrases, used by customer service representatives, that irritate your customers. Positive influence words, phrases that encourage interaction and that create an interest, are offered as alternatives.

What Sets This Book Apart

Most books on telemarketing offer ideas, but they don't offer a step-by-step approach. Others only provide bite-size pieces. Therefore, in order to make one's telemarketing efforts more successful, several books are required to grasp the whole picture of what needs to be done. This complete handbook teaches you how to get started and offers ideas of how you can project the cost factors. You are given information regarding legal issues to examine prior to and while you are running your operation. In addition, the book provides a step-by-step implementation and maintenance procedure for an ongoing profitable call center. Whether you are setting up a new call center or improving the one you already have, solutions that are well-developed and proven are provided to take the guesswork out and help you to simplify the process.

2
Telemarketing Industry Overview

Telemarketing Overview

The information and statistics provided in this chapter will reinforce what those who are actively involved in the telemarketing industry already know—telemarketing will be around for decades to come. This chapter addresses not only some of the legal issues of telemarketing both at federal and state levels but also the public's perception of telemarketing and the misconceptions consumers have about this explosive industry. For those who are unsure about the industry, the information will reinforce that telemarketing, whether it be inbound or outbound, is a profitable marketing solution in any economy. You will learn the advantages and disadvantages of the following: direct sales compared to telemarketing, direct marketing with or without telemarketing, the toll-free industry, and its phenomenal breakthroughs. Finally, for those who are not using telemarketing as a marketing media—this chapter shows how you can get started. This chapter will lay the foundation necessary for anyone involved or uninvolved in telemarketing. The chapter also provides a clear understanding of the industry, making it easier to set up a telemarketing center or enhance one's current telemarketing efforts.

What Is Telemarketing?

Telemarketing is a fairly low-cost yet highly efficient method of conducting business. Applied properly, telemarketing increases sales, establishes new markets, and offers greater efficiency to businesses (i.e., reorders and customer service departments). Telemarketing can produce quality advertisement, professionally presenting company image and can be more cost-effective than radio, television, magazines, and other media advertisements. Simply stated, telemarketing is using the telephone as a *professional marketing tool.*

As a child, I remember my grandmother telling me that she had conducted telemarketing in the early 1900s for a local radio station. In that era, telemarketing was not the industry it is today. The latest figures, according to a study conducted by AT&T, is that telemarketing now generates over $280 billion in goods and services, and experts predict that over 8 million people will be employed as professional telemarketers by the year 2000. Telemarketing is making its way as the fastest growing industry in the world!

Today, thousands of companies use telemarketing to market their products and services: it's more cost-effective than an outside sales call. Most companies can effectively sell any product over the telephone providing they have all the tools necessary to help with the selling process. With our advanced telecommunications technology, computers, peripherals, databases of information, and highly skilled professionals, it's no wonder that the outside salesperson may feel slightly threatened by telemarketing.

The Marketplace

In the early 1980s, many companies implemented inbound and outbound services and quickly uprooted every market. The investment required to enter the market was minimal. The implementation of inhouse telemarketing on a corporate level was a major improvement over boiler-room type operations. During that time, phone costs skyrocketed, and the demand for sophisticating telemarketing services increased, forcing companies to close down their operations, since it was no longer cost-effective to keep up with the demands of quality in order to compete and satisfy their client base. In addition, many companies were not in a position to spend more money on the sophistication of their operations, such as computer hardware, software, autodialers, and so forth.

Today, telemarketing is no longer inexpensive. Sophisticated phone systems, monitoring devices, advanced training computers, full automation, and higher telemarketer and customer service representative salaries have tremendously added to the investment required to develop a competitive and successful telemarketing program. Just about everyone is trying to capitalize on the telemarketing industry boom!

Telemarketing in today's competitive environment has led to a high level of sophistication and marketing efficiency. Only a few years ago, inbound telemarketing consisted of inquiries, taking orders, and providing dealer location services. Advanced technology consists of highly automated systems capable of delivering marketing information and consulting, selling products, and providing technical information and training that can give product information, benefits, and support. Inbound telemarketing is becoming an increasingly flexible marketing tool that delivers strong bottom-line results. Many companies today who conduct outbound telemarketing have highly trained and motivated staffs who are able to market almost any type of product regardless of its complexity or price.

In today's marketplace, many companies who have incorporated telemarketing are part of an overall marketing mix. These companies see the value of radio advertisement and other media advertisements working in conjunction with telemarketing as a form of advertising for their company. Whether it is promoting a product, targeting new markets, cross-selling existing clients, or following-up on a mail piece, telemarketing has led to a global increase in responsiveness.

Who Needs Telemarketing?

Every company needs telemarketing, whether it is in direct sales, is an entrepreneurship, a small business just starting out, or a large *Fortune* 500 corporation. Direct sales people, entrepreneurs, and small businesses need *immediate exposure*—what better way (direct and faster) to advertise and offer more of a personal approach for your products or services! For example, when contacting business-to-business applications, a telemarketer can reach an average of 5 to 15 contacts each hour, depending on the type of business to be called and the time of day. In direct sales calls, how many businesses can one reach sending an outside salesperson on a "cold call"? In residential applications, a telemarketer can reach an average of 20 to 30 consumers each hour compared to an outside sales representative who can effectively reach a fraction of that number in an hour. Don't forget, come rain or shine, with telemarketing your business doesn't have to slow down.

To illustrate this further, recently we all heard about the earthquake Los Angeles experienced at 4:30 a.m. on a Monday morning. I was there (I had a two-hour training seminar that I was conducting) in a deep sleep, and all of a sudden—wake up call!! Earthquakes must follow me around, I was in San Francisco during the one in which part of the Oakland Bay bridge collapsed. Unfortunately, these earthquakes were devastating; many people were left without homes and lost their loved ones, and businesses had to close down. However, many companies used telemarketing as a means to stay in business. Their employees conducted their business activities at home using the telephone to stay in touch with their existing clients and so forth—today, we call these "home-based" businesses. Because of this experience, more companies are realizing that telemarketing is a profitable way to do business. It's just too bad that a tragedy had to occur for companies to get a taste of using the telephone as a major marketing media.

Another benefit that telemarketing can be used for is in conjunction with advertising, direct mail, catalogue sales, direct selling, and many more communication modes. When telemarketing is properly implemented, it enables telemarketing sales representatives (TSRs) to effectively communicate with their prospects, to maintain their company's exposure with their clientele, and to reach business opportunities beyond their borders. Telemarketers increase sales for a company without ever having to leave the office, or the home.

Other Ways You Can Benefit by Telemarketing

Telemarketing eliminates costly sales calls by keeping repeat visits to a minimum. Depending upon the product and where one is traveling, a company can spend an average of $300 or more for each outside sales call. These figures are progressively increasing. Because of this, the affordability of an outside sales call is affecting current corporate profits. Combining the direct sales, the professional outbound telemarketing approach, and the inbound customer service center increases company productivity so that sales overhead decreases and profits improve. A company that implements a quality inbound and outbound telemarketing operation in conjunction with a direct sales department, fulfillment center, and other media advertisements will have all the marketing tools necessary to capture today's marketplace!

Types of Companies That Have Benefited by Telemarketing

Many companies have seen the cost-effectiveness of telemarketing. Statistics prove that telemarketing is very efficient. For example, a particular company that markets technology products and services increased its advertising revenue for several of its high-technology publications by more than 500 percent and their subscription revenues by 100 percent in just six months without having to add new employees. This extraordinary increase in sales was achieved during the most recessed economic conditions and in a period when other publications reported losses in their advertising revenue.

One of the top five life insurance companies in the world, prior to an effective telemarketing training program provided to its agents, was generating an average of one appointment out of every 30 to 50 residential contacts prospecting from a preferred list. Once telemarketing training was implemented, each agent had an opportunity to follow the skills and use the tools provided along with effective scripts. When using the same type of lists, agents averaged one appointment out of every 3 to 10 contacts. This increase of appointments per contact ratio is phenomenal when one considers that the insurance industry is unquestionably more difficult to prospect by telemarketing because of high competition in the market and heavy consumer prospecting.

Studies have shown that consumers who shop by mail are likely to become shoppers by phone. This will result in the continued growth of the inbound telemarketing industry. Approximately 60 percent of the respondents from a survey who shop by mail and not by telephone said they would use the 800-number service if given the opportunity. This response definitely validates the belief that—if given the opportunity—consumers would rather shop by phone than by mail. This should encourage many companies to offer their potential customers an 800-number service—this will increase their business.

Through aggressive inbound and outbound telemarketing programs, hoteliers are using telemarketing to increase their occupancy rate, especially during traditionally slow periods, thereby improving their bottom lines in the process. Nationwide reservation centers run by lodging companies often utilize telemarketing primarily for special promotions or as a way to advertise. The objective for the hotels is to set themselves apart from their competitors. The desire for distinction from other hoteliers has increased the growth of telemarketing within the hotel and lodging industry with the increase of sophisticated computerized automated systems and network services.

The Sheraton Corporation became one of the first companies to implement the 800-number service as an effective way of doing business. Today, every large hotel and lodging chain offers an 800 number as a convenient and economical way for customers to do business. Hoteliers are increasing the sophistication of their 800-number services with menus of departments or services when customers reach the reservations center. These systems are also providing minute-by-minute reports by tracking inbound performance and its effectiveness.

Telemarketing Acceptance and Future Growth Expectations

Telemarketing has rapidly expanded to a $90 billion industry. Opportunities for the professional telemarketer are virtually unlimited. With proper training, telemarketing can help companies maintain a leading edge in a competitive and technologically complex marketplace. The telemarketing industry is destined for explosive growth in the remainder of the twentieth century, and U.S. business has clearly recognized that the current competitive climate, increasing sales costs, and urgent need for higher return on sales expenditures all make telemarketing cost-effective. Indeed, employment in telemarketing is increasing faster than in any other area of business; by the year 2000, telemarketing will be one of the country's largest industries.

During the early 1980s, telemarketing operations in many medium and large businesses were considered experimental. Most of the attention paid to telemarketing originated from management to the outside sales force. Today, telemarketing is used at the corporate level. Companies have sent top management to receive professional telemarketing training outside the company. More than ever before, decisions are made daily, in all types of industries, to introduce telemarketing as a major marketing strategy. The increased use of this marketing strategy is the most significant change in the telemarketing industry today and the greatest contributor for continued growth for the future.

Public Perception of Telemarketing

As those who are involved in telemarketing understand, telemarketing in most applications is a very effective, productive, and vital tool for selling products and services. According to the American Telemarketing Association (ATA), the telemarketing industry spends more than $60 billion annually on telephone marketing. Billions more are spent on equipment, furniture, hardware, software, and the support services necessary to operate efficiently in this industry. As the telemarketing industry improves its telemarketing techniques, consumers will receive even greater benefits. Companies that use telemarketing are able to reduce their marketing cost. Cost reduction enables companies to meet the consumer's individual needs by lowering prices and customizing products and services.

However, due to the explosive growth in telemarketing (including unprofessional and fraudulent telemarketing operations) legislation is cracking down hard on the industry to protect individuals from culprits who are taking advantage of the industry and consumer. Unfortunately, this causes more suffering for those who are legitimate. If the politicians keep pushing issues that don't distinguish and protect the legitimate telemarketing operations from the fraudulent ones, regulation could cause an upheaval in our industry that would damage not only those businesses conducting legitimate activity but the consumer as well. Later, in this chapter, you will have a greater understanding of what the legal issues are. The understanding will help you take the appropriate steps to ensure that you are in compliance and that you are better prepared when changes do take place.

Much has been said regarding the positive aspects of telemarketing. There is no doubt about it, telemarketing works! However, there is another side to this industry, the perceptions of consumers and how they view telemarketing. What are their misconceptions? If telemarketing disappeared as a result of consumer demand for tougher regulations, how would that affect our economy? Moreover, how would that affect the consumer?! For now, let's look at how consumers feel about telemarketing.

What is the consumer's perception of the telemarketing industry? Is it as negative as we think it is? Do consumers really differentiate between the legitimate and the fraudulent telemarketers? How can consumers really identify who they are?

In 1990 an independent research company, Walker Direct Marketing L.P. from Indianapolis, looked at consumer attitudes. (Walker Direct specializes in telephone and database marketing programs for fundraising and business-to-business applications.) Walker Direct donated research that was featured in *Telemarketing* magazine's March 1991 issue (*Telemarketing* magazine is published by Technology Marketing Corporation, Norwalk, CT). Since then, new findings were determined in 1992 that updated the research, again funded and donated by Walker Direct. Steve Walker, CEO, spearheaded both research projects to determine how consumers feel about this profitable and productive industry and, based on their responses, where this industry is going as it stands today. The research enables those involved in the telemarketing industry to determine what changes should take place to address today's consumer issues to ensure a long-term healthy relationship with the consumer market of tomorrow.

Walker Direct's research results show some positive findings and some areas where telemarketing needs to improve the industry's image in the eyes of the consumer. The message that the research clearly brings to those involved in this industry is to *listen to the public*, to be *sensitive to consumer needs*, and to *take necessary steps to address these needs* in a positive and proactive manner. Access to the public is the telemarketing industry's only nonrenewable resource. Telemarketers should consider carefully what people are saying about the industry and should design strategies to position this industry favorably for the future.

The objectives of the research were to:

Measure and quantify the volume, participation, and refusal levels of telemarketing calls

Determine consumers' attitudes toward and acceptance of telemarketing

Determine how consumers evaluate the telemarketing process

Measure the impact of consumer telephone answering machine technology

Evaluate the acceptability and appropriateness of different telemarketing applications

The uses of the survey were to:

Defend the value of the industry by keeping public opinion in perspective

Analyze the gaps between public perception and industry reality, and design strategies and tactics to better educate the public

Suggest ways in which we can change techniques to implement programs that positively impact the public's perception

Take proactive positions on issues of importance such as legislative and regulatory issues

Twelve specific conclusions were drawn from the 1992 survey findings, which were compared with the 1990 survey to show whether there have been improvements made or changes within the telemarketing industry according to the consumer's perspective. These conclusions are presented along with data to support each conclusion:

1. *Consumer telemarketing is a massive industry that is growing fast and reaching a very high percentage of the U.S. public.*   Nine in 10 U.S. households (90 percent) reported that they have received a telemarketing call at some time. This is up from 82 percent in 1990. More than 8 in 10 (85 percent) reported receiving a telemarketing call in the last year. This is up from 70 percent in 1990. Thus roughly 118 million Americans are receiving more than 3 billion telemarketing calls each year.

2. *The efficiency of consumer telemarketing as an advertising medium and sales channel has held steady over the past two years.*   Based on the 1990 survey, virtually no change is observed regarding how consumers report the result of the last telemarketing call they received. Six percent of the sample reported that their call resulted in a completed transaction over the telephone such as a sale, an appointment, a donation. An additional one-third of all calls (32 percent) are taken to

completion of the presentation. Combining the above two findings indicates that, on average, telemarketing will generate 38 percent awareness and recall in a single exposure. These figures, reported by consumers themselves, demonstrate the efficiency and productivity of using the telephone to convey a product or service message. They also illustrate the accountability of telemarketing. Few direct-mail campaigns generate a 6 percent response rate, and, due to the inundation of direct mail and other advertisements, it's difficult to believe that 32 percent of direct mail and any other forms of similar advertisement is comprehended by the reader. Therefore, it is valid to conclude that few advertisements are generating a 32 percent awareness in a single exposure. Add to these impressive statistics the fact that only through telemarketing can you obtain selling advantages such as immediate feedback from the consumer and the ability to change the message during the call.

3. *Public opinion of telemarketing calls is* not *always perceived as unpleasant.* Results from the survey showed that more people characterized their last telemarketing call as "pleasant" rather than "unpleasant." Less than half (42 percent) of all telemarketing calls received are viewed as unpleasant. This percentage is exactly the same as observed in 1990. The degree to which calls are perceived as "pleasant" has dropped slightly from the past two years from 44 to 39 percent, and 19 percent responded that the call was neither pleasant nor unpleasant or the person didn't know. The 1990 research indicated that the leading causes of an unpleasant experience were:

√ Unprofessional/poorly trained TSRs
√ Computer-generated messages
√ Inconvenient timing
√ Poorly targeted or no perceived need for the presented product or service

Based on these responses, a follow-up question was asked to determine the fourth conclusion.

4. *The image of consumer telemarketing calls has declined slightly in the past two years. This is due to the frequency of unfavorable reports the industry has received.* Nine in 10 (90 percent) view telemarketing as just another way to sell. This is up slightly over the 1990 survey which indicated 80 percent. Four in 10 (40 percent) see telemarketing as serving a useful purpose. This measure is basically flat from two years earlier at 41 percent. Three other attitude measures show decreasing agreement from 1990 to 1992: In 1990, 57 percent said telemarketing is an opportunity to provide feedback compared to 47 percent in 1992. In 1990, 40 percent stated telemarketing helps produce better products and services, and in 1992 that number decreased to 43 percent. Finally, in 1990, 18 percent said that telemarketing is a good way to buy things compared to 13 percent in 1992. Two other conclusions came about regarding the consumer's perspective concerning "invasion of privacy" and telemarketing being "misleading": Respondents agreed that telemarketing was an "invasion of privacy"—this agreement held steady at 70 percent in 1990 and 1992. The 1992 survey indicates a 10 percent increase (to 61 percent) in the number of consumers who believe telemarketing calls can be "misleading."

Two new image statements were introduced in 1992 that were not used in the 1990 survey to assess the degree to which consumers understand why telemarketing is a growing industry. It concluded that the respondents did not appear to recognize that telemarketing is popular because it is efficient from a marketing standpoint. The first new question added asked: "Do you agree or disagree that telemarketing is a more efficient method of selling where savings are passed on to consumers?" Out of 200 total respondents, 73 percent disagreed, 17 percent agreed, and 11 percent didn't know or were not sure. The second question asked was: "Do you agree or disagree that telemarketing calls should be regulated by the government?" Out of 200 total respondents, 49 percent agree, 39 percent disagree, and 12 percent didn't know or were not sure.

5. *The extent to which a consumer telemarketing call is accepted by a household has much to do with the purpose of the call.* Figure 2-1 highlights the broad range of "acceptability" of different types of telemarketing calls. Acceptability of a specific call application ranges from a high of four in five people (79 percent) to a low of one in four (26 percent). A customer service call, described as a follow-up on a product or service purchased, was considered the most acceptable form of telemarketing call at 79 percent. This was followed closely by constituency-based fund-raising calls (schools, 69 percent; hospitals, 53 percent; religious organizations, 51 percent). Business-to-consumer applications where an existing relationship was not clearly established were near the bottom of the scale (household

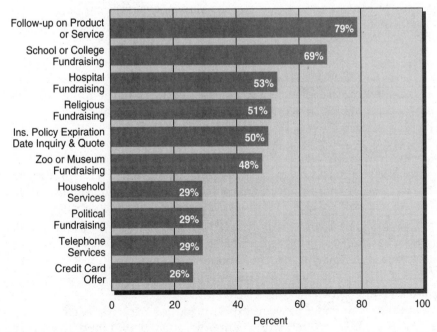

Figure 2-1. Acceptability of the types of telemarketing calls.

services and telephone services, 29 percent; credit cards, 26 percent). Political fund raising was also rated at the low end of the scale at 29 percent acceptable.

As an interesting aside, the pending legislation to regulate telemarketing tends to exempt charitable fund raising, which has *high acceptability* with consumers, and political fund raising, which has *low acceptability* with consumers.

6. *Inbound consumer telemarketing has emerged as a large industry.* Nearly two-thirds of U.S. households (64 percent) have called a toll-free number to buy something or inquire about buying something. Over half (52 percent) have done so in the past year.

7. *The overall image of inbound telemarketing is extremely positive.* This relates to the fact that consumers initiate the contacts at their convenience. The great majority (93 percent) of inbound telemarketing calls are perceived as "pleasant" by consumers. Six percent had an "unpleasant" experience, and 1 percent didn't know.

8. *Respondents acknowledge that sometimes they represent the other side of the telemarketing equation.* They report that their employers, as well as organizations they support, use telemarketing. Nearly one in three (32 percent) respondents employed outside the home reported that their place of employment used some form of telemarketing; 64 percent stated their place of employment was not using any form of telemarketing. The majority of that 32 percent of respondents reported that the type of calling was business-to-business. However, when business-to-consumer was reported as well, these figures were only 4 percent for both business and consumer calling, 3 percent for consumer calling only, and 4 percent were not sure. Of the respondents who do volunteer work for charitable work organizations, 13 percent were aware that telemarketing was being used, 6 percent did not know, and a whopping 80 percent said they were not aware if telemarketing was being used.

9. *The acceptability of telemarketing calls increases with circumstances and perspective.* It appears that telemarketing is more acceptable when one is the seller and when business-to-business telemarketing is the application. The following figures show the acceptability of two other applications of telemarketing. More than four in five (85 percent) of those whose employers use telemarketing find the use in their organization acceptable. Most of these respondents were referring to business-to-business applications. More than half (53 percent) believe it is acceptable for a company to contact them if they originally inquired about a product or service but did not buy during the initial contact. Both these applications would fall into the top one-third of all applications measured for acceptability.

10. *The data suggest that respondents' ages and experiences have an impact on the attitudes they formulate about the telemarketing industry.* Figure 2-2 shows how the age of a respondent affects the image statements. Young people tend to be more favorable.

Figure 2-3 shows how the last telemarketing experience impacts image. A positive experience will improve the consumer's attitude.

Note that those who had a pleasant experience during the last telemarketing call were twice as likely to listen to the entire presentation and more than three times likely to buy.

11. *Consumer telemarketing calls represent a small percentage of the total phone traffic into the average household.* Approximately 200 households surveyed were requested to use a diary to record over 11,000 incoming calls to their households over a two-week period in July 1992. Nearly 9 in 10 calls (88 percent) were of a

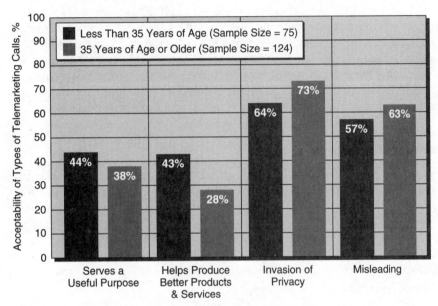

Figure 2-2. How age of a respondent affects the image statements.

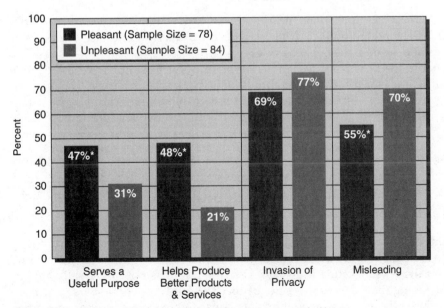

Figure 2-3. How the last telemarketing experience impacts image.

"personal" nature. Telemarketing calls defined as specific requests for "sales or donations" represented only 1 in every 20 calls (5 percent). "Wrong number" calls were reported as 4 percent of all calls received, 2 percent were "other," and only 1 percent were "survey/political."

12. *Telephone answering machine ownership continues to proliferate. This technology is increasing the percentage of screened calls.* More than half (53 percent) of U.S. households now own a telephone answering machine, more than double the 1988 figure of 25 percent and a higher percentage from 1990 (37 percent). More than half of all answering machine owners use their machines to screen calls at least some of the time. Those who screen calls report that on average they screen 32 percent of all possible calls. Doing all the math and projecting, about one in four U.S. households (28 percent) is screening roughly 9 percent of all inbound calls into households.

Limitations of Findings

The findings of the 1992 study (and the previous one) are limited by the normal statistical errors inherent in any sampling process. Because this research was conducted by telephone, it is not necessarily representative of non-telephone-owning households.

The findings of the consumer telephone diary have the same limitations as the public study. Diaries may be affected by incomplete or inaccurate recording, although our experience suggests that these factors have minimal impact in a study of this type.

Summary and Recommendations

What do these 12 conclusions mean to our industry? How can we improve our image with the U.S. public? What steps can be taken to enhance the positive feelings and reverse the negative ones?

Probably the best place to start is by attempting to summarize the conclusions into one concise statement about the image of the industry. The telemarketing industry is "misunderstood." Although telemarketing improves marketing productivity and ultimately benefits the consumer, the image of the industry does not reflect these benefits. This occurs for two primary reasons:

1. The illegitimate element incorrectly classified as telemarketers, which use fraudulent and deceptive practices, has eroded consumer confidence.
2. Other than the telemarketing call itself, no significant messages are helping to form the public's image of the industry.

There are, however, some very positive indicators for the industry. Young people are significantly more comfortable with and positive about the technology and the telemarketing industry. Also, the public is not universally against telemarketing. Based on the results of the first study, several steps or actions make sense. These recommendations are consistent with what other concerned industry leaders have been saying for some time.

Steps You Can Take to Resolve
Consumer Misconceptions

Make a commitment to stick to standards for ethical and legitimate telemarketing as outlined by various industry organizations. Adhering to these standards will decrease the percent of consumers who feel that their last telemarketing call was "deceptive."

Promote and support education and marketing efforts to communicate the positive aspects of the telemarketing industry. Increase the public's ability to distinguish telemarketing from fraud. For an industry made up of people who are good at selling, improving the industry's image would be an interesting challenge.

Target some educational efforts to the young people who are already more positively disposed toward the industry. This long-term strategy will leverage inevitable demographic changes and maximize the value of such efforts.

Continue to employ technology as a means of increasing productivity, but also emphasize ways that reduce the number of calls (and thus unqualified calls) being made. Better database analysis, segmentation of lists, and more extensive testing will increase the percentage of calls that are on target.

Recognize the critical role played by working telemarketing service representatives. Despite technology, selling is still relationship-based. Become obsessed with developing and training TSRs. When well-trained TSRs interact with the public, the chances of positive experiences increase.

Later in other chapters, you will be given training concepts that address these issues while overcoming the prospect's fears when being telemarketed. The ideas and concepts given are in compliance with the legal issues being enforced with regards to what you can say on the telephone. Moreover, the prospects are very receptive to the approaches the training chapters provide.

Legal Aspects of Telemarketing

Like any other business enterprise, telemarketing is subject to certain federal, state, and local laws and regulations. Depending upon the size and nature of the telemarketing operation, applicable regulatory requirements may literally run the gamut from A—the Americans with Disabilities Act, for one example—to Z—local zoning ordinances, for another. But apart from laws and regulations that generally apply to all kinds of businesses, a number of special regulatory requirements are intended to protect consumers from certain telemarketing practices that are considered to be harmful to consumers' interests:

- Unwarranted intrusions on personal privacy
- Fraudulent advertising and sales practices
- The abusive use of certain telephone technologies
- Marketing campaigns that directly target children

While some of these matters are addressed by federal laws that have nationwide applicability, many are governed by state laws and regulations that differ from state to state. In some cases, state laws may differ from applicable federal laws. Moreover, each of the laws and regulations in this area may apply in different ways that depend upon the particular facts and circumstances involved.

The following summary discussion is intended to provide an overview of the regulatory landscape for telemarketing. It is designed to introduce telemarketers, trainers, and business owners to certain specific legal aspects of telemarketing activities and to alert them to the need for prudent inquiry regarding the actual or potential applicability of various laws and regulations to their particular operations, activities, or personnel. It is *not*, however, intended or designed to be relied upon as legal advice or as a substitute for the advice of legal counsel when any determination of regulatory applicability is required.

Federal Regulation of Telemarketing Activities

On the national level, the Federal Trade Commission (FTC) has been the primary source of federal regulation of telemarketing activities through its jurisdiction over "unfair or deceptive acts or practices in commerce" and its implementation of the so-called mail-order merchandise rule, which was recently amended to extend FCC delivery, refund, and other consumer protection requirements to purchase orders placed by telephone.

In addition, the Commodity Futures Trading Commission, the Securities Exchange Commission, and the various federal bank regulatory agencies all exercise their respective jurisdictions to address telemarketing fraud in the context of transactions that are otherwise subject to their regulatory authority (i.e., involving commodity futures or options; stocks, bonds, or securities; and credit cards or consumer accounts, respectively).

Nevertheless, growing congressional concern over a number of consumer problems with telemarketing during the past five years has generated proposals for the enactment of federal laws specifically intended to regulate telemarketing:

1. *The Telephone Consumer Protection Act.*   In 1991, Congress enacted the Telephone Consumer Protection Act (TCPA) to protect residential telephone subscribers from what Congress considered abusive uses of certain types of telephone equipment and to give consumers the ability to avoid unwanted telephone solicitations as a matter of choice. Together with implementing FCC regulations, which went into effect in December 1992, the TCPA:

- Imposed restrictions (subject to exemptions) on the use of "automated telephone equipment" (i.e., "automatic telephone dialing systems" and "artificial voice or prerecorded voice" messages) and the transmission of unsolicited advertisements to facsimile (fax) machines;
- Imposed time-of-day restrictions (8 a.m. to 9 p.m., local time of the called party) and telemarketer "do-not-call" list maintenance requirements to help

residential telephone subscribers avoid receiving unwanted telephone solicitations (i.e., calls to encourage the purchase or rental of, or investment in, property, goods, or services, but *not* including calls made (a) with the prior express consent of the called party, (b) to a person with whom the caller has an "established business relationship," or (c) by a "tax-exempt nonprofit organization")

- Established both a right to sue in state court for violations of restrictions on uses of "automated telephone equipment," and a private state cause of action and a state attorney general's federal cause of action for violations of FCC regulations regarding "telephone solicitations"
- Prescribed technical and procedural standards for facsimile (fax) machines and systems that are used to transmit artificial or prerecorded voice messages via the telephone

The provisions of the TCPA govern all *inter*state telemarketing activities and preempt related state laws to the extent they impose less restrictive requirements on *intra*state telemarketing.

2. *The Telephone Disclosure and Dispute Resolution Act.* In 1992, Congress enacted the Telephone Disclosure and Dispute Resolution Act (TDDRA) to regulate interstate 900-number, or pay-per-call (PPC), services. As these caller-paid information services have grown in diversity and popularity, consumer complaints have also increased, focusing on excessive or hidden charges for such calls, improper billing, and false or manipulative advertising, especially with respect to children. Together with separate but complementary sets of implementing regulations issued by the FTC and the Federal Communications Commission (FCC), the TDDRA:

- Requires a "preamble," or introductory message, which will disclose the name of the service provider, the nature of the product or service provided, the cost of the call, the right to disconnect without charge, and a "parental consent" warning
- Requires long-distance carriers to provide, upon request, the name, address and customer service telephone number of the service provider
- Requires local exchange carriers to offer telephone subscribers the option of blocking access to interstate 900-number PPC services, where technically feasible
- Prohibits both long-distance and local exchange carriers from disconnecting subscribers' basic local or long-distance telephone service for their failure to pay charges for any interstate PPC services
- Prohibits "signaling tones" in PPC broadcast or cable advertisements and imposes minimum standards for PPC service providers, PPC "call-blocking" requirements, and specific restrictions and requirements regarding the advertising of goods and services sold through PPC transactions

3. *Pending Telemarketing Fraud Legislation.* As this publication goes to print, two other major pieces of telemarketing legislation are expected to be enacted by Congress before the end of this year. Both the House and Senate have passed legislation to strengthen civil law enforcement efforts against telemarketing fraud.

In addition, the Senate has added provisions to its omnibus crime bill which would establish telemarketing fraud as a separate and distinct federal crime.

The pending civil enforcement legislation would require the FTC to issue rules that prohibit "deceptive (including fraudulent) telemarketing activities" and bar telemarketers from undertaking "a pattern of unsolicited telephone calls" which the reasonable consumer would consider coercive or abusive of such consumer's right to privacy.

The legislation would also require the FTC to "consider" inclusion of rules on refunds for delivery problems, customer cancellation rights, "hour-of-day" calling restrictions, record keeping, and computer calls that do not permit automatic disconnect when the called party hangs up. Like the TCPA, the telemarketing fraud legislation would give consumers and state attorneys general the right to go to federal court to sue telemarketers who violate the FTC rules.

The separate criminal telemarketing fraud legislation would, among other things, provide enhanced criminal penalties for fraud by telemarketers; apply criminal forfeiture and victim restitution requirements to telemarketing fraud offenses; and broaden the scope and application of federal mail fraud and credit card fraud statutes for use in appropriate telemarketing fraud cases.

Telemarketers should also be aware of several other federal laws which are applicable to telemarketing activities but not specifically intended to address them. These include the Fair Credit Reporting Act, the Fair Debt Collection Practices Act, and the Truth-in-Lending Acts—all require sellers to make certain disclosures to consumers or to otherwise deal with them in a fair, respectful, and reasonable manner.

State Regulation of Telemarketing Activities

Most states have a variety of laws which directly regulate telemarketing or "telephone selling," as it is often termed in statutory language. These state-regulated activities are listed below:

Home Solicitation Statutes. Originally designed to address door-to-door sales, these statutes have been amended, interpreted, or incorporated by reference in other state legislation to regulate telemarketing that is initiated by or on behalf of the seller. Although their terms vary, these state laws generally require the disclosure of certain information about the caller, the seller, and the products or services being sold; the observance of a "cooling-off period" during which the consumer may cancel a transaction; certain restrictions on the form of agreement for purchase; and notification of the consumer's right to a refund and other considerations.

State Fair Trade Practices Statutes. Sometimes referred to as state FTC acts, these statutes often provide the same types of requirements found in "home solicitation" laws. Like the latter, these laws place a heavy emphasis on required disclosures by the seller or persons acting on its behalf, including those intended to help the consumer to identify, locate, and contact the seller and to otherwise obtain necessary relief from a regretted transaction. Like the federal FTC act, the state laws also address questions of unfair and deceptive trade practices and false and misleading advertisements.

Registration and Bonding Requirements. Sometimes found in home solicitation and fair trade practices laws, registration and bonding requirements frequently appear in separate statutes regulating telephone selling. The requirements are a common feature of state law, although there are currently no registration or bonding requirements for telemarketers under federal law.

At least fifteen states now have *registration laws* which typically require telemarketers to provide a particular state agency or official with certain information, certifications, fees, and materials before they may legally use the telephone to solicit prospective purchasers of goods or services from any location within the state.

These laws usually specify requirements for identification, location, and contact information regarding the principals, managers, and soliciting telephone service representatives of the "seller" entity, and any information regarding criminal convictions, civil action liabilities, or injunctions lying against such persons. In addition, the laws typically require information regarding the legal structure and organization of the seller, including the filing of corporate by-laws and articles, partnership agreements, and the like and the identity and address of an agent of the seller who is authorized to receive service of process on its behalf.

Registration filings usually require descriptions of the goods or services to be sold or advertised by the telemarketer, together with disclosures regarding any prizes, gifts, or promotions offered by the telemarketer and all terms and conditions for any purchase. In some cases, the filings may even require any calling scripts and other advertising literature used by the telemarketer.

Such filings, which must usually be accompanied by the payment of a registration fee, are required to be renewed on an annual or other periodic basis. Supplemental filings may be required in the interim if there are changes in any of the information required.

Most state registration laws contain exceptions or exemptions for telephone solicitations performed by the holders of certain state-issued licenses, tax-exempt entities, and callers whose sales are completed in face-to-face meetings with purchasers. In many cases, these laws also exempt sellers of newspapers, cable TV and magazine subscriptions, as well as book and music clubs and catalog mailers. Sometimes there are also exemptions for sellers whose calls are only to previous purchasers. Exemption schemes, like other registration requirements, vary from state to state.

Failure to comply with registration requirements will, in most instances, constitute an unlawful practice of solicitation which is punishable under both criminal and civil law. Civil fines and injunctions are the usual penalties, and sellers who fail to make required filings may be subject to subpoena for such materials or information.

Many states enforce *bonding requirements* in conjunction with their registration laws. Pursuant to such requirements, a surety bond for a specified amount (e.g., $10,000 to $50,000) must typically be posted with the state treasurer to be held in trust for the benefit of any person who suffers financial damage as a result of unlawful telemarketing conduct by the seller or its solicitors. The bond will usually cover only monies paid to the seller or solicitor by the injured purchaser, plus reasonable attorney fees.

Do-Not-Call or Asterisk Laws.   Intended to permit telephone subscribers to opt out of receiving telemarketing calls, these laws have been enacted in many states and are regularly proposed in the state legislatures where they have not yet been enacted. They typically require the local telephone company to put a mark (i.e., asterisk) next to the subscriber's listing in the local telephone directory to indicate that the person does not want to receive telemarketing calls or to compile a separate do-not-call list of persons who object to receiving such calls and make the list available to any persons who would be subject to such restrictions. Another option, similar to the one adopted by the FCC in implementing the federal TCPA, is to require telemarketers to mark or delete the names and telephone numbers of such individuals in connection with their own solicitation lists.

It should be noted, however, that most asterisk or do-not-call laws exclude certain types of solicitation calls from these requirements. These exclusions, like those in the federal TCPA, typically cover calls by political, charitable, and other tax-exempt entities; opinion and research polling calls; and calls to persons with whom the caller has an existing business relationship.

ADRMP/ADAD Laws.   The state counterpart to the automated telephone equipment provisions of the federal TCPA, these laws restrict the use of automatic dialing, recorded message players (ADRMPs) or automatic dialing announcing devices (ADADs), both common references to computerized equipment which selects and/or dials telephone numbers and then plays a prerecorded message when the called party answers. Although some state laws simply limit or prohibit the use of ADRMP/ADADs for certain types of calls, others regulate call disconnection requirements, hour-of-day call restrictions, random and sequential dialing usage, and many of the other disclosure, identification, or do-not-call requirements usually imposed under separate laws or regulations.

As is the case with the federal TCPA and state asterisk or do-not-call laws, state restrictions on the use of ADRMP/ADADs are usually subject to exceptions for calls by tax-exempt or government entities and calls made in furtherance of a previous transaction, in response to a request from the called party, or based on an existing business relationship.

Interception, Monitoring, and Taping of Calls

Periodic monitoring of the calls handled by telephone service representatives is generally considered to be an essential tool for any telemarketing manager or supervisor who wants to ensure customer service, provide effective employee training, conduct fair job performance evaluations, and maintain compliance with federal and state consumer protection laws and regulations. However, the monitoring of telephone conversations is subject to various restrictions under federal and state laws. Whether monitoring in the telemarketing context is subject to specific restrictions will depend upon the nature of the monitoring activity and where the call originates and terminates.

Federal Laws and Regulations.   The so-called federal wiretap laws apply to both interstate and intrastate calls and generally prohibit the interception (or recording) of a telephone conversation by a third party unless one of the parties to the conversation has consented. However, the wiretap statutes contain a so-called business call exception, which has generally been applied by the federal courts to permit employers to monitor work-related employee calls if such monitoring is conducted in the ordinary course of business and is limited in its duration and scope. Although the exception has been construed to permit the employer to record, as well as listen in on, such calls, a tariff regulation issued by the FCC requires a "beep tone" to be used when taping of a telephone conversation takes place without the consent of both parties to the telephone conversation. But the federal criminal statute, which is regarded as having greater weight on this issue than the agency regulation, does not require that notice of the monitoring be given to the customer or consumer who is speaking to the employee.

State Laws and Regulations.   Apart from the federal wiretap laws, most states have their own laws restricting employer monitoring of employee telephone calls. The federal statute generally preempts state laws which are in conflict, but states may supplement the federal laws, especially with respect to intrastate calls. Given the possible applicability of both federal and state laws in some instances, the advice of legal counsel should be sought before undertaking a monitoring program.

Some of the state laws are more restrictive than the federal statute, including requirements for the employee's prior consent and minimization standards to ensure that personal, non-work-related calls are not overheard. About a dozen states require employers to inform employees when their calls are being monitored, typically by means of a beep tone or some other signal. Like the federal law, most states permit such employee monitoring without requiring notice to the customer or consumer who is speaking to the employee.

Conclusion

The regulatory landscape for telemarketing involves a variety of jurisdictions and authorities, as well as diverse laws and regulations. Careful research of applicable laws and regulations, prior to engaging in telemarketing activities, may prevent unwanted legal headaches.

Telemarketing versus Outside Sales

The cost to support an outside salesperson is high and will continue to escalate forever. The average salesperson can make anywhere from 4 to 8 business contacts face to face each day and 2 to 4 residential contacts each day. However, a TSR can make a business contact with a decision maker anywhere from 5 to 15 times an hour and in residential markets anywhere from 20 to 30 contacts each hour. It is proven that a TSR can generate more business in a single day than any outside salesperson, simply due to the fact the TSR can reach more contacts in less time.

Most outside salespeople are not trained to prospect by telephone. In fact, the typical comment I receive when consulting and training outside salespeople is, "I do better face-to-face." This is primarily because they feel they have greater control in a face-to-face presentation compared to over the telephone. The outside salesperson's philosophy is, "It's easier for prospects to hang up the telephone than close their door in my face." The salespeople don't realize that if they would learn the telephone as a skill with the same attitude, attention, and motivation as they learned their outside selling skills, they would have just as much control at prospecting by telephone as door-to-door selling. However, the benefits go beyond door-to-door results. Not only can you have control in your presentation when telemarketing but you will reach more prospects in a shorter period, thereby having more opportunities to close more sales! This is the kind of bottom line a company wants to achieve.

Telemarketing allows you to do more business and cut cost. It also allows anyone to contact their primary, secondary, and other potential markets on a local and/or international level. Below is a list of some of the most common problems in a business and why telemarketing is so vital to anyone's business opportunities:

- The cost for maintaining an outside sales force is increasing. Gas prices are going up, not down. Insurance protection and workers compensation are skyrocketing. Certain companies are not making enough profit margin due to the high commissions and expenses of an outside salesperson.

- Companies are feeling the pinch of a highly competitive marketplace, and they need to expand their market share quickly without the rising cost. They need to reduce cost to lower their overhead in order to make a reasonable profit.

- When a company must have an outside sales representative, the best time for prospecting is usually when the salesperson is in the field meeting with and/or servicing clients. The salesperson needs more qualified leads. The TSR can bridge that gap by conducting a market research and finding prospects who are qualified and have a need for your products and services. This allows the salesperson to concentrate on what they believe they do best—sell!

- When a company generates leads through direct mail, trade shows, and other sources that bring in massive amounts of suspects (potential prospects), salespeople don't have the time to follow up, and in most cases they don't. These leads end up getting very cold, and the money and time made to obtain these type of leads has been wasted. The TSR can weed these leads out, generate a greater interest, mail out more of a customized brochure or information so the leads remain warm for the salespeople to properly conduct their own follow-up calls, or the TSR can complete the process.

- When making an outside sales call, it often requires a two- or three-call close. This is time-consuming and costly. The TSR can conduct the same two- or three-call close in less time, especially with faxes and modems, for less cost to the company.

- Keeping in touch with the customer and thereby gaining referrals and repeat business is becoming a thing of the past for salespeople, who are obsolete in today's market. With telemarketing, existing customers can be suspensed (placed in a tickler file) and followed up easily and with accountability built in. Having the telemarketing center automated will speed this process.

- Determining customer satisfaction is an activity that salespeople may never engage in. By having a phone blitz or conducting after-sales support with a customer service representative (CSR) contacting existing customers 30 to 90 days after a sale has been procured would enable a company to identify any unforeseen problems and rectify them before losing the customer altogether.

- Controlling an outside salesperson's time and expenses can be difficult, and validation is not easy. All activity is easily monitored and tabulated with a telemarketing department. You have complete control of time management and access to daily, weekly, and monthly reporting of each TSR's activity and cost analysis.

- Outside salespeople are hard to track down for training and supervision. The TSR is trained continuously and provided with constant supervision to ensure quality control and professional representation.

The other advantages to telemarketing are too numerous to list. Not only is telemarketing effective and beneficial for a company, the customer benefits too. For example:

- Customers receive fast, reliable, and convenient service.

- Customers gain a more personalized service that can be tailored to their individual wants and needs due to the continuous contact and hands-on decision capability.

- Customers get the latest information and won't miss out on special promotions or discount rates.

- Telemarketing reduces a company's overhead, and this savings can be passed on to the customer. It is a "win-win" for you and customers; they get a good deal, and you remain competitive.

■ For inbound servicing, the customer can call and get service and even ask for an inside salesperson (TSR) for better and more personalized servicing. This provides an inside contact for the customer.

Surveys have shown that people would rather be contacted and sold over the telephone than door-to-door because it is less informal, prospects feel less pressure, and they have the illusion that they have more control of the process. This is not to say that you would eliminate the outside salesperson altogether, but with our technology and ability to increase our level of communication, who knows, maybe in the year 2020 the position of the outside salesperson will be a thing of the past!

Winning Your Sales Force's Approval of Your Telemarketing Department

For many telemarketing departments the primary function is to assist a field sales force by generating appointments or leads. The telemarketers often encounter resistance from the salespeople whose responsibility it is to run the appointment or follow up on those leads. This is due to several factors. First, the outside salesperson feels threatened by the telemarketer who is generating the leads. The outside salespeople either feel that one day they may be replaced by inside salespeople (TSRs) or they feel inferior to the TSR primarily because they have not acquired the phone as a part of their marketing tool. Often when the outside salesperson runs an appointment that the TSR generated, if the salesperson did not close—make a sale—the blame will go on the quality of the lead and thus on the TSR instead of on the salesperson's lack of ability to close.

In some situations, an outside salesperson who is running appointments that the TSR generates will treat the appointments and/or leads as if they were candy as opposed to gold. This causes the salesperson to sell strictly on the numbers games and not concentrate on the quality of presentation. If the TSR is on a bonus system based on sales produced by the outside salesperson, the TSR's income will greatly depend on the salesperson's closing percentages. If the salesperson's percentage isn't very high, the TSR becomes unmotivated to continue generating leads. Both departments end up working against each other as opposed to working for each other, costing a company time and money. It's vital for the outside sales force to recognize the tremendous opportunity to work as a team with the telemarketing department.

Once a company has made a decision to integrate a telemarketing program into an existing sales plan, certain steps need to be taken to help achieve positive and long lasting results. In any relationship strong communication between the telemarketing management and the sales management is essential. All who are a part of the two departments need to have a clear understanding of the objectives and commitment level of each other and of the company.

Announcing to the sales force that telemarketing will be implemented needs to be handled in such a way that the salespeople are excited and ready to offer their support to ensure success. Upper management must demonstrate its total, long-term support to implementing telemarketing and must communicate to the sales department that the addition of a telemarketing department will benefit everyone. Be sure to open the lines and allow the flow of communication to move freely. This ensures that the sales force has communicated personal concerns or lack of understanding of the telemarketing department's function. The sales force needs to realize that the goal of the telemarketing department is to allow salespeople to better utilize their time to do what they do best—sell! When the sales force understands this, salespeople can easily translate it into terms for their own financial gain.

If the responsibility of the new department is to prequalify prospects for the sales force, this needs to be introduced to the sales force as a benefit. The salespeople need to understand what's in it for them. One way to reach the sales force "hot button" is to appeal to a weakness, "cold calling." If the sales force understands that the telemarketing department will prequalify leads for the salespeople and will provide information that will further assist salespeople in the selling process, not only will their selling time be more productive, but they will have an edge over their competition. Clear the air by communicating to the sales force that the telemarketing department is not to phase salespeople out, otherwise they will do everything they can to abort the idea of telemarketing and make it cost-prohibitive.

To help ease the transition, invite the sales force to spend some time on the phone, conducting telemarketing activities. This will help salespeople gain a better perspective of the function and appreciate what the telemarketing department will be doing for them, how they will be supported. Also, having the sales force spend time performing what the TSR is doing day in and day out will allow the salesperson to really understand what TSRs go through, and the salespeople will be less critical of the leads generated for them. When the sales force is more familiar with the difficulties that are involved in generating leads, this overcomes the misconception that telemarketing is just a "number game." In reality telemarketing is a skill that needs to be respected, and when this happens, the sales force's attitude changes, and salespeople become more positive about telemarketing and will be more supportive. Salespeople don't like to cold-call, and when they understand that the TSR will have to do the dirty work of finding that "needle in the haystack" on an ongoing basis, they will place a higher value on the leads provided by the telemarketing department and will less likely "burn" the leads provided.

Another problem with the sales force is allowing salespeople to confirm or contact the prospects prior to a scheduled appointment. Salespeople fear that the lead may not be qualified enough to make the sale, so they will overqualify the prospects and end up disqualifying them in the process. There needs to be a clear understanding that the telemarketing department needs to have full control of the confirmations and dispatching of all leads generated. The sales force needs to concentrate on being on time and on running the appointment as scheduled. In the event that the salesperson runs late, the telemarketing department needs to be informed immediately by the salesperson and allow the TSR to contact the prospect to communicate the information to the prospect. The TSR is trained to effectively handle resistance over the telephone and handle objections. TSRs are prepared with canned answers to address any fears a prospect may have at the last minute prior to the appointment. This also allows the telemarketing department to have full control of the scheduling process and be able to reset any appointments to another time that is more convenient.

When the sales force is running appointments generated by the telemarketing department, a system needs to ensure that the salespeople receive the leads promptly and accurately and, more important, provide their management with timely reports to keep track of each salesperson's follow-up and results. These results need to be provided to the telemarketing department for validation and correction of any problems that may have occurred that could have been prevented by better training or of errors that can be easily corrected internally.

When adding a telemarketing department, the sales force will play a major role in every phase of the program's growth, and the communication of the two departments needs to be flowing with constructive and positive feedback. Accountability factors need to be built in for improving results, and the sales force needs to keep an open mind and not feel intimidated by the telemarketing department and its role in assisting the outside sales force to do its job more effectively.

Telemarketing versus Direct Mail

The cost per contact of direct mail is considerably less than telemarketing. Of course, this cost varies depending on the type of mail piece and how expensive the piece is to print and to mail. However, telemarketing is more effective. Direct mail provides an average response from ½ percent to 7 to 10 percent depending on the nature of the mail piece and any incentives that will bring in a higher response. Combine direct mail with telemarketing, you gain up to a 40 to 60 percent response when you follow up on those who did not initially respond. Below is a list of the disadvantages of direct mail and why telemarketing is more of a valuable tool for marketing:

- Direct mail is noninteractive. First, there is no guarantee that prospects will look at your mailer. Second, if they do, there is no control of whether they would respond and inquire.

- Direct mail may captivate a certain percentage of those prospects who are in the market but not those who may be or would be if only they had immediate interaction to respond to their objections or questions. With direct mail, it is impossible to customize the message to meet the prospect's individual needs.

- The tracking of a direct mail response is difficult. You can only track those who call in. With telemarketing you can track every contact and gain feedback. This helps a company determine how to enhance its marketing efforts or improve its product and stay ahead of the competition.

- Direct mail is not as persuasive or personalized as telemarketing. Most people will buy on emotion, and the TSR has a greater opportunity to appeal to the prospect's emotion than with a mailer.

- With low-volume accounts, it is not very profitable to market by direct mail only or through an outside salesperson. Telemarketing would enable you to sell low-end accounts faster and cost effectively, conduct volume client contact per hour, and still provide a personal service to your customers.

Direct mail has it's benefits. When a company needs to get out into the masses, direct mail is an excellent medium to contact a prospect base that is too large for telemarketing, especially if there is a short timetable involved. Direct mail is very beneficial for offering the visual that prospects need when making a final decision. This is why I recommend that you combine your telemarketing efforts with direct mail. By calling first, create the interest and the need for your products or services. Once you have accomplished this and your prospects seem interested, then send your direct mail piece with a commitment to conduct a follow-up call; then you can sell to close! You may opt to send your direct mail first, then follow up. However, you will experience a greater impact and leave a more positive and professional image by doing the former than the latter. Adding an 800 number to your direct mail piece will help increase your response levels. And targeting your market and offering incentives for the prospect to call will bring up your response rate.

800-Number Inbound Telemarketing

Today, consumers are very receptive to the 800-number phenomenon. With infomercials, customer service support, mail order, and a credit card society, 800 service represents roughly $9 billion of the $55 billion annual revenue of the domestic U.S. long-distance industry. It's clear that the 800 service plays an important role in business, and this role is growing. The 800 service is growing one-and-one-half to two times the rate of the rest of the telecommunications industry.

There are several benefits to providing a toll-free telephone system to encourage and handle service calls. These benefits are necessary to provide the quality service consumers want in today's marketplace, regardless of the size of company or corporate structure. Some of these benefits are increased consumer brand loyalty and positive word-of-mouth advertisement. By offering an 800 number, existing customers can call in for complaints as well as to bring forth additional business.

With a professional, fast, reliable 800 service, these customers feel they have a resource to turn to when they are unhappy or satisfied with a product or service. The company can then proceed to monitor the inbound activities, to cross-sell, to deal with the complaints quickly, and to try to satisfy the customer's needs. By offering an easy and uncomplicated access for the customer when a problem occurs, potential customer liability claims are reduced.

800 Number for Lower Costs to Service Goods and Warrantees

Manufacturers of durable goods have found that 30 percent of the products returned for service or requiring a service call usually have nothing wrong with them. With the high cost of service today, a toll-free 800 system can prevent many unnecessary warranty or service expenses. Some companies can detect 20 percent of the problems over the phone by providing an 800-service direct line between a consumer and a service representative.

800 Number for After-Sales Support

Many companies are placing 800 numbers on their product labels, service manuals, or warranty cards. This is to provide an after-sales support to handle dissatisfaction or offer product information and to educate their customers. It is important for a company to identify any service or warranty problems as soon as possible. This is because a customer is less likely to purchase that product or any other product from that company/manufacturer again. A customer is more inclined to try a new product if responsive service was made available on a question or problem with another product produced by the same company and if the quality of that service met the customer's needs. A customer who has had good service in the past from a bad experience is more likely to take a chance on new products. Good service means the service representative was able to provide solutions for the customer and the company was willing to stand behind its products and services, ready to assist the customer.

Benefits of a Toll-Free System

Not only does the customer benefit from the 800 service but the manufacturer and the dealer or distributor benefit as well. Here are a few examples of ways to use 800 service:

Advertising the 800 service for customer complaints

Providing general product and specific use-of-product information

Implementing market research on new and existing products

Providing assistance to customers over the phone

Giving immediate attention to possible liability claims

Providing quality assurance

Tracking data for growth of aggressive marketing

There is an enormous potential for continued growth for the inbound telemarketing industry. Statistics prove that more consumers in today's marketplace prefer to shop by phone compared to mail order. Companies can sell more products by phone because of the convenience the phone offers compared to the mailing process. Distributors can quickly process orders and fulfill incoming orders, and customers are happy to receive their orders quicker. This increases the profitability of the company along with the time saved by the consumer. Inbound 800 service is a growing industry and will continue to grow in the years ahead. It could make the mail order industry inferior given that the inbound 800 industry will ensure that quality assurance is always kept at high standards internally and externally.

Getting Started—How to Set Up a Successful Telemarketing Operation

Providing you have selected an individual to spearhead the telemarketing program for your company who is dedicated to the project full-time, you are on your way to the first step. Considerations for financial support to ensure an ongoing program are critical. Later in another chapter you can learn about the hardware, software, and furniture selection and how to determine how sophisticated you want your initial start-up.

Once you have made a commitment to incorporate telemarketing into your company, it is wise to include the upper-level managers in sales, marketing, customer service, credit, and shipping management to gain their support. It is important to work together in controlling the communication between other departments that would be affected by telemarketing. You can present your ideas and projections with proposals and reports and even conduct special workshops to educate others who will be involved or affected by telemarketing. To ensure that you have everyone's support, you need to provide validation of your information with statistics and case studies from other similar companies. One way to gain the most recent and updated reports for your industry is to contract with a telemarketing consultant who may already have that information or can easily research and compile it for you. The main objective is to gain support from everyone involved.

Set up a project plan as you would a business plan. You need to define what you want to do, where you will go with it, how you are going to get there, and how you will know when you have arrived. Determine where you are now and begin from there. Assess your company with regards to your marketing objectives, the products and/or services you offer, your organizational structure, and how each department will reflect each other and support the telemarketing operation. Once you have the basis of your foundation, then set realistic goals for short term and long term. Be flexible. Just because you have started out with an idea, there is still room for change. In fact, count on it! You might as well get used to change, because telemarketing is growing and changing rapidly. Be sure to record all your adjustments and why, so that you can refer to your notes if you need to change things again. This is extremely helpful since you don't want to repeat the same mistakes, and you may be able to see a pattern that will help you to go in the right direction. Once you have determined your project, plan how you need to educate yourself and others regarding the legal issues of the telemarketing industry.

3
Hardware Selection

This chapter provides education on the best hardware selection available for today's call center. Whether you have an outbound or inbound call center, the selection process can be extremely difficult. There are a vast amount of products available on the market with prices ranging from one extreme to another. This chapter will offer solutions to maximize your software applications and increase production by using automatic call distributors (ACDs) or predictive dialers. You will have a better understanding of the different types of telephone equipment that range from a PBX to a key system and includes other associated hardware that needs to be considered when making a final selection. Regardless of your call center's size or the budget you have to work with, this chapter helps to clear up some of this confusion and will enable you to make the best decision for your company.

Predictive Dialers and the Benefits for Outbound Telemarketing

As previously discussed, technology and automation have created a number of conveniences for call centers of today, including online scripting with infinite branching capabilities, sophisticated online and back-end reporting, unlimited list manipulation capabilities, and improved list penetration. The benefits of automation can only be maximized if the hardware components are properly interfaced with customized system and application-specific software.

Although the technology designed for the inbound and outbound telemarketing industry is highly sophisticated and has surpassed many expectations in the area of hardware and software applications, experts say that it's unlikely that vendors will ever offer a total turnkey solution. Therefore certain call centers must have the appropriate technical expertise and resources to be successful in a sophisticated, automated environment. With this in mind, the following information focuses on a specific system component that is the "hot topic" of the mid-1990s—the predictive dialer.

What Is a Predictive Dialer and How Does It Increase Productivity?

A predictive dialer is a computer system that dials a list of phone numbers and presents a steady flow of successful "connects" to available TSRs for outbound environments. The system configuration consists of a telephone line to TSR ratio of 3:2 or greater. For example, 16 TSRs could use a system with 24 phone lines dialing. The calls are dialed in anticipation of a TSR being available. Through a formula preprogrammed into the system, the dialer predicts the number of lines to dial at any point in time. It is an intelligent, self-adjusting system that selects the optimum number of lines given the abandon rate set by the call center manager. Alternatively, the manager can override the system and select the number of lines dialing to achieve maximum contacts per hour without regard to abandon rate.

The TSRs do not dial, do not listen to busy signals or rings, no answers, or operator intercepts. Only calls that have been answered are passed to the TSRs by the system. Once a call is received, the TSR screen displays the prospect's name, address, city, state, zip code, and telephone number. With predictive dialers, TSRs spend their time selling because the need to dial numbers manually, listen to busy signals, and ring no-answers has been completely eliminated.

There are other options, depending on each manufacturer; one is called *progressive dialing.* This permits the dialer to operate on a line-for-line basis using the same number of phone lines as there are TSRs. Otherwise, all the same features operate as described above. The system still has tremendous speed and capabilities in the progressive mode. There are no abandoned or dropped calls. Since the calling pace is slower, it may be better suited for smaller calling files or new TSRs in training.

Another feature option is called *preview dialing,* which is similar to progressive dialing in that it is line-for-line; the major difference is that the system displays the name and address before dialing. The TSR can select or opt to skip the record after review of the displayed information.

Maximizing List Penetration

Predictive dialing enhances list penetration by creating more contacts for TSRs to convert to successful sales. Proper list management and predictive dialing allow you to penetrate a list to its fullest potential. This is increasingly becoming an issue as companies try to get the maximum return from their limited number of customers/prospects. By utilizing predictive dialing and sophisticated list management, you are giving your program a higher probability of success by maximizing the number of contacts.

Improved Program Performance Evaluation

Predictive dialing has caused clients to analyze their results more closely. Let's take service agencies for an example. Typically, a client measured the cost effectiveness of outbound telemarketing service agencies based on the cost per sale for a specific program. This was calculated by taking the average sales per hour divided into the telemarketing cost per hour to equal the cost per sale. Since most service agencies do not guarantee their production when charging their hourly rates, the service agency with the lowest cost per sale would typically be awarded the majority of business.

With the rise of automation, clients can now thoroughly evaluate a program's performance. Predictive dialers allow list performance to be more completely analyzed. With the profitability of program lists now more complete, accurate, and readily available, companies are realizing that the "net revenue generated" from a given list is the most valid measurement for gauging the success of the program. Net revenue is defined as the actual net dollar amount generated from a given list after the outbound telemarketing expense is removed. Basically, automation has allowed companies to realize that the cost per sale is not as important as the profits the program generates.

Shop Around—Not All Predictive Dialers Are the Same

It's obvious that predictive dialers represent tremendous advantages and improvements compared to manual dialing. However, not all predictive dialers and the systems they are interfaced with are the same. Hardware, software, and human expertise all are vital aspects when it comes to the performance of the dialer as well as the automated system.

Before making an investment in predictive dialers, be sure that you are fully aware of the advantages and disadvantages. For example, legislation is toughening the requirements on the don't-call list, and with predictive dialers you need to be careful not to include these numbers when entering them into your database. Reputable firms that sell predictive dialers have features that can assist you in purging these "don't call" numbers. Also, consider the cost-effectiveness of the predictive dialer when determining the time factor involved in purging these numbers.

Another disadvantage to predictive dialers is the dead silence it may have for prospects answering their telephones with no one available yet to pick up the line. The prospect is annoyed at having been contacted by a machine and having to wait for a live and breathing body to make the introduction. Many consultants in the telemarketing industry have a negative view of predictive dialers and anticipate these devices to be more of a nuisance that won't survive very long. However, others love predictive dialers and wonder how we ever got along without them. Again, you be the judge. Get all your facts, test the information, and determine whether it meets your objectives and company's philosophies of doing business.

What Is the Cost of Predictive Dialers?

Cost depends on how sophisticated you want to get, how many lines and stations your predictive dialer will service, what you already have in hardware, and what you don't have. Also you need to consider, whenever you are determining cost, the set-up and installation fees and of course the training, which is absolutely essential unless you have someone on staff who is capable of addressing and handling these added issues. This of course doesn't include the software rights and the manufacturer's customized software for other add-on functions, future software upgrades, and the ongoing software maintenance fees.

The cost may range from $12,000 to $19,000 for just the basic kit with up to 24 lines for 16 TSRs. If you add this with all the other equipment such as TSR stations, supervisor station, file server, predictive manager, 9-track tape drive, external modem, battery back up, voice-monitoring kit (up to 30 lines), software add-ons, set-up and training fees, software maintenance agreement, Novell Netware, and so on, the cost can range anywhere from $36,915 to $100,360 (7 to 28 stations, 12 to 48 lines). To break it up further by cost per station, it is $5416 to $3584 with the same stations and lines.

Remember, consider what you think you need by determining first what your call center's objectives are. Only then can you make an informed decision on what you really must have now, and at least you'll know that some purchases can wait until your call center is solvent and moving forward!

Computer Hardware Requirements

Selecting your software and hardware go hand-in-hand. Many will think that they should determine the software first, then buy the hardware that will run that software. However, this is not a good strategy when choosing a mission-critical business application like telemarketing software. In a LAN environment, your hardware and software requirements should be dealt with simultaneously, hopefully by one organization that can make the equation between your needs and the hardware and software that will support them.

Some considerations are straightforward. The number of TSRs you have or will have determines roughly how many work stations you will need. Your responsiveness needs will determine whether you can use a lower-cost networking technology like ARCnet or you need a higher-speed system such as Ethernet or Token-Ring. Many hardware and software consultants recommend Token-Ring for any online telephone processing (OLTP)-oriented system because it has the ability to support larger numbers of users without having a lot of network traffic colliding.

Other hardware issues are more complex. If you are choosing a simple file-server-based telemarketing system, then a single LAN file server will be adequate. However, if you are choosing an OLTP-based system, you may need to purchase more than one server to handle different functions such as call processing and interfacing with a PBX switch. As stated, unless you have significant computer hardware expertise on staff, you need a consultant or systems integrator to help select both your hardware and software.

Although there are an infinite number of complex issues to resolve when choosing the telemarketing software system that best supports your organization or call center, some of the most important factors in making the right decision have been addressed in this chapter. You should be able to find a package that runs on state-of-the-art PC LAN hardware, is powerful enough to support your immediate and future needs, and will grow as you grow without requiring a significant reinvestment of capital. Once you've chosen the right system, you will be on the road to total telemarketing.

Automatic Call Distribution (ACD)

The basic automatic call distribution (ACD) is a device that takes inbound calls on any of a number of lines and distributes them evenly among telephones or extensions on the system. An ACD is ideal for taking orders, making reservations, or handling other situations where numerous inbound calls are fielded by a number of CSRs, as is common when 800 numbers are promoted. Most ACDs will do the following:

- Automatically answer calls on any line
- If all CSRs are busy, answer with a recorded message urging the caller to wait and then place the call in "queue" (holding pattern in order received)
- When a CSR is available, route the call to the appropriate extension based on the length of time CSR has been available
- Give priority to calls that come in on certain lines, channel calls to certain extensions, or signal which line the caller is using
- Automatically compile data and provide reports on system status, including call traffic, delays, and problems
- Allow supervisors to silently monitor any line on the system

The primary benefits of an ACD is it allows numerous inbound calls over many lines to be handled efficiently by fewer CSRs. The customer, the CSR, and the company benefit by evenly distributing incoming calls among two or more CSRs. ACD ensures that the inbound call is answered by the CSR quickly with minimal hold time. For those whose job function is servicing customer calls, taking orders, inbound selling, or providing technical support, ACD makes their jobs easier by evenly distributing the incoming calls to these departments. Without ACD, inbound calls would have to be answered and routed by a receptionist or switchboard operator who would then transfer the caller to the first available CSR or would be answered by the CSRs themselves.

The bottom line for a company is that ACD is cost-effective due to increased productivity and sales because of improved customer service.

ACD is available in a range of systems: large, stand-alone systems, ACD capabilities that are resident within telephone systems, and independent add-on systems for telephone systems. Whereas large corporations and call centers have relied primarily on stand-alone ACD systems for their operations, these systems remain too expensive for small- to medium-sized companies and in-house call centers. However, due to the demand from small- to medium-sized companies and in-house call centers, ACD now offers smaller systems. This gives small to medium companies the opportunity to afford the same benefits that the advanced features of the large systems offer but at a more cost-effective price.

ACD improves call-handling activities and increases productivity. The latest industry research indicates that the fastest-growing segment of ACD applications are the smaller call centers ranging from 1 to 20 stations. Today, virtually any business that performs inbound telemarketing activity can benefit from ACD. Whether your operation is staffed with one individual or you have 100 stations, ACD plays a critical role in ensuring that incoming calls are answered efficiently and effectively.

What to Consider Prior to Investing in an ACD System

Not all ACD systems are alike. There are different methods for adding ACD to an existing business telephone system, as well as the feature and operating differences between ACD systems. When shopping around for an ACD system evaluate the following criteria.

Evaluate Each System's Features.   In your evaluation, consider your specific requirements. For example, do you have problems with staffing and scheduling your CSRs especially during peak hours of inbound activity? Does your business get affected by bad weather that prevents CSRs from reaching the call center during critical periods? Does possible high turnover cause you to lose customers? If you face any of these challenges, choose an ACD that offers telecommuting. This gives the CSR the ability to handle inbound call activity from a remote location, even a CSR's home! Telecommuting is not a standard feature offered by all stand-alone ACDs; it's part of what distinguishes one ACD from another.

Review Every Standard Feature and Available Option.   Many vendors will try to convince you that the number of product features is the differentiating factor. But it's not the number of features that's important. Instead, it is the ability of theses features that's important. Your primary goal when selecting the right ACD technology is to enhance your customer service. You don't want a customer waiting in queue for someone who ultimately turns out not to be the person or department the customer should be speaking with. Another situation that wastes the customer's time and causes poor customer service is if the CSR doesn't have all the information needed to handle the call. CSRs spend unnecessary time searching for and verifying customer information needed to complete the call or transaction. If this is a major problem in your call center, then invest in a front end integrated voice response coupled with simultaneous voice and data presentation. This saves a lot of time and money for the customer, especially if the call is on their dollar!

When selecting your ACD, don't spend time looking at just the features as your basis of determination; it is more important to determine what features the ACD has to offer that provide solutions for your particular situation. Take time to identify all the business problems facing all the individuals with a stake in your ACD selection including CSRs, managers, supervisors, and, of course, the customer! Once you are aware of the problems, then collectively choose an ACD that solves those business problems. Below is a checklist of features you may want to consider.

√ Be sure the ACD has the capacity to handle present and future lines and extension needs and is easily upgraded.

√ Insist on an automatic call forwarding where the CSR merely has to pick up the line to take the call rather than having to press a button.

√ Choose the flexibility of creating "gates" or "groups" for directing certain calls through certain extensions and assigning priorities.

√ Depending upon the size of your call center and your objectives, you may need a means to obtain identification that is either visual or audio so that when calls come in on certain lines, the CSR can be better prepared to answer the call in a certain way.

√ Look for CSRs that can access outbound lines, transfer calls, put calls on hold, set up conference calls, and contact others internally via intercom lines.

√ Ask about recording special messages for prospects on hold and having a second message played if prospect remains on hold for too long.

√ Require easy reprogramming by user for changing gate assignments, routing priorities, acceptable hold time, and call traffic before warnings are given or emergency routing procedures are used; make sure it is easy to activate and deactivate phones and lines on the system.

√ Ask for full data compilation and reporting of call activity on each line, group, and extension, including maximum number of calls waiting any hour of the day, length of time calls were waiting at any time, number of calls lost, times when all lines were busy, and any problems detected on any lines, line groups, or extensions.

√ Look for an easy-to-use CRT and printer for programming the ACD and for generating reports.

√ Insist on power failure security and self diagnostics.

If you are unclear about the direction of ACD and what you should consider, hire a consultant who can assess your needs and determine the route you need to take and how much of a system you really need within the first few years of your call center. The main key here is expandability!

Get Everything Up Front Prior to Making Your Final Selection, Because Prices Vary.   Many features are similar between ACD systems; however, there are substantial cost differences in how ACD is implemented with an existing system. For telephone systems with system-resident ACD options, the cost for adding complete ACD capabilities averages about $3000 for the software. Additional hardware is usually not required. Adding MIS capabilities averages an additional $3000 for the software and another $1200 for a personal computer. So the total cost for adding complete ACD/MIS capabilities can be as low as approximately $7200.

The cost is higher when adding ACD to a telephone system without system-resident ACD. Adding ACD requires adding a PC, at about $1200, plus the ACD software at approximately $10,000. Basic ACD capabilities, then, average $11,200. Adding MIS and reporting capabilities costs an additional $4000, bringing the total cost for complete ACD/MIS to approximately $15,200.

Adding ACD to another telephone system can be cost-effective for large systems. The cost for adding a new telephone system with ACD capabilities varies depending on the existing system and the new telephone system selected. Adding complete ACD/MIS capabilities via a new key system for ten CSRs can cost as little as $15,000, compared to the $40,000 it can cost to add ACD and MIS capabilities to a large PBX.

Interview Reputable Suppliers.   These suppliers know and understand ACD systems and their installation. The most cost-effective way for you to obtain information regarding ACD suppliers and the requirements you need to consider is by getting a list of suppliers from trade magazines or by contacting companies that have similar-size call centers to yours. Ideally, if you can budget for this, contract with a consultant who specializes in hardware and software for call centers. They are there for you and have your best interest in mind. It may cost you up front to retain a consultant's services; however, in the long run it can save you thousands more while saving you time and unnecessary confusion when each supplier will be promoting its preferred features and functions.

Get References and Check Them Out!   If you are going with a consultant or a supplier direct, get references. Of course you will probably be getting the "cream of the crop," since no one will be giving *bad* references. Ask for a variety of references, for example, clients dealt with in the past 30 days, clients that are a year old, and finally clients that are three or five years old. What you want to look for are clients that are still happy with the service after sales support was provided, the recommendations that accurately assessed any difficulties, and if there are any inconsistencies in the attitude, service, and philosophies in how the supplier conducts its business.

Adding ACD to Your Existing Telephone Systems

Currently, companies can add ACD to their existing telephone systems in three primary ways. Selecting the right method for your application requires an evaluation of your existing telephone system, your business requirements, and a thorough cost analysis.

Existing Telephone System Upgrade.   First determine whether your telephone system has system-resident ACD capabilities. If so, adding ACD is accomplished through a simple software or firmware installation. Telephone systems with resident ACD capabilities offer an advantage over those without because all call-processing functions are performed by the telephone system which ensures a smooth implementation of ACD. Due to the demand for ACD, most telephone systems today feature resident ACD capabilities.

Third-Party Add-ons.   Should you have a telephone system that doesn't have system-resident ACD capabilities, you may be able to add ACD by a third-party add-on system. These systems can be either a personal computer with ACD software or a proprietary system. With these add-on systems, ACD call processing is handled by a PC or proprietary system that works together with your existing telephone system. However, should system problems arise, this approach makes it difficult to identify and correct the failure.

Adding a Telephone System to an Existing System.   To meet the ACD requirements of a department within a corporate environment, adding ACD capabilities to the existing telephone system can be more expensive than adding a new telephone system dedicated to ACD activities. For example, if your business uses a large PBX, adding a key system specifically for ACD and connecting the two systems by tie lines is often more economical than upgrading your existing PBX with ACD capabilities.

Essential ACD Features

Sometimes the age and technology of your existing telephone system make it difficult and very expensive to add ACD capabilities. In this case, you may want to examine the cost of replacing your existing telephone system. Although the three approaches to implementing ACD using existing telephone systems vary, they all offer a range of essential features, including the following:

- *Optimal Call Distribution.*   The ACD provides even distribution of incoming calls to ensure that incoming calls are quickly answered.
- *Call Overflow Support.*   Most systems allow users to program the length of time acceptable for callers to remain on hold before being connected to a CSR. If a call is not answered during the programmed time, the system will automatically reroute the caller to someone else for service.

- *Remote Log-In.*   This feature is useful during peak call periods because it allows others within your organization, from any telephone, to log into the ACD group and function as a CSR.

- *After-Call Work Time.*   ACD systems typically allow users to program the amount of time CSRs have between calls. CSRs use this time to complete paperwork and other duties. This time can range from a couple of seconds to minutes, depending on the application.

- *Messages on Hold.*   While callers are on hold, they may be provided messages encouraging them to continue holding and notifying them that their call will be quickly answered in the order received. Messages may be customized to provide the caller with instructions that will help expedite the call when it is answered. Other companies prefer to use this time to advertise their company's products and or services. Another alternative is music from the system's music-on-hold device. When using music other than what has been provided and published by companies who specialize in "on-hold music," be sure that you have written permission so that you don't infringe on copyrights without authorization. Many companies use radio for their on-hold message; again, a lack of authorization and obtaining, in most situations, an annual licensing fee to tap into the radio's air time could lead to a serious federal offense if not handled properly.

- *Auto Answer.*   Many ACD systems allow CSRs to receive calls without pushing a button. Most feature *zip tones,* which are brief tones that notify CSRs when they are about to receive calls.

- *After-Shift Service.*   This feature permits the routing of incoming calls received after work hours to another destination, such as a message center or attendant.

- *Supervisor Displays.*   Some ACD systems can provide supervisors of small call centers (five people) with necessary information about call center activities using the telephone set display. These telephone sets can display such information as the number of calls waiting in the queue, how long calls have been waiting, how many CSRs are logged into the ACD group, and individual CSR status.

- *Adding Additional ACD Groups.*   In most cases it is cost prohibitive to invest in ACD for every department on an individual basis. Therefore to ensure your company gets the most out of ACD, consider adding additional ACD groups. These groups can include an in-house help desk, credit department, or secretarial pool. Teaming up with other groups to take advantage of ACD capabilities is much more cost-effective. With most ACD systems, additional ACD groups are added by a simple programming change.

Management Information System (MIS) for Effective Tracking

Complement your ACD by adding a management information system (MIS) internally or externally to the telephone system as a PC or as a proprietary processor. The MIS takes ACD information and processes that information to provide a complete series of real-time displays and reports, as well as historical reports.

Through the MIS, department supervisors can track the status of each CSR, the status of each group, the number of calls on hold, the time that calls are on hold, the number of calls taken daily, and a range of performance information. Reports are typically available by shift, hourly, daily, weekly, monthly, and annual periods and can be displayed at the supervisor's terminal or output to a printer. The MIS can also be used to identify and track the types of calls received, a feature that is particularly helpful if the call center is funded by multiple divisions within a corporation.

The MIS is invaluable to department managers and supervisors when it comes to managing call center operations, as well as setting and measuring customer service goals. Historical reports combined with real-time displays provide the information needed to accurately plan for staffing requirements— a capability essential for businesses that are subjected to occasional high-volume call activity brought on by special events or promotions. The MIS reporting capabilities contribute to improved customer service by identifying poor service and low productivity areas.

Although the up-front price of ACD can be costly, when weighing all the options and benefits that an ACD offers to a call center, it is cost-effective for any type or size of operation. Those who choose to add ACD to their system will find that ACD will more than pay for itself through reduced holding time and hang ups, reduced WATS service charges, increased productivity, improved customer service, and a higher level of profit.

Wrapping It Up with the Biggest Mistake

You have been thoroughly educated regarding the different aspects of computer hardware and software and it's advantages and disadvantages, in order to help you make wise selections that are cost-effective and profitable to your call center. However, one area that has not been discussed yet is the biggest mistakes companies make when attempting to automate their call centers. This mistake is not being committed to the implementation of the technology. As a consultant, I see many companies making huge investments in computer hardware and software packages and yet not able to utilize their functions to the fullest potential. These companies are losing out on greater heights to improved performance, faster production, and more reliable and accessible information, simply because they are not fully educated on the computing power they have invested in.

Having initial and ongoing training together with clear communication and support from the beginning for the new technology is key to the success of automation. There is no use in spending a great deal of money on automating your call center if you are not willing to invest in the initial and ongoing training for the end-user. If you are unable to invest in either an on-staff MIS person or an independent consultant and/or an on-sight technician, trainer, then you may not be ready to fully automate. You can start out small and work your way up; however, it will cost more later when purging and massaging information that wasn't initially done because no one was trained properly to do so or no one was aware that the particular function even existed.

Again, take your time, shop around, negotiate your needs, and acquire technical assistance when making your final selection and implementation. Doing so could save you a tremendous amount of dollars and for the long haul, it is worthwhile because of its long-lasting bottom line results!

Now that you have the hardware and software section down, it's time to set up your call center. The following section discusses how to set up a call center that provides you with basic information on tools you will be needing when setting up a desk—ideas that will increase TSR and CSR motivation, lower stress, and ensure greater success with their production.

Phone Switch and Telephone Equipment

After estimating the number of lines you need and how they will be used, you should begin to examine your equipment needs. Like services, equipment selection and installation can be a lengthy process, so don't delay this task. Your search for equipment should closely parallel your search for telephone services. You can generally get both from the same vendor.

The equipment you choose can dramatically affect the number of calls that each TSR can handle in an hour. The right equipment can remove all need for TSRs to leave their work stations while in their prime prospecting time because they have to fax a letter or create and send a proposal. Certain equipment can reduce or eliminate the time spent on paperwork, dialing, and other manual tasks. Other equipment can direct call traffic in and out of the telemarketing center to ensure productive use of each TSR's time and each phone line. If a single TSR can make 20 to 30 calls per hour with an ordinary telephone, it is possible the same TSR could handle 30, 40, 50, or more calls per hour with more capable equipment.

If you have dedicated TSRs, the extra calls your TSRs can make are worth the extra cost for the equipment. Even one more call per TSR per hour can have a dramatic effect on your bottom line. However, the equipment investment can be very expensive, and selecting the wrong equipment at the wrong time can be a costly mistake. Therefore, if you are starting small with your call center, keep it simple until experience shows you what you need and how it would affect your results. However, if you are making a large capital investment into your call center now, then making the right choices at the right time are your key objectives to making cost-effective decisions when selecting and purchasing your equipment.

The right equipment can also save hours of work tracking results, compiling data, analyzing data, and generating reports. To do this manually is tedious, and accuracy can never be ensured. Computers can help in a variety of capacities, from displaying customer data to using the call guide (discussed previously). The equipment you use can also save you money on your monthly bill for phone services. Some equipment, for example, will automatically route calls onto the least expensive lines available, depending on time of day and destination. Finally, some equipment will warn you when a line is down and even tell you what is wrong with it, saving much time and money to locate, diagnose, and repair the problem.

The only piece of gear you must have for telemarketing is the ordinary telephone. You can get good results with one plain vanilla telephone per TSR. However, if you want the best results possible, you will have to get a little more sophisticated than that. You can choose from literally thousands of phone accessories, systems, and computers available from a few large and hundreds of small phone equipment vendors. All the diversification of products and services now available can be a bit bewildering. To make your first step a little easier, first decide what you need; then try to group the equipment that is available into major categories. This section of the chapter will help you define those categories and begin to sort the items you need from those that will only have marginal impact on your success.

Determining Your Equipment Needs from *A to Z*

Telecommunications technology has advanced so far so rapidly that you should be able to find a telephone system that will do just about anything you might reasonably want it to do. Therefore, you need not limit your equipment expectations. It's best to decide what you want to do first, then go find the equipment that will do it, because chances are it's available.

Of course, you might find yourself having to compromise to get a price you can afford. Everything costs, but competition is fierce, and there are good bargains available if you are a good negotiator! You may be able to find a vendor that offers everything you want in one neat package, or you may build your system by integrating components from many vendors.

What to Know before Getting Started

If you are already have a call center and you want to enhance it, first examine your existing situation before you begin searching for equipment. Start by answering the following questions:

What kind of equipment do you already have?

What are the features your equipment has to offer?

What is it used for and how much is it used?

How many phone lines and phone sets do you need?

How many calls is each TSR going to handle per hour? Per month?

What is the total call volume expected for the program per month?

Will TSRs be handling inbound calls, outbound, or a combination of both?

What level of technical knowledge will you require TSRs to have?

How many phone numbers will be recalled frequently by TSRs?

Will the TSRs coordinate with customer service, sales, credit, etc.?

Will TSRs need to coordinate with various services while on the phone with prospects?

What information will be needed for TSRs to do their jobs?

Where is this information stored? On computer? CD? Manually?

Will TSRs need this information while on the phone with prospects?

Are the TSRs, their intracompany contacts, and information they need to do their jobs all in the same location? If not, where are they?

How long is the program planned to last?

How will all of the above change in six months? Three years?

How much money has been budgeted to equip the program?

With the answers to the above questions, you can now speak more intelligently about your particular situation with your vendor and cut through the first level of what you may need.

How Complex Does Your Phone System Have to Be?

Do you need a technologically advanced system to benefit from telemarketing? No, but the level of sophistication you will want depends on the number of calls the center will handle each hour. To be most effective, telemarketing must be organized. The more calls handled by the center, the more difficult the task of organization becomes. The more sophisticated your system, the more it helps you organize and simplify your program for doing things like scheduling outbound calls and call-backs, processing orders, mailings, collecting data, and using the database.

The system needs to be easy to use. Advanced, multifeature systems tend to require a more sophisticated user, although skilled technicians can sometimes program the system so that users of the system may not need to be so computer literate, and many companies have on staff a management information systems (MIS) person available at all times to handle the technical aspects of the job.

Simple, unsophisticated systems tend to be less powerful and limited in the things they can do. Somewhere in between are a multitude of powerful systems that are relatively easy to use. However, each vendor's system is different, and equipment developed just two years ago may be far more difficult to use than equipment with the same features today. In the end, do not assume a system is difficult or easy to use by its features; instead it is always best to try it before you buy it.

Develop a Specifications Sheet

As you learn about the equipment and features that are available, together with the questions you asked yourself earlier, begin to compile a specifications or "spec" sheet of the capabilities you want in your phone system. Later, this spec sheet can be reviewed with equipment vendors who can then try to meet all or a portion of your specifications with the equipment they sell. If you do not specify what you want, vendors will gladly tell you what they want you to get. When this happens, you should welcome their suggestions. Listen very carefully, take plenty of notes so you'll have them to compare and use later for validation and accountability if needed. But remember, vendors are biased; the capabilities they suggest will be influenced by the capabilities they can provide. So consider their advice, but start out knowing what you want and present it to the vendors intelligently, which will give you a greater edge during the negotiating process.

What Happens When You Already Have Equipment—Can It Be Used?

Certainly. Just make sure the phone (and an open line) is available whenever your TSRs need them. Otherwise, you are wasting their time, probably adding to their frustrations, and costing yourself money. However, you may want to consider changing or improving your current system if one of the following conditions exist:

- Your TSRs have to wait to use an open phone or line more than just a few times per day.
- Too many inbound calls are on hold too long during peak hours.
- Too many inbound calls are blocked or detained at peak hours.
- Your telephone receptionist has a hard time keeping track of those who are holding and for whom.
- Inbound callers have difficulty reaching TSRs who are away from their desks.
- Your TSRs frequently have to get up from their desks to get information, or often need information that others have, especially while on the phone with prospects.
- Your personnel frequently complain about the phone system or, when asked, think it should be improved.
- Your TSRs frequently abuse the system (for example, by making unauthorized calls).
- You feel you need to curb telephone spending or you are unaware of how and on whom your money is being spent.
- You are aware of plans to add personnel or other factors that may affect phone usage in the future.

Even if you can satisfy all these criteria with your present equipment, you may be surprised to find what is available. Shop around and see what is available, go to computer or telemarketing trade shows, subscribe to the industry's magazines; you might discover many worthwhile ways to improve your system. If nothing else, you should always remain on top of developments in telecommunications technology. The industry is advancing so fast that to wait until your need is pressing could mean you are missing substantial opportunities for maximizing your potential and increasing your profit margin.

The Telephone System

The single line phone, common to most households, is just that—a phone connected to a single line. There may be more than one phone connected to that one line, but only one call can be handled at a time. Certainly, single-line phones can be used for telemarketing. You could equip each TSR with a phone and phone line, and that's that. It was extremely workable in the "boiler room" days, when telemarketing was just a hole in the wall, and TSRs were calling from the white pages of the phone book; the single-line system was the ideal phone system to use. It's simple, inexpensive, and it makes a connection from your line to the prospect's line. But this is not a telephone *system*.

With a telephone system, more than one phone line can be accessed from a single phone. Also, since everyone who needs a phone may not be on the phone at the same time, a system can minimize the number of lines that must be rented. For example 15 phone sets could share four lines, which is fine as long as no more than 4 sets need to be used at one time. In addition, systems can be enhanced with a multitude of time- or cost-saving features.

The Components of Systems

A telephone system is made up of components. The basic components are the phone sets themselves. However, there may be different kinds of phone sets within the system, each of varying capability. All the phones of a system may be connected to a central control unit, which has its own capabilities; peripheral devices can be online to enhance the system. New features can be added to most systems just by adding another phone or peripheral device. Some devices are designed to do something very specific. These are called *stand-alone devices*. Devices that combine many features into one unit are called *integrated devices*. You can find a device, either stand-alone or integrated, that will do almost anything you want. The cost per feature tends to be less in integrated devices, but the overall price for the device is more.

The trend in telecommunications equipment today is toward integration, packing as many features as possible into one device. Many features once reserved for stand-alone devices are now being integrated with other features, which makes it hard to categorize telephone equipment. In a sense, they're all the same in that you can usually find the features you need in almost any type of equipment. However, there are two generally recognized types of telephone systems: the key system and the PBX. But even here, the distinctions are growing fuzzier all the time. The main distinction today is primarily size. A PBX is generally larger than a key system, but there is overlap here too.

Key Systems

A key system is a network of phone sets, each having direct access to any number of phone lines on the system. It's the phone system used in the offices of most small businesses today. Most key systems range from 2 to 25 or so lines and 2 to 100 or more phone sets. The phone sets of a key system are distinguished by the row of buttons on the set called *keys*. Each key allows the user to access a different line. Most sets can access any line on the system. In other words, if there were 12 lines in the system, each phone would have at least 12 keys. However, you can get sets that do not have access to all 12 lines if you want. Many sets also have other buttons for various features, such as intercom lines, hold, or speed dialing.

When users of a key telephone want to dial a number, they usually pick up the receiver and press a button (key) that represents an available line. The user can tell which lines are available by small lamps on the set that light up or blink indicating the status of each line (busy, on hold, etc.). If all lines were being used, the user would have to wait until a line became free as indicated by the lamps. A key system may be equipped with two kinds of lines:

1. Outside lines, for calls to or from outside the key system (also called *central office* or *CO lines* because they are connected to the central office of the phone company). Each outside line on a key system is assigned its own outside phone number.

2. Inside lines, for calls to and from other phones within the key system (also called *intercom* lines). Each telephone in the system is assigned its own one- or two-digit number to be reached via an intercom line.

On a key system, inbound calls can be answered from any phone, though only a designated phone or phones may ring. However, the call will *flash* and can be picked up at any other phone on the system. Larger key systems can be equipped with an *answering position,* which is a special key telephone designed for use by a telephone receptionist. All inbound calls would ring at the answering position. The receptionist would then use an intercom line to alert the recipient that a call is waiting. If the receptionist is out, incoming calls can be automatically programmed to ring at various other phones, rather than at the answering position or go to voice mail (which is discussed later).

Most key systems today have a central controller, called a *key service unit,* to provide the entire system with more advanced features. On some key systems, the service unit is packed into one of the phone sets. Each phone on the key system may vary in its own features and capabilities. Other stand-alone devices can be added to the system for features not available, perhaps to record data on call traffic.

What to Look for in a Key System

Aside from direct access to any phone line on the system, the most useful features of key systems are shown below. Descriptions of these and other features is given later on.

- Visual indication of lines and features in use (LED or LCD lamps)
- Outside and intercom lines
- Line hold
- Call transfer
- Call forward

The Advantages of a Key System for Telemarketing

Key systems are ideal for a small- to medium-sized telemarketing center. TSRs can be assigned phone lines to which they have direct access at all times. Another reason is that a key system, because of its relatively small size, can be dedicated entirely to the telemarketing center, eliminating interference or delays due to sharing the system with other departments, unless this is a function they will be required to do. Another attraction is that key systems today can be equipped with almost any feature available on much larger PBX systems.

The Disadvantages of a Key System for Telemarketing

The disadvantages of a key system in telemarketing are that it is a relatively small system, so TSRs may not be able to reach others in the company for information when needed unless they too are on the system. This is not a problem for small companies with fewer than 50 or so phones, but the problem can result in communications isolation in larger companies. However, some companies solve this by using both a key and PBX system.

Line Capacity Requirements

In terms of capacity, make sure there are enough lines on the key system, not just enough phones. If your TSRs are to be on the phone all or most of the day, all TSRs should have dedicated outside lines to their phones that no one else has access to. If TSRs are on the phone only part of the time, and some phones are occasionally idle, fewer lines than phones will be needed. On the key system try to separate the lines that are to be used for telemarketing purposes from others. The number of lines you need depends on use. Normal office (nontelemarketing) usage averages are about one in three persons using the phone during peak time.

Use Two-Lines Phones

Although each full-time TSR may need a dedicated outside line, TSRs may also need access to other lines on the system. At a minimum, it is best if each TSR has access to at least two lines—one outside line and one inside line for communications within the company or department. Inside lines are needed for fast communication between the supervisor or manager and TSRs, if not to others in the company as well. Since they would not be used all the time, only a few inside lines may be shared between all TSRs. To make one inside and one outside line accessible to each TSR requires at least a two-key phone for each TSR, plus a hold button. However, you may also consider additional keys on each phone so TSRs can access the lines of fellow TSRs so that one TSR can answer for another who is absent. A TSR can also use other lines during an emergency or failure.

PBX Systems

A private branch exchange (PBX) is a system where each telephone user has only indirect access to the outside lines on the system. Each inbound or outbound call is routed through a central controller (switchboard) within the company before reaching its destination. PBX systems are used in larger installations where the number of phones the system can handle usually exceeds 100. Each phone on the PBX system is connected to one or more inside lines (extensions) that run from the phone to the PBX but not to outside lines. The phone sets themselves may resemble single-line sets, if they are connected to only one extension line, or key telephones, if connected to more than one extension. Outside lines connect the PBX to the central office of the telephone company. On a PBX, outside lines are called *trunks*.

How a PBX System Works

When a user on the PBX makes a call to somewhere outside the system, the trunk that is used is chosen by the system, not the user. Instructions can be programmed into the PBX on how and when to choose various trunks. Inbound calls may also come in on any trunk. The trunks on the PBX may be accessible from the outside by dialing individual numbers; more typically, in what is called *trunk grouping,* many trunks can be grouped under one number. An inbound call by that number could come in on any line in the trunk group. The switching is done at the telephone company's central office. If the first line in the group is busy, the call is automatically switched to the next available line in the group. This is called *hunting.*

The inbound call does not ring at anyone's desk until it has been switched to the proper extension by the PBX, which is usually a manual procedure. Inbound calls are only answered in one, sometimes two, places on a PBX, called *answering positions* or *switchboards* that must be staffed by a telephone receptionist who actually answers the calls and routes them to the appropriate extension, as requested by the caller. Therefore, using a PBX usually requires one or two dedicated telephone receptionists to answer and channel inbound calls unless you are using an ACD system (automatic call distributor) which would reduce the number of receptionist or switchboard operators. (ACD was discussed in the hardware/software section.)

Many PBX systems can provide certain phones on the system with direct access to an outside line (called a *direct-in* line). The PBX can only handle as many outside calls at a time as it has trunks. Although there may be a thousand extensions on the system, there may only be a hundred or so trunks. If all trunks are busy, the caller would get a busy signal. To place an outside call usually requires that the user dial a special number or code first (usually a *9*) before dialing the outside number. Different codes may be required for calls to different areas (as in local versus long-distance calls), and the areas that can be called from certain phones can be restricted.

Making calls within a PBX system is easy. Each phone is assigned its own extension number. To dial another phone on the system, one simply dials the three- or four-digit extension number. Some phones may have access to more than one extension number on a key phone, with lamps on the phone indicating the status of each extension. Though many phones may have access to a certain extension, calls on that extension may only ring on one phone, for example, at the secretary's desk.

A PBX could range anywhere from 20 to 4000 trunks. In fact, the equipment at the telephone company's central office that serves your city or exchange is in essence just a huge PBX. Some companies' PBX systems are so large that they are granted their own three-digit exchange. Calling into such a company requires a normal seven-digit phone number with the last four digits being the extension number within the PBX of the person dialed (this is called a *centrex* system). Two or more of a company's PBX systems can be tied together via *tie lines* which can make the whole system operate as one huge network.

Advantages and Disadvantages of a PBX for Telemarketing

The greatest advantage of a PBX over a key system is it enables TSRs to contact anyone within a large system very quickly. This is extremely important where TSRs must frequently get answers from others to handle prospect inquiries on shipping, credit, inventory, product applications, troubleshooting, service, or other subjects.

The first disadvantage of a PBX is the price tag. It can seldom be justified by the telemarketing center alone and therefore the PBX must be shared with others outside the telemarketing program, which may cause delays or blocked calls during peak usage hours. If the PBX does not have the capacity to ensure a free line whenever needed by TSRs, you should consider upgrading your PBX or dedicating a key system to the telemarketing program.

What to Look For in a PBX System

Almost any feature anyone could want can be found in a PBX. Features programmed into the PBX are available to all users on the system. The features that are most relevant to telemarketing are shown below. You may have a need for any or all of them in your center. Individual phones on the system may provide additional features to the users of those phones.

- Least-cost routing
- Automatic call distribution
- Toll restriction
- Call transfer
- Call forward
- Call pick-up
- Call accounting
- Direct-in Dialing
- Trunk queuing
- Call waiting and split
- Data communications
- Self-diagnostics and power back-up

PABX Systems

Private automatic branch exchange (PABX) is another term often used to describe a PBX with integrated features for both voice and data communications. Whereas the PBX can handle voice communications (which are analog signals), the PABX can also handle communications between computers (which are digital signals) at high speed. Using devices built into the PABX called *modems,* a PABX allows a computer to be hooked right into the phone system, enabling it to send data to other computers on the system or to computers hooked into phone systems anywhere in the world. A modem translates the digital signals of a computer to analog signals that can be transmitted across telephone lines. Another modem at the receiving computer translates analog signal back into digital signals. You should look into a PABX if your TSRs need to access data on computers located off-premises.

Hybrid Systems

Hybrid systems are key systems that are so large that they are like small PBX systems and can be equipped with many of the same features. Key systems with more than 25 lines are sometimes called *hybrid* systems.

Miscellaneous Equipment and Options

Recording and Monitoring Devices

You may wish to record or monitor the calls of your TSRs for training and quality control. Usually, the best way to critique a TSRs' skills is to observe them without their knowledge of your observance, because TSRs may not act the same when they know their call is being monitored, generally due to nervousness. The main thing to look for in recording and monitoring devices is the ability to do it silently. Be careful to abide by local regulations regarding silent recording and monitoring of calls before investing in this kind of equipment.

A variety of devices are available for monitoring or recording the conversations of TSRs. Telephone tape machines can be connected to individual phones or can be part of a central device. Monitoring can be accomplished from a key telephone on the supervisor's desk that provides access to each TSRs line. The supervisor can just pick up any line and listen. The problem is TSRs will know when their call is being monitored by an audible click when the supervisor taps into the line. Plus, the TSR (and prospect) will hear any noise the supervisor makes. However, devices are available for silent monitoring. Be sure the devices are *listen-only*, and that there is no click or loss of volume that the TSR can perceive when the supervisor tunes in. Silent monitoring is a feature of many ACDs.

Uniform Call Distributors (UCD)

A forerunner of the ACD, which is still available from used equipment dealers, is the *uniform call distributor* (UCD). The UCD does not distribute calls evenly among TSRs or extensions. Whereas the ACD will distribute the first call waiting in queue to the TSR that has been available the longest, the UCD will always route the call to a particular extension if it is open. Only when that extension is busy will it route the call to a different extension, and only if that extension is busy will it route the call to a third extension. This means that TSRs with high-priority extensions will get most of the calls while others remain idle except during times of peak traffic.

Automatic Call Sequencers (ACS)

Another forerunner of the modern ACD is the *automatic call sequencer* (ACS). The ACS may route several calls to a TSR using a key phone. Rather than automatically connecting the TSR to the first caller, the TSR must select the call to be answered by pushing a button on the key set. Requiring the TSR to pick up like this can result in some callers waiting longer than is appropriate or fair.

Station Message Detail Recorders (SMDR)

Station message detail recorders (SMDR), also called *call accounting systems,* automatically compile, store, and format data into reports that help the telemarketing manager monitor call traffic and costs. SMDR capabilities are built into many devices, such as advanced key systems, PBXs, ACDs, and computers. Stand-alone SMDRs can be added to just about any phone system that does not have these capabilities. Specific SMDR capabilities vary, but most include the following:

- Number of inbound and outbound calls on each line or extension recorded
- Number dialed and destination of each outbound call recorded
- Date, time, and duration of each inbound or outbound call recorded
- Number of outbound calls blocked (busies), no answers, disconnects, transferred calls recorded
- Call statistics stored on disk or tape
- User-definable reports (on calls/costs per day, per line, per account code, per carrier, per number dialed, etc.) generated

Basic SMDR capabilities are highly recommended for every telemarketing program. Call statistics provided by the SMDR can help identify faulty lines and monitor TSR effectiveness. It can also help curb unauthorized use of the phones. Most importantly, the SMDR can be used to plan line requirements, equipment needs, and work schedules and to verify the call reports compiled by your TSRs. Most phone service carriers provide basic call statistics on your monthly phone services bill or will do it for an extra fee, but they will only provide basic, uncompiled information.

What to Look for in an SMDR

The main thing to look for is the amount of data that can be stored by the system and the reports that can be generated. In terms of storage, find out how many bytes of data are required to store data on each call. If, for example, each call requires about 100 bytes of disk space, a system with a 5 megabyte disk could record information on about 50,000 calls. Before 50,000 calls are made, you would have to print out the reports and data you need so that the disk can be erased to make room for more data. In this case, you would want to determine how long it would take before you make 50,000 calls. You should get an SMDR that can handle at least one full month of calling activity. Otherwise, you will not be able to automatically compile statistics for a full month and you will have to work with the system too often. Also, look into these features:

- Number of account codes that can be programmed into the system, number of lines and extensions that can be handled

- Speed dialing of account codes assigned to each phone or person
- Reports that can be generated on demand, without halting system's ability to keep recording data ("real-time," not "batch")
- All reports time and date stamped, information sorted chronologically, by phone, line, account code, or by other logical sequence as defined by user
- Easy-to-use system generating nonstandard reports
- Compatibility with existing key or PBX system

Integrated Voice/Data Terminals (IVDT)

An *integrated voice/data terminal* (IVDT) is a device with capabilities somewhere between a key telephone set and a personal computer. In essence the IVDT is a telephone that can be used in place of a standard telephone set. It has a screen, keyboard, storage and data communications capabilities similar to a computer. Most IVDTs are equipped with the same capabilities as an advanced key system:

- Direct access to more than one line
- Speed dialing, on-hook dialing, last number redial
- Call accounting (SMDR capabilities)
- Line hold, call forward, call transfer

In addition to these capabilities, the IVDT is equipped with a modem that allows the user to log onto a computer and access or update its database. This means that the user can view customer files, product information, or prospect lists on the screen while talking to a prospect on the phone line. The IVDT also has the following features:

- Recording of messages while unattended (electronic mail)
- Available display of phone directory, calendar, scratch pad
- Speed dialing by menu selection (select number from list on screen)

Guidelines for Evaluating Equipment Vendors—Buy, Rent, or Lease

The options to buy, rent, or lease are available from most, but not all, equipment vendors. The decision depends primarily on the length of time you expect to use the equipment and your available capital. Be sure the vendor you choose can provide you with the option you want.

Manufacturers, Carriers, and Dealers

Equipment vendors come in three varieties: manufacturers, phone service vendors, and dealers. The equipment of some manufacturers is available only through service vendors and dealers. Other manufacturers use dealers in addition to marketing their products directly. Phone service carriers tend to be large. Dealers tend to be smaller but with more experience in selling and installing private systems than many carriers. If you are a small company, or your telemarketing program is small, you will probably get more attention and service from a small dealer. It will be difficult to find knowledgeable assistance on a small SMDR from a vendor that makes most of its revenue from large PBX systems, for example. However, if you are a large company, a large vendor would have more resources to provide the extra services you may require.

Procedure for Evaluating Vendors

After you have learned what you can about what is available and have drawn up a spec sheet on what you think you need, do the following:

1. Call and speak to representatives of several vendors. Describe your needs as completely as you can. Do not be embarrassed to ask questions. Have them mail you literature on the equipment they recommend.

2. Read the literature and prepare specific questions for three or four vendors selected from those you contacted. If you plan to spend over $10,000 to $15,000 or so, most vendors will come talk to you. Otherwise, you may have to do your questioning over the phone, unless of course you insist on an in-person visit. Like you, vendors try to save money by using telemarketing. Things you may want to find out include:
   - Original manufacturer of equipment in question
   - Background and credentials of manufacturer and supplier
   - Size and financial standing of manufacturer and supplier
   - Number of systems installed
   - If dealer, is it authorized and supported by manufacturer
   - Capacity and upgradability of equipment (phones, lines, etc.)
   - Pricing, warranty
   - Speed and costs associated with service and repairs
   - Extent and quality of training and documentation provided.

3. Have two or three selected vendors submit a written proposal of the equipment they recommend. Specify that the proposal should contain sections on these items:
   - Your needs as they see them
   - Specifications on recommended equipment, including physical size, phone and line capacity, and features

- Some kind of productivity analysis compared to present equipment, plus an analysis on the ease of using the system
- Itemized prices for mandatory and optional features (make sure prices include *all* necessary parts and services)
- Service, installation, and training capabilities and costs
- Length of time until equipment could be installed
- All warranties, guarantees, methods of payment
- A list of customer references

4. Check on references and others who may be able to comment about each vendor and its equipment.

5. Go to see the equipment working. Try to use it yourself to get a feel for how easy or difficult it is to use.

6. Make your selection.

7. Draw up a contract. Get *everything* in writing, including:
   - All information included in the proposal
   - Delivery time, installation schedules.
   - Responsibility for installation (should be coordinated completely by the vendor)
   - Payment plan (the last payment should not be made until at least one month after the equipment is installed)
   - Penalties for delay of installation or inability to meet expected performance standards

Preparing for Installation

The equipment vendor should coordinate the installation of your phone system, including all wiring, carpentry, and electrical work. You will have to supply an area for all central control units and telephones. Be sure to ask the vendor how much space will be required. Some large PBX systems can require a whole room. Be sure that any room housing computer equipment is ventilated and humidified to manufacturer's specifications. Where computer terminals are used, natural or fluorescent lighting is usually best. Try to read about the equipment you are getting before it is installed so that you can start using it right away.

The telephone equipment you use in your telemarketing center does not have to be complex, but it should provide each TSR with a push-button telephone connected to one line for calls outside the company and to one for calls within. The system should have the capacity to make sure a line will be available whenever a TSR or prospect will need to use one.

Equipment is available that can do almost anything you might need to do. Therefore, you should start your search by evaluating your needs and decide what is best for your program. Decide on the type of phone sets your TSRs should use and, if possible, provide them with headsets if they want them. Depending on the size of your program and your approach, you may also want to look into automatic call distributors, station message detail recorders, integrated voice/data terminals, computers and telemarketing software, automatic dialer recorded message players, and data communications capabilities via modem and multiplexer. Some of the most notable features to look into for your system include least-cost routing, speed dialing, line hold, call forwarding, call transfer, call pick-up, volume control, and toll restriction.

Once you have decided what you think will serve your needs, talk to several vendors about these needs and see if they agree. Have them submit detailed proposals on their recommendations. Make sure to ask about all hidden costs and delivery schedules. When you make your selections, put everything in a contract before agreeing to buy, rent, or lease any equipment.

Phone Switch and Telephone Equipment

The telephone system you select is obviously where the train meets the track in your call center management. The successful call center depends on this feature, so be sure to save the biggest portion of your investment dollars for your telephone system. There are hundreds of telephone manufacturers to select from, so make your selection carefully. Some basic guidelines have been included for your reference, but be sure to use a telephone or business consultant to assist you with your selection.

The first step in determining the proper telephone switch manufacturer to purchase your telephone system from would be to look at the number of TSRs or stations that you will have today and any expected growth within the next three years. This simple factor can save you thousands of dollars by focusing you on the proper telephone switch to purchase. Some manufacturers have focused on a specific size business audience, and you might be able to eliminate many telephone companies immediately.

Once you have determined the number of stations you will have in the foreseeable future, you must determine the number of telephone lines that you will need in order to accomplish your goals. Be sure to consider in this estimate fax lines, inbound lines (including 800, 900 numbers, etc.), outbound lines, and possible lines required for future growth. The number of stations and the number of telephone lines are two of the most important factors in selecting your telephone switch. The next task is to find manufacturers that can provide and maintain that size of a system. You should also consider the vendor's approach to your size system—not all vendors want to work with all system sizes.

Unless your account is huge, you may not be dealing with the manufacturers themselves. Typically you would call a local vendor or vendors to do the bidding for your system. In this way (even with the same product) you can receive the best value for your investment.

The reputation of the manufacturer and vendor is the most basic function of the operation. If your telephone system goes down, you're out of business. Therefore the manufacturer of the telephone switch that you select will determine your success or failure. Be sure to thoroughly check references of both the manufacturer and the vendor involved.

Warranty of both the manufacturer and the vendor is a vital aspect of making your final selection. What happens when there is a problem with the equipment? You need to know you have made a wise investment prior to the investment, which will give you peace of mind knowing you are getting after-sale support. Always insist on an agreement in writing describing what you can expect from each party in the event of failure. As time is money for all parties involved, be sure your specific time needs are attended to in the contract. If necessary, purchase an on-site service agreement with the vendor, and again be sure all expectations are outlined specifically.

When making your selection, have the vendor not only demonstrate the product but also allow you to determine if it is user-friendly so anyone in your call center can use it. Therefore, be sure that the system can be user-maintained and not just maintained by the vendor. For basic needs such as adding another station or reprogramming some system options for a TSR, determine whether you can perform this operation without required vendor support.

Anticipate that you will expand and make a projection for the first three to five years. Doing so will help you to select the equipment you need not only today but for the future growth you're anticipating for your call center. Always insist on expandability of the system. You do not want to spend your most valuable resource (money) only to find that months later you have outgrown your system. Be sure that your system can be expanded (either lines or stations) without having to purchase an entirely new system.

Explore the financial options that the vendor can present. In this competitive environment, there often are exceptionally good deals and creative financing options available such as "12 months same as cash," leasing, or other financing alternatives that might be attractive to your budget.

Miscellaneous Items

Several optional miscellaneous items could be effective in giving you the tools necessary for a fully functional inbound and outbound call center. It is wise to do some research on them and get the best prices you can; again, negotiate or go with one vendor that can offer you a volume discount.

Battery Backup. This is probably one of the most forgotten items in a telephone system, but upon your first power outage, it becomes the most important option. Do not buy a telephone switch without a well-tested, reliable battery backup option. If the power goes out, your TSRs are not out of business. Remember, while you may be having power problems in your area, the rest of the world is still operating as normal. Make the power outage an inconvenience rather than a catastrophe.

Message on Hold (MOH). These devices look like miniature cassette players that play messages to your callers when they are placed on hold. Most of these

MOHs are relatively inexpensive; however, the production costs should be considered as part of the whole cost. Most of the MOH companies do not make their money on the machines but on selling you their production services. Most of these companies will recommend changing your message monthly, quarterly, or even each time you wish to make a special offering to your customers. Obviously the more frequently you change your message, the more it will cost for productions. When creating a production, the MOH company will usually offer voice type (male or female) or background music (jazz, rock, etc.) and of course, your message. An MOH is an extremely effective means of communicating with your clients and prospects, giving them a preview of what you have to offer along with any special promotions and helping to pass the time, since we all spend some amount of time on hold, even in the most effective call centers.

Voice Mail.   This is one feature that you should seriously consider for your call center. It is a necessary part of your telephone switch for a high-volume inbound call center. For outbound organizations, this will not have as much importance. The voice mail system provides a holding cell for overflow calls. It should only be used when all other live routing is busy and the caller wishes to simply leave a message. These systems can get costly depending on the features required. These features include decision branches required, number of in/out telco lines handled, and hardware limitations.

Call Transfer.   Call transfer allows the receiver of a call to switch the call over to another phone within the department or company if the call was received by the wrong person or department by mistake. Call transfer is also used when a prospect needs to talk to more than one person in your company. For example, after speaking with the customer service department, the prospect may need to be transferred to the sales department. If prospects have to hang up and call again, they may not bother, especially if they are paying for the call.

Call transfer is required on any system where a receptionist fields inbound calls. With the press of one button, the receptionist should be able to both put a call on hold and transfer the call to any phone on the system. *Timed transfer* is a feature that will automatically transfer a call to another extension if it has been waiting on hold longer than a specified period of time.

Conference Calling.   Conference calling provides the ability to call two or more persons with the same line and converse simultaneously with all of them. The ability to do this may require not only special equipment but also special wiring in the local telephone company office. The applications for conference calling in telemarketing are limited. Some high-level business-to-business negotiations that involve different companies, branches, or departments may be able to benefit from conference calling. Otherwise, it is not needed.

Direct-in Dialing.   Direct-in dialing is a feature of a PBX system that allows users on the system to have direct access to an outside line rather than having to compete for an outside line with other phones on the PBX. This can be very helpful in telemarketing where it is important for prospects to reach the telemarketing center without having to be routed by the company receptionist. Direct-in lines also ensure that TSRs will have access to an outside line, for inbound or outbound calls, whenever they need it.

Distinctive Ringing.   On some systems, calls that come in on certain lines may be programmed to have a different ring than calls on other lines. For example, intercom lines may ring differently than calls on outside lines. Distinctive ringing can be important where call preparation, or a specific greeting, is required for calls that come on certain lines.

Grouping, Hunting.   Any number of lines can be grouped into a common circuit called a *line group* or *trunk group*. There are several reasons for line grouping. One is to set up a *hunting* arrangement which enables an inbound call to a particular number to be handled by any line in a group. For telemarketing, this means that more than one prospect can call at the same time and still get through. The second call comes over a second line in group priority.

Other reasons for grouping lines are to simplify call accounting and problem identification. If hundreds of calls are made each day over many lines, keeping track of call activity on each line can be difficult. It is easier to review activity over a group of lines instead. Lines may be grouped according to type of service, type of users, or any other scheme that makes analyzing call data easier. Identifying a problem within a particular group can also be easier than finding a faulty line among many possibilities. Once isolated to a group, the faulty line is easier to find and fix.

Intercom Lines.   Managers, supervisors, telecommunicators, clerical staff, and others within the telemarketing center can communicate with each other in a couple of ways. One is to assign each phone in the group an extension within a PBX, which of course, requires a PBX. With either a key system or PBX an intercom line can be used for the same purpose. Dialing extensions within a system using intercom lines usually requires only one or two digits. Some method of intragroup communication is highly recommended for any department with more than five people or where members are not physically close to each other.

Least-Cost Routing.   Least-cost routing (LCR) is a feature of many PBXs, key systems, telemarketing computers, and stand-alone devices. It is recommended for any outbound telemarketing program using several phone lines to call many different parts of the country or where more than one kind of phone service is used. A system with LCR will automatically select and use the least expensive line for every call, based on the time of day, call destination, and other factors affecting the rate structure of different services. Ideally, a system with LCR should be able to do the following:

- Change routing patterns at different times of the day
- Respond in a variety of ways if the least expensive line is unavailable, such as, place the call in queue for a certain time until the line is free; route the

call to other lines based on priority; or send a warning signal to the person placing the call that the most expensive line is being used

- Allow users to easily enter and change line priorities and assign at least 16 priority levels
- Automatically revert to higher-priority line if it becomes available while searching or waiting for lower-priority lines
- Restrict toll calls

Line Hold and Mute. Putting a call on hold means to put it in a temporary waiting state. A TSR may want to put a prospect on hold in order to answer or dial out on another line. Another reason is to prevent the prospect from over-hearing something happening around the TSR, like a conversation with the supervisor. *Exclusion hold* prevents others from picking up a line holding for a specific phone only. With mute, the prospect will not be able to hear activity on the TSR's end as long as the TSR holds down the mute switch. Hold capability is necessary anytime a TSR may need simultaneous access to more than one line. When hold is available, mute is not necessary.

Some systems sound an audible warning when a line has been on hold for longer than a set time. Other systems will ring the phone again. Some kind of safeguard is useful where many inbound calls may be handled at once by a telephone receptionist.

Paging. The page feature allows any user on a key system or PBX to send messages to other phones on the system, usually over a speakerphone, to locate people who are away from their desks. All-call paging allows the user to send a message to selected phones on the system. External paging allows the phone to be hooked up to the company PA system.

Speakerphones. Hands-free operation can be accomplished with speakerphones, headsets, or shoulder rests. With a speakerphone, the TSR can speak from anywhere within several feet of the phone, and words are picked up by a microphone in the cabinet of the phone set. The words of the prospect are projected through a speaker on the phone and can be heard at the same distances. Speakerphones allow the TSR to hang up the receiver while talking to a prospect; unfortunately all sounds around the phone are easily picked up and heard by the prospect. In a busy telemarketing center, this can mean a lot of noise, which can be distracting and may appear unprofessional. In addition, the sound of a TSR's voice may sound funny to a prospect when captured by a speakerphone, making it more difficult for the prospect to feel at ease. Better methods for achieving hands-free operation are via headsets (discussed earlier) or shoulder rests (not as effective).

Speed Dial. Many phone systems include features that enhance the dialing of phone numbers. Speed dialing allows the user to store a string of numbers under a button or short code which allows an entire phone number to be dialed by pressing one button, entering a one- to three-digit code, or selecting from a menu on the screen of a computer. Speed dialing can reduce the amount of time required to look up and dial the number from 30 seconds to less than 1 second and eliminates the chance of a misdial. Numbers that can be dialed with the speed dial feature may be available to all phones on the system or to particular phones only.

Sound Controls.   Not every connection with a prospect will be the same quality, especially long distance. Some calls will sound soft and weak, and others may come through loud and clear. It is critical that both parties are able to hear clearly to prevent misunderstandings and to avoid the need to repeat oneself. If the prospect cannot hear your TSR, the TSR should hang up and call back, but a volume control on the TSRs phone can help the TSR hear when a connection is weak. Some phones, with a feature called *auto gain,* will adjust volume automatically based on the quality of the connection.

As said before, background noise from the telemarketing center can also be a problem and should be avoided. Some systems are equipped with background noise reduction features that block out all sound except the strongest, which would presumably be the voice of the TSR.

Toll Restriction.   Outbound calls to certain places can be prohibited from particular phones in the center if the system has a *toll restriction* feature. All phones, or just certain phones on the system, can restrict the exchanges or area codes that can be called. *Dialed restriction* goes a step further by restricting calls made on a certain phone to a specific set of authorized numbers only.

Toll restriction ensures that calls are made only to areas where they are supposed to be made and reduces the expense associated with unauthorized long-distance calls. If you plan to call within a local or regional area only, toll restriction can be a useful feature. However, allowing a few calls to go through can indicate professional trust and regard for your TSRs who do not abuse the privilege. A good call accounting system will tell you how many calls are going to unauthorized places anyway.

4

Software Selection

For companies who plan to become automated, this chapter will provide education on the best software selection for a particular call center. When conducting outbound telemarketing, as opposed to inbound, the software selection process is quite different, and prices range from one extreme to another. This chapter, written in a language that can be understood by anyone embarking for the first time on a more sophisticated and high-tech call center, is designed to take away some of the confusion and to provide easy and useful ideas.

Automation

Automation has a positive effect on the profitability and effectiveness of telemarketing. Technological advances have definitely made an impact on the changing structure of the telemarketing industry. These changes include increased cost effectiveness, controlled operations, increased productivity, and marketing effectiveness. Initially, automation made a greater impact on inbound telemarketing primarily because inbound applications are more standardized than outbound applications. This automation has become flexible with decreased cost and increased effectiveness.

Today, outbound is reaping the benefits of automation, and more software companies are designing their packages to meet the demands of the outbound industry. List compilers, who are placing prospecting lists on diskettes, are also considering the automation needs of outbound telemarketing operations.

Automation in the Sales Environment

One of the primary goals of every company is to reduce the high cost of making a sales call. In December 1990, *Harvard Business Review* estimated the cost of a computer industry sales call to be $300/h.* Since that time, the airline and hotel industry rates have risen steadily. This increase in travel expenditures is just the tip of the iceberg. The average sales and marketing department can demand up to 35 percent of the total budget for a company. It has become apparent to corporate America that it has lost control of these external expenses. The business community must find a way to drastically reduce the high cost of sales meetings without losing the "personal touch." In response to this dilemma, sales and marketing managers are turning to telemarketing and sales software to reduce costs and increase productivity.

Lately, everything we hear concerning the economy is negative. But there is one bright spot in the "black hole" of economics—sales and marketing automation (SMA). Companies have found that the best way to reduce the sales and marketing per-hour sales ratio is by automating these departments. In companies that have automated, it is estimated that sales have increased anywhere from 10 to 30 percent, and the return on the initial investment of the software and hardware is 100 percent in the first year. With this obvious can't-lose guarantee, it is amazing that companies have taken so long to realize the advantages of automation. Even in the computer industry, sales and marketing departments are the last area to be automated.

There have been numerous reasons for this procrastination. One major hurdle can be attributed directly to the salespeople themselves. Many prefer to function outside the daily restraints of the office. They have enjoyed the freedom to pick and choose how and to whom they will sell. Their primary goal has been to make sales, not gather or input data for other divisions of their company. With the present economic challenge—to increase productivity while decreasing expenses—we can no longer enjoy this luxury.

Objections raised by the sales department can easily be dispelled with the obvious improvement automation will provide to their earning potential. When the sales cycle is automated, productivity increases, making it possible for salespeople to reach more prospects each day. Some companies have found that the average salesperson can make more than 50 telephone calls per day. Together with the right phone presentation and an automation environment with a high contact rate, sales undoubtedly increase.

By utilizing "telesales," a company is able to reduce the number of times the salesperson must visit a customer before closing the sale. Just reducing these on-site visits cuts drastically into the per-hour cost ratio.

Another objection raised by opponents of automation can be attributed to the very word *automation*. *Webster* defines automation as, "a system or method in which many or all of the processes are automatically performed or controlled by a machine." In many industries, such as manufacturing, automation precipitates a reduction in the work force. Fortunately, automating a sales or marketing department will have the opposite effect. Increased productivity produces more revenue, which in turn enables companies to expand their

---

*Rowland T. Moriarity and Ursula Moran, "Managing Hybrid Marketing Systems," *Harvard Business Review*, December 1990.

sales forces. Telemarketing gives management the ability to effectively monitor sales and marketing strategies and to make the necessary changes that affect the bottom line.

Most companies rely on contact and activity management more than any other feature of SMA software; however, marketing automation is also an important aspect of sales, and marketing software should not be underestimated. Marketing has a great influence on the bottom line—marketing not only affects the accounts receivable (sales), it also has a direct correlation to the accounts payable (expenses). With the proper marketing information, a company can evaluate its competition and customer information, as well as marketplace data. This information not only is essential to the sales force but also is invaluable to the company's decision makers. Marketing managers must have the ability to evaluate their past promotions and trade shows to see if the leads-to-sales ratio has met the company's objectives. In the past, it was difficult for managers to determine if a particular advertisement or direct mail piece was successful. With the right SMA software, all this is possible.

The most important challenge to be met by sales and marketing professionals is in purchasing a software package that will meet their company's particular needs. The packages available to the consumer today are many and varied. The search for an SMA software application should start with a list of internal criteria developed by everyone who will use the new system. Input should be received not only from sales and marketing but also from upper management, accounting, and technical staff. All these departments will be affected by the purchase of the software and should have a say in its design and implementation.

Definitions in the Industry

Before getting into the hardware and software side of this chapter, it is important to understand the definitions that are frequently used in the industry. The hardware and software world is a foreign environment for those who are new to the telemarketing industry. Also this book is for those veterans who have been locked in time and have not had the opportunity to keep up-to-date with the new technology this industry is thriving on. The following definitions will help you make a quick reference rather than referring to the glossary at the back of this book.

Activity Management: The process of cycling through one's actions for a day or a period of time. Some software applications can manage both contact and activity in one integrated solution.

Automatic Call Distributor (ACD): The basic ACD is a device that takes inbound calls on any of a number of lines and distributes them evenly among telephones or extensions on the system. An ACD is ideal for taking orders, making reservations, or other situations where numerous inbound calls are fielded by a number of CSRs, as is common when 800 numbers are promoted.

Automatic Number Identification (ANI): The process whereby the long-distance carrier provides its customers with the phone number of the incoming caller. ANI is typically delivered from 800 service and integrated services digital network (ISDN) lines. When a telephone call arrives at your home or office, the beginning of the call is a series of digits which tells you the number of the phone calling you. These digits may arrive in analog or digital form on the same circuit or on a separate circuit. You will need some equipment to decipher the digits and do something with them. ANI can be used to automatically retrieve database records from your software and have the customer record automatically presented to the CSR, who may answer "Mr. Jones, how can I be of service?" The CSR can look at Mr. Jones' history knowing what he buys, how often, when his last order was, etc. With ANI the calling party does not pay for the 800 call; therefore, the call information belongs to the called party. No regulation is under consideration to limit dialed number identification service (DNIS).

Calling Line Identification (CLID): Unlike ANI, CLID is delivered on a local basis. Linked with your software, the caller's data record can be delivered with the call to the CSR at the same time. CLID is facing heavy regulation across the country. Consumer groups feel that since the calling party is paying for the call it should be private. CLID blocking is available on a per call and/or per line basis for a monthly fee.

Cathode Ray Tube (CRT): This term has been used in the older systems, and it implies the computer screen or monitor from which the representative reads. Today the terms more commonly used are *monitor* or *computer monitor.*

Computer-Telephone Integration (CTI): The merging of computer and telephone technologies to provide users with strategic communications applications such as telephone network capabilities, voice and data switching, computer applications and databases, and voice processing.

Contact Management: Management of the people we come in contact with is integral in a call center application. This is the primary function of a successful call center that should be automated.

Database Management System (DBMS): This is a generic term in the computer industry to imply a database system. There are hundreds of DBMS; however, most companies do not concern themselves with the actual DBMS a software system uses. The company really is looking for the application and its related functionality.

Dialed Number Identification Service (DNIS): The process whereby the long-distance carrier provides its customers with the 800 number the caller dialed. Knowing the number dialed lets the customer know how to answer the call.

Direct Inward Dialing (DID): The digits a caller dialed can identify the type of call. This saves money and time by avoiding the need to set up different physical incoming trunk groups for different departments. The switch knows which department to route the call to by identifying the DID digits.

Disk Operating System (DOS): The basic operating software for all PCs.

Electronic Data Processing (EDP): A general term for techies and their industry.

Front-End Integrated Voice: Usually thought of as an IVR (interactive voice response) or as a voice computer. An IVR uses a digitized, synthesized voice to prompt the caller through a menu of created options. This menu can include other menus, information on anything that has been prerecorded, or options to move calls around an organization or to voice mail.

Integrated Services Digital Network (ISDN): This represents what the world's telephone system should be. This would provide a standard (which does not exist today) for voice, data, and signaling.

Local Area Network (LAN): This hardware/software allows multiple PCs to communicate with a central machine (file server) to facilitate the sharing of information among the entire company. This platform makes sense for smaller call center applications.

Microsoft Windows (MS Windows): A front-end graphical user interface to the standard DOS system. This software allows the user to talk to the computer through a mouse (a pointing device that attaches to your computer) and application software.

Midrange: In between a mainframe and a personal computer. It has been said that this level of computer represents what may be the high end of computer horsepower in the near future.

Network Operating System (NOS): This is the core code that the LAN network uses to implement its file sharing. Some of the common brands of NOS include Lantastic, Novell, and Banyan.

On-Line Telephone Processing (OLTP): This term is usually to reference credit card verification and/or credit reporting. The capability for such is important for most inbound catalog or mail-order shops.

Private Branch Exchange (PBX): A telephone switch for private business; found primarily in large organizations that have a pool of telephone lines and share the pool within the organization. Most PBX systems require the dialing of the familiar prefix of *9* as opposed to direct dial telephone systems.

Proprietary System: Used to imply that the application has its own database management systems and the data are not accessible easily to other applications. Most companies want to seek out an application that uses an "open architecture" rather than proprietary database.

Systems Integrators (SI): An SI usually provides a large turnkey system to an end user that includes multiple vendors' products. SIs are especially geared to work with the government.

Tie Lines: Two-way transmission voice circuits that directly connect PBXs or LANs.

Voice Response Unit (VRU): Think of this as a voice computer. The VRU uses a digitized, synthesized voice to read the options to callers and branch them to the proper options.

Automation Software for Inbound and Outbound Applications

With the right software, a personal computer or minicomputer work station can increase TSR productivity substantially. Computers enable this improvement by automating routine, repetitive, or mundane tasks such as dialing phone numbers or scheduling calls. Anything that a computer can do can be done manually by the TSR. However, since the computer can do all these things faster and more efficiently, automation is recommended for any company with large or small, high-volume or low-volume, and experienced or inexperienced programs. A lot of thought and preplanning goes into making a determination for software that meets your call center's objectives. These suggestions are not absolute, since everyone has different objectives in mind, but they will get you moving in the right direction.

Keep in mind that much of the discussion about the automation of telemarketing is directed to software rather than hardware, since the software is more complex and is your major consideration prior to investing in your hardware. Although some of the information may sound similar, many software applications are better designed for certain kinds of call centers, from the very small one-person operation to the thousands.

The suggestions given are broad enough to help you through your particular needs regardless of where you're at in the process or how small or large your call center is or will become. It is my objective to keep the information as simple as possible while opening your eyes to another side of telemarketing containing aspects vital to the success of your call center. In this way you are better equipped when making your decisions of how you'll set up your operation.

Platform Considerations
Choosing A LAN-Based Software System

Technology has made significant advances to meet the demands of the telemarketing industry, and because of this demand, we are soon entering an era in which the very definition of telemarketing and how it is done will change. Now is the right time to get acquainted with what is available, so that when this new era hits, we'll be ready for it! Finding the right software that meets this demand and is capable of handling the new era is essential when setting up your call center. You don't want your software to be obsolete before the end of its time.

In the following information are some key considerations when selecting and purchasing a telemarketing software package. Systems based on personal computer local area networks (LANs) are mostly discussed in this segment, since many companies believe that LAN alone has the potential to handle what the future has in store for telemarketing and is capable of meeting the needs for just about any company. In any case, it is wise to discuss your particular platform considerations and what you need to consider in selecting hardware and software for your call center.

The Local Area Network (LAN)

In the mid 1970s, the minicomputer brought the idea of affordable computing to U.S. businesses, and later in the early 1980s, the personal computer (PC) advanced this idea even further, making it possible for an individual to tackle computing power while being more productive in the job. Now, the PC LAN is able to combine individual computing power with the information and resource sharing of a network. Companies in every industry have the ability to tap into the potential that the PC LAN represents.

Computerized telemarketing has undergone a similar transformation. After building its foundation on mini- and mainframe systems, it was only natural that computerized telemarketing would revolutionize the PC market. Because of the low cost for a PC purchase and installation, many smaller companies have the opportunity to afford computerized telemarketing for the first time, and software vendors have responded quickly with a variety of excellent packages that increase the power of this new computing platform.

The cost of the personal computer hardware is decreasing over time and presenting a low-cost entry point for a small call center. The major issues to address here would be speed. Though one can purchase 486, 586, and soon to be 686 machines, there is still a limit to the speed of the software because of the architecture of the PC hardware. The environment (even in Windows) is still a single-task world, unlike those environments found in midrange solutions.

For the telemarketing industry, the PC LAN is more than a vehicle for connecting PCs to share programs, data, and communications devices. Because the PC LAN is a connected set of computers, a LAN-based telemarketing system has the potential to process, distribute, and collect telemarketing data, utilizing the full processing power of every work station on the LAN. In some circles, this is called *parallel processing*; in others it is referred to as *client/server*, or *distributed, computing.*

Hardware, software, and training will range from $2500 to $3000 per station for initial implementation. The additional costs that one must consider are ongoing hardware/network maintenance, software upgrades, technical support for both hardware and software, and ongoing training and retraining.

Midrange Solutions

This level of computer falls between the expensive, large mainframe computer and a personal computer. The midrange computer represents what may be the high end of computer horsepower in the near future. Many mid-size to large call center applications use the midrange because of its speed in handling a high volume of users. The IBM AS/400 is a popular midrange computer that provides an excellent platform for call centers due to its architecture, speed, and flexibility in interfacing with the telephone switches. There are also Unix-based midrange computers such as Sun, HP, and DEC. The typical costs for hardware, software, and training will be approximately $5000 per station.

Vendor or Value-Added Dealers

Vendor and/or value-added dealers should be available to assist your continuing needs when you select a particular application. This assistance can come from many sources, but be sure to check out the availability of such assistance beyond day one. Markets change; your application will change; the bottom line is that everything will change. You need to be able to get assistance within a reasonable amount of time so that you can have the software adapted to the changes that have occurred. This assistance can include end-user training, technical training, system design, report creation, custom programming, and management consulting.

Computer-Telephone Integration (CTI)

CTI, or computer-telephone integration, appears to be the hottest topic among call center professionals. But what exactly is CTI and how does it work?

Computer-telephony (telephone) integration, commonly referred to as CTI, has become a way of life for many leading companies. It is not uncommon to find computer systems and telecommunications equipment functioning side-by-side, in integrated environments that provide levels of productivity and customer service that were unheard of just a few years ago.

What exactly is CTI? It is a highly sophisticated system that functionally integrates TSRs and CSRs with telephone network capabilities, voice and data switching, computer applications and databases, and voice processing. Today's CTI encompasses all the technology used in a call center. By integrating all of the technologies such as ACD, intelligent network services, MIS, TSR and CSR workstations, voice processing, LANs and mainframe computing, the telephone transaction can be streamlined to reduce holding times and after-call work times and to eliminate many errors. CTI also has the ability to effectively process each outbound and inbound call. To put it succinctly, CTI links telephone switches with computers to coordinate computer information and intelligence with inbound call handling that automatically incorporates pertinent data, fax, graphics, and/or video-to-voice communications. All calls are enhanced according to the availability of selected services or equipment that passes identifying information with a telephone call.

CTI, which is relatively expensive, is designed to improve customer service and a TSR's and CSR's productivity. Therefore, in the long haul, CTI saves a company potentially lost revenue because it increases communication while generating a higher revenue due to a TSR and CSR handling more calls quicker. According to vendors, and certain end users, CTI return for early stage inbound applications is less than one year. Also the investment for predictive dialers designed for outbound applications which replace the TSR's manual operations can be realized in only a few months.

CTI is making a significant contribution to increased productivity and improved service at a number of business firms and, properly implemented, can do the same for many more. In addition to improving service, building stronger customer relationships, and increasing consumer loyalty, CTI can also generate a positive impact on a company's profitability.

How Does CTI Work?

Before CTI revolutionized itself, the most common application of CTI was "screen pops" to synchronize the arrival of voice and caller data at the work station. Take the example of an inbound customer attempting to determine the shipment status of an order. In most cases, the customer can obtain this information in a number of ways: (1) By calling directly to the CSR; the CSR enters the customer's number on their terminal and retrieves the information. (2) By calling a voice response system; the customer enters the customer number and retrieves shipment status directly from the host database. These two options are similar to the banking industry. When you call into the customer service center, you have the option to either gain information directly from the CSR or to enter your account number and with a series of other numbering options gain information about your account such as balances, deposits, deposited checks, and so forth.

Using CTI, this process can be streamlined by eliminating one or more of the steps the customer or CSR performs. CTI can use caller information or the nature of the call, which is captured through automatic number identification (ANI) or dialed number identification service (DNIS). Through communication between the switch and the host database, CTI enables the call to be automatically linked with the caller's customer account number, eliminating the need to enter the account number when using a voice response system.

A more advanced call center application of CTI uses ANI to simultaneously pass both the customer and the customer's current account status to a CSR's telephone and terminal. Using CTI in this way eliminates having the CSR obtain, enter, and retrieve the customer record from the database, thus improving customer servicing by providing the customer faster service. By cutting down the CSRs' time per call, they are able to handle more inbound calls each day. CTI encompasses the integration of many functions into the work station, implementation of automated outdialing, and the integration of reports from many technologies into one set of comprehensive transaction reports.

Implementing CTI into Your Call Center

Because of CTI's complexity, the high cost of owning such technology, the diversity of each customer requirements, and the variety of existing PBX/ACD, voice processing and computer systems, virtually every CTI implementation is different. Implementing CTI requires a great deal of thought to determine the best uses that meet your internal operation and company objectives. Identify your business requirements. Determine whether you need functionality at the work station (e.g. screen synchronization) or better management tools. Then compute the cost and determine justification for the project. When CTI solutions focus on functionality (i.e., work station automation), it is easy to justify costs. With a large amount of initial investment and ongoing dedicated resources, as well as multivendor cooperation, you should research your options. Take careful considerations prior to making your final determination; in the long run this will save you unnecessary frustration, time, and exorbitant costs.

Once you have identified your needs, decide if your internal information services organization has the time and, better yet, the skills required. If not, you need to choose a third party to act as a systems integrator. Someone who is experienced can often modify standard platforms and applications to fit almost any data processing environment and get your system operational faster than internal resources who are first-time performers. Most existing CTI installations are custom-designed by either value-added resellers (VARs), system integrators, management information system (MIS) personnel who develop their own personalized solutions, electronic data processing (EDP), or telecom departments.

Just like anything new and innovative, once a product or idea as unique and high-tech as CTI has been out for sometime, when improvement has been made in the area of distribution, and when system integration and application development techniques become available, you can expect the process to be less time-consuming and more cost-effective. But watch out; in the next few years something else will come on-line that is even more innovative, something that does *everything* but make your morning coffee, and if you're not slightly overwhelmed now, you will be!

How Are Call Centers Using CTI Technology?

You can use CTI to update your existing inbound and outbound telemarketing operation. By integrating voice and data systems, a company is able to provide simultaneous call/screen switching for both inbound and outbound calls. TSRs receive the corresponding screen of prospect information as the call is connected, and the application is designed so that sales data, such as competitive information, is available to TSRs by keying in the specific code for whatever particular information they are requesting. You can use CTI not only to improve the quality of your telemarketing contacts but also to provide your company with better control and monitoring of the telemarketing effort of each TSR.

Another way to use CTI is when the TSR is conducting outbound call activities. As a prospect is connected, the TSR receives a screen of the customer's purchase history, the prospect's qualifications or any other pertinent data that will be useful for the TSR to effectively prospect for appointments, upgrade, or sell.

Also CTI has the ability to capture specific information on every caller and to route selected special customers to the next available TSR. Not having this feature could cause a company to lose a tremendous amount of revenue from customers who do not like to wait for a representative to answer their calls.

What's Ahead for CTI and How Can You Benefit?

According to the experts within the hardware and software industry, CTI has just begun to pave the way and earn its mark globally. With telemarketing on the rise, CTI will definitely continue to play a major role for our future; we've just begun to see the power of CTI technology. Most of the examples mentioned use the most obvious call center productivity aspects of CTI. However, CTI has the ability to send fax confirmation and to automatically fax relevant product or service brochures and data sheets to callers based on database information. The incorporation of image processing into the CTI mix is able to provide on-screen images so you can actually view photographs. The future holds the possibility of adding full-motion video to the host of information that can be accessed with CTI. Call centers are able to improve service to their customers and to save a measurable amount of time in the process.

Implementing a computer-telephone integration system can be outwardly expensive, with costs routinely running into the high six- to seven-figure range. However, if you are budgeted to spend the dollars and are planning to have a fairly large ongoing call center, and if you see the future telemarketing has for your company's growth, then CTI is something you need to seriously consider.

Choosing a Software System for Your Call Center

There was a time when a company seeking PC software for telemarketing automation didn't have far to look because only a handful of software systems available on the market could do a creditable job. Choosing one software over another was mostly a matter of comparing features lists to see who might come out on top. Now there are more than 150 telemarketing systems on the market, aggressively vying for your business. What's even more confusing is that all these systems include the basic features telemarketing managers want and need for their call centers. The following are issues to consider in choosing a telemarketing software system, and obviously these factors are geared toward a system that effectively increases the power of the PC LAN as a vehicle for telemarketing.

Open versus Closed Architecture.   One major consideration in choosing a telemarketing software system is whether the system has what is called an *open* architecture. An open architecture software system will allow data to be used flexibly rather than rigidly and allows the user to be in control of dictating how the data are used rather than the system dictating to the user.

For example, you have an incoming lead list containing names of prospects for office products. The open architecture software system allows you to prospect those names for their original purpose and later go back and retrospect them in a different fashion, for example, to sell them an inexpensive telephone service, without having to alter data files dramatically or incur massive software changes. The open system allows you to easily integrate telemarketing information with other business applications, such as sales support and customer service systems.

Questions to ask in this category include:

- Will the system allow data to be easily exchanged with other information systems?
- Is it fairly simple to import and export data?
- How flexible is the system in using the data as information? In other words, can you easily change how you use lead lists, what you market to prospects, how you choose prospects from lead lists? Are the data flexible enough to be used as information?

If the answer to most of these questions is no, you are probably dealing with a *closed* architecture system. For many people such a system may be perfectly adequate, especially if your telemarketing organization is fairly small, you don't have a heavy processing load, and you process fairly simple lists. For others, however, an open architecture system should be considered.

Inbound versus Outbound.   The issue of inbound versus outbound might seem insignificant or even too obvious. After all, there is inbound telemarketing software and outbound telemarketing software, correct? This is incorrect. With an open data architecture, and proper use of LAN resources, a telemarketing software package can combine inbound and outbound telemarketing—you don't have to sacrifice one for the other.

The traditional view of outbound telemarketing in which TSRs call lists of prospective customers to try to sell them a product or service is well supported by the outbound packages on the market. Similarly, inbound telemarketing, which deals with incoming sales calls and existing customers, is well represented by a number of packages currently available. In each of these cases, however, software has been designed to support one or the other type of telemarketing. Most can't be used interchangeably for either inbound or outbound; very few, if any, could be used for both inbound and outbound telemarketing simultaneously. If your software application has been designed with a flexible, open data structure, it is possible to do either type of telemarketing, or even both.

Consider this scenario. You have an outbound telemarketing group dedicated to selling advertisement for a trade magazine to targeted businesses. After prospects have been converted to customers, you'd like to have the names in a customer service database, without going through an unwieldy exporting and reimporting process, and especially without having to completely transfer from one hardware platform to another. You should be able to use the exact same data for outbound telemarketing and easily transfer it into a customer database for customer service. Then, you should be able to take prospects who didn't buy anything and set them off separately for a future callback. Combining inbound and outbound in one system means being able to do all this in one place—and it is possible.

List Management versus List Processing. Another key consideration in choosing a telemarketing software package is whether you are doing *list management* or simple list processing. For many organizations, telemarketing is a simple process: a lead list comes in; TSRs call the names, determine which leads are prospects, or actually sell product; and at the end of the process, you end up with either a list of sales prospects or a list of customers who have bought your product. That is what we call list processing, and it equates to the standard definition of computer-based telemarketing that many organizations have. List processing is all they will ever need, and software that supports list processing is perfectly adequate.

However, you should consider whether your telemarketing needs are more complex, whether you will have to maintain a history on each call so you know when to recall or whether to recall at all. Similar to the inbound/outbound question, will you want to easily transfer call records to a different system after they've been telemarketed and reuse the records or market a different set of products to the people on your lists? This is list management, which should be supported by your telemarketing software if it is designed with an open data architecture.

Size of Telemarketing Group. A major consideration in choosing a telemarketing software package is the size of your telemarketing organization, group, or call center—and what your expected growth rate will be. Again, this might seem obvious, but the answer as to how well software supports different size organizations and groups is not simple or obvious at all.

The main factor involved here is how many TSRs you expect to have on your system. In the past, especially with minicomputer-based systems, the answer has come down to how many users the system will support for what dollar investment. If you wanted to upgrade x number of users, it would cost you x number of dollars (often many tens of thousands of dollars), and there was usually a rather low theoretical limit to the number of users a single system could support.

The PC LAN has reopened this question. Theoretically, the LAN can support a very large number of users, and when you connect a series of LANs, a single system could support many hundreds of users, correct? This is incorrect. A LAN running a high-speed file server, a high-speed network like Token-Ring and the most advanced version of Novell Netware available might theoretically be able to support 50 to 75 users or more, but that doesn't automatically mean a software package running on such a network will be able to support that many users. In fact, the design of the network and the design of the software have to fit together hand-in-glove, or performance degenerates rapidly once you start to add users. Telemarketing is a form of on-line transaction processing (OLTP) similar to a bank's check-processing system. A LAN software system that supports a large number of users has to be designed with this in mind.

Many LAN telemarketing systems are built upon the primary data and file-sharing capabilities of the network operating system (NOS), and this simply is not adequate to handle extremely high volumes of information. Of course, if your group or call center is relatively small, say 10 to 15 or fewer TSRs, then you may not be doing OLTP-style telemarketing. In this case, a system that leverages the NOS's own information-sharing capabilities will be perfectly adequate. But any medium- to large-size telemarketing operation needs to carefully consider how well the telemarketing software fits the network environment. You don't want to purchase a state-of-the-art LAN and then put a low-performance software system on it; it's like buying a Rolls Royce and putting a Volkswagen engine in it.

Responsiveness.   Related to the issue of how many TSRs you will have is how responsive you will need your system to be. In part, this is a performance issue, because the number of users can affect how fast the system works, which, in turn, can influence how quickly a new call record is presented on the TSR's screen. However, if performance is important, you want to make sure your software and hardware fit each other as well as possible. Nothing is more unproductive than finding out that the system supports 25 users, but when you added users 21 through 25, you start seeing TSRs sitting around chatting or reading a magazine while waiting for call records to appear on their screens.

Some telemarketing operations, of course, are not so concerned with responsiveness, so waiting a few seconds for the next call record to appear isn't crucial. But for those who need to have TSRs on the phone 100 percent of the time, the software package must be responsive.

How do you measure responsiveness, or more important, how do you gauge if the vendor's claims about performances are true? Start with the direct approach: Ask the sales rep to be honest and give you an accurate measure of the maximum number of users the system will support while still maintaining subsecond response time. If you're uncertain about the vendor's response, ask for a reference site with a similar layout to yours. You're going to be relying on this system for some time to come, so it's worth extra research to make sure you are getting what you need.

Flexibility in Scripting.   Another major consideration in choosing a telemarketing software package is the design of the system's "scripting engine." To an extent, this issue depends on whether the software designer has married data and scripting or has considered the two completely separate parts of the application. If the two have been integrated well, the software should support both global and localized branching logic; if not, usually only global branching is supported.

Many telemarketing software packages treat data storage and scripting as separate functions—scripts are specialized program code, somewhat data-dependent, that control how information is presented to the TSR. Most branching logic in such a system is global; that is to say, the flow from one question to the next is determined in advance by the answer to the current question.

A more flexible approach is to treat scripts and data together, so that localized branching logic is also possible. Localized branching allows information collected during the process of the call to be used in conjunction with global branching logic to determine the direction of questions, if that is appropriate. In other words, the script itself can actually change while the call is being made. For example, with global branching logic, only the immediate answer to the question, i.e., yes or no, can be used to determine the next question. With localized branching logic, information about the contact could be combined with the question's response to determine the direction of the script.

Like an open data architecture and list management capabilities, flexible scripting is a strategic business benefit: it means that a greater variety of products can be sold to a given list, and that TSRs can appear much more knowledgeable about the products or services they are selling. One only has to guess what impact the latter will have on your lead-to-prospect conversion rate.

Contact Management Software

Perhaps the most exciting area of automation in businesses today is the contact and activity management software arena. Various experts in the industry have said that this is the "spreadsheet of the 1990s." In order to better understand the impact that this statement really represents, one needs to understand briefly the recent history of computers:

- The birth of the IBM PC occurred roughly in 1980 or 1981.

- First applications of PCs were primarily for the accountants using the VisiCalc and eventually the Lotus spreadsheet.

- The late 1980s brought about word processing and document creation.

- The 1990s are about contact and activity management (hence, the quote above).

What Is Contact and Activity Management?

Simply put, contact and activity management is the software that will manage your daily "who do I call today?" "what did we talk about the last time?" and, "what appointments do I have?" Furthermore, the following questions will hit home the importance of such a system: Can you easily recall the last time you spoke with one of your hot sales leads? Can you remember what you spoke about or when you need to get back to this individual? What if you (like many business professionals) had hundreds, if not thousands, of contacts—would you be able to keep track of all these people effectively?

Traditionally, people have relied on scribbled notes and good memories to keep track of contacts. Unfortunately, this method makes it all too easy to let contacts fall through the cracks. Since the old way relies on keeping time-consuming manual records, you may be spending more time keeping records and less time doing what is productive, such as selling or serving your customers and prospects.

Originally developed to help salespeople automate their prospecting efforts, now contact management systems are designed to automatically track, schedule, and report interaction between you and your contacts. These systems maintain a database of your contact information: keeping track of names, addresses, telephone and fax numbers, and usually plenty more. Many contact management systems allow you to record extensive notes on individual contact interactions such as phone calls or letters mailed. In general, these systems will allow you to post a call back date and then automatically remind you to make the call. In addition, contact management systems allow you to classify contacts. You may choose to group certain sales contacts as "hot leads" or you may want to classify contacts by geographic region.

The following is a scenario to best describe how a contact management system might work for a typical call center in taking an inbound call:

The telephone rings, and the CSR answers the call. The caller identifies himself or herself as an individual who has seen an ad in a magazine and would like more information on the product the CSR's company sells. Using the CSR's contact management system, the CSR records the caller's name, address, telephone, and fax number. The CSR also records the source of the lead as this specific magazine and promises to send further information to this highly interested prospect. The CSR decides to classify the caller as a "hot lead" and indicates to the system that a follow-up phone call should be made in one week. The CSR then uses the system to automatically print a mailing label and a personalized cover letter for this particular lead. A few minutes after terminating the call, the CSR has a personalized information package ready to be mailed.

Another example for the TSR conducting *outbound* calls would be:

Whenever the TSRs are conducting follow-up calls, they would use the contact management system to retrieve all leads scheduled for a follow-up call today. A TSR would go through this list one at a time and attempt to make contact. If unable to make contact, the TSR would schedule another follow-up call. Upon closing a sale, the TSR then classifies the contact as a "customer" and records a brief note in the notepad provided in the software.

Finally, when filing reports for the supervisor to submit to the vice president of sales, who needs to know how well the magazine ad campaign is going, the contact management system produces a report summarizing the number of calls generated by the new ad and the number of new customers achieved by the ad. This helps to determine how successful the new ad campaign is while also determining how well that particular TSR or CSR is performing.

Contact management enables your call center to think with one mind and speak with one voice. You get increased results because it's faster but also because, with everyone on the same system, your call center has more continuity in performance and reliability of information.

Minimum Functions Required in Call Center Software

The following are functions needed in any call center software:

- *Autodial (also known as power dialing).* The ability for your software to dial the telephone number for the contact on the computer screen is called *autodialing.* This process can also initiate a timer for each call and provide various call-handling options. When ending a call, your software applications will also request a call result code and will store the times, results, and caller information for later reporting.

- *Tickler files.* Once a call has been completed, an entry in a tickler file would be the next action to take on an account. The ability to add more than one action per record can be found in certain software applications. This is important when the CSR takes a call that requires some assistance from multiple people in the organization; rather than setting a meeting for all these parties, the simple action of documenting what is required in the notepads and setting *FYA* (for your attention) activities for the proper people will get the job done quickly and efficiently. This also accomplishes the documenting of each action in the notepad for future retrieval and review on the account.

- *Activity management, including group activities.* As defined above, this is the management of your activities (calls, meetings, personal, etc.), as well as your activities in relation to your group. This is an essential ingredient in the "think with one mind" concept so that if I have a question if you are available, all I would have to do to get this information is to view your calendar.

- *Word processing (single letters or mass mailings).* The creation of letters, whether single letters or mass letters to groups of people, produces the written follow-up which is another key component in the success equation. The more you keep your name, product, and/or service in front of your prospects, the more likely they are to buy from you!

- *Faxing.* Either an internal capability or a link to other faxing products is mandatory to stay competitive in the 1990s. TSR productivity levels are directly tied to their ability to generate letters (word-processing and facsimile) quickly.

- *Notetaking.* Every conversation, every letter, every fax, every thought (internal or external) should be noted in the contact's notepad in the software. Certain software applications offer this feature which is extremely useful as the notes appear on the first screen when you call up a contact record. Many other applications require the paging through information to get to the notes which are the essence of the account history and should be the first thing viewed. If it is not in the notes, it did not happen.

- *Flexible database for creating different campaigns.* As call centers (inbound or outbound) have different campaigns that they work on, different data elements and screens should be made available for the representatives. These data fields can be entered through the use of scripts. There are software applications that are extremely capable in this area. The benefit is that the user has the ability of designing both the fields and the screens in all databases.

- *Scripting.* As important as a flexible database is in the campaign process, so is the ability to script the CSRs/TSRs for these different campaigns. Scripting should include logical branch scripting; as data are entered into the script by the operator, these data should be captured in fields in the database for later reporting. Look for software that provides optional modules for the scripting facilities.

- *Flexible, fast sorting.* Speed is everything. If sorting your data takes forever, do you really think that this would be an effective tool? Software is available that provides an open-architecture sorting tool called *filters* that allow the user to specify fields or parts of fields to search through; there are unlimited numbers of filters that can be created to this end. The sorts are fast, and the software allows you to page through records in the sort with ease.

- *Flexible reporting.* The key here is garbage in equals garbage out. This function comes complete with interfaces to capable reporting tools that allow users to create what they want. No matter where you are in an organization, the automation tool you use should enable anyone to answer any question from a client or prospect. If it is not in the computer it did not occur. The sharing of information among all people in an organization is an essential part of the success of the organization. The goal is to keep the internal communication flowing accurately and swiftly.

- *Cycle-of-action handling.* Most software applications are capable of handling the standard in/outbound *cycle of action.* The components of such a cycle of action are listed above, but to tie it all together, the following will reiterate these steps:

Inbound
- Take the call
- Take notes
- Terminate the call early
- Complete call status/results

- Send letter (optional)
- Set next action date
- Take the next call

Outbound
- Initiate the call
- Take notes
- Terminate the call early
- Complete the call
- Send letter (optional)
- Set next action date
- Move to the next call

- *Good performance.* Obviously the success of the automation effort is directly linked to using the software in the first place. Though it is a fact that any system will never be fast enough for most users, barring the unreasonable, if a system is unusably slow, it will not be used. Therefore, in your selection of the platform and/or software, speed should be one of your key criteria.

- *User friendly.* Is the system usable by operators (not computer junkies)? This point would lie just behind good performance, since the most sophisticated piece of software is not worth anything if your users cannot use the software! User friendliness involves several factors:
  - Can the user understand the options available in the software?
  - When the user is stuck, can she or he find an answer quickly?
  - Are there unusable portions of the program where the program just does not work?
  - Are the options intuitive?

Additional Optional Functions

The following are optional functions to consider:

- *Graphic calendars.* Beyond the obvious, the graphical design is often more appealing to a user than a boring, standard printout of appointments. Most Windows applications will provide this feature.

- *Integration to other packages common to the platform.* This becomes important in non-Windows applications. The ability to share data between different applications could be the difference between a successful system and failure. However, do not let this rule your decision-making process. The software you select should be a standard database design that would allow one to move data between applications. The Windows environment has this inherent ability without any special coding.

- *Links to predictive dialers.* This can be a hot topic and in some specific applications could be a "must-have" rather than a "nice-to-have." However, if you are a fairly small to even a medium-size call center, especially if you are just starting out, consider the cost versus benefit of such an investment thoroughly before jumping to the conclusion that you must have it. (Predictive dialers are discussed later in this chapter.)

Are Telemarketing Features Really Enough?

Comparing lists of features such as those just mentioned may prove to be helpful in sorting through your many choices of available software. But feature lists by themselves can often be misleading and never tell you the whole story. For example, potential software vendors may all answer yes to a feature you request. But the quality of performances that various software systems can actually deliver may be as different as night and day.

Many companies enter into a telemarketing software search without full awareness of their real needs. Paperwork overload and inefficiency in a telemarketing department is often the problem that demands the benefits of computer technology. Instead of looking narrowly for telemarketing software to solve that immediate problem, companies need to see the much larger picture of a software system that can contribute to a broader solution: *sales and marketing automation.* If a telemarketing department can become more productive through automation, consider how much more beneficial it will be to automate the entire company's sales and marketing activities through an integrated system, powerful enough to make database marketing a reality.

Today most companies are involved in telemarketing. But most companies are also involved in a variety of other marketing functions at the same time such as, field sales, customer service, technical support, collections, sales and marketing management. With a fully integrated software system, all these functions can be coordinated from a central database to deliver much higher levels of power and productivity throughout the company.

New Technology and Advanced Capabilities

Not many software systems on the market can perform as a fully integrated sales and marketing automation solution. However, this is not a negative factor, since with fewer limited choices you can evaluate the quality of the available systems in greater detail. Companywide sales and marketing automation requires several advanced features and functions that only a few vendors can offer:

- Automated scoring system to assign a priority level to a client based on profiling information and sales potential, providing more accurate target marketing

- Automated, multistep marketing system to guarantee that prospects receive multiple sales impressions (letters, faxes, calls) over the length of the sales cycle

- Connectivity between the corporate office and the field sales force with a system that provides fully automated transfer and merging of information between remote sites (essential for efficient lead distribution and tracking and timely sales management reporting, enabling the field salesperson to function as a real extension of the corporate office)

- System interface capability that allows two-way exchange of data between the sales and marketing system and other micro, mini or mainframe applications

- Fax transmissions directly from computer work stations to send letters and digitally scanned product literature

- Direct hot key interface with order-entry modules of leading accounting systems

- Automated dealer referral and lead distribution system to match and assign a prospect with the best qualified dealer in the closest geographical proximity

- Marketing campaign planning and budgeting integrated with lead response and return on investment

- Availability of sales and marketing automation project consulting and custom software development to fully meet the organization's needs

As you can see, these kinds of sophisticated sales automation functions will give you an incredible advantage over more fundamental solutions, yet the relative cost difference will be more than covered in increased marketing productivity.

Keep in mind that when you are selecting software to automate your company's sales and marketing functions, you are selecting a long-term business partner. You should be able to relate to the vendor organization as one that supplies quality performance, reliable function, and available support. These issues cannot adequately be measured on a comparison chart, but they are just as important for you to consider as features and pricing.

If the feature lists start looking pretty much the same and you are confused about what to do, the following guidelines should help in making your decision about which software vendor to select:

- Is the vendor's product new to the industry, or has the company proved its stability through longevity and good reputation?

- Check out the vendor's installed client base. What kind of companies have entrusted their business to the system? Do the big-name users represent isolated, single-user systems, or have these companies made major investments in multiuser installations?

- How well does the system run in a real-world environment? Ask for references and check them out. Does the system require frequent file rebuilding?

- What levels of security does the system provide?

- What advanced functionality does the vendor offer for your future system growth? Is there any chance you will outgrow the system's ability to serve your needs?

- How easy is it to customize the system for your own business?

- Is the vendor prepared to work with you? Are consulting staff and technicians available to help you plan your project and to provide special customization services if you need them?

- What training is available for users and system managers?

When you ask vendors to submit proposals, they require in-depth information from you. When preparing this try to understand your company's "big picture" needs and project beyond the immediate productivity crises of individual departments. Avoid asking vendors for just a yes or no on availability of features. Require the vendor to define the scope of the system and to spell out how the features provided will fulfill your needs. Ask if the feature is currently available or will have to be developed after the contract is awarded.

Once you select a software system vendor, automating the sales and marketing processes in your company is a major undertaking. Give yourself and the vendor adequate time to prepare on the front end to make the project a success. Remember that your client database is your most important company asset. Selecting a sales and marketing automation software system deserves your best effort and your most careful planning.

One Final Recommendation

Whenever you are starting out and/or making any large investments into your call center's computer hardware and software needs, it is best to hire a nonbiased consultant. A professional consultant can objectively sort through the various software packages on the market. Most software companies have "demos" you can purchase at a reasonable cost that covers the research work and hard cost of the demo. Test several demos and see for yourself which one is user-friendly and able to meet your objectives in your automation environment. Using some of these measures when selecting your software packages might save you 10 to 20 times the cost of taking these precautions.

5

Setting Up an Effective Call Center for Inbound and Outbound Applications

Some companies' budgets do not allow for retaining professional consultants to set up their call centers. This chapter will help you get started and know all the facts before you start hiring TSRs. Methodical planning and implementation will determine the success of your call center. This chapter will include the steps to consider when setting up and laying a strong foundation for a successful call center.

A variety of information is provided: the role of a call center manager regarding the technical aspects and the estimated cost of setting up and maintaining a call center of any size. The chapter will also discuss the causes of stress and injury in call centers today and how to select ergonomic furniture and the miscellaneous hardware that will reduce the risk of injury in addition to how to provide appropriate lighting and create the ambiance of a call center designed to increase TSR motivation and their production. Also included are descriptions at the variety of headsets available on the market and what to look for depending upon the different type of phone equipment you have. You will also learn how to select the perfect headset to ensure hardware-software compatibility and increase its life span.

Before delving into the technical aspects of setting up your call center, it's important to start this chapter by discussing your call center's objectives. In this way you can determine cost justification for your hardware and software and other technical items that add to your call center's bottom line.

You can invest a great deal of money in order to have the most sophisticated equipment designed to increase speed and to provide accurate reports in a professional environment for your TSRs and CSRs, which are important aspects of setting up an effective call center. However, if you do not know the role of a call center manager, or what your objectives are and how to calculate the production to ensure your investment is being spent profitably, then all the technical investing was in vain. Therefore the following information will help you to set your objectives, determine your production needs, and decide what it will take to meet those needs so you can financially support your call center for continued success.

Once you have studied the first portion of this chapter, then you can proceed into the other aspects that are important when setting up call centers effectively. Again, this information will assist you in the selection process when setting up and designing your call center to support your staff and offer a professional environment that they can and want to work in.

The Role of a Call Center Manager

Gone are the days when the call center manager's job was simply to keep sales representatives on the phone talking to customers! The infiltration of sophisticated technology and integrated marketing now demands a call center manager who is adept at achieving top productivity from systems as well as from people. Since salary can easily be the largest expense for the center, investing in the right technology, under a proficient call center manager, can dramatically increase productivity without adding human resources.

Of course, call centers come in all shapes and sizes. Management skills in a large service agency call center may be applied differently than in a small, two-person telesales team. Either way, there is a certain knowledge level that must be acquired if the center manager is to be effective in developing the department.

Depending on the complexity of systems in use, the call center manager may need to be someone with a high knowledge of technology and with the style of a team coach. Combining these two roles can be difficult, simply because the managers personalities' will most likely cause them to favor one over the other. Those managers who are more people-oriented often find their technology skills must be developed, honed, and even self-disciplined into use. Those managers who are more technical may need to brush up on interpersonal skills.

Call center managers should have their management and leadership styles profiled to confirm their strengths and to give suggestions on how to develop skills in the areas they are lacking. Experience is the best teacher, but specific training may be in order.

Know Your Call Center's System

One of the call center manager's challenges is to correlate the center's activities with the related department, such as customer service, field sales, and distribution. Selling over the telephone is an inclusive activity, and the effects of sales in call volumes on other departments must be monitored. To this end, it is critical for the call center to be managed by someone who understands what data are important for performance measurement and how to prepare data for top management. This includes knowing how to track and interpret specific information from ACD reports, sales reports, distribution reports, etc. Trends should be followed and extreme fluctuations treated as warning signs that attention is needed. For example, a two-week delay in product shipment can cause a flurry of incoming customer complaints. By knowing in advance that shipments are delayed, outbound calls can be made to alert customers before they become irate.

In today's call center, the manager must also understand how, or at least why, the technology in use such as ACDs (automatic call distributors), telephone system and switch, predictive dialers, interactive voice systems, and the like should be monitored for improved performance. It's not that the manager has to know every detail of how to maximize the use of the technology, because sophisticated users will have some level of technical support in the company to help them, but the manager shouldn't be afraid to ask vendors about expanded use or increased productivity from the system in place. That's how you get your money's worth!

To gain a basic foundation of technological knowledge, the manager should consult vendors, professional publications and trade associations and should attend trade conferences. The call center manager must be proactive and read all relevant literature to stay current. The company must take responsibility for providing the support for trade organizations and providing a training budget to develop the manager in a fast-paced, changing industry!

Inbound Call Center Management

Most companies have the need for inbound call management as well as outbound call management. Inbound calls are managed through devices called *call ACDs* or through manual (personal) call management. The customer service representative (CSR) handling the inbound call activity can answer the telephone call and would have information about callers, for example, who they are, where they are calling from, why they are calling, and what prompted their call. The information not only is vital for monitoring and managing the effectiveness of an advertising campaign but it also saves time in production. The user interfaced with the proper software is paramount to the success of such inbound call handling. The software should offer various scripting techniques that can be used to keep all CSRs thinking with one mind and with one voice. These scripts can guide a company in the implementation of a "one call" approach, which is discussed in depth in Chap. 4.

Defining Your Call Center's Objectives

There are three areas that you need to focus on when you want to define your call center's objectives. First you need to estimate the effectiveness and cost factors of your telemarketing campaign. Then you need to list meaningful and

realistic objectives for the telemarketing campaign. Finally, you need to prepare a cost justification for the campaign. Once you have defined your telemarketing opportunities, you will be more confident of your direction. As you
make your journey, you need to know when you have reached your destination, if it was successful, and how successful it really was. The way to accomplish this is by establishing *objectives* which provide both a definition for and a
way to measure success.

In order to measure something, it must be quantifiable. This means that your
objectives should be assigned to a goal and that goal should have a value to it.
For example, if your objectives were to sell 50 manuals for the week and you
achieved that goal 100 percent, you have successfully met your objectives. If you
had only reached 25 out of the 50, you met only 50 percent of your objectives. If
you had sold 75 manuals, then you were 25 percent more successful than your
original objectives.

There are however, two different types of objectives that need to be defined.
The first is your *effectiveness objectives.* The previous example illustrated this type
of objective. The second type of objective is called a *cost objective,* which defines
how much you want to invest into your campaign to meet your effectiveness
objectives. Both these objectives work hand in hand; the more you invest, the
more effective you can be. What is important is to be cost-effective in the process!
When you know the cost effectiveness of your campaign, you can set more realistic objectives.

How does setting objectives benefit the TSRs? Having objectives and setting
them realistically and measurably has motivational value for the TSRs who are
often more productive when they have been given a specified goal to reach.
Also, allowing them to participate in the process of setting those goals is
extremely effective in motivating them. Therefore, what is the starting point
for defining your department's objectives? It is whatever you want it to be.
Every company is going to have a different answer to this because each company has different perspectives and goals in mind for its call center. As you
define objectives on an ongoing basis, you will learn from experience, and that
will help you to redefine those objectives later on. The more knowledge you
gain through your own experiences and the experiences of others, the more
you will be redefining your objectives.

When setting your objective, start with realistic goals that you feel are obtainable; measure how long it takes to meet the objectives and what took place to
achieve them; based on that information, gradually make the objective tougher
and more challenging to reach. Be sure not to make objectives unrealistic, which
can be demotivating and crippling to future objectives you introduce. When setting future objectives, the right mix is between what is ideal to *reach* and what
has already proved to be *obtainable.* There are two fundamental components of
every objective: it's *quantifiable,* which represents the goal you have in mind,
and it has a *time frame* in which it is to be accomplished. By having these two
components, your objectives are workable; without them, you will not be able
to measure your success, monitor the progress, or control your costs. Below are
a few examples of the right and wrong way to use these two components:

Wrong Way	Right Way
Cross selling existing clients	Cross sell to an additional 20 percent of our clients
Make a lot of calls to our primary market	Contact at least 2000 prospects each week in our primary market
Increase our sales	Increase our sales by 20 percent in the next 30 days
Lower operating cost to a reasonable level	Confine operating cost to under $20,000 each month

Quantifying and suggesting time-limited statements are the basics of an objective; however they are not conclusive. Also included is defining observable actions: identify who is responsible for meeting the objective and provide a list of prerequisites or milestones that must occur before the objective can be successfully met. Let's break this down further so you can clearly see each of these elements to apply to any objectives you define in the future:

Train Two TSRs to Sell 30 Seminars and 50 Speaking Engagements Nationally for This Fiscal Year

Prerequisite	Train two TSRs
Observable action	Sell
Quantification	30 seminars, 50 speaking engagements
Specifics	Nationally
Time frame	This fiscal year

When creating your objectives, write a list of exactly what you want to do and how your plans will assist you in achieving them. This will help you to visually establish perspective and ensures that your objectives are in harmony. Conflicting objectives would be too confusing and would defeat your campaign. Instead, establish your priorities and adjust your objectives so they work together, so they enhance each other.

Another area of setting up your objectives is to define what you want your company to gain from your department. For example, *generate 40 percent of the company's annual revenue by conducting outbound calls to secondary markets*, or, *generate 30 appointments each day per TSR*. This second example is more difficult to relate to company objectives other than by having a predetermined number of appointments to generate for the outside sales division which might enable your company to reach it's $2.5 million goal. Each year when the company increases it's goal, you would increase yours to meet those objectives.

Be sure your objectives identify an action that can be accounted for and measured; otherwise it will defeat your purpose for having objectives.

Setting Up Short- and Long-Term Objectives

Just like setting your TSRs' goals or personal goals for yourself, you also need to set your objectives in a similar way. Your short-term objectives may be daily, weekly, monthly, or quarterly. Be sure to set your objectives to be attained within the first year of the program. When setting your long-term objectives, you can go as far as 5 or even 10 years. Planning your long-term objectives early will help you to know what steps you need to take in your short-term objectives that will meet your long-term ones. Remember, make sure your objectives enhance each other and learn to be flexible in adjusting your objectives whenever your experience tells you to do so.

Define the Cost of Your Objectives

You need resources to help meet your objectives; without them, your objectives will not happen for you. You need financial support and the right personnel, and you must determine how much you will need and are willing to invest to meet your objectives. Make sure that your investment does not exceed your return; otherwise, you have gained nothing. If you are just starting your call center and you have a limited budget, remember, all you need to start is a telephone, dial tone, desk, person, prospecting list, and a place to put them. Once you have generated enough capital, then you should invest it back into your call center for a more sophisticated call center, such as a computer, software, headphone sets, and so forth. Better technical equipment will increase whatever production you had with just the basics by a minimum of 30 percent, which will help you reach your objectives quicker and more cost effectively.

Build in an early warning system into your objectives. For example, divide your medium long-term objectives into segments, called *subobjectives*. Let's say you want to generate 3000 sales in one year. You divide that figure by 12 months, giving you 250 sales per month. To break this down further, you will need 62.5 sales per week with an average of 12.5 sales per day. Knowing this in advance, you will have a better handle of what is required and if you fall behind within a few days of the objectives, it's time to assess the situation and readjust! If you want to have control of the potential losses ahead of time, you don't want any surprises at the end of the first quarter, finding you have a great financial loss. Early reassessment will enable you to adjust before the losses accumulate. Keep in mind that your daily, weekly, and monthly figures will differ based on seasonal buying patterns and other factors that you know are typical either for your industry or your company. By adjusting along the way, you can allow other days, weeks, and months to make up for those particular off or low peak times.

Too often, managers are slow to react to problems because they are unable to differentiate a problem from normal or acceptable results. One of the reasons that this happens is that managers are so engrossed in managing their day-to-day operations that they are not paying close attention. Having objectives for every program in your call center will keep you abreast of what is happening and why, as well as when and what you can do to combat problems. Also, it is okay not to hit the objectives precisely as you projected, but you need to set an acceptable range. For example, if your objectives are 100 sales, an acceptable range may be between 80 to 100, with 80 being your warning signal. Anything under 80 would be unacceptable, endangering successful completion of your objectives. It's time to regroup and analyze the circumstances that may have prevented you from being within your range.

The key here is to do something when you see your objectives failing. Predetermine what your actions will be based on where your range is failing. Below is an example of what you can do to predetermine what your actions will be:

Below 50 percent: Reassess your program objectives. Include products, services, and your market.

50 to 69 percent: Reconstruct your telemarketing approach, rebuttals, and offering.

70 to 79 percent: Evaluate your prospect list and find a different one.

80 to 89 percent: Alert upper management about problems and gain feedback.

90 to 109 percent: Program on target, continue as planned.

110 to 129 percent: Consider revising your objectives or increasing objectives and targets.

130 percent +: Definitely raise your objectives and TSR quotas.

You may decide to change the temperature of your actions based on your company and its financial ability to support the objectives. Don't panic; you learn by your examples. By monitoring and tabulating each campaign from the beginning of the project to the end, you will always improve your results each step along the way.

How to Set Realistic Objectives

Setting realistic objectives is difficult unless you have an idea of the kind of results to expect. There are many variables that affect results: your product, your market, company structure, company support, TSR staffing, compensation plan, prospect list, presentation script, equipment, environment, and the skills of your TSRs are all critical aspects of whether you're successful or unsuccessful with setting realistic objectives for your call center.

Whether you are operating a new call center or have had your center for some time will greatly affect the cost factors of supporting your call center's objectives and thus determining its effectiveness. Unless you have previous experience, you should try to get as much information from other sources, beginning with the ideas this chapter is providing. Other resources you may use to gain information are your related experiences, the experience of others, telemarketing consultants and service agencies, periodicals specializing in telemarketing, dry runs, and test calls. These will give you a start if you have nowhere to start.

How to Define Cost Effectiveness

You can define cost effectiveness in many different fashions. Three particular ways to define it are the following:

1. Number of calls made or received per TSR-hour (C/TSR-h)
2. Number of complete presentations made per TSR-hour (P/TSR-h)
3. Number of obligations accepted (sales or appointments) per TSR hour (S/TSR-h)

The TSR-hour represents what one TSR can accomplish in one hour of telemarketing. From the three ways to define and calculate, you should be able to determine cost-effectiveness ratios such as the number of sales per 100 calls, the cost per sales, hours per sale, or the sales per TSR. Let's take each of the three and break it down so you can calculate your cost factors and define the cost effectiveness of your objectives.

Calls per TSR-hour (C/TSR-h).   The number of dials each TSR is making per hour or the number of inbound calls TSRs are receiving per hour will tell you what the minimum and maximum requirements you know your TSRs can do each hour based on the equipment they are using. A change in these figures will tell you how effectively your TSRs are handling their time and how hard they are working. When you compare this figure with the sales per TSR-hour (S/TSR-h) and your cost per hour for each TSR (including the hard cost such as the telephone bill for each hour of operation), you will be able to determine the cost effectiveness of your campaign.

Presentations per TSR-hour (P/TSR-h).   Determining the number of calls your TSRs are able to make is important, but it only reveals the limits of what can be done each hour per TSR. What's really critical is to determine the number of complete presentations per hour per TSR. When a TSR completes a presentation he or she has presented effectively and can ask for the order or a commitment. Another way to look at this is the number of *selling opportunities* the TSR performs each hour. Let's face it—you cannot sell anyone unless you are in a situation that asks for it. A TSR's presentations will be different each hour depending on the type of calling she or he is doing. For example, if TSRs are contacting executives, their contacts per hour are significantly fewer than calling homeowners during prime-time calling.

Sales per TSR-hour (S/TSR-h).   This measures the final outcome of how successful your campaign is. Determining the number of prospects' commitments each TSR-hour allows you to compare this success to the number of calls and presentations given in an hour. You can better assess the number of calls and presentations given each hour and predict the sales or commitments you can expect daily, weekly, monthly, quarterly, and annually. Also it helps you to determine how many TSRs you require to reach a specific sales goal or your department sales objectives.

Conclusions

After you have identified these objectives and performed this analysis for a certain period, results will become fairly consistent and predictable, providing you are offering the same product or service in the same market and using the same caliber of TSRs to perform the task, and so forth. As you compare current results with previous figures you will find that the calls per TSR hour will relate directly to the number of sales or commitments received. Therefore, if you want to increase your sales, you either need to increase the calls per hour or add more TSRs if increasing calls is not feasible. You can also reduce the amount of paperwork your TSRs are doing so they have more time to make calls. However, as a training step, you can have new TSRs make the actual first contact and utilize your more experienced TSRs to conduct the follow-up calls, thus maximizing your "closers" to their fullest potential while training new TSRs on the basics. Whenever you experience a drop in production, the first area you want to look at is the number of calls being made each hour. If there has been no drop, then look at the number of presentations they are doing each hour and whether they have fallen short in those numbers. If you have an unexplained drop then you can determine it is due to one or a combination of these three areas:

1. The effort of your TSRs
2. The TSRs' presentation
3. A change in your product or service, market, or company

Changes in product, service, market, or company is something over which your TSRs have no control, and you need to determine for yourself what those changes are. However, the best indicator of your TSRs' effort is going back to the number of calls they are making per hour. To determine the quality of the presentation, you need to know how many prospects are listening to it. By keeping track of how many presentations per hour the TSR is conducting, you can test the effects of changes to make in the script. You may need to go back and retrain your TSRs who are falling short of your objectives; they may be incorporating some of their own methods into the presentation that you did not originally instruct them to use. Prior to making adjustments into your objectives, you need to understand the level of a particular call the TSR will face each hour.

There are seven levels of a quality call; outbound calls encounter all seven levels while levels 3 to 7 deal with inbound calls:

Level 1. No connection—no answer, disconnected number, or busy signal.

Level 2. Connected but no contact with decision maker. Decision maker is unavailable, caller got voice mail, answering machine, child home with no parent, etc.

Level 3. Contact made, but prospect cut TSR off prior to heart of presentation. Either prospect didn't have time to talk and TSR has permission to conduct a follow up, or prospect was disinterested in the early stages of presentation and refused to allow TSR to continue or hung up.

Level 4. Contact made to unqualified prospect. Prospect listened and, during TSR's probing step, prospect was identified as not qualified or was not able to create the need for offering.

Level 5. Qualified prospect listened to full presentation; made attempt to close on something, but no offer was accepted.

Level 6. Qualified prospect listened to full presentation; made attempt to close on something, but only secondary offer was accepted—information to be sent with a willingness to accept a follow-up call.

Level 7. Prospect accepted primary offer; a commitment or sale was made.

When using this level chart, you can determine the strengths and weaknesses of your TSRs' presentations. For example, if more than 10 percent of your prospects cut your TSRs off within the first 30 seconds of their presentation (prior to probing) then it's the TSRs' style of presentation that needs to be evaluated or they may not be following the script as you instructed. Another area that you can evaluate is your prospecting list; if you find too many that are unqualified, then you need to reassess your list and get another that is more targeted to your call objectives. If your TSRs are getting the prospects to accept the secondary offer as opposed to the primary offer, then either they are not following the script or you need to rewrite the script, changing your approach or the offering.

Determine How Long You Will Need to Meet Your Objectives

Once you have determined the cost effectiveness of your objectives, you can estimate the number of total TSR-hours needed to meet your objectives. First you need to translate your objectives into the number of sales you want. For example, if your objective is to generate a revenue of $2 million in one year, how many sales does this represent? You can use your sales per TSR-hour objective to determine the total TSR hours needed. The formula to calculate this is as follows:

Sales objective ÷ dollar per sale = Sales needed to meet the objective

Take the total sales needed and divide it by the number of sales obtainable per TSR-hour to get hours needed to meet the objective:

Total sales needed ÷ sales obtainable per TSR-hour = hours needed to meet objective

Then take the next step to determine how many total TSRs are required to meet the amount of hours it would take to meet the final objective. You accomplish this by dividing the total hours by how many realistic telemarketing hours each TSR will perform per year and—Bingo!!—you now know how many TSRs are required to meet the objective. The following is an example:

	$2,000,000.00	Objective
÷	$125.00	Product sale cost
=	16,000	Sales required to meet the objective
÷	2	Sales per hour per TSR
=	8,000	Total hours required to meet the objective
÷	1,440	Hours per TSR in one year, based on 30 hours per week per TSR
=	5.55	TSRs required to meet the objective

Another example: If your objective is to generate 10,000 leads and you estimate that each TSR can generate 5 per hour, then it will take you 2000 total hours to generate those leads:

$$10,000 \text{ leads} ÷ 5 \text{ leads/TSR-h} = 2000 \text{ TSR-hours}$$

To determine how many weeks it would take to reach your objective, you would first determine how many TSRs you have to work with and multiply them by how many hours they can work each week; then divide the total hours required to meet the objective by the total TSR hours for one week, and you have your time status determined to meet the objective:

$$5 \text{ TSRs} \times 30 \text{ hours per week} = 150 \text{ hours}$$
$$2000 ÷ 150 = 13.33 \text{ weeks required to meet the objective}$$

Keep in mind that these figures are not realistic, since several issues were not factored into them. For example, sick leave, vacation, holidays, etc. were not taken under consideration, and time off is inevitable. Therefore, when you calculate your time tables, be sure to add the other figures that will reflect time off. It is better to add more hours for time off, since this is not under your control. Unfortunately you depend on your TSRs to come into work when they are supposed to, and reality proves they will not always do so. Setting your figures on the high side will give you a more realistic low figure of what it would take to meet your objectives.

Some of the areas where you may need to add or make changes to ensure you meet your objectives are the following:

Increase the number of leads that can be generated per TSR hour

Add more TSRs

Have TSRs spend more time on the telephone, less time on paperwork.

Increase the leads per TSR hour, by advancing your equipment, providing better training and motivation.

Be sure to evaluate the cost factors of hiring additional TSRs as opposed to advancing your equipment or retraining them and so forth.

How Do You Calculate the Cost of a Single Telemarketing Call?

When you know the cost per telemarketing call, you can compare the revenue generated per call to the cost per call. If the cost per call is higher than the revenue, your telemarketing is not effective. Chances are you are not following the guidelines that have been provided in this book. Go back to the TSRs you have hired and ask yourself several questions. How is your compensation plan structured? Are you training TSRs on the 12-step process in the training chapter of this book? What kind of motivation and ongoing support are you offering your TSRs? Theses questions will help you to determine where you are going wrong in your program. Many companies that fail at telemarketing believe it's because their product or service is not marketable by way of telemarketing, that it is more of a direct mail piece or direct sales approach. In some situations this could be true; however, for most, telemarketing is for everyone, but not all telemarketing campaigns are the same for everyone. You may need to do telemarketing to generate quality leads for your outside sales force, or to follow up on your mail piece. The *way* you use telemarketing will make a difference in your success.

In order not to complicate things, the following examples will help you in determining revenue per call based on a direct sales call. The revenue generated by each call can be figured as follows:

1. Figure the number of calls required to make one sale:

$$C/TSR \div S/TSR\text{-}h = \text{number of calls required per sale}$$
$$30 \text{ calls per TSR-h} \div 2 \text{ sales per TSR-h} = 15 \text{ calls required per sale}$$

2. Calculate your revenue per call:

$$\text{Average value of each sale} \div \text{calls/sale} = \text{revenue per call}$$
$$\$125.00 \div 15 \text{ calls per sale} = \$8.33 \text{ per call}$$

Based on the above examples, your cost per call must be less than $8.33 in order for you to make a profit.

Calculating Your Cost Per Call

To determine your cost per call, you need to add everything related to the cost of making that call. These costs may vary depending on each campaign you are doing. The TSRs' compensations and bonus structures and how they are supervised on the phone equipment, phone services, and the list management system used will add to this variance. When figuring your other overhead costs, put them into a cost-per-hour figure so you can easily calculate your cost per call. An example would be, add up each TSR's total phone cost for the month, and divide the hours the TSR worked on the phones, which will give you an average of a single hour. Your lists cost you x amount, and you have purchased 5000 names per TSR. Determine how many names each TSR can contact per hour, divide that figure to the total names, and you will have a cost per hour on your lists. Do this calculation with all other costs analysis. Realizing these are not exact figures, it is better to exaggerate your figures so you don't underestimate your costs. Below is an example that will show you a picture of how to make your cost per call calculation:

TSR compensation	$10/h ÷ 30 calls/h = 0.33 cents/call
Telephone service	$10/h ÷ 30 calls/h = 0.33 cents/call
Equipment	$ 5/h ÷ 30 calls/h = 0.17 cents/call
Administration	$ 5/h ÷ 30 calls/h = 0.17 cents/call
Lists, database	$ 2/h ÷ 30 calls/h = 0.07 cents/call
Overhead	$10/h ÷ 30 calls/h = 0.33 cents/call
Total	$42/h $1.40/call

These figures are based upon paying your TSRs only $10 per hour with no consideration of bonus and incentives along with other underlying costs such as employer contributions, workers' compensation, benefits, and so forth. It is also based on TSRs conducting an average of 30 calls per hour; however, in certain telemarketing applications the calls per hour could decrease considerably. For example if your TSRs are contacting executives, who are more difficult to reach on the first call, the contact ratio would drop to as low as 5 calls per hour. When this happens, you need to adjust the other cost factors, and your cost per call could go up as high as $10 to $20 per call. When comparing the cost per call to your revenue per call, it will enable you to determine whether your telemarketing program is working. If you want to project your total cost in order to meet your objectives, then multiply the calls you need to make by the cost per call to get your total figure. Using $3 as an appropriate figure for cost per call, if you need to make 3000 calls to meet your objectives, then it should cost you about $9000 to meet your objectives (3000 × $3 per call = $9000).

Determining Your Telemarketing Call Center's Budget

It is recommended that before you set up your call center, you consult with an accountant who specializes in assessing your budget figures. There is a rule of thumb which you can go by that will give you ball-park figures. But every situation is different, and your budget depends on how much you want to allocate for salaries, commissions, benefits, and other compensations. The compensation plan will be the most expensive part of your budget.

Your second most expensive item is the telephone line usage charges, and if you are automating, your third highest expense, which ties hand in hand with the list and database, is your computer, peripherals, phone-related equipment, and equipment maintenance. Other factors in determining your budget are as follows: rent, utilities, furniture, security, training, outside vendors, consultants, supplies, travel, bad debt, taxes, cancellations, returns, accounting, administrative cost, shipping, packaging, and of course your production cost of any products (if products are what you're offering). This list is quite extensive, but with an expert assisting you, each list item will be given a percentage placed by them. When using your cost per call, per revenue, per objectives, experts will assist you in meeting your budget cost. Everything ties in and works in meeting the end results, which is to become—solvent!

Don't feel dismayed, telemarketing has already proven itself to be a cost-effective and productive means of starting and expanding one's business opportunities. Enough companies have been through the trial-and-error syndrome; there is no need for *you* to have to go through that again. We all have the opportunity to learn from the mistakes of others as well as their successes; that is precisely why this book has been written—*for you*, to offer you a cost-effective means of getting started. As it has been said many times you don't have to start out elaborately; start small, and work your way up to a more sophisticated call center. You want first to be able to prove to yourself that you can support the call center.

Now that you have the information needed to support your call center financially and ensure its success, you need to know what other options you have available to further support it in the area of headsets, lighting, ambiance, and ergonomic furnishings.

Environmental Planning

Incorporate a Positive Environment.   Creating a positive telemarketing environment involves the consideration of many factors: the TSR's individual work space, the layout of the office, and the location of the building. Environmental planning also includes the ease with which TSRs can interact with each other and the tools of their trade.

Set-up an Environment Where TSRs Feel They Are Important.   Nothing is more motivating than a company that shows it cares about its employees. An important way to show this concern is to provide a good environment. Supply a good ergonomic chair and ample work space. Provide a safe, comfortable, and convenient environment. Ensure that all procedures, technical hardware, software, and people are supportive and friendly. Pay attention to details. Having headsets and terminals are important to your call center, but don't neglect to provide personal phone directories, extra pencils, or wastebaskets. It's the little things that count to your TSRs.

Is It Worth the Cost?   When TSRs are not given the things they need to be comfortable, have to wait in line 10 minutes to use a copier, or have members of other departments walking through the center all day, they tend to feel temporary or insignificant to the company. Your TSRs' attitudes affect the company, your customers, and your prospects. TSRs may become uncooperative and unproductive or may become discourteous to your prospects. These aggravations will increase a TSR's frustration and decrease motivation. The cost of these things will far exceed any costs you may incur to provide a safe, comfortable, and friendly environment.

If the environment is particularly unbearable, turnover will be very high. Some experts estimate it costs four to six times as much to hire and train a new TSR as opposed to keeping an experienced one, not including lost sales while the new TSR gets up to speed. In addition, most experienced TSRs can spot a boiler-room environment and will not want to work in it. Not only will the manager spend a significant amount of time hiring, but the firm also may not be able to attract the most qualified candidates.

Always remember, your TSRs are very important to the success of your company. If they're engaged in direct sales, they are at least as important as an outside sales force. When you compromise on environment, you compromise on motivation, enthusiasm, and productivity. And when you compromise on these, even a little, you compromise on the potential success of your call center.

Avoid Common Mistakes. There are several aspects of a telemarketing environment that commonly hinder a TSR's efforts to be motivated:

- Too much paperwork, or forms take too much time to complete
- Information needed to do the job well is not easily accessible (customer, product, shipping, inventory, credit, specials, etc.)
- Too much noise or traffic—interferes with concentration
- Unable to interact with other TSRs—too much isolation
- Too many policies, procedures, and red tape to meet objectives
- Unpleasant personal habits of fellow TSRs allowed to continue
- Inconvenient to find or use things that are needed frequently (files, copiers, supplies, mail room, bathrooms, etc.)
- Inability to escape to a personal area or break room (when necessary)

Create an Environment That Looks Professional. Since you want to project a professional image to prospects, you should make TSRs feel like telemarketing professionals. You should create an environment that looks like it is inhabited by people who are serious about telemarketing, who are good at what they do, and whose careers are in telemarketing, sales, or marketing. Telemarketing is a fast-paced growth industry. Therefore, the office should be clean and efficient with a modern business style.

Provide a Dedicated Environment. If possible, try not to have to share your telemarketing space, equipment, phone lines, supplies, and so forth with other departments and functions. The company attitude should be to place TSRs in a position of status, a class by themselves, which should be reflected in their own office space. Also, the needs, pressures, and attention of a telemarketing department are much different than any other department you have in your company. Sharing facilities could be the least expensive way for you to start the program but may be the most costly to long-term productivity.

Provide Easy Channels for Escape.   Phone work is tough, and sometimes TSRs need to get up and remove themselves from the environment for a few minutes. This should be encouraged as long as it's not abused, because a few minutes off the job can make the time on the job several times more productive. The channels of escape have to be convenient. Retreating to a personal, at least semiprivate, work area is one way to escape from others and think things through. A nearby window provides an opportunity to clear the mind. Also, a nearby secluded break area is important. TSRs should be encouraged to go to the break room during breaks to sit, talk, get a drink, or just relax, so they will be much more likely to start again refreshed, optimistic, and successful.

Ensure Balance Between Social Stimulation and Privacy.   Stimulation from others in the group can be very powerful and should be used in the modern, professional telemarketing environment. Social interaction with peers and recognition for sales should be encouraged. TSRs need to be aware that others are doing well so they know that it's possible to do it themselves. They also need to develop good social relationships with their peers to feel comfortable, for encouragement, and for an escape when needed. However, social interaction needs to be balanced with a measure of privacy as well.

Too much noise and visual distraction interferes with the TSR's ability to listen effectively. TSRs must guide the prospect, be sensitive to what should be presented, know when to close, and be able to negotiate calmly and reasonably, all of which requires concentration.

Provide an Environment That Increases TSRs' Motivation.   The main purpose of a positive environment is to allow motivation to exist and flourish. However, environmental factors can be used as rewards to increase motivation as well. Recognizing the efforts of your top performers by granting them a larger or more private work space gives them something to strive for. Granting preferred locations, an extra work table, or desk pad might be symbols of increased status and make good rewards.

Designing an Effective Call Center on a Tight Budget

The following information is designed for those companies who are on a tight budget or not ready to invest a great deal of money toward furnishings until they see the call center has proven to be a profit center. The objective here is to ensure that you provide a clean, safe, and professional environment. Once your call center is generating a profit, devote a certain percentage of the profit toward modernizing it and making it ergonomically safe.

Minimum Work Space Requirements

Like most other issues about telemarketing, you can spend a little and get good results or spend a little more and get excellent results. However you need to consider two criteria. First, if you make any investment, even just a little, make a wise investment. Don't just settle for anything; quality is important, but keep the TSR or CSR in mind when making your selections. The second criterion is your budget and confidence in the program. For testing and during the initial phases of the program, you may not want to invest too much on each work space. This is fine until you begin to know what you can accomplish with telemarketing. However, you should plan to finalize your work space requirements within the first two or three months of the program. After that, it may be too easy to settle for less than maximum performance, and changes will be more disruptive.

The minimum TSR work space requirements are the following:

- Desktop or table for writing, phone, call guide, etc.
- Shelving for product information, reference materials
- Ordinary, push-button telephone
- Comfortable, adjustable (height, tilt, swivel) chair on casters

The Ideal Work Space

As the success and permanence of the program become evident, and telemarketing is advancing leaps and bounds into technology for more productive work stations, you should move toward the "ideal" work space. The ideal work space depends, in part, on the equipment being used by each TSR, the amount of reference materials needed, customer file space needed, and space and privacy required to accommodate your type of telemarketing. The more automated you become, the less work space is required for paperwork and reference books etc. For example, account executives who manage large or important accounts by phone and who may be visited by customers on occasion, may require their own offices. But, as a guideline, the following is representative of the ideal work space for most telemarketing programs, though you should modify it to suit your particular needs.

U-Shaped Cubicle. A cubicle of ample size to accommodate everything the TSR may need is best. The cubicle should be bordered on three sides with partitions about 4.5 feet high and open on one side. This type of cubicle provides privacy when TSRs are on the phone, yet there is stimulation of an open atmosphere since they can see around the entire room by just standing or moving out of the cubicle. Most cubicles are lined with a sound absorbing material or foam backed carpet, and the colors can be custom-designed.

The cubicle may be the size of a small office if the TSR needs a large desk, file cabinet, terminal, and bookcase, or it may be no larger than a work surface and chair for simpler telemarketing approaches.

Work Surface. Within each cubicle should be a flat surface with ample room for call guides, lists, objection sheets, reminders, a writing area (for filling out call reports, orders, etc.), and a little room to spread out. This usually requires a surface about 4 feet wide by 30 inches deep. Additional surface area would be required to accommodate a CRT terminal or PC. The work surface may be a simple table or a desk with drawers for files, office supplies, and so forth.

Shelving and Bins. Each cubicle should be equipped with shelving or bins for organizing paperwork forms and stationary, product literature, and other information. There should be a bin for every kind of form that is needed for your telemarketing campaign—such as call reports, order forms, and credit applications—and enough of each to last at least a full day. The shelving should be within arm's reach of the TSR when seated, not tucked away in a drawer or somewhere across the room. Bins for completed paperwork should also be within arm's reach to be collected at the end of each day. Shelving for reference books, product manuals, and phone directories may also be needed at arm's reach. Most shelving and bins can be built a foot or so above and to the back of the work surface.

Computers and Printers. Computer users need storage facilities to protect and organize diskettes. Also needed are a copy holder and a cart or stand capable of supporting the printer and for storing printer paper. Effective and efficient design calls for

- A keyboard drawer that saves valuable desk space while providing storage for a mouse and small office supplies
- A copy holder for source documents, positioned at the same height and plane as the screen
- A mobile, space-efficient printer stand that allows the user to back- or bottom-paper-feed and furnishes a range of features for trouble-free printing.

Supplies

You should have your clerical staff make sure that each cubicle has enough supplies each day, or have each TSRs replenish their bins at the beginning of each day. Necessary supplies may include

- Prospecting lists
- Forms such as appointment, callback, suspense, market research, and sales

- Files
- Call report forms, order forms, contracts, and other paperwork
- The usual desk supplies (pencils, pads, paper clips, etc.)

Arranging Work Spaces

When you know the approximate size of each work space, you should begin to think about how work spaces will be arranged in an open room. Arranging cubicles in an open room should allow acoustical privacy and personal space, without making TSRs feel isolated. Keep in mind that distance is the best way to reduce noise from other TSRs, but proximity is the best way to stimulate enthusiasm. The best approach is to arrange TSRs in clusters of four to six. This provides distance from most others but still allows for the necessary interaction. It also provides ready-made teams for contests; plus members of each cluster can cover for each other when one is out or on break. To help TSRs concentrate, it is usually best not to arrange cubicles so that they oppose each other directly.

Assess Existing Company Resources

Before making any decisions, you should take inventory of unused office space in your company that could be used by a telemarketing department or to set up phones. You may find several opportunities to save money. The following is a list of questions you need to answer. Once you have answered the questions, go through them again to be sure this is what you really want. It is wise to gain a second and third opinion so you won't make mistakes from not considering other options that could have been more cost effective and beneficial.

- Is there any office space currently unused?
- Could any be made available?
- What furniture is already available?
- What common facilities are already available, such as break rooms, lunch rooms, bathrooms, parking lots, shipping and receiving docks, and so forth?
- How many more phone lines can I put on my existing system?

After you check for what is available and compare it to the criteria for acceptability as listed in this chapter, then make your decision about whether to use it.

Determine Space Requirements

After the size and arrangements of each TSR work space is determined, you should be able to determine your total office space requirements based on the following:

- Number of TSRs now and in the future
- Number of supervisors
- Office space requirements for each TSR
- Office space required for managers and supervisors
- Space needed for clerical areas
- Space needed for reception area or call switchboard operator
- Space requirements for meeting and training room(s)
- Supply and storage requirements
- Space for break room, restrooms, coat room
- Requirements for telephone equipment room, if needed
- Requirements for mail room, if needed
- Other facilities as required

Design a Floor Plan to Ensure Optimum Productivity

After you have decided on the facilities you need, sketch a floor plan that will ensure optimum productivity from the group. Just make a rough sketch of what would be best if you do not already have a facility. You will probably have to change it later based on the particular office space you choose. After you have rough sketches of the desired floor plan in the selected office, you should consult facilities experts for drawing formal floor plans. While sketching floor plans, keep these guidelines in mind:

- The goal is to put the facilities TSRs use most often closest to them so that they never have to spend too much time walking around the office or building while on the job.
- Supervisors should have a view of the TSRs from their offices and, if possible, be able to see if a TSR is on the phone or not. The supervisor's office should be close for frequent conferences with TSRs in private when needed.
- TSRs should be close to secretaries and all office equipment they may need such as, copiers, word processors, printers, faxes, etc. Some of this equipment generates a lot of noise and should not be too close, or better still, placed in a separate room. Electronic printers can be especially annoying because the sound is choppy, not constant. If possible, TSRs should have exclusive use of the equipment so they don't have to wait in line to use them.
- All common and frequently used files and reference materials should be close by and quickly accessible. Make sure there are enough copies of everything in the event several people decide to use them at once.

■ The restroom and break room should be close to each other and not too far away. Otherwise, it will cost TSRs several minutes of travel time to use them.

Office Space Requirements

After you have sketched the basic floor plan you would like, begin looking for office space that will fit the plan. The criteria to make your decision include the following:

■ *Isolation from too much noise and interference.* Noise, from either outside or inside the building, should definitely be controlled. Noise above 60 decibels will interfere with concentration as will sudden or high frequency noises. To keep noise down, the center should be isolated from interoffice traffic and other departments. The floor should be carpeted (static-free carpeting). A drop ceiling of 2- × 4-ft sections of sound absorbing material is best. If possible, the work space around each TSR's phone should also be lined with a sound-absorbing material. Be careful that the center does not become completely quiet, or TSRs may feel isolated. A low hum from TSRs voices is desirable.

■ *Good ventilation.* A good flow of fresh air is very important. Stagnant air causes lethargy and irritability, which can effect a healthy telemarketing atmosphere. Good ventilation is particularly important where computers and other office equipment are used. These equipment generate heat and make the air stale.

■ *Comfortable temperature and humidity.* It is hard to concentrate on work when temperature and humidity levels are not comfortable. Also, computers tend to malfunction when temperature and humidity exceed the manufacturer's recommendations.

■ *Adequate power and cabling ducts.* Some older buildings are not wired to handle the power requirements of large computers and a lot of office equipment. Not only may there not be enough power, but also the channels and ducts for all the required cabling may not be adequate. The costs to add power and to drop the ceiling or raise the floor to run new wiring may not be worthwhile. Keep that in mind when selecting a location.

■ *Access to windows.* Windows may seem like a small matter, but it is little things such as this that can make all the difference in a TSR's comfort and attitude. The only problem windows may pose is that sunlight can increase glare on CRT/PC screens. Venetian blinds reduce glare and still allow a view of the outdoors; tinted windows are good, providing they are not too dark, just light enough to reduce the glare.

■ *No barriers for the physically impaired.* Check with OSHA and find out what the recommendations are for allowing space for wheelchairs and movement.

■ *Expandability for future growth.*   It is best to leave your options open and assume that growth will happen. Make sure the facility you choose can absorb that growth in all the ways listed above.

Consider Location

You can make telephone contact with your prospects from virtually anywhere. Therefore, if you do not already have office space, you should have many options to choose from. Before signing a lease, make sure that local ordinances do not restrict telemarketing as you plan to practice it. Another consideration is where your employees are likely to live. It will be harder to attract good job candidates if your office is in a remote location. If you do not have a cafeteria in your facility, you should also consider the availability of places for your TSRs to have lunch. Consider the neighborhood. A good neighborhood projects an image of a clean, modern enterprise and exciting opportunities. Finally, consider the location of your market, since calling to a local market will be less expensive than long-distance.

After selecting your office space, you should revise and finalize your floor plan to reflect the space you have chosen. Now begin to consider decor or the style of your office interior.

A Professional, Relaxing Interior for Your Call Center

Decor is important for the image you want to project, because this image will be reflected by your TSRs to their prospects. The image should be professional, modern, interesting, with a touch of energy; although decor does not have to be expensive, colors, wall-hangings, plants, and furniture are important.

Colors.   Colors should be fairly neutral, not too dull or excessively vivid. Lighter, modern, softer tones are best.

Ambiance.   The ambiance of the environment can add little cues to the success of your operation. There are hundreds of motivational phrases and pictures that can be placed strategically throughout your office in order to influence proper attitudes among your staff. Having your company and department mission statements is an appropriate motivational piece that will add to the ambiance of your call center.

Interesting wall hangings are important. Looking at them can provide relief from a monotonous bad day, and they help define office image and atmosphere. Modern, intricate designs are nice, as are photographs of people in exciting places or doing exciting things. Wall hangings can also stimulate pride and effort, professional photos or samples of the company's products, for example. Plaques commemorating the top TSR of each month or posters advertising sales or contest leaders and winners can be real morale boosters. Wall hangings can also be educational, such as those that highlight products, benefits, or work slogans. To maintain their value, wall hangings should be changed or rearranged every three to six months to ensure that TSRs always have something refreshing to look at.

Plants.   A few plants are definitely recommended for every office. They look nice and make an otherwise sterile environment look more natural and comfortable. A few tall plants around the room are enough, but a small plant for each TSR's workplace is always appreciated. Some TSRs will enjoy having plants to nurture and care for.

Furniture and Fixtures.   Furniture should be ergonomically designed, modern, modular, should look professional and should blend nicely with the colors of the office. The entire TSR workplace or cubicle should be modular too. This means the partitions, shelving, drawers, and everything else should be able to be taken apart piece by piece for easy movement or rearrangement of the office. Simple, functional furniture is fine. It does not have to be fancy. Along with cubicles, file cabinets, and other standard office furniture, the office should include the following fixtures:

- Large white board (for daily and on-going messages, reminders)
- Large bulletin board (for permanent information, policies, etc.)
- One or more wall clocks (for recording time of each call, breaks)
- Clocks for different time zones (if you're calling other time zones)
- Coat rack, if there is no closet
- Water cooler

Making Site Preparations.   You should consult with office design vendors before undertaking any major renovations. Have potential vendors visit your site, and show them your plans and requirements. Make sure the vendors you choose can accommodate all your needs, and have them supply quotes for materials and labor in writing. If you shop around, you'll find a wide variety of prices; once you have an understanding of the varied prices, you'll have more power to negotiate some of the vendors down, but never sacrifice quality and service just because of a few dollars difference in price. Consider resources you already have, and if cost is a major concern, consider used furniture. As long as it is in good shape and does the job, that's all you need to get started.

Before making any final selections, consider the anticipated length of the program. If you plan on a short-term program, don't bother creating the perfect telemarketing environment. Anyone can withstand a less-than-perfect environment for a while. It's the over-a-length-of-time part that you have to be concerned about. The same is true for a start-up call center. There is nothing wrong with starting modestly, with the intention to improve your center quickly once the program is under way.

Headsets Are a Necessity

Initially, all headsets were manufactured to a standard specification for carbon microphones and the standard plug-prong connectors and wiring. But the industry changed in the early 1980s, which caused a breakthrough for the telecommunications industry; however, now end-users can be confused by the multitude of choices. For example, new equipment with new specifications and connectors that allowed easy connection to all types of telephone sets flooded the market. New styles of modular telephone sets were introduced along with new hands-free applications. Since these new applications were now being developed around telephone station sets and not operator consoles or plug boards, the modular handset port became the place where headsets could be easily connected.

The office automation explosion drastically changed the business environment, and the demand for hands-free communication increased. Today the computer is a common desk accessory, next in line to the telephone set. Soon, the need to talk on the telephone while having both hands free to key the computer increased the demands for headsets in environments that had never before required them. Marketing, collections, customer service, and other business functions proved more efficient via telephone. Also users needed to interact with sophisticated and extremely interactive databases while on the line with customers. This made the headset an even greater necessity and an asset for the telecommunications industry.

Today, more than ever, the demand for highly sophisticated and efficient systems is crucial globally. It is necessary for the headset to be capable of transmitting and receiving information clearly and in universal environments in order to succeed as the final connection between the caller and the system.

Even though telephone switching systems can cost millions of dollars, they are worthless if they fail to effectively send and deliver voice information between two users. The needs of those on the receiving end are relatively simple—they need to hear and be heard, clearly, comfortably, and safely. Unfortunately, as simple as this requirement sounds, most of the time this doesn't occur. Although it makes common sense that the handset or headset forms the most vulnerable link in the system, not enough serious thought has been given to design. In spite of this, headsets are replacing handsets as the primary voice interface because they offer hands-free productivity that pays for the extra equipment costs within a short time.

Consider the Work Environment When Considering Headsets

Today's headset wearers are often working close together in offices with hard surfaces that reflect noise; equipment such as impact printers have significantly added to the noise level. Close working environments and poor acoustics due to low-quality building materials also add to the problem. Unfortunately, people automatically raise their voices in a noisy room, thereby increasing the noise level to an even higher degree. Add to the increased noise level the fact that many cheap telephone terminals and headsets have been introduced since the early 1980s. It's no wonder the end-users have complained that they cannot hear or be heard.

Most equipment problems stem from minimal specifications and standards compliance on the part of manufacturers. Headsets in today's environment are also subject to more physical damage and abuse and, therefore, need to be sturdier to survive the abuse.

Headset Selection and What to Look For

Because of the history of headsets and the variety of features and functions available, headset selection is extremely important. Although there are many headset manufacturers, all manufacturers choose their own way of implementing a successful headset. As selecting a headset type or manufacturer is an extremely personal decision for your TSRs, no one can do it for you. However, there are some guidelines and information regarding some of the major aspects of a headset that can assist you in selecting the headset manufacturer that will provide your company with the desired success. Before you begin learning all the different aspects of selecting a headset for your TSRs, the primary decision you must consider is to purchase only a name-brand, industrial grade (not consumer grade) headset; by doing so, you enable your TSRs to be on their way to enjoying their hands-free environment. Now that you have decided where to get your headset, the following will give you information you need to determine what you need.

Cosmetics Are Important

The design of a headset determines the comfort level of the user. Though the designs of available headsets are similar, each headset manufacturer chooses its own style. These styles seem to pervade the entire line of headsets produced by any one manufacturer; therefore, the design could influence your buying decision. The cosmetic effect is far more important than with most business products—users can become attached to the look, feel, or style of a particular headset. Communications managers often make the mistake of attempting to impose a single headset style that does not address different head sizes, shapes, and user preferences.

Below are some of the special features that are available and can assist in making your decision (not all headset manufacturers provide these features in their headsets):

- *Wireless design.* This does not require a cable to connect the headset to the telephone unit; this feature is not yet widely accepted due to interference, static, and the bulkiness of the battery pack to be attached onto the TSR.

- *Quick disconnect.* This feature allows TSRs to move freely without having to remove the headsets whenever they move from their desks.

- *Mute switch on the base amplifier.* This allows the TSR to listen to the conversation, yet mute out any noise or background conversation on the TSR's end (not to be confused with noise-canceling headsets).

- *Noise-canceling headsets.*   These are of tremendous value in the typical call center environment where many TSRs are in the same room. This feature provides a facility that will lower or eliminate background noise when the TSR stops speaking.

There are other considerations when selecting a headset and having a clearer understanding of what they are, and what they do, will help in securing your ideal headsets.

Universal Amplifiers (AMPS)

Headset tops may be varied in style, but the amplifier used to connect to the system should be as universal as possible. Just as you would never expect the handset on your business telephone to work on your telephone at home, headsets may work on one telephone but not on another. Many newer amps are battery-powered and will work on almost all telephones and station sets. Battery life and the difficulty of field replacement should be considered before choosing such amplifiers. A minimum or lowest-case battery life of one year, constantly on, should be required.

If you use one amplifier and use a quick disconnect connector between the headset top and the amplifier, you can get several styles of tops that work with the same amp. By leaving the amp connected to the console or station set, employees wearing their own personal headsets can share the same amp. This can reduce headset costs by 30 to 40 percent.

Durability

An amplifier that's carried around by the user because the headset is not equipped with a quick disconnect in the cord is liable for damage and failure. However, when an amplifier is left connected to the system at all times, very few amp failures occur. Headset tops, unfortunately, are the most vulnerable to physical damage. Most headsets fail as a result of being dropped, run over by chair wheels, or closed in a desk drawer. Because these and other similar hazards are normal occurrences in most work environments, headset failures occur four times more often than amp failures.

Until recently, the challenge for headset designers was to reduce size, weight, and exposed metal surfaces. In addition, they endeavored to make headsets less delicate and, therefore, less prone to breakage. Now because of the rise in the telemarketing industry, a new generation of headsets has become available. Many of the new headsets are stronger, less bulky, lighter, and smaller. Because of the competitiveness in the industry, many suppliers and manufacturers offer extended warranties. With smaller, newer cables, some binaural (both ear) versions use a single cable instead of a Y or yoke.

As a result of these improvements, you can now purchase headset tops that provide better sound quality and are lighter, stronger, more comfortable, safer, and warranted for a longer time. Whether you're purchasing new or replacement headsets, seriously consider these new headsets, because they can significantly lower overall costs while providing improved performance and safety.

Determining Sound Quality

The sound quality of a headset depends on the quality of the microphone and receivers. Frequency response and how that response is modified to reject noises and enhance voice reproduction is essential to optimum sound quality. In addition, the headset design must efficiently couple the sound to the ear canal. When the receiver cushion or ear piece fails to do its job, more noise from the surrounding area gets to the ear and the sound level drops. The frequency response also deteriorates, which causes the user to turn the surround level too high, just to overcome these effects. Some recent designs attempt to use proximity or air-gap receiver coupling. Except for very quiet office environments, these headsets are usually not efficient. In addition, they have been designed with increased sound output which can reach potentially dangerous levels.

Hearing Safety and Requirements

Does this sound familiar? Sound levels are either too loud or too soft. The listeners on the receiving end complain that they can't hear or that some sound levels are too high. With current amplifier technology, this is no longer a problem; more signal amplification is easily achieved, but as the recent Americans with Disabilities Act (ADA) proves, modern telephone equipment serves many purposes. In addition to providing voice communication, it must protect users from loud signal bursts that were never meant for the human ear. It is ironic that the 300-baud signal burst from the deaf telephone user's TDD terminal may cause discomfort or even danger to an operator's hearing. The ADA mandates that government service and businesses must accept TDD communications. Unfortunately, the telephone operators are the first to hear the 300-baud burst that alerts them to switch over to the TTY Deaf communications link. Add to this fax and data bursts, one can understand how "too loud" and "can't hear" complaints can be present at the same time. Because of this problem, a new form of compression, called *trilevel compression* (TLC), controls voice and sound burst separately. It monitors the incoming signals and controls them at two separate levels. Data bursts are intercepted and automatically reduced to OSHA-recommended levels. Peak voice signals (conversation) are short in duration and, therefore, permitted to go to higher levels, since they present less danger. However, even peak voice signals are not permitted to exceed OSHA limits.

Voice Clarity

Quality headset systems are designed to reduce noise and enhance voice clarity for the best possible sound performance on telephone networks. Controlling the level of certain frequencies or tones can improve voice transmission.

The frequency response of the headset output is limited to a range between 300 and 3300 hz. This is done to improve articulation of those sounds that help people distinguish one word from another, so that customers don't need to ask the TSR to repeat. The lower frequency sounds toward 300 hz are necessary to give the voice sufficient power so that the TSR can be easily heard. Both acoustic and electrical techniques are used to accomplish this frequency shaping. When combined, these advanced technologies create a headset with the sound quality full-time headset users desire.

Where and What to Purchase

Usually manufacturers are attempting to cover low-end consumer use and high-end TSR/call center use. These lines can often be blurred, but with the proper research, you can determine which of these lines you are considering. The first determination is the source of the headset. As most industrial grade headsets (business use) cannot be purchased in general purpose stores (such as your local department or office products stores), do not attempt to purchase your headsets from these places. You should seek out specialty headset stores or sources (telephone consultants, phone vendors, and the like). Your other option is to contact the manufacturers directly and query as to where you might try their headsets. Often vendors will allow you to try their headsets for 30 days to ensure that you want and feel comfortable with their products. If you are not satisfied, then you are not obligated to purchase them. Most headset distributors will work with you; they want your business, and, if you're sincere in investing in a headphone set, they will work with you to ensure your satisfaction.

Issues to consider include:

- *Quality.* Quality considerations include the manufacturer's status in the industry, manufacturer warranty, and availability of national repair centers in the event of breakdown.

- *Flexibility of selection.* Most of the name-brand headset manufacturers have a wide array of headset choices or varieties from which to select. The many types of headsets include in the ear, over the ear, over the head, one and two ear varieties (stereo sound)—and each of these can include noise canceling. Most who use headsets prefer the two-ear, stereo sound, which enables the user to hear the prospect or customer from both ears and is less distracting.

- *Weight of the headset.* A very important feature to your TSRs is the weight of the headset. The lighter headsets made today are typically the ones that go in your ear; the heaviest ones are typically the ones that go over your head.

The TSR might compromise some weight in order to accommodate their other comforts and needs. If your TSRs are not accustomed to using a headset, they may complain at first; give them 30 days and they will wonder how they ever got along without them.

- *Compatibility with your telephone system.* If the headset manufacturer does not produce headsets that are compatible with your telephone system, then there's no need to continue looking at those headsets. Usually the key here is to verify with manufacturers that their base (or amplifier unit) can be connected and used with your specific telephone switch. The problem of compatibility is diminishing with time; however, it is better to verify this information to be safe.

The Ergonomics of Your Call Center

The word *ergonomics* means to adapt the workplace to the human being, and it is the new buzzword for the 1990s. When your employees are uncomfortable, they are unhappy, which causes them to be nonproductive, and the company can lose a tremendous amount of dollars by not making wise investments in the initial phase of setting up their call center. Implementing ergonomics in your call center is a smart choice—workers who are comfortable are more productive and more willing to work longer and harder to reach your company's objectives. Since the job of a TSR is tedious and stressful, it is important to ensure they are comfortable. You need to make your call center ergonomically sound; in the end, you will be rewarded by happy, productive, and long-term employees.

Before getting into the ergonomics of your call center, you need to understand why ergonomics is the new buzzword for the telemarketing industry. The following will provide you with information of the injuries that are stressful and dangerous to a TSR's and CSR's health. This information will shed new light on making any furniture purchases. Hopefully, you will keep in mind the workers having to sit behind that workstation and make or receive those numerous calls each day. They need your full support, and this doesn't mean monetary support; it's the other support that many are not even aware of—ergonomic environment!

Repetitive Stress Injuries

In the past, job-related injuries were generally confined to areas such as assembly-line and industrial work that involved repetitive and high-speed operation of machinery. The resulting injuries fell under the category of *repetitive stress injuries* (RSI), referring to upper-limb discomfort or pain associated with the performance of repetitive tasks.

Today, such injuries are becoming increasingly prevalent in the office where affordable technology, particularly the video display terminal, has become a standard fixture. The availability of VDTs has been a boon to industry, enabling managers and executives to streamline their operations and achieve a higher-than-ever level of cost effectiveness. But VDTs were only the first step in the workplace revolution begun in the early 1980s.

Increased job specialization is also on the rise as companies seeking to reduce operating costs find that additional savings can be realized by narrowing the scope of workers' responsibilities and intensifying their concentration in a single area. Executives in industries that require these types of highly specialized jobs, such as telemarketing, must be attuned to how the workplace is changing and carefully monitor the impact on workers.

Stress and the Modern Workplace

Physical and mental stress on workers have increased dramatically. Physical stress can result because VDTs allow workers to perform their jobs without leaving their chairs—most needed information can be accessed and entered right at the keyboard.

Uninterrupted spans of time working at a terminal can result in a number of health problems, from carpal tunnel syndrome (CTS) to back injuries. Mental stress can occur because the decreased variety of job tasks may not be stimulating to some workers. Also, pressure to perform is up because VDTs allow more information to be processed at a faster rate. Both mental and physical stress increase the potential for injury.

Cumulative Trauma Disorders (CTD)

Cumulative trauma disorders are illnesses of the musculoskeletal and nervous system that involve damage to tendons, tendon sheaths and related bones, muscles and nerves of the hands, wrists, arms, back, or legs, and they account for 40 to 60 percent of the work-related injuries and costs. One of the disorders, carpal tunnel syndrome, has made its way from the assembly line into the office. Those who are behind the computer each day and are keying in 20,000 strokes per day are susceptible to this type of injury. What can be done about this problem? By making some changes in our thinking regarding selection of office furniture, we can make the primary important furniture the chair.

Selecting the Right Chair

Without proper chair support, your TSRs are prone to poor circulation, leg, shoulder and neck pain, and frequent headaches and fatigue. By not having a suitable chair, especially for those having to sit in one throughout the day, eventually back injuries will occur for many, slowing production and causing loss of work time and increased medical costs. Those who claim that it costs too much to invest in an ergonomically designed chair are not looking beyond the initial cost. A typical back injury claim can cost $20,000, and the cost for a carpal tunnel syndrome claim can cost approximately $5700. With these figures in mind, how cost effective is investing in a chair which runs about $300 to $600? When configuring the dollars, also keep in mind lost production, medical coverage, and time out from work.

Selecting a chair isn't as simple as buying something that adjusts for height and backrest. It's not a one-size-fits-all anymore. The seat and back of the operator's chairs must be adjustable, and the front of the seat, called the waterfall, should be rounded. If it's not, pressure on the thighs of the seated operator causes the circulation to be cut off to the lower part of their legs, thus causing the sensation of cold feet.

Look for a chair that offers flexibility, because we are all built differently, and you need to have adjustability together with freedom of movement. The following is a check list you want to consider when selecting your chair:

- Height adjustments, back height, and angle adjustment
- Forward-slide seat pans to accommodate different leg sizes
- Seat tilts
- Height- and width-adjustable armrests and elbow supports
- Diverse backrests and seat configurations to accommodate the user's individual needs
- Rocking motion for relaxation

Another area of concern is a ruling by the ADA effective January 1992 which instructs employers to provide disabled workers with safe office equipment and chairs to fit their needs and tasks.

The main concern when selecting the right chair is that it prevents "static" sitting. A static chair forces the body into a position, whereas a dynamic chair offers the flexibility of adjustment. You want to give users the freedom to move and reposition themselves during their working hours. This freedom will improve circulation and prevent muscle pain, back pain, and other repetition motion injuries.

By not providing the most advanced ergonomic seating available, the employer can be sued by the user (for up to five years) for installing inadequate, hazardous office equipment—chairs. This in itself should give every employer the incentive to investigate options and ensure compliance with an ergonomically safe environment! One last suggestion, if you are going to invest in new chairs, be sure to train users how to operate this equipment. Show them the proper way of adjusting the chair; if they have never sat in an ergonomically designed chair, they will never know what it should feel like.

By making this a serious priority when selecting your office furniture, it will be a win-win situation for everyone. You have a comfortable environment, happy workers, higher production, reduced turnover, less time off, and you have saved on unnecessary medical expenses or a potential lawsuit!

This is only one example of how the use of ergonomics, sometimes called biomechanics and human engineering, combines engineering, medicine, and psychology to optimize worker performance, safety, and health. When ergonomic installations become part of a company's safety and modernization program, the design of the workplace and the procedures and tools used not only increase employees' skills and productivity but also safeguard them from overexertion and stress.

By applying ergonomics to the design and layout of work stations, you can considerably improve the comfort and well-being of TSRs. Furniture construction and placement, along with recognition of human body, wrist, and hand weaknesses, are the primary bases on which to build improvement programs. Following are the major functions and factors that are involved in the effective use of ergonomics in computer operations.

Seating and Work Desk Considerations

Because almost all sustained terminal operation is performed from a seated position, seating posture deserves particular attention. Proper posture ensures both comfort and accessibility to the keyboard. For operator comfort and a minimum of stress, ergonomic features of the furniture should include a chair with an adjustable back rest and seat to provide low-back support and to control the amount of pressure on the back and thighs. The chair should have five legs for stability and wheels to enable the operator to easily change position at the work desk.

Although the average work desk in most offices is 30 in high, which is too high for the placing and operating of a keyboard, an operator has a choice of a wide range of adjustments to position the keyboard and monitor to suit his or her needs. The best ergonomic design of desks and work surfaces requires:

- A desk that is between 23 and 28 in high, depending on the operator's height. The desk should allow for knee clearance over the full range of body movement required to operate all accessories.

- A work surface that holds all work materials and permits efficient work flow. The operator should not have to stretch or get out of the chair to pick up or place material.

Consider the Keyboard and Screen to
Reduce Carpal Tunnel Syndrome

An incorrectly positioned keyboard that encourages bent wrists and elevated elbows, combined with the tendency of many VDT users to pound the keyboard, is likely to produce discomfort. Carpal tunnel syndrome, an inflammation of the wrist tendons, is an ailment most often associated with VDT work. Symptoms can include pain and numbness that generally start in the thumb and work outward into the fingers. Left untreated, CTS can result in muscle inflexibility to the extent that the sufferer may be unable to pick up objects. CTS can be treated with therapy and surgery, if necessary, and is not permanently debilitating. But CTS and other forms of RSI, including pain and stiffness in the shoulders and arms, ultimately result in time lost from work and medical expense. Thus, keyboard design becomes central to putting together a comfortable and ergonomic workstation.

When selecting computer-support products, it is important to make sure they provide the maximum degree of flexibility and articulation. Items such as keyboard supports or monitor arms should swivel, tilt, and move vertically and laterally to best accommodate the needs of different workers. Computer support tools should be easy to use, without sharp or rough edges to snag clothing or stockings. When not in use, workers should be able to unobtrusively stow them away. Effective keyboard and screen design include:

- A detachable keyboard that can be positioned for efficient keying. The top surface of the front row of keys should be no higher than 2 to 3 in above the work surface. With the operator's elbow at 90° and his or her forearms parallel to the floor, the keyboard should be at the level of the person's thumb joints. Wrists should not be bent up, down, or sideways.

- An elevated, cushioned support to help align wrists to the keyboard. This device relaxes muscle tension in the operator's wrists, arms, shoulders, and neck to ease the discomforts of repetitive motions.

- A monitor stand with an arm that extends, retracts, rotates, and lifts the monitor, allowing it to be positioned to eliminate glare and reduce neck pain or backache. The monitor should be located 18 to 24 in from the operator's eyes for easiest focusing.

Standardizing telemarketing workstations with computer-support products will help employees perform their jobs better and in greater comfort. And that's an edge that will benefit your company's bottom line.

Conclusion

A positive physical and social environment for your telemarketing program is critical to productivity of each TSR. Without a positive environment, motivation and job satisfaction do not have a chance to happen. The environment should help make the objectives the TSR must meet each day reachable, despite the monotony and rejection that the job may involve at times. The physical environment should be professional, modern, clean, safe, convenient, interesting, and dedicated to the department's objectives.

6

Selecting Your Prospecting Lists

This chapter will assist you in selecting the proper list for your outbound tele-marketing campaign. Together with the expertise of a professional list broker, Melodye DeWine, president of Abstract Records Services Inc., and the timely research from a mix of other available resources, the chapter offers definitions and tips that are critical when selecting prospecting lists. The objective is to increase your selling and marketing opportunities.

Many companies use a local directory in the belief that this is an acceptable means of obtaining a list. For those who are not able to afford the investment of a professional and a more defined list, the local directory is an alternative. However, lists are very important, and Chap. 6 looks at how a company should select a list for its particular marketing campaign. Issues raised include: Who is your market (such as, primary, secondary, and so on)? Where is the best market? How should you select the right list? Where should the list be ordered from (broker versus distributor versus manufacturer)? What are the cost factors, since a list can range from one extreme to another for business and consumer markets. How much information is required? What size order? Including labels or diskettes?

The *mailing list* is one of the most misunderstood terms in business language today. Often businesses will select the source on which their livelihood depends in the same fashion that they would select a loaf of bread in the local grocery store.

Before any selection of a mailing list is decided upon, the business must identify *who it wishes to reach*. In making this decision, one shouldn't have to reinvent the wheel. Instead, you can utilize what markets have been most successful for others, and evaluate your own potential and existing client base that would typically have more of an interest level in your offering. You can also evaluate your competitors' positive experiences and use them as a basis to begin your quest for determining and obtaining your own prospecting lists!

The following are different types of lists that you can consider; however, prior to deciding on a list, you need to break it down further by defining what your specifications are so you can better target your list to your particular market niche, thus making your prospecting efforts easier.

How to Target Your Market When Prospecting Business to Business

If your market is business-to-business, the first step in reaching the right target market is knowing who you need to be speaking with. This could be either the decision maker, the one who signs the check (not always the CEO), the influencer (if you are doing a two-step close), or the one who has the information you need when conducting surveys.

So many individuals miss their mark because they fail to truly know their market. You have your primary markets—this is the type of profile or customer that you are accustomed to doing business with, and it's your existing customer base. If your business is new, it is a base from which your industry conducts a greater percentage of its business activities.

Once you have your primary market identified, you need to know who your secondary markets are. This market could be the expansion of your existing client base to similar industries or reaching an industry or consumer profile that has previously proven to be successful for your product or service. For example, if your primary market is chiropractors, then your secondary market might be, podiatrists or physical therapists. Again, your offering determines your ideal markets. Other types of secondary markets could be your networking organizations or associations you belong to, or a referral base. These could also be third markets.

The objective is to determine what your potential market opportunities are and never put 100 percent of your energy into just one market. Doing so will reflect in your bottom line, especially when that particular market isn't doing very well.

There are telephones for every single business firm listed in the *Yellow Pages.* The net number of firms has been estimated to be approximately 9.5 million. This huge file comprises about 6000 different business categories. Enterprising mailing list companies are constantly calling these firms to verify the company name, address, and telephone number. Additional information is obtained from the answering party to verify the name of the chief contact, president or owner, the SIC code (type of business), and number of employees. Therefore, should a telemarketer wish to narrow its primary market defined as, say, office supply retail stores, the list company will program the SIC pertaining to this exact category. There is a standard rate charge for the company name and mailing address. When telephone numbers are included, the rates increase, and they continue to increase when you keep adding more information such as the contact name of the CEO or owner; you can even get the contact name broken down by departments. Each additional selection you require costs you a little more, since additional time and labor has been taken to get the information and keep it current.

The cost will vary depending upon the geographical area, the volume of the list order, and the format provided (tape, diskettes, labels, etc.). The rates may vary slightly from one list house/compiler to another, so it's best to call established companies and compare rates before placing your order. Should you need a list of compilers, the Direct Marketing Association (DMA) will provide the names of list companies that are members of this large trade association.

Some important points need to be considered when renting a list of businesses that originates from the *Yellow Pages*. The primary consideration is the *date* of the *Yellow Pages*. The last research date is critical. Since about 80 percent of all business firms employ fewer than 20 workers, there is a high turnover in the names of your contact person and the business itself. So, let your list provider guarantee that the list it supplies is accurate. Get the statement in writing that at least part of your money will be refunded and the list exchanged if it is not 92 percent mail deliverable or 85 percent telephone accurate.

Why is there a percentage distinction? Simply because list compiling procedures are performed by data-entry clerks. If a street address is keyed incorrectly, the mail carrier will probably try to deliver the mail anyway. However, if a telephone number is improperly entered, there is no hope of reaching your prospect, and the cost for directory assistance is too costly. There are telephone *look-up* services, and if you are trying to obtain telephone numbers that your list company doesn't provide, you may be able to get these telephone numbers from a look-up service. Should the list company provide these numbers, its job is to keep them current. Some list compilers update only every 18 months, and others update every month to 6 months. This will either cost you more for the current data, or it's a service that sets the list compilers apart from others. Again, research it, interview your list compiler, and whatever claims it's making—get them in writing!

There are several lists to select which should be predetermined when ordering your business list. Again, before making your selection, know what it is you want to achieve and who will have a greater interest in your type of offering.

What Is an SIC Select

SIC select is a national standardized code for each type of business. This is broken out by three major divisions: manufacturing, wholesale, and services. Under the major three divisions there are numeral codes for each separate type of business under the three divisions.

Generally, when ordering the business list the selection is chosen by the general classification of manufacturing, wholesale, and service, rather than hundreds and hundreds of the subclassifications. If the target market is a specific type of business under the general classification, then additional selects must be made under one of the three general classifications using the specific SIC select subclassification number.

What to Delete When Ordering Your Lists

One of the most repeated mistakes made in ordering business lists is forgetting to omit the type of businesses that are irrelevant to the individual's market. For example, if an insurance agent orders a small business list and forgets to delete insurance, sure enough, it will be in its order. For this reason, before ordering any list, the first step is to decide who you want to reach and who you don't want to reach. This saves you time and the unnecessary expense of paying for names you cannot use.

Size of the Company Helps to Determine What List

If your market is small businesses, it would be foolish to order a business list with a large number of employees. In most cases, the larger the company, the longer the decision time will be for buying your goods and services. In this market, your competition is accustomed to marketing itself to large businesses and has the ability and experience to bid competitively. If this is the case, and you are not prepared to be price competitive, you may be wasting your time and expense for not defining your list properly. Most larger businesses are not as interested in relationship selling as they are in discounts, discounts, discounts! They usually have tougher budgets, and if you're not in a position to lower your prices and stay competitive, you may be out of your league.

Although many companies market themselves only to very large companies, they have structured themselves to be extremely competitive with other low bidders. This greatly depends upon what you're selling. For example, if you are in the training industry, then price to your prospective market is usually not a major issue. Of course, to some extent it is an issue, but the quality of the training and the results it can achieve generally outweigh the cost factors. However, if you are selling a commodity item such as paper products or other office supplies, then price could very well be the *only* issue. This is why you need to predetermine who you should be marketing your offerings to and if you don't know the answer, then you need to do some research work and find out.

Branches, Trademarks, and Chains

If your sale depends upon reaching the prime decision maker you may want to consider whether you will need to have all the branches of a given company included in your list order. You may also want to consider if all the stores of a given chain or trademark are needed. Time is money, and a good lead source will save you invaluable time by enabling you to go right to the decision maker without the unnecessary effort of finding who and where the decision makers are.

Government, School, and Nonprofit Organizations

Business lists include government, both state and local, as well as the federal government under the service classification. Schools (both private and public), are included in nonprofit and private organizations. When ordering your list, it is essential that you know who you want to reach, so you can avoid ordering undesired categories.

Getting the Most from Your Consumer Lists

If your market is consumers, you should know whether they are homeowners, or residents, their ages, if they're married, if they have children and if so how old their children are. Do they live in a given geographical area? How long have they been living in their home? Did they respond to a magazine article or are they mail-order buying? All these questions should be asked before you approach the purchase of the mailing list. Unless you know the answers to these questions you should do diligent research before ordering your list.

The cost of the list is only one element in the cost of lead generation. If your list is not on target, the back-end cost of the lead generation program can become so expensive all profits could be absorbed through wasted time in telemarketing to the wrong prospects as well as the high price of mailing to the wrong individuals. When ordering your leads it is essential you know exactly what you want or you could end up with thousands of names and addresses you do not need or are unable to profit from.

A consumer list, like a business list, has many selects that should be considered before the order is made. Consumer lists are overwhelming in their size, but computerization has enabled anyone to narrow the audience gap and fine-tune the potential calling list. Here are some of the ways in which you can target a market more precisely, yet maintain expansive coverage.

Major list compilers can provide the names, addresses, and telephone numbers of 90 million households. Selections include *demographics* and *psychographics* (lifestyles). Demographics include your choice of age group: 18 to 24, 25 to 39, 40 to 59, 60 to 74, and 75 plus. Most age information is obtained from driver's licenses and voter registration, but this is not conclusive. In many instances ages are not included. Other sources that can help fill this gap include credit bureau records, motorcycle registrations, warranty card information, and the Donnelley-sponsored Carol Wright questionnaires, to name a few.

Lists with telephone numbers that combine age, income, and lifestyles of the consumer will further breakdown the market you wish to target. For example, you may request that your list provider-broker locate a file of families, aged 35 to 49, with income between $50,000 and $125,000, who are health conscience such as owning exercise equipment. Other major lifestyle categories not only include health, but also sports, hobbies, interests, religion, financial investments, contribution, electronics, insurance, ethnic groups, and mail-order buyers. There are as many as 60 different lifestyle choices you can select from.

If you want to define your prospect group further, you can select multiple lifestyles, such as wealthy households that purchase investment advisory information and own equities, in a particular age and income bracket, in a specific geographic area. This is more costly. However, the benefits may outweigh the cost factor if your TSRs have more time to conduct effective prospecting and spend less time weeding out than they would have with a less concise list. By being very specific as to who your target market is, you will save your TSRs time, and they will encounter less resistance. Another possible selection is the occupation of the prospect. Hundreds of trade and professional occupations can be married to the investor profile just described. In this case, you can select top or middle-management executives, plus business owners and professionals. This is really isolating a narrow market.

Beware of Bargain Lists

If a mailing list is priced well below other lists with the same list requirements, purchasing such a list may cost you dearly. Quality leads will not be sold much below market value. Once a list is created, it will be of value to you only if it is accurate. This means the compiler of quality lists must continually merge-purge the information to keep the data fresh and correct, frequently running all new data against all old data. This process is labor intensive as well as costly due in part to the computer time. These costs will always be reflected in the retail price of the list.

In addition to the merge-purge procedures, there is another charge for "list overlays." This is when additional data are purchased from one compiler to enhance the data of another. For example, one compiler may have information that will include new homeowner's real estate transactions, closing date, purchase amount, lender, square footage, and the like and wish to purchase additional demographic information such as age, income, and children in household from a second source. The cost to buy additional overlay information once a compiler buys from another compiler will always be factored into the retail price of the list. Therefore, when a reseller offers a mailing list price too good to be true, it usually is. The consequences from purchasing a poorly compiled or irregularly updated mailing list means the buyer pays less up front but surely loses after the initial purchase.

If direct mail is the means by which buyers wish to target their markets, they could spend needless money on stamps that will never get to the individual or business, as well as the cost for the mail piece that will be thrown away with the stamp. If the target is to be reached by phone, think of all the wasted hours in telemarketing time the client will spend, not to mention the dollars lost.

Renting a Mailing List and the Allowable
Use of the Rented List

Mailing lists always remain the property of the creator of the lists. When buyers purchase lists, they are purchasing them for "one time" use unless otherwise agreed upon in writing. The buyer is a leaser, not the owner, of the data and does not have any exclusive right to multiple usage. This also means the buyer may not resell the list or share the list unless the compiler or list manager has so agreed.

There is an ongoing debate over who *owns* the list after an individual pays for it from the compiler or reseller. This argument rests on the misconception that because a company has bought the list it now should have the right to use it in anyway it pleases. If a compiler sold its product on a nonexclusive agreement to all who purchased the list, no one in America could afford the data. This is the same concept of a protected article or book that has a copyright. The copyright helps the owner who performed the work protect the work from anyone who purchases it, preventing duplication and distribution to friends, colleagues, and so forth. Such distribution would keep the owner of the protected work from making the revenue expected when the owner initially performed the work. Not protecting the compiler's list would allow anyone to reuse or recompile the information into a data bank.

Unfortunately, some are in the business of reselling compiler's lists, this is called the *black market*. The black market is getting very serious, and heavy legal actions are being inbounded for those who get caught. Another problem compilers face is that many individuals purchase their list inexpensively such as a list prepared on cheshire (paper). They only order their list once and reprint the list on pressure-sensitive labels themselves. This enables them to do their direct mail without having to re-order another list.

Compilers put in many hours and invest a great deal of labor cost to compile their lists and keep them current; they would not be able to stay in business if they were not protected. To offset the great cost of compiling information, the data must be sold over and over in order for the creator of the list to afford the processing cost of compiling. Should a customer wish to use the data more than once, the number of uses is agreed upon at the point of order, and additional copies of lists are shipped. Usually someone ordering second and third copies of the same list can obtain it at a reduced price. This applies to lists on pressure-sensitive labels, on cheshire (paper), bar coded, or on cards. Buyers should not expect discounts on new orders of the same data other than when they specify this and pay at the time of their first shipments.

Using a Response List

A *response list* is a list that is broken down into buyers who purchase through mail order of certain products and services. They are subscribers to particular types of newsletters and magazines. However, it isn't always easy to get these lists, since the owners are reluctant to provide them because they don't want their customers receiving high-pressure telemarketing promotions and because of their customer's privacy factor. Customers' privacy should be respected, especially if consumers request that their information remain private, but there are ways to get permission. You can have the consumer fill out a registration card or questionnaire that gives permission to be contacted by other related industry products and/or services.

Once the customer allows information to become public knowledge, then it is ethically acceptable to call. With the new laws coming into effect that protect the buyers (consumers) from having their number published without their permission, it is wise to have documentation in the event validation may be required.

Response lists are extremely valuable to your prospecting efforts. It's entirely possible that many of these buyers are not on a host of compiled lists, such as the resident or business files. Therefore, TSRs experience less sales resistance, better response rates, and increased profits. It is important that you negotiate with the list manager, the list broker, or the list owner so that you will not jeopardize the integrity of their list. If you can prove that your offer is genuine, noncompetitive, free of high pressure, and beneficial to the customer, then you may be able to persuade the list owner to do business with you.

Generally, these lists do not contain telephone numbers. Therefore, use a *look-up service,* and it will perform this at a reasonable rate, providing the quantity is at least 5000 to 10,000 records at a time. Since the match rate usually is around 50 percent, be sure to take this under consideration when you are negotiating the list with the list owner or manager to allow for this shortage.

Another feature you can bring to the negotiating table is to offer an exchange of each other's lists. All such transactions should be placed through a list broker or manager. By doing so, you'll receive impartial and expert representation at a nominal cost. Also, you want to be sure you are not purchasing a list that was previously rented and not the true ownership of the person whom you are negotiating the list with.

The primary reason that response lists are effective is because they contain names that are proven to respond to solicitations for mail-order merchandise, to offers of services (financial), or to subscription offers. Should you be able to obtain this type of list, you'll be able to locate and use the list of prospects that best matches the lifestyles and demographics of your target market. Demographics (gender, age, income, type of dwelling, presence of children, year and type of auto, and so on) and lifestyle information are fundamental elements in your marketing program. This knowledge leads us to the art of selecting data from large existing lists, and if possible, attaching these data to your own database.

For instance, once you've determined the demographics and lifestyles of your best prospects, you may approach any large list owner with either the residential database or the business data bank. These firms will match your customer characteristics with their files, including telephone numbers, of potential buyers. Again, for each additional information you require, there is an added cost. You can request that selected demographics and lifestyles information be added to your customer database.

The cost of adding data is directly related to the quantity of records passed and located and the amount of information to be added; for special rates, you need to negotiate with your supplier. Be sure to research this thoroughly, since you can get competitive prices that are cost effective when you check around. Use a list broker to help in your negotiations, since most list companies don't advertise this type of service due to the variance of their fees.

Marketing to Executives at Their Residence

Another type of list you can get is for executives at their place of residence. Telemarketing to business executives at home in the evening can be beneficial, providing your offering is consumer related. You should never attempt to call executive at their home if it is business related. Calling executives at home when it is consumer related permits longer conversations, and generally the prospect feels more relaxed and less controlling; you're not having to deal with the secretary screening process, and you have a higher probable response rate factor. Prospecting these executives at their place of business for consumer marketing will more than likely irritate the executive.

Hard-to-Find Resources

As telemarketing programs are getting more and more sophisticated, the demand for new sources of previously unavailable names becomes greater. One example of this harder-to-find source are the names and telephone numbers of businesses that are listed only in the white pages of the telephone directory as opposed to the yellow pages.

Today, due to our economy, many entrepreneurs, small businesses, and certain employees of larger corporations are working from their homes in so-called *home-based businesses.* Most of these workers are white-collar employees, managers, or professionals. They include people in sales, administration, or technical jobs. Their home phone number is a desirable selling feature.

Many are not advertised in the yellow pages, yet they are a viable resource for many types of other businesses to market their products and services to. Because of this new and rising market, many list compilers are locating these firms and are adding their names and phone numbers to their data banks to set themselves apart from their competition by offering additional sources of information that others don't take the time to do. Because this is fairly new, it has not yet been determined how many of these small operations are located at home or business addresses, yet they make up a major portion of a business file, numbering about 1 million records, or around 10 percent of all business firms in the United States.

Eliminating the Deceased from Your List

When prospecting consumers, you must make certain that the names of deceased individuals are not on your TSR's calling list. Unfortunately, these names have a tendency to remain on lists long after the individual has died. Primarily because the surviving spouse either forgets to make the appropriate changes or refuses to make these changes on a vehicle registration. Surviving spouses may never send in the death certificate to the drivers license bureau, and, most commonly, they never inform the telephone company to change the name of the phone owner. Because of this, the list owner is never notified, unless a market research has been done to update the list, but this is very costly to the list compiler. It's easier to get the information from other avenues.

Over 2 million deaths are reported each year. There's a possibility that a senior citizen file will contain a significant quantity. Some suppression files of deceased persons go back more than 30 years and include 45 million names. More recent suppression files have 4 million records. These lists consist of a social security number, zip code, name, date of birth, and date of death.

Service agencies can construct a match code of some of these data and run the file against your existing customer or prospect lists, significantly updating your file, reducing the size, and eliminating embarrassing calls to the surviving spouses. It's important to make your calling list as accurate as possible; insist on this with your list compiler or broker.

800 and 900 Responder Lists

The 800 and 900 responder business industry has been growing by leaps and bounds, and it's predicted to continue to grow for decades to come. All names from an 800 or 900 list were gathered through an emotional inquired response, rather than a carefully considered response. However, the response can vary between an 800 "inquiree" list and a 900 "buyer" list. Remember, 900 number responders are paying for the call. Therefore, they probably are more qualified buyers. The 800-number responder list may simply be inquirers who make free calls and are just "looking" more than buying. Finally, be sure that if you use either an 800 or a 900 list, you get current names, because these lists get out of date fast. Usually a good guide is somewhere within the first 2 or 3 months, after that, you can consider the list out-dated. It is best to invest in the most recent files, made within the first 30 or 60 days of buying or when an inquiry was made.

Telephone Numbers on Mailing List

Deliverability on phone numbers will not be as great as deliverability on mail outs. The consumer file may have several reasons for nondeliverability. Families may move after the most recent update or the person may have died. If the phone number belongs to a female, she may have been married after the last update. The owner of the phone number may have changed to an unlisted number.

National averages on incorrect telephone numbers can range from 15 to 30 percent depending on geographics. For example, from 1989 to 1993, Californians lost over 500,000 jobs in the aerospace industry, and many families moved out of the area and even out of state. Then the General Motors plant closed down in Fremont, California. Many of the military bases were also ordered to shut down, and so forth. This gives you an idea of why the telephone numbers have such a low deliverability factor.

The business list telephone number contact rate ranges somewhere between 70 and 80 percent deliverable, and these lists subject to the business climate of their area. As a rule, good times mean more correct numbers and bad times mean fewer connects.

List Pricing

The cost of the mailing list will vary and depend upon the production cost by the compiler, marketing cost, broker, and list management fees. The more information you need, the higher the cost. Each compiler will have its own pricing options. However, the more volume or larger the size of your order, the greater your chances are of negotiating the cost down.

Base Price

Most compiled lists will have an established base price. This price is the no-frills starting point. Both business and consumer list prices will start around $65 to $75 per 1000 names. This is known as the base price. No matter what else you select on your list, you will always pay a base.

Select Price

Different pricing options are based on the quality of the list and how extensive the information is. The following is a list of the types of select lists and price considerations. Keep in mind that there are many brokers and compilers to chose from, so do your homework, interview them extensively, and get plenty of references. Look for references in a similar industry so you can really get a more accurate comparison.

Consumer Selects.   You may wish to know the homeowners' income and age, if there are children in household, and so on. Each time additional information is requested, expect to pay anywhere from $1 to $20 per 1000 for that information. A rule to remember is: the more specific and uncommon the request, the greater the cost.

Hot-Line List.   A hot-line list will be one of the most expensive lists because of the continual updates on the information. You should expect to pay from $90 per 1000 all the way to $500 per 1000, depending on the compiler's cost to retrieve the information on a monthly, weekly, or daily basis.

Respondent Lists.   Respondent lists are used when a client wants to reach market segments with established buying patterns and strong prospects for a particular product or service. Respondent lists are compiled from magazine subscriptions or catalog buyers, and, as a rule, will cost 10 to 15 percent more than a compiled list.

Diskettes Format. Anytime a mailing list buyer purchases the list on diskettes, the compiler assumes that the buyer will use the mailing list more than once. As mentioned earlier, in order for the compiler to be able to provide an affordable price for the list, the list must be sold or turned several times. Diskette usage can be used as often as the buyer wishes. For this opportunity there is an additional charge. The buyer's cost for the diskettes will be higher than labels or cheshire print outs. Usually the charge for a mailing list on diskette will range from 1.5 to 3 times the base price, including the selects of the mailing list.

Other considerations that increase the sale price of mailing lists on diskette are the download charge, which is the charge for converting the mailing list to diskette, as well as any additional programming that must be done to make the list compatible with the buyers' computer program.

Don't-Call Lists and How They Affect Your Market Opportunities

The Direct Marketing Association (DMA) makes available a Telephone Preference Service (TPS) list of about 486,000 businesses and residents that have registered themselves to not receive solicited telephone calls. You can provide this TPS list to your list broker or compiler and have these records deleted from the calling file. This will not only acknowledge the privacy requests of these people but will also increase the response percentage, since fewer calls will be made.

Many companies believe that the *don't-call list* regulation will greatly affect their marketing opportunities. On the contrary, what the regulation does is further scale down your list so you are contacting those who don't mind this type of approach and are usually more receptive. It is highly unlikely that the majority of consumers and businesses will take advantage of this regulation and most consumers are conducting this activity themselves or through their company. Proper education about the positive facts about the telemarketing industry will keep the don't-call list to a minimum.

When the rules get tougher and it seems to have a negative effect for your call center, it is better to look at it with a positive attitude. Just consider these rules as an opportunity for those who are managing their call centers legitimately to be representative of those who are respected as marketers as opposed to solicitors!

You now have a better idea of the different types of lists that are available to you and how you can narrow them down to be very specific to your company's market. Your next step is to find an expert in assisting you to help secure your selection.

Using a List Broker

The list broker is a reseller of information. Using the services of list managers or brokers is a win-win situation for you: the list owners pay their commissions, not you; you get the best list at the best price possible; and you're not restricted to one broker—a host of brokers and managers out there will analyze your offer, your price, your timing, and even help with your script. But always remember, the list you choose will spell success or failure for your marketing program.

Mistake in Orders

Because of the nature of the mailing list industry, mistakes are made. These mistakes may be due to computer overruns, missed selects, incorrect addressing to the client, wrong zip codes, and delay in deliveries rendering the list useless to the client. Good brokers can minimize mistakes by keeping hands-on experience in managing hundreds and even thousands of orders throughout their career.

Experienced brokers will know how to guide clients in the purchase of their lists, and brokers can make certain that nothing has been overlooked in the order. Knowledgeable brokers can recommend adding information to the base list which may not have been apparent to the buyer until the suggestion, information which could make a significant difference in the results of the list. Also, a quality broker knows the strength and weakness of a given compiler, which will eliminate mistakes through extra caution in writing up the order.

Brokers as Marketing Consultants

Due to the vast experience through working with hundreds of different types of businesses through repeated orders, professional brokers will have a broad knowledge of many industries. They will know what works best in a given market through reorders of a given list, because what has worked in the past will be ordered again.

Over time patterns will develop for each industry. A good broker working with many types of businesses daily will learn all the in's and out's of a given market and be able to pass the information on to the client. Some brokers will have the ability to give the buyer suggestions on offers, type of mail piece, and seasonal mailing schedules.

For example, a landscaper may need to mail to the new homeowners 30 days after the move, rather than immediately. A good broker should be able to suggest through experience when other landscapers have been mailing most successfully. A good broker learns the characteristics of each market through repeat orders and continually refines information through observation. This information is valuable to the buyer of the list and justifies the additional effort on the buyer's behalf to seek an experienced broker with a respected reputation.

Order Takers

List brokers are sweeping across America. However, only a handful are considered truly qualified professionals to represent you. Therefore, it is significant for you to recognize an "order taker" immediately. This feat may not be apparent to a novice in ordering lists, yet there are signs which will give away the order taker. The following is a list for you to take notice when interviewing a broker:

- When the broker seems to know everything about your needs without asking questions, move on.
- If the broker makes few or no suggestions, be in doubt.
- How long have the brokers been in business? Experience is essential, you want a track record and their knowledge regarding the market trends and the like.
- What are the guarantees they offer? If no guarantee at all, find someone else. You want a long-term relationship with your broker and someone whom you can trust.
- What are their references? Do they have experience in your field?
- Listen for their "lingo," do they seem up-to-date and knowledgeable?
- Will they allow you to do a small test prior to placing a sizable order? This is important when you are making a large investment up front for your list. If they are not willing to allow you a test, don't use them.
- Are they rushed and do they put you on hold frequently? They are probably too busy to handle orders in a precise manner, and this is imperative in the mailing list business. One overlooked select could change the entire target market.

Mistakes made by a nonprofessional list broker cannot recover monies made from mistakes on his or her behalf. This leaves the buyer in a vulnerable position because in many cases the broker has already paid for the order and has spent a sizable portion of the money to buy the list. This money cannot easily be recovered from the compiler or list manager if the mistake was a broker error. Where does this leave you? You are probably going to be stuck with a list you cannot possibly use. Time and money have been wasted, and your TSRs who are prospecting from the list are discouraged. Do your homework before you approach the broker, have a list of questions prepared in advance, and don't just shop for the lowest price—you'll end up paying for what you get! Remember if your broker is not a professional, his or her mistakes could be at your expense.

How to Find a Qualified Broker

Professional Organization. Step one in securing a competent broker is to inquire as to what professional organizations brokers belong to. The Direct Marketing Association (DMA) is a national organization of professionals that combines all the facets of direct mail advertising: direct mail advertisers, advertising agencies, telemarketing organizations, list brokers, mail houses, printers, envelope companies, and any and all suppliers to the direct mail markets.

When networking with professionals, you have an excellent opportunity of finding a qualified mailing list broker. Professionals usually associate themselves with other professionals. A knowledgeable broker will typically belong to one or two work-related groups. Ask brokers what organizations they belong to. If you do not have a DMA charter locally, call the national headquarters in New York to find the nearest chapter.

Personal Referrals.   A referral is an excellent method for finding a qualified broker. Always examine the referral source; is it someone you respect? Has the source's mailing list broker placed orders more than once? If your referral has only used a broker once, you may want to get additional references on that particular broker.

Broker Referrals.   Ask the broker for references. If brokers can supply more than three satisfied customers who have ordered more than once, there is a strong chance you can count on them to supply you with accurate information in a timely manner.

Business-to-Business Yellow Page.   Another method of finding a broker is the business-to-business yellow page advertising. If this becomes your method of choice, it would be extremely wise to devise a questionnaire to interview potential brokers in order to weed out those who are unqualified. The following are some questions to consider:

1. *How many years has the individual been a broker?*   Because brokers need a vast amount of knowledge about dozens of industries in both consumer and business markets, it is important that the broker you select has repeated hands-on experience in your marketing area. This type of experience can only come with time. Therefore, the longer an individual has been a broker, the greater the chance that broker knows what he or she is doing. The inexperienced broker may have good intentions but lack the necessary knowledge to direct the prospective client if the client has missed a demographic or geographic select which is essential to the success of the list.

A qualified broker will also be able to guide the buyer of the list toward additional information which will strengthen the list. Ask brokers how many years they have been in business. Usually experienced list brokers will have 8 to 10 years in the list business before they truly know their way around most industries.

2. *What organization does the broker belong to?*   As discussed earlier, professionals have a tendency to belong to work-related organizations. When they are associated with these organizations and are active, they are usually on top of what's happening in their industry and are up-to-date.

3. *Can the broker provide references?*   A successful broker should be able to supply at least three solid references—clients who have previously ordered from the broker more than once. When calling the references, check if mistakes were made on the orders which were not the fault of the buyer. Did the broker make good

on that order? How long did the replacement order take? Remember, time is money, and if replacement orders are not dealt with swiftly, the list could be deemed useless to the buyer. As a rule, mailing list delivery should run somewhere around 7 to 9 working days from the order date.

4. *How deliverable are the data?*   When talking with the reference, ask what was the deliverable rate on the mailing list of the actual contact rate on telephone numbers. A standard mailing list should be 90 to 93 percent deliverable if the list is updated regularly. Telephone numbers vary, but it could be estimated as follows: business list, 70 to 80 percent deliverable; consumer lists, 65 to 80 percent nondeliverable.

5. *How often is the list updated?*   Ask the broker how often the list is updated. Compiled consumer and business lists are usually updated quarterly. Hot line lists are lists that are continually updated. One example of this type of list would be "new homeowners," which can be updated monthly, weekly, or even daily depending on the compiler. It is essential that the mailing lists are regularly updated or the telemarketing and mailing efforts will incur additional costs through wasted time or nondeliverable mail pieces.

Enhancing Your Lists and In-House Leads Through Database Marketing

Today we have such an enormous amount of computing power that is moving to desktops. Management and TSRs are usually preoccupied with leads—how to go after them, how to generate enough to drive sales. TSRs usually are thrilled when large stacks of reply cards arrive in the mail and are plopped on their desks. However, sometimes TSRs go through the leads too quickly and do not incorporate database marketing into their prospecting efforts. When leads come in by the boat load, they're not getting the maximum usage they are entitled to, and that is what database marketing is all about.

For example, successful promotions draw prospects who not only wish to purchase your company's product or service once but also want to establish a long-term business relationship. There are many ways telemarketing, integrated with other marketing vehicles, can be highly effective in cultivating customers. Using technology to execute targeted campaigns and manage these interactions with prospective customers improves your success rate. After all, the main propose in lead management is to generate customers.

What Database Marketing Is

Database marketing is nothing more than commonsense fundamentals. It's about finding customers faster, more strategically than your competitors. According to the National Center for Database Marketing, database marketing is "transforming raw data into powerful, accessible, actionable marketing information systems." It's discovering everything about your customer or prospects and what their needs are. Database marketing is storing the information gained from your prospects and customers in a central database so it can be converted into reports. Finally, database marketing is using the knowledge previously gained from potential prospects and customers to address your presentation to meet their needs better than anyone else. The bottom line is, database marketing is using data-driven marketing decisions to find and sell to the greatest number of prospects at the lowest possible cost.

How Do You Begin Maximizing Your Database?

First of all, sales and marketing personnel or departments need to agree on the definition of what is a qualified lead—a prospect that would have an interest on your product or service. Once defined, your prospect will determine your target list for promotions. You can obtain these lists as described earlier in the chapter, and you should use a reliable broker who can offer you assistance in targeting your market. If you have an existing customer base, this is a good place to start. Think of your best customers, your primary market, and consider what they have in common. For example, in a business-to-consumer market, your best customers might be women between the age of 25 and 40 who have children and an annual income of $75,000+. Or, in a business-to-business market, these customers might be the vice president of sales at medium- to large-size companies.

When customers and their traits (demographics, type and size of company, location, psychographics, financial capabilities, publications read, personality) are managed in a database, the segmentation process can be easily completed by reporting from customer profile information. If you do not have a marketing database list, you can build one by purchasing prospect lists that fit the ideal customer traits. Sometimes the information you need isn't always on one particular list; therefore, you need to have several relevant lists that can be merged into the database for cross-referencing. Gathering the desired data will take place over the telephone in the form of qualifying, selling, and servicing contacts and survey respondents. As you gather your data and record them in your database, a profile of your customers begins to take shape.

You need database software that will record and store the gathered data and keep it continually updated (this software is discussed in Chapter 4). Just remember that the data you store will continue to change as you gain experience. Learn to produce reports with the information in your database (the software has a function to help you in this process).

Developing your database is an ongoing process. It is a long-term investment in the future of your business. By continually using database marketing, you now have the power to make data-driven marketing decisions that not only reduce your lead costs but also increase sales from your direct marketing, public relations, and advertising efforts.

7

From a Human Resource Perspective

This chapter is full of information to assist a supervisor and/or department manager from a *human resource* perspective. Those who are in personnel have set guidelines for compliance with state and federal issues regarding labor codes for hiring and terminating employees, but each company has procedures that set a standard for department managers to follow. Having set standards allows a company to have better control of its internal operations and to maintain consistency in operational procedures when new employees and middle management come aboard.

Much of this chapter highlights ideas for setting up a new department. Those who have had their departments for some time should consider whether they are following some of the basics when it comes to dealing with and handling employees. This chapter will not give you details about your particular state, and every state is run differently. Instead, the chapter provides you with ethical procedures that address some of the more important issues that are common and are a standard method of practice. Go to your local labor board for the most up-to-date information so you are always in compliance with local requirements.

One of the main reasons for employee turnover is lack of communication between employee and management. Good management of information removes barriers by advocating that communication be in writing and flow freely from one department to another. This chapter provides samples on how to train and educate a newly hired employee about a company's history, the importance of a mission statement, the channel of command (accountability with titles and positions and their responsibilities), and conditions of employment. These topics enable employees to have a better understanding of the company's expectations and procedures in all facets of their job function. This information will remove the lack of communication between management and staff and ensures consistency in performance and actions.

Also included is a summary of procedures and a format to follow to assist in the development of a new department. Each section suggests ways to hire and advance internal employees to other positions that become vacant due to resignation, termination, or newly created positions. When a company is hiring within, there is usually an air of internal competition. Dissension among employees and departmental heads can arise if this competition is not handled properly. Therefore, recommendations are made for recruiting and interviewing internal employees. Furthermore, supervisors learn how to organize their personnel interview file and personnel processing to employee termination procedures.

Company Information

All employees need to have information regarding their company. This information briefly educates them about the company's background, how the company stands today, and where its plans are for the future. This information helps employees feel secure about those for whom they work and that they are a part of the company's plans for their future. Also, whenever the employee is asked about the company and its background, the employee can confidently communicate the information to others. Company information should be a part of the new employee's orientation packet and in the employee handbook.

It isn't necessary to give several pages of information, make it as brief and succinct as possible. You should include a one- or two-paragraph statement about the company. This statement is philosophical in nature and speaks to what the company is, what it does, its ultimate goal, and its attitude toward personnel. This is similar to a company's *mission statement* but has a little more information.

Department Mission Statement

What is a mission statement? Your company mission statement defines who you are as a company—your purpose for being in business. A department mission statement is precisely the same concept narrowed to a department focus: Your department mission statement defines who you are as a department— your purpose for existing as a department. A good company mission statement reveals why someone should buy from you rather than your competitors. The department's statement is the way you handle your prospects and how you want those prospects to perceive you. A department mission statement talks primarily about the goals and standards of departmental customer servicing practice and what the results are to the company and its customers.

Although it is important to have a company mission statement, it is extremely beneficial to have a *department mission statement*. Although most telemarketing departments do not have their own mission statements, those that do have an enhanced level of focus and synergy that runs through the department because all department members know what their mission is—their departmental objectives. This isn't the objective that the supervisor or company decides to set, this is a standard that the employees of that department strive to achieve together. When they do achieve it, not only does the department and the company benefit, but, more important, the customer! Below is an example of a mission statement that enhances the TSR's presentation training:

Mission Statement

> We as a department strive to win our prospects over by using excellent communication and effective listening skills. Although we will try to keep it simple and direct, we will always use professional language in our verbiage and positive phrases that create an interest that will inspire and impress our prospects.
>
> We will fully introduce ourselves, our company, and how we acquired our prospect's name. We will always respect their time and give them the purpose of our call. Our survival is to *farm*, we accomplish this by planting seeds for our future harvest. We understand and are never offended that some prospects will not have time to spend with us at the time of our call.
>
> We will never treat our prospects like numbers, because we look forward to our future harvest. Instead, we gladly send information that is of interest to our prospects, this is how we plant seeds. Once enough seeds have been planted and we have provided plenty of water—information and proper follow-up calls—we will have a plentiful harvest to reap from.
>
> Our most important objective is not to sell our prospects, it is to *service* them. We understand this and we make it our priority to communicate this message to all we are in contact with.

Employment of Personnel

Employment is based solely upon qualifications and competence for the position being sought. There will be no discrimination in hiring, promotion, advancement, termination, or other personnel action based on race, color, creed, religious or political beliefs, ethnic or natural origin, age, gender, or physical disability. Each employee has the responsibility to uphold all policies and procedures in order to maintain a good working relationship within the company with all staff and administration.

Staffing

The supervisor shall have the responsibility of recruitment, employment, and dismissal of all employees. However, portions of this responsibility may be delegated to appropriate staff or contracted personnel.

Contracted Employees

All employees of company shall be subject to the adopted personnel policies. The company and/or certain departments within the company may individually contract with persons under conditions of employment which differ from those described herein. In addition, these individually contracted persons or companies may be eligible for employment benefits which vary from regular employees. Should the company exercise its prerogative in this regard, said variations must be expressly written into that employee's contract of employment.

Conditions of Employment

All staff are either regular employees (paid by salary and/or commission and either full-time, permanent part-time, or part time) or contracted employees. Newly hired, regular employees will be informed in writing of their date of employment, salary, job title, and other pertinent conditions of employment. Unless otherwise stated in a personnel employment agreement (contract), all personnel are employed subject to the employment practices of the company, which will be made available to and discussed with the prospective employee. Policies will be specified for the following:

Hours of work

Pay periods

Time keeping

Probationary period

Performance evaluation

Unsatisfactory work performance

Promotions

Substance abuse policy

Grievance policy

Reimbursable expenses (optional)

Termination of employment

Termination with Notice

All regular staff members wishing to resign shall give at least 2 weeks' advance notice to their supervisors in order to be eligible for their severance benefits. If company and/or department feels it is necessary to terminate an employee because of poor work performance or because of an unsuccessful disciplinary action, the employee shall receive 2 weeks' notice, or 2 weeks' pay in lieu of notice, or a combination not to exceed 2 weeks' pay.

Termination without Notice

Any employee who has not completed her or his probationary period may be terminated without notice. Any employee who violates the following policies will be immediately dismissed with no recourse: sexual or romantic involvement or harassment with an employee or client that would jeopardize contractual obligations or substance abuse without refusal of treatment. Acts of direct insubordination, illegal acts, and unethical practice are also grounds for immediate dismissal.

Employee Benefits

The company will provide vacations to all full-time and permanent part-time employees. The accrued vacation is determined every 6 months as follows:

Full-time wage employees—Every 80 clocked hours worked earn 0.5 days. Employees can cash in accrued vacation every 3 months.

Full-time salaried employees—Every 6 months worked earn 7 days. Employees can cash in accrued vacation every 3 months.

Permanent part-time employees—Every 160 hours worked earn 0.5 days. Employees can cash in accrued vacation after 6 months of employment.

Notice that full-time employees are able to cash in their accrued vacation earlier than permanent part-time employees. This is because full-time employees need more frequent time off to reduce job burn-out, and they perform better when they are less stressed.

Sick Leave. Paid sick leave will be granted to all full-time regular employees up to a maximum of 12 days a year and cannot be accrued. Employees who intend to be absent from work due to illness or recuperation must notify their supervisors as soon as possible. Failure to do so may result in loss of compensatory pay for sick leave taken. A statement from a physician to verify illness may be required. Sick leave in excess of 12 days annually can only be granted by special permission of the department supervisor or head of personnel and is determined on an individual basis. Paid leave for medical or dental appointments may be taken in lieu of sick leave if desired. In this case, employees must give 24 hours advance notice to their supervisors, unless it is an emergency.

Special Leave. A paid leave of absence for personal reasons may be taken only when authorized in writing by the department supervisor prior to such a leave. Under no circumstances will a paid special leave exceed 10 working days.

Educational Leave. Educational leave with pay is only authorized by the vice president or the CEO of the company and must be signed by the department supervisor and submitted by the personnel department. The education must benefit the company and a reimbursement by the company is made only upon proof of certification. An employee can opt to use accrued vacation to pay for this time off.

Parenthood Leave. A paid parenthood leave of a maximum of 6 weeks can be granted to cover the period of childbirth/adoption and early infant care for all full-time regular employees who have been employed continuously for at least 3 consecutive years prior to the request for leave. This paid leave is granted upon returning to work for a minimum of 90 days. Accrued vacation may be taken consecutive to parenthood leave, if desired. In addition, a disability claim may be submitted for the 6 weeks. Requests for parenthood leave must be submitted in writing 90 days prior to the time requested. This must be submitted to the employee's supervisor and reviewed by personnel for final approval.

Leave without Pay.   Approval for leave may be authorized by the departmental supervisor and is dependent on the circumstances in each case. The basic purpose of leave without pay is to preserve an employee's continuity of service through emergency or planned periods of absence. In each case of leave without pay, consideration will be given to the company's needs. Employee's requests must be submitted in writing, in advance of the desired leave, to both the employee's supervisor and personnel.

Worker's Compensation.   Each company is required by law to be insured for worker's compensation. This is a state-regulated fee, and the amount is obtainable from most property and casualty insurance firms, or you can obtain this directly from the state. Once you have the protection, you need to post the sign in an area where everyone can see it, such as the lunchroom and rest rooms.

Unemployment Insurance.   This is required by the state your company operates in and pays its employees in. All employers are required to pay a percentage of their employees' incomes to the Employment Development Department (EDD). This is insurance for the employee in the event that the employee is terminated, laid-off, or no longer working for the company. Each employee is accountable for why he or she is no longer employed and must meet certain requirements to collect this insurance; it is for a designated period of time.

Medical and Health Insurance.   Many companies provide this for their full-time employees only. Laws may soon go into effect that would force companies to provide this benefit regardless if they could afford to or not. Instead of giving generous bonus or monetary incentives, specific to each employee and to her or his motivation and level of importance, you may opt to use the medical and health benefit package as the incentive—the hook. This is used primarily to draw key employees to come and work for your company. Some employees prefer the cash in their pockets as opposed to paying their medical plans, and they may have coverage on their own or through their spouses' place of employment. In any case, this type of benefit should not be overlooked, especially for the career-minded individual.

Holidays.   The company recognizes 7 major holidays: Christmas, New Year's Day, Independence Day, Easter, Labor Day, Memorial Day, and Thanksgiving Day. These are paid by the company to full-time and permanent part-time employees. Employees who wish to observe any other holiday due to religious, ethnic, or political beliefs, may do so with pay as long as they are not extending the 7 days already allotted with pay. Employees requesting other paid holidays do so by submitting in writing (2 weeks in advance) a holiday request. This request will be reviewed by the employee's supervisor and personnel.

Outside Professional Activity. The company encourages all employees to maintain membership and participation in pertinent organizations which benefit both the employee and the company. Part-time employees are welcome to use their outside hours as they see appropriate, provided the activity does not conflict with company hours, does not represent a conflict of interest, and is not for a competitor. Full-time employees requiring time away from work to pursue such affiliations must have the sanction of the employee's supervisor and may, under unusual circumstances, be paid in full or in part by the company upon the authorization of personnel. This request must be submitted by the employee's supervisor.

Outside Employment Activities. Outside employment activities shall not conflict in hours, duties, and responsibilities with the employee's position.

Salary Range. Salary ranges are set by the supervisor in conjunction with personnel. Recommendations for salary ranges may be made by employees, managers, and others for the salary review committee.

Confidentiality of Personnel Records

All written records pertaining to an individual employee's performance evaluation and other personnel actions of a personal nature will be kept in a secured administrative file. Access to this file will be limited to internal management, administrative staff, and personnel selection committee members. Employees may examine their personnel file and are advised to do so once a year (during their annual review). Personnel records will not be made available to sources outside the company without approval of personnel. All information released from a current employee's or previous employee's records must be authorized in writing by the employee.

Employment Vacancies

As vacancies occur due to resignation, termination, or newly created positions, the following procedures are utilized.

Nonadministrative or Supervisory Positions. When these positions become available, the vice president and/or the CEO shall meet with appropriate administrative and/or supervisory personnel to review:

- Whether the position should be filled
- What the current job description is

■ Recruitment, interview, and hiring procedures to be used

If the vacancy is to be filled, recruitment is primarily conducted through preparation and distribution of a formal job announcement. It is the responsibility of the appropriate supervisory personnel to prepare the job announcement, whether for inside or outside the company.

Administrative or Supervisory Positions.   When administrative and/or supervisory vacancies occur, the vice president and/or CEO shall review the current job description or function and recommend to the chairperson of the board and/or personnel committee whether the position should be filled. The vice president and/or CEO may also meet with administrative and/or supervisory personnel for input regarding filling the vacancy.

Recruitment Procedures

Recruitment of personnel is conducted through the preparation of distribution of a formal job announcement. Job announcements are distributed to staff, posted on public and staff bulletin boards, and sent to a variety of employment agencies. A job announcement mailing list is maintained by the company and is located in the administrative office. Periodically, the local newspaper may also be utilized to advertise staff vacancies. Individuals with résumés on file will also receive job announcements when appropriate. Recruitment for vacant positions is generally a combination of both in-house announcements and advertising outside the company. However, upon consultation with the vice president and/or CEO, recruitment may be limited to an in-house announcement only. All applicants are required to respond with written résumé and references within the time specified.

Preinterview Procedure.   The interview process at the company involves two steps: (1) preinterview and (2) interview. The general responsibility for the coordination of preinterview tasks and activities lies with the supervisory personnel in charge of the department in which the new employee will be placed. The format used shall be in accordance with the following procedures:

Letter to All Applicants.   A letter is prepared by the appropriate supervisor and sent to the applicant to acknowledge receipt of a résumé. Copies of this letter, with a list of the applicant names and addresses, are kept on file for future reference.

Résumé Screening.   Résumés are screened for qualifications by the appropriate supervisory personnel. A committee composed of the company's personnel (two to three members) may be established to assist in the screening of applicants. Screening criteria (including notes) should be retained for reference. Résumés will be screened to five to nine applicants per one employee hired.

Qualified Applicant Notification.   All qualified applicants will be notified by telephone followed by a letter confirming the date and time of the interview. The interview confirmation letter should include a copy of the job description. Copies of this letter are kept on file for future reference. Generally, it is the responsibility of the appropriate supervisor to contact, schedule, and arrange for interviews with the applicants. However, this task may be delegated to the executive secretary or department manager.

Interview Committee. It is the responsibility of the appropriate supervisor to establish an interview committee. The interview committee shall have a maximum of three to four members. Membership of the interview committee is varied and may include line staff, supervisory personnel, and/or administrative personnel. As deemed appropriate by the vice president and/or CEO, an outside resource may be asked to participate on the interview committee. At least one line-staff representative shall be a member of the interview committee for line-staff vacancies, and such representative may participate in interviews for administrative and supervisory position vacancies.

Interview Procedure. The general responsibility for candidate interviews lies with the interview committee. The functions of the interview committee include:

- Review and develop a standard set of interview questions.
- Interview candidates and prepare written comments using a rating scale on the interview questionnaire form. This form is periodically reviewed.
- Provide verbal input regarding top candidate(s) to the supervisory personnel responsible for coordinating the interview process.
- Reconvene to review outcome of reference checks and, if necessary, for second interviews.

Function of Supervisor. The functions of the supervisor are varied and can extend beyond the limits suggested below. This is up to the company and how it wants to structure its organization. Supervisors may

- Participate in interviews
- Collect interview materials and reviews committee input
- Rank qualified candidates(s)
- Make reference checks and report finds to the interview committee
- Review and make recommendations regarding top candidate(s) to the vice president and/or CEO

Candidate Interview. The procedure used at the company is an oral interview with candidates. The following describes the format for conducting oral interviews:

- Supervisory personnel involved with the interview shall have primary responsibility for ensuring that the interview is conducted in a consistent and relaxed manner.
- Interviews are generally scheduled for approximately 30 minutes for each candidate.

- A member of the interview committee (generally the supervisor) shall be assigned the responsibility to inform each candidate about the interview process, to introduce the candidate to the interview committee members, to regulate the interview time, to ensure that interview recordkeeping functions are complete, and to guide the interviews by keeping them focused on evaluating job-related factors.

- Time shall be set aside at the end of the interview to allow the candidate to ask the interview committee job-related questions.

- At the end of the interview period, each candidate is thanked and told when and how he or she will be notified of the results of the interview.

- Following closure of the interview, the interview committee members shall discuss the candidates' qualifications as they relate to the job. Comments and ratings are individually recorded on the interview questionnaire form by committee members.

Interview Follow-Up. Upon closure of candidate interviews, the supervisory personnel responsible for the coordination of the interview activity shall:

- Collect all interview materials from the interview committee and rank the top candidates.

- Conduct reference checks on top candidates. Comments from reference sources are recorded on a job employment reference form.

- Arrange for a second interview if necessary with the appropriate candidates.

- Contact each candidate to notify him or her of the outcome of the interview; send follow-up letter to candidates not hired for the position.

- Contact top candidate to ascertain whether he or she will accept the position of employment. A letter of employment confirmation is prepared for the vice president and/or CEO's signature and forwarded to the new employee. This letter shall include date of hire, position, starting salary, and assigned supervisor.

- Arrange and schedule employee orientation for newly hired employee.

Personnel Interview File. A personnel interview file containing all pre- and postinterview materials is organized by the supervisor responsible for the interview activity. The file is forwarded to the administrative office and includes:

- A copy of the job announcement
- Résumés of nonqualified applicants
- Copy of letters acknowledging receipt of résumés
- Résumés of qualified candidates
- Copy of letters confirming interview date

- Interview questionnaire form
- Interview materials completed by the interview committee members
- Job employment reference check forms
- Follow-up letter to candidates

The personnel interview file is reviewed for content by the administrative department supervisor upon receipt. The personnel interview files are filed in the personnel file cabinet in the file drawer labeled "job interviews." Personnel interview files are retained by the company for a 1-year period.

Personnel Processing and New Employee Orientation

Upon hiring approval by the vice president and/or CEO, a letter of employment confirmation is prepared and forwarded to the new employee. This letter will include the date of hire, position, starting salary, and assigned supervisor.

It is the responsibility of the appropriate supervisor to ensure that new employees are provided with an employee orientation and that proper personnel forms are completed in an accurate and timely fashion. All orientation and personnel forms are available in the administrative offices. The orientation should be conducted on the first day of employment with the following documents and policies reviewed and completed as necessary:

1. *Payroll change sheet.*   It is the responsibility of the new employee's supervisor to complete a payroll change sheet, indicating the employee's name, date of hire, and starting salary. The document will be cosigned by the vice president and/or CEO and will be forwarded to payroll and recordkeeping through the department supervisor.

2. *Personnel policies.*   Each new employee will receive a copy of the personnel policies. Areas to be reviewed with the employee include:
- Probationary period
- Job performance evaluation
- Grievance procedures
- Termination (including termination without notice)
- Substance abuse policy
- Client interaction policy
- Outside employment policy
- Vacation, sick leave, and holiday time off

3. *Job description.*   Each new employee will receive a copy of her or his job description with specific duties reviewed and clarified.

4. *Salary and commission step schedule.*   Each new employee will receive a current copy of the salary and commission step schedule.

5. *Time sheet and leave forms.*   The new employee will receive copies of the employee time sheet and leave forms with instructions regarding completion.

6. *Job performance evaluation.*   Each new employee will receive a copy of the job performance evaluation and an explanation of the evaluation process. A description of this process is contained in the performance evaluation section of the personnel policies.

7. *Affirmative action plan.*   Each new employee will receive a copy of the company's affirmative action plan.

8. *Personnel employment agreement.*   In cases where employment is connected to, or contingent upon, a contract for service (a project), the new employee is required to complete a personnel employment agreement. This will be completed in consultation with the supervisor and will indicate work schedule, funding source, and contract termination date. Any questions on the completion of this form or the details therein should be directed to the department supervisor. The supervisor will forward the completed document to administrative office for review and filing on the new employee's first day of employment.

9. *Employment record.*   It is the responsibility of the supervisor to ensure that new employees complete the employment record form during the initial orientation. The supervisor will forward the completed document to the administrative office on the day of orientation.

10. *Résumé.*   It is the responsibility of the new employee's supervisor to obtain a current résumé from the employee. This should be accomplished prior to the orientation. However, in no event shall the orientation pass without the submission of said document. Upon receipt, the supervisor will forward the résumé to the administrative office for filing.

11. *Issuing of keys and equipment.*   In the event that the supervisor determines a need for keys and equipment, the new employee will be issued said items through the administrative office.

Housekeeping Items

Personnel File

It is the responsibility of the administration department (or executive secretary) to ensure that a personnel file is established for new employees upon receipt of initiating documentation. The personnel files shall be established in accordance with the procedures and timetables outlined below:

1. Upon receipt of the letter of appointment confirmation, employment record, personnel employment agreement, W-4 (withholding allowance certificate), and résumé, the executive secretary will type a *red-tipped* file label indicating the employee's last and first name in the aforementioned order.

2. In the event that the executive secretary does *not* receive *both* the employment record and personnel employment agreement from a new employee, the secretary will contact the appropriate supervisor and request submis-

sion of the missing documents. The executive secretary will continue follow-up until all required documents have been submitted by the supervisor. Should the executive secretary experience any further difficulty with obtaining personnel documents, the matter should be brought to the attention of a supervisor for appropriate action.

Maintenance of Personnel Files. It is the responsibility of the executive secretary to initiate (upon receipt of proper documentation), maintain, and update the personnel file folders. In addition, the executive secretary ensures that the contents of each folder is in accordance with the requirements stated below.

Each personnel file should contain the following documents. All documents should be secured in the folder with file fasteners:

- *Employment record.* The employment record form should be affixed to the *left jacket* of the file folder. The employment record should *not* be covered with other documents and should be visible when the folder is opened.

- *Staff development form.* The staff development form should be affixed to the *left jacket* of the file folder, directly under the employment record form.

- *Personnel employment agreement.* The personnel employment agreement should be affixed to the *left jacket* of the file folder directly under the staff development form.

- *Job description.* The job description should be affixed to the *right jacket* of the file folder. Copies of job descriptions, employment record, staff development, and personnel employment agreement forms are located in the administrative office.

- *Letter of employment confirmation.* A copy of the letter of employment confirmation should be affixed to the *right jacket* of the file folder directly under the job description form.

- *Résumé.* A copy of the employee's résumé should be affixed to the *right jacket* of the file folder, directly under the letter of employment confirmation.

- *Miscellaneous personnel forms and documents.* All personnel-related forms and documents other than those described above should be affixed to the *right jacket* in the order of entry into the file folder, for example, the W-4, job evaluations, awards, and job-related disciplinary action documentation.

File Update Responsibility. It is the primary responsibility of supervisory personnel to ensure that job performance evaluations, payroll change forms, job-related disciplinary action documentation, and other personnel-related documents are completed on time and in accordance with the company's personnel policies. The administrative department supervisor and/or executive secretary may periodically remind supervisory personnel of pending document due dates.

Upon completion, personnel-related documents shall be forwarded to the administrative offices, to the vice president and/or CEO, or to the executive secretary for review and appropriate disposition. The following are some personnel-related documents that require updating:

- *Payroll change form.* The payroll change form is forwarded to the executive secretary by the bookkeeper through the administrative offices. The executive secretary shall record information (e.g., salary and/or position change and date) from the payroll change form on the employment record located in the personnel file folder. Following the completion of this task, the executive secretary shall forward the payroll change form to the bookkeeper's office for permanent filing.

- *Leave request forms.* The originally signed copy of the leave request form shall be forwarded to the executive secretary by the appropriate supervisory personnel. The executive secretary shall file the leave request form in the employee's personnel file.

- *Job performance evaluation and miscellaneous disciplinary action documentation.* All job performance evaluations and job-related disciplinary action documents are to be forwarded by the supervisor to the vice president and/or CEO for review prior to incorporation into the employee's personnel file.

Personnel Files and Confidentiality. All written records pertaining to an individual employee's performance evaluation and other personnel actions are considered confidential in accordance with the company's personnel policies. Employee personnel files are kept in a secured administrative file. Employees may inspect their own files and may request copies of the contents of their respective personnel file.

Staff Development and Training. An optional opening statement could be included as follows: "It is the goal of the company to enhance its employees' quality of service by requiring a minimum of 30 hours a year of additional outside and/or in-service training, workshops, or seminars. The focus of this training must be job-related."

It is the responsibility of supervisors to assess training and skill development needs of their staff. When appropriate, staff shall receive release time and be assigned to attend outside or in-service trainings, workshops, and/or seminars. Supervisory staff will submit a list of staff members assigned to attend training and/or workshops to the vice president and/or CEO for review. A description of the event, dates, times, and location (brochures, etc.) should also be attached for reference. This material will be forwarded by the vice president and/or CEO to the executive secretary responsible for updating personnel files. Training information will be recorded on a staff development form and attached to each employee's personnel file.

A file will be maintained in the administrative offices for the purpose of keeping record of all trainings, workshops, and seminars assigned and/or granted to the staff during the year. This file is maintained in the personnel file drawer.

Payroll

Upon receipt of the new employee's payroll change form, it is the responsibility of the bookkeeper to contact the new employee and schedule a payroll orientation meeting. This meeting should be scheduled as soon as possible after the date of hire and in a manner consistent with the processing deadlines of payroll input documents.

During the payroll orientation, the bookkeeper will instruct the employee about the W-4 (Employee Withholding Allowance Certificate) and the health insurance enrollment forms (if appropriate). The bookkeeper will also provide general payroll information, including (but not limited to) the length and conditions of payroll, company health insurance stipend, and amount the employee pays. Upon completion of the payroll orientation and the appropriate forms, the bookkeeper will update the payroll system in accordance with the procedures outlined in "payroll procedures."

Termination of Employees

It is the responsibility of each supervisor to notify the vice president and/or CEO of a pending employee resignation or termination. It shall be the responsibility of each supervisor to ensure that the following documents are completed upon receipt of an employee's notice of termination and forwarded to the executive secretary as soon as possible:

1. *Termination with notice (company-initiated).* Refer to the following sections in personnel policies: Conditions of employment, termination of employment, and termination without notice.

2. *Termination without notice.* Refer to the following sections in personnel policies: conditions of employment, termination of employment, and termination without notice. The procedures for completion of the exit interview and payroll change form are outlined below.

3. *Letter of resignation.* Terminated employees will be required to submit a formal letter of resignation. The letter should contain the date of initial notice, the termination date, and reasons for resignation (optional). It is the responsibility of the supervisor to ensure that the resignation is submitted within 2 working days of the verbal notice. The letter of resignation will be attached to the payroll change form upon completion and forwarded to the administrative department, executive secretary, or the vice president and/or CEO in their absence. Procedures for completion of the payroll change form are outlined below.

4. *Exit interview form.* The supervisor of the terminated employee should provide the employee with the exit interview form for completion. The exit interview is normally conducted by the president and/or CEO but may be assigned to the terminated employee's supervisor in their absence. The completed form will be attached to the payroll change form and forwarded to the administrative department or executive secretary.

5. *Payroll change form.* Prior to completion of the payroll change form, the supervisor should contact the administrative department or executive secretary (or aide in their absence) for the terminated employee's current vacation leave balance. In the event that the employee is owed vacation leave, arrangements should be made with the employee to exhaust the accrued leave time prior to the termination date. In the event that this is unfeasible, the president and/or CEO should be contacted to pursue other arrangements. When vacation leave time arrangements have been made, the balance remaining at the termination date should be entered on the payroll change form. Upon completion, the payroll change form is forwarded to the bookkeeper through the administrative department.

6. *Payroll final completion check out.* Upon receipt of the payroll change form, the bookkeeper should:

- Check for *equipment control* notation and arrange for the employee's surrender of *controlled equipment,* such as keys.
- Arrange with the employee the date the final paycheck will be paid; explain that the final check will not be issued until all controlled equipment has been surrendered. In the event the employee desires to have the final check mailed, all controlled equipment must be surrendered prior to the mailing of the check.
- Terminate the employee from the payroll system in accordance with the procedures outlined in "payroll procedures."
- Forward the payroll change form to the executive secretary within 4 working days of the written notice of termination.

7. *Personnel File Update.* Upon receipt of the payroll change form, letter of resignation, related correspondence, and exit interview form, the executive secretary should:

- Remove the terminated employee's folder from the personnel file.
- Enter the termination date in the *status stamp* area on the jacket of the folder.
- Check the *equipment control roster* for assigned equipment (such as keys) and note on the payroll change form.
- Forward the payroll change form to the bookkeeper.
- Type the employee's name on a yellow-tipped file label, place in the personnel file folder, and file in the inactive personnel file.

8

Increase TSRs' Motivation Through Your Compensation Plan

Any telemarketing manager and/or company needs to have an understanding of the various ways of compensating TSRs. With the right compensation plan you can effectively motivate your TSRs and help to increase their production levels above the minimum standards. However, the wrong compensation plan is a sure way to demotivate your TSRs right out your doors and into the hands of your competition.

This chapter focuses on the compensation and bonus structure for TSRs, whether they are selling or servicing. You'll have a better understanding of what the industry is willing to pay for a telemarketer and what a company, depending on the type of telemarketing being conducted, should realistically pay. Also included is a script on "How to Sell the Compensation Plan." Whether it is a great plan or mediocre, this how-to-sell feature walks the applicant through the plan with confidence. And no matter what plan is offered, whether it is commission, salary, hourly, or bonus, the applicant will see its benefits.

By now you realize that your telemarketing program depends on the success of your TSRs. When they meet their objectives, you meet your objectives, and the company meets its. Not only is the success of the TSR determined by skill and knowledge, motivation is also high on the list. Motivation is not defined only in terms of "rah rahs" and cheers and whistles, and how TSRs are compensated plays a key factor in their motivation. A good product, a targeted list, call guides, and the most advanced hardware and software are all very important to help run a professional and effective telemarketing center. However, without motivation, these material things don't matter. Your telemarketing campaign will go straight down the tubes if you have a room full of *unmotivated* TSRs.

Many factors affect one's motivation. For example, take the TSR's environment. If the environment that the TSR is to work in is poorly designed and lacks ambiance, that could effect one's motivation to sit there day in and day out. Lack of training could also affect a TSR's motivation. If you expect a certain amount of production and there is no training to support the anticipated numbers, this lack of training could possibly demotivate the TSR from continuing on with that activity, especially if TSRs cannot meet the quotas that are set for them. But one of the most important factors for motivation is the compensation plan. A high-tech environment and all the rest that comes with the territory can help increase production, but if you do not provide the TSRs with an opportunity to earn a sizable income, with incentives to go beyond their quota, then be prepared for your TSRs to eventually look elsewhere for that opportunity. It's too costly to have spent hours training and coaching your TSRs to lose them because they were not compensated fairly or properly.

Every telemarketing department has a budget. If your budget for compensation is lower than your competitor's, then you need to cut costs elsewhere to allow more dollars for your compensation plan. Think about what a company would pay for an outside salesperson and the cost to support him or her in the field. This should give you some idea of what you need to consider when developing your TSR compensation plan. Although you would probably not pay your TSRs equally or more than your outside sales force, depending on the extent of their job function, you may need to modify your plan to increase your TSRs motivation. Your objective is to encourage your TSRs to be consistent and to decrease your turnover. In this way, you are spending more time enhancing and maximizing your department rather than being a full-time recruiter.

Your operating cost will be spent more on your compensation plan than on any other area within your call center. The key factor when compensating your TSRs is to concentrate on the way your TSRs are compensated rather than the amount of compensation to be awarded. Compensation is the primary reason that applicants accept a position. Your compensation plan is an important contributor in determining your TSRs motivation regarding effort, production, and length of employment.

Your compensation plan isn't always defined in terms of money—there are other ways to motivate your TSRs rather than increasing their income. Later, you will be given ideas that will help you to compensate, in the form of incentives and bonus structures that are cost effective and will have a positive impact to get you the results you're looking for.

Determine TSRs' Basic Income Needs

The amount of compensation you offer your TSRs should be based on what will motivate them to accept employment, meet and surpass their production requirements, and remain in your employment. First you need to consider what type of telemarketing they are expected to perform. For example, an outbound telemarketer has a more difficult job to perform as opposed to someone handling inbound calls. Furthermore, a TSR who is expected to sell has a more intense task than making appointments. However, conducting market research is less difficult than generating appointments. Therefore, the compensation plan will differ according to the job that is being performed.

Another area of consideration is the size and complexity of the project requested of the prospect by the TSR. If a TSR is selling a $5000 product or service compared to a product or service that is selling for $100, then the TSR who is selling the larger amount should be compensated more. This is also true for the TSR who is asking for a commitment from the prospect, whether it is an appointment or to participate in a taste-test; consider also TSRs who only ask the prospect to answer a few quick questions as opposed to those conducting lengthy surveys.

If the TSR is conducting business-to-business as opposed to consumer prospecting, this is a determining factor in your compensation plan. In general, business prospecting is more time consuming and competitive in nature than consumer prospecting. Although consumer prospecting is getting tougher every day with regard to whom and when you can make contact, it is more tedious than business prospecting, and you need to consider this when developing your compensation plan. When TSRs are expected to develop long-term clients who take more contacts than a one-call close, then a higher compensation will be paid to the TSRs having to take more time to cultivate business. This is because these TSRs are responsible for developing ongoing relationships with their prospects and/or customers and are responsible for repeat sales. After a few months of recontact, it becomes easier for the TSR, but the value of the TSR is greater due to the relationship developed with the customer. Again, your compensation plan could change after the first or second sale from the same prospect, but some compensation should be awarded to motivate the TSR to keep up the activity.

Complexity of Product, Market, and Offer

The knowledge required by the TSR regarding product, competition, and market acceptance greatly affects your compensation plan. Expecting the TSR to understand the technical aspects of your products and services and to communicate that information intelligently to the prospect requires more aptitude of the TSR. This may require the TSR to spend more time studying in order to become more versed. In most cases, you do not have to pay TSRs to learn the information, but the compensation will provide them with that reward. Of course, this requires you and the TSR to have an understanding prior to roll-out of your telemarketing campaign. Provided you have hired the right individual who is interested in doing what it takes to get up to speed, and you have offered a compensation plan that makes the job worthwhile, you have developed a win-win situation. Just remember, the more experience, skill, and knowledge you require from your TSRs, the more you need to compensate them. The level of experience, skill, and knowledge is determined through the interview process. You need to have these elements as part of the TSRs job description so that your applicants will reflect on what it is you require of them. Keep in mind, the number of qualified applicants is reduced by the greater expertise you require of your TSRs. The more difficult it is to find the ideal applicant, the more you need to compensate the successful one.

A Competitive Compensation Plan

When attracting TSRs, you need to be competitive with what the competition is offering. This doesn't mean the same type of business as yours, rather it means anyone who is vying for TSRs and who is willing to offer an attractive compensation plan for the ideal applicants. Scan through the classified ads in several newspaper publications, call around and ask what they are looking for and how they are compensating their ideal applicants. If you're able, find out what kind of turnover factor they're experiencing and why. In order to gain the information you are looking for, you can approach this in two ways. One is to make these calls as a survey approach, be sure to state your information honestly with regards to your name, company name, and what your call objective is. Below is an example of how you can present yourself:

> **Good morning, I need to speak with the person who is responsible for recruiting applicants in your telemarketing department. Who would that be? Hello, this is** (*your full name*) **and I am with** (*your company name*) **and we're located at** (*your landmark or location*)**. I am the telemarketing manager, and my company requested that I conduct a survey to determine your compensation plans. I hope I haven't caught you at a bad time** (*Wait for response.*) **In order for us to ensure that we are fair and attract the right individuals, I need to ask you just a couple of quick questions if you don't mind** (*Wait for response.*)
> **What kind of applicant are you looking for?**
> **When developing your compensation plan, what part of the compensation plan seems more important to your ideal applicants?**
> **How cost effective is your compensation plan? Please share with me if it motivates your TSRs to meet your quota requirements?**
> **If you could improve your compensation plan and your company supported you with this change, what would you do?**
> **Thank you for sharing this information. It was very helpful. Would it be all right with you if I recontact you another time to exchange ideas with you?**
> **Thank you for your time, and I wish you success!**

This script can be modified to meet your specific situation. But the idea is to contact others in your position and get ideas. For those who are receptive to speaking with you, keep the door open, you never know, they may refer others to you or be working for you someday! Be sure to give them your name and telephone number so they do have an opportunity to get in contact with you. This is a good networking tool for both of you.

The second approach is to be up front with them from the beginning and say:

Good morning this is (*your full name*) and I'm the telemarketing manager for (*your company name*). I hope I haven't caught you at a bad time have I? I am in the process of reconstructing my compensation plans for my department. I'm contacting other telemarketing managers to get an idea of what they are compensating and how effective it is for motivating TSRs and encouraging increased production. Would you please help me answer a few quick questions?

Wait for their response and, if they are positive, continue with the questions listed in the first example. Otherwise, just close off and try contacting someone else.

How Should You Compensate TSRs?

The typical questions of telemarketing managers are: "Should I pay salary, hourly, or commission?" and "How much of a bonus is profitable and what kind of incentive should I offer?" Below are some definitions of different types of compensation plans; based upon your telemarketing objectives, you should be able to determine how you should compensate your TSRs.

Salary

Salary is a fixed income paid on a regular basis. This is usually given to full-time employees with the minimum requirement being a 40-hour work week. However, should the job require additional hours from time to time, the employee doesn't get paid overtime. Salary is ideally designed for the more career-oriented individual and requires a level of income that such a person is willing to work for based on the job requirements. It is a more professional way to compensate compared to a wage compensation plan. The psychological benefits of paying a salary is that TSRs feel they are considered professionals and major assets to the company—it's a status recognition. In addition, with a salary compensation plan you can provide benefits. The size of the company and annual revenue will help determine how lucrative these benefits can be.

This package could include paid vacations, sick leave, maternity leave, and a comprehensive medical and dental plan. Bonuses and incentives can be added to the compensation plan, especially if the TSRs are expected to sell and bring in a high volume of production. This will compensate them for having to spend additional time on a project for which they are not receiving additional money in their salary.

The disadvantage of salary depends on the function of the TSR. The telemarketing industry is known for having a higher level of TSR burnout, and with a salary compensation plan, you may be paying too much for nonproduction and extra time off. When paying salary, you cannot "dock" time off TSRs' pay as you can with a wage compensation plan. Most companies will pay salary for middle or top management. This is not to say that salary is ineffective for your TSRs. You may want to consider a lower base salary and pay higher on the bonus and incentive plans to compensate for the difference, encouraging more production. A salary compensation plan is easier to preplan for budgets, it allows for more difficult assignments to TSRs, and you have greater control of quality and integrity of your TSRs—*you* can expect the best from them! The disadvantage of a salary-only compensation plan is that it only provides a general level of motivation, there are no special incentives to work harder toward your department's objectives, and there are no offers to reward your salary-based TSRs for accomplishments of specific tasks.

Hourly Wage

A wage compensation plan is paid on an hourly basis for a certain amount per hour. The hourly rate needs to meet a certain percentage above the minimum wage requirements that are set by each state in which you operate a call center. Never pay minimum wage only, this attracts individuals who will be using you as a stepping stone for opportunities elsewhere. In essence, you will be paying TSRs to train them; once trained they will advance themselves and move on. Although the wage amount could increase as performance levels are increased, basically they will have little effect on the TSRs motivation. You can offer the same benefit package as discussed for the salaried TSR; however, without other incentives or bonuses, you will experience the same attitude as with the salaried TSR. Therefore, it is not recommended that salary or wage be the only means for compensating your TSRs. Instead, it is highly recommended that you offer these two types of plans as a part of your compensation plan, but you should incorporate other ways for your TSRs to earn additional income. You can accomplish this by offering bonuses and/or incentives, to be discussed later.

Commission

There is another method of compensation, called *commission*. This is based on what and how much is sold by your TSRs and is paid primarily when the TSR is strictly conducting inside sales, replacing the outside salesperson. A commission is paid based on a percentage of the company's gross income from the sales made by the TSR. Commissions have always been and are still the best possible method of motivating TSRs to make sales. However, if you don't provide TSRs with proper training in the area of product awareness, competition, and presentation skills, you will encourage poor sales tactics that are high in pressure and misrepresentative of your company or TSRs may offer claims that cannot be met.

This doesn't mean you shouldn't pay on commission, you need to go about it by a different approach. The typical methods are those used for the outside sales force. For example, when interviewing applicants, you can offer two types of compensation, such as hourly or salary, along with commission. Do not offer all three but make a decision on whether you are going to pay salary or hourly wage. Once you have made your final decision, sell that one with the commission plan. Let TSRs choose which one they feel more comfortable with. A TSR with experience in your industry selling the kinds of products or services you offer who has developed a good track record may choose the commission. Others who choose the salary or wage compensation plan are unsure of their personal production, especially for your company. They may not want to risk not having an income for a few weeks, and in this case would defeat your objectives in getting production results within the early stages of your TSR's employment.

You could offer a wage for the first month with a review to allow the TSR to switch compensation plan to commission. This is with the understanding that a review would not take place for another 6 to 12 months. You don't want your TSRs to think that they can change at any given time, this would cause too much chaos, and you would lose your position of control. Your primary objective is to ensure you have the most cost-effective department regarding compensation and production possible. Your second objective is to provide a compensation plan by which TSRs are able to meet income expectations that motivate them to keep up with their production and remain employed with your company.

The benefits of a commission compensation plan are that it only costs you based on revenue brought to the table, it's not fixed, and it reduces your liability for paying too much for nonproduction. Commission motivates high achievers to meet and surpass their sales objectives. TSRs will see their rewards based on the size of their checks. The reward keeps them motivated and encouraged to continue with the activity.

The disadvantages of commission-only is that it may encourage the TSR to go for the numbers only and not concentrate on quality selling and establishing long-term relationships. This can be corrected by the design and direction you present to them on a daily basis. Unlike outside sales, you don't have as much control unless you run the sales calls with them. A commission compensation plan can cause TSRs to have high and low peaks in their production, especially if they're not having a productive day, and they start to develop a negative attitude. This could increase low peak times to more than what is considered normal peaks and valleys. For new TSRs and moderate achievers, this demotivates them, and the call center experiences higher turnover. If they were on salary or an hourly wage plan, if they were moderate achievers, how much more would they cost you? Are you confused yet? The following will help you to decide which plan is better suited for your company and those you are hiring to perform the job.

What Compensation Plans Should You Choose?

How do you decide on a compensation plan? All can be effective only if you have done your preliminary work. First, you need to hire the right individuals for the positions. Subsequently, offer your applicants two compensation options to choose from (hourly wage or salary and commission). If you are decided on either the hourly wage or salary, you need to offer some type of bonus and/or incentive to increase TSR motivation to do better and to be able to earn more than base pay.

If your TSRs are in sales positions, pay more on the incentive and bonus and less on the salary or hourly wage. Give them enough on their base to meet their minimum requirements to come into work each day and represent your company. This also gives you greater flexibility to interchange their tasks and incorporate other functions within their job. Be sure to be sensitive to adding too much clerical work and less time for selling, as this will quickly demotivate them.

When your TSRs are doing more on the servicing side, then raise their base higher and pay them lower on the incentive and bonus plans. However, pay for results in meeting their production quotas each hour, day, week, or month. Never pay your TSRs based upon the results of someone else, make sure your plan is designed to pay for their own personal production and or abilities. For example, if your TSRs are required to conduct market researches (lead generation), then you pay for every completed market research or lead they conduct. In advance, set up an agreement of what constitutes a quality lead and have your TSRs sign it so they are clear as to what you require of them. You can also pay them for any number of completed surveys they conduct per hour as long as these can be verified later. You don't want to encourage your TSRs to generate poor quality. As long as you set up the parameters in advance and make them sign an agreement that they understand and will comply with, you will not encounter problems with this type of bonus plan. Be sure to build in a *charge back* system in the event you have TSRs who will try to get away with it. This kind of bonus plan is called *production* and is very profitable for the TSR and for your call center.

Should your TSRs be strictly involved in the sales process, and they choose commission, then you need to ensure that you provide them with the proper training, skills, and tools necessary to be successful. Tools include not only scripts, head sets, and automation but a good list so they don't have to spend all their time weeding out. You should have someone else internally generate qualified leads for the inside salespeople, because their time is more valuable spent in selling—closing sales instead of cold calling. Again, you don't want the inside salespeople to have the attitude that they are "closers," this would be very dangerous to your company, since selling today has become "relationship selling." Be clear on your specifications as to what you expect of them and have them sign an agreement that they understand this and are accountable to follow through.

Developing a Winning Commission Compensation Plan

There are many ways in which you can compensate your TSRs on commission; the idea is to keep it simple, fair, and easy for accounting purposes. The most accepted plan is that the TSR be paid on a percentage of the gross dollar amount sold. This is easy to measure and motivates the TSR to sell more. Decide on the percentage TSRs are to be paid, because it greatly depends on what your immediate costs are. Most outside salespeople are paid anywhere from 10 to 20 percent of gross sales; however, in the real estate market they are typically paid 6 to 10 percent, since they are dealing with a highly competitive marketplace and the dollar amount of sales are large. The best way to determine the percentage you should be willing to pay is to ask whoever handles the budgets what you have available after meeting your other costs and ensure you are still making a 15 to 20 percent net profit margin. On average you can range the figures anywhere from 3 to 20 percent.

Incentives

Rewarding your TSRs is extremely powerful for motivating them to increase their performance levels. Incorporating a well thought out incentive program will help you on your way to having a continuous flow of production on an individual, departmental, and team basis. Rather than just focusing your incentive program on an individual level, it is more advantageous to instill some of your incentive programs through a team effort to improve the overall production of your call center.

Before you implement your incentive programs, you need to develop a sense of trust within your department so that all are aware of what is expected of them and believe that management is fair and honest with everyone. Many companies try to hide what they are paying each TSR. This discretion makes TSRs feel like they are being divided into low, average, and top producers. This is not to say that you need to reveal each individual's exact weekly or monthly pay, instead you want to impress upon your TSRs that you have carefully planned your compensation plans and list them in writing so everyone concerned will be properly informed. You need to list not only the compensation, but the policies and guidelines as well. In this way you can eliminate hearsay. Also, have each of your TSRs sign her or his plan for accountability. This type of system builds trust within your call center and establishes a clear understanding of how TSRs are to be compensated.

When designing your incentive programs, you can use several options that would be used for certain telemarketing campaigns and production objectives. This adds variety to your incentive programs, and TSRs become excited by the new adventures. Incentives not only improve production but can also serve to reinforce your TSRs' desire to learn new skills. They will strive to learn how to do their job better when they know there is an incentive that rewards their efforts. The following are ideas for implementing incentive programs for your call center. These are ideas you can customize depending on how your company operates, the size of your center, and whether TSRs are selling or servicing.

Rate Scales for Increasing Sales Volumes. Offering rate scales that are based on volume selling not only can be used for the commissioned TSR but also if you're offering incentives to your salaried or wage TSRs. By offering incentives, you will encourage your TSRs to go beyond the minimum requirements. For example, if the TSR sells 50 units of whatever in 1 month, you might award an additional 2 percent above regular pay. But if TSRs sell 51 to 100 units in 1 month, that rate would go up to 4 percent, and so on. Don't make this retroactive or it will cost too much. You also must be specific as to what is to be sold, how many are to be sold, and in what time frame. Once the time frame has been achieved, the sales cycle starts over again. This will further encourage your TSRs to produce more sales. It is an opportunity to shoot for goals and a means for accomplishment that yields personal satisfaction.

Instead of using a certain amount of units to be sold, you can use a sliding scale to pay for extra bonuses. This encourages the TSR to strive for higher goals, thus making the rewards higher when reaching them. The following is an example of how a sliding scale works:

Under $5000   = 0 percent

$5001–10,000   = 3 percent

$10,001–15,000 = 5 percent

$15,001–18,000 = 7 percent

Bonuses That Help Reach Your Sales Objectives.   A bonus typically consists of additional money awarded for reaching a certain quota or goals predetermined by the supervisor or manager. Bonuses are small amounts of money and are usually provided on a daily, weekly, and monthly basis. Everyone in the department can earn bonuses. Be sure to make the goals reachable and to pay well for the more difficult goals. You can pay your TSR a bonus based on sales volume just as it was described for the commissioned TSR. For example, if the quota to reach the first sales goal is $5000 and the TSR made the quota, you would pay an additional $50 for reaching that goal. As the dollar amounts go up, so do the bonuses. You can also provide bonuses based on quality of performance, on specific tasks, or on job functions they perform well. Bonuses are not awarded on the basis of per dollars or units sold, that is commission. On the contrary, bonuses are designed to reward your TSRs for meeting or surpassing objectives.

Offering Prizes as a Means for Rewarding Achievements.   Prizes can be awarded for achievements your TSRs accomplish. You don't have to award these on a consistent basis; however, it is ideal to provide this monthly or quarterly so TSRs can see the benefits. Your operating budget should allow a certain amount of money for prizes. This energizes your TSRs, and they really look forward to cashing in. An effective way to offer prizes is by using a point system. For example, give 1 point for every time your TSRs come to work and complete a full day; each time they meet their minimum quota offer them 5 points, and so on. Produce a catalog of what they can cash in their bonus points for. Have the catalog available where TSRs can see it, such as in the lunchroom or break room, on the bulletin board, or make one for each of your TSRs as a part of their employee handbook. The catalog can have items such as dinner for two at a nice restaurant, a weekend away with travel and hotel expenses paid, or to purchase your company's products. The possibilities presented in the catalog can be endless. Allow your TSRs to cash in their points at a scheduled time, perhaps once a month, so you are not always involved in taking orders. You don't want to be a retail store.

Another way to offer prizes is by having a contest with teams within your department. Besides having your other built-in incentive and bonus programs, you can offer a contest for the month or for the day. This is encouraged whenever you want to increase your department's numbers dramatically or if you want to have a special promotion to rid possible monotony from your TSRs daily activities by having a "blitz day." This enables your TSRs to participate in a special incentive program that is specifically designed to reach a particular goal. Depending on how extensive this contest is and what numbers you're reaching for, this goal can either be determined by the marketing department during the beginning of the fiscal year or by the manager if it is on a last minute basis. Depending on the project, the program could last for several months, and toward the end of the campaign a new cycle for another promotion or target goal for increased sales would begin to take shape. This cycle could take place three to four times per year. You would need to plan the more aggressive contest thoroughly in order to ensure its success.

The following is an example of a contest that is very aggressive and designed to reach a high volume in production: The size of your call center and how you are set up, whether you are national, regional, or local, would determine how your teams are set up. For illustration purposes, let's just say that your telemarketing center works on a national level. You would need to divide your TSRs into specific territories. Have your TSRs pick four team leaders with each team having its own name and representing four parts of the entire country. For example, Easterners, Westerners, Southerners, and Northerners. The team name not only identifies each of the teams and its players, but they could also get carried away by having T-shirts made, buttons, pendants, and signs—anything that would spur on more competitiveness between the teams. Once they have formed their four teams of eight TSRs, they agree to reach a certain goal. They need to determine the exact dollar amount that each team needs to generate and the time frame in which the goal could be reached. These figures should be based on previous statistics provided by a supervisor, and the goal needs to be achievable in order to motivate future campaigns. Again, depending on the project and the dollar amounts that marketing or the manager would decide upon, it will typically take 6 weeks to accomplish the goal. The incentive for the TSRs is the ability to earn extra dollars for themselves and for their team. This happens when a team reaches their goal earlier than the 6-week term. Should a team reach the goal sooner, TSRs on that team will be compensated individually for each additional sale they personally generate in the time left in the campaign.

The department can opt to suspend all other regular work during these special promotions with the exception of handling existing customers, inbound calls, or certain emergency situations. The department is aware of these projects in advance and is prepared. Therefore the teams plan how they would meet their goals. This would take place in a meeting during a designated time, and each team would make it an event. In some instances, other departments may get involved by cheer leading the teams, which further heightens the events and causes greater motivation to succeed. Certain teams that are more aggressive than others will experience greater success. These aggressive teams might meet during the campaign to figure out ways to increase their chances to reach their goal and to ensure that they reach it sooner than the time frame given by marketing or management. The more aggressive teams who really take the time to strategize their game are more than capable of completing their goal in half the amount of time allotted, thereby generating an extra 2 weeks of additional compensation possibilities.

The rewards are great with this type of incentive because everyone benefits. It is a win-win result for all. TSRs will have fun creating the incentive program. Some TSRs could go so far as to have paraphernalia that would advertise and promote their team, even to the point of having their own cheerleaders. This of course adds more excitement and recognition to what they are accomplishing. The teams get noticed by everyone within the company! Because of this high energy level, they are still full of energy and motivation during regular routine projects, and they continue to excel in other areas. This type of incentive has been known to reduce turnover to almost zero and in the process satisfies both middle and top management. Management doesn't mind doling out the large pay-outs during these campaigns, because it is also netting sizable increased revenues and meeting the demands of superiors.

A Synopsis for Developing and Implementing the Compensation Plan

The one area that is not discussed very much is how management will reinforce and make a firm commitment to the compensation and incentive plan. The plan is only as good as management's willingness to carry it through and to be on top of the situation to ensure TSRs are benefiting by the plan. Below is a list to get you started:

- Decide how much total compensation you can and want to pay your TSRs.

- Determine the production of what you want your TSRs to accomplish. Set goals for new TSRs, average, middle, and finally for your top producers.

- Decide on what compensation plans you will be implementing and how you will structure them to meet your pay-out requirements.

- Set provisions for problems and be flexible when they arise. Be sure the provisions are in the best interest of your department while meeting your company's guidelines and procedure. Include how you will make adjustments and when you will review your objectives.

- Define the methods of how you will measure your TSRs' results and how you will assist them in achieving their minimum requirements.

- Define how you will determine and implement charge-backs.
- Get your TSRs to read and sign the compensation plans they have agreed to.
- Evaluate your TSRs and coach their performance to help them reach their goals.
- Occasionally, or when necessary, have a meeting on an individual basis and with the group to discuss how they are doing and what they would like to see happen to help them and to further support their efforts to meet their goals.

9

How to Attract, Interview, and Select Your Telemarketing Staff

In this chapter you will learn how to attract job applicants, screen, interview, and hire the right telemarketers for your call center. An applicant who has many years of experience may not always be the ideal person to hire. The job function, your products, services, the target market, and whether the applicant is handling inbound or outbound calls will determine what you look for when making your selection. An applicant may have fewer skills and less knowledge than another applicant in certain areas but may possess other important qualities; you have to assess the critical qualities and those you can improve with training. The objective when hiring your telemarketing staff is to ensure that you lower the risk of turnover. You want to avoid losing a hired and trained applicant or having to dismiss one because of a hiring mistake. You want to minimize the costly process of searching, hiring, and training your telemarketers.

Chapter 9 provides ideas to assist in determining your ideal TSR and to develop a job description for them. After defining the ideal applicant, determine what kind of ad to place to attract the appropriate applicants. Keep in mind that you are competing with other ads vying for the same ideal applicant. In addition, knowing what to say in your ad and how to run your ad are vital aspects for your recruiting process.

This chapter also covers how to conduct an effective telephone interview before asking the applicant to come in for an interview. Let's face it, you're not hiring on the basis of how well they project themselves visually, it's their voice and how they present themselves over the telephone that's important. Vocal presentation is more important during the telephone interview process, and visual presence is important during the personal interview in the office. Conducting telephone interviews saves you and the applicant time. If an applicant doesn't pass the first phase, you have time to conduct more interviews to search for your ideal candidates.

Providing you have found several applicants that fit your job description, you now need to sell them the job for which they have applied. It is probable that your ideal applicants will be interviewing other job opportunities. Therefore, you need to set your company apart and sell them on why they should work for you instead. This needs to be handled delicately, because you want to keep the upper hand and never allow applicants to think you need them more than they need you. Ideally you want an amicable relationship that is productive and long lasting.

Finally, once you have chosen your TSRs, you must inform others that they have not been chosen. A standard declined-applicant letter is provided in this chapter to help you to decline applicants tactfully while encouraging them to continue seeking a job elsewhere.

Overall, this chapter gives you the nuts and bolts of your recruiting process. The objectives are to ensure that you are getting the right people to do the right job and to reduce the turnover factor.

Telemarketing as a Career Choice

When telemarketing was not very sophisticated, most companies would hire with only two criteria in mind: they could speak and they could get to work. When I was first hired as a telemarketer in the mid-1970s, it was a quick interview. I was hired on the spot, and I reported for work the following day. In fewer than 3 months, I was promoted to telemarketing manager. Unfortunately, this promotion did not occur because I earned it, the previous telemarketing manager was caught lighting the telephone wires on fire so we didn't have to work on the phone! While the telephone company came to repair the so-called short in the wiring system, that telemarketing manager and the TSRs would eat pizza and get high in the rest room! After a few times the owner became suspicious about the frequency of such incidents and the lack of production. At the time I was only 18 years old, I loved my job, and I did not want to be unemployed. Therefore, I 'fessed up and explained what had occurred. I was promoted to telemarketing manager because I told the truth, and the rest is history! What a way to get promoted.

Fortunately, today we have come a long way and developed a more sophisticated industry for ourselves. Telemarketing is no longer hiring anyone who speaks well enough to read from a script and able to get to work. It is more complex than that. With automation paving the way toward a more sophisticated form of telemarketing, telemarketing sales-service representatives (TSRs) require experience and/or knowledge of data entry. They must have excellent communication and verbal skills including professional language, customer servicing techniques, selling background, and, in many environments, a college education—this is especially necessary in the area of business-to-business marketing. Also, depending upon their specific job function, TSRs can earn a substantial amount of income (see compensation chapter).

The requirements of a TSR are more stringent today, and because telemarketing is an uprising and acceptable industry, you can find many qualified applicants vying for a qualified position. Telemarketing today has gained widespread acceptance as a new and dynamic career choice. Although the boiler-room type telemarketing operations have decreased in number, the quality of the telemarketing work force has increased tremendously. No longer are companies forced to hire anybody to fill the room and hope that the TSR will stay long enough to learn the program. Today, a steady supply of professional, trained telemarketers are seeking permanent employment. These career-oriented telemarketers have helped reduce the turnover that boiler-room operations face daily. Choosing the right candidate for the telemarketing position adds greater stability to the marketplace for the telemarketing industry.

Personnel Planning for Building a Strong Call Center

Planning for your TSRs is a big responsibility, and careful thought and research are essential to ensure that very few mistakes are made. Part of this planning includes improving your recruiting and hiring methods to ensure you obtain the ideal applicants for your call center. Using written job descriptions and implementing ongoing performance management are all part of this whole process. The objective is to be able to improve the quality of your telemarketing team and decrease hiring mistakes. You want to improve the efficiency and productivity of your department and focus upon your TSRs' efforts to accomplish the goals and objectives you've set for them. This can be difficult if you don't first find ways to seek and recruit ideal TSRs to assist you in meeting your objectives for running a profitable call center. One must determine exactly how many TSRs one needs in order to meet department goals and objectives.

Recruiting, hiring, and training new employees is time consuming and can be very expensive. Making mistakes when hiring is counter-productive and costly, not to mention stressful. Therefore, taking it slow and being careful when making decisions on who you hire are very critical. Don't get desperate and hire anyone who is eager for the job. This can cost you more money than not hiring anyone at all!

As you begin recruiting, you must be constantly on the alert for competent individuals. Your primary objective is always to find the most productive TSRs that your budget permits you to afford. Never hire out of desperation or because of a crisis situation, you will spend more time and money and receive very little for your efforts. If your attempt to find ideal TSRs fails, try again. Place another ad, contact an employment agency, go to other resources, but don't ever settle for less than what you're expecting.

Hiring Requirements

Before you place your ads in the classified sections and before you write the TSR's job description, you need to define exactly what it is you will be looking for and what particular job functions TSRs will perform. Below are factors to assist you in developing your hiring requirements. Be flexible if certain criteria don't apply to your company's guidelines; however, as you read along think in terms of how you will apply the factors to your recruiting process.

Knowledge and Skills

Knowledge and skills are developed in an individual through experience and education, skills such as marketing know-how, data entry, and recordkeeping. All these qualifications can be taught to an individual. You will either hire someone who already possesses these skills, or you will teach them yourself. The decision is based solely on how much time and money you want to invest. A higher salary paid to the applicant who already has these skills may outweigh the cost of training. Determine what is more important to you before viewing applications. The following are considerations in the area of education and experience:

- What is the applicant's work experience?

- What formal education and training have applicants received? How long and how recent was their last time training?

- Other than their advanced education and training, what basic education and experience do they have that may be important to the skills you require?

Natural Communication Skills.   *Natural communication skills* mean abilities to communicate that are not easily taught to others. For example, a quality voice projection, good listening skills, the ability to relate and to get along with others—you want to find applicants who were born with these qualities. When interviewing, look for the following:

- Telephone voice—how well do they project themselves?

- The command of language—look for negative or irritating words or phrases. Do applicants incorporate professional language or terms and positive phrases that create interest?

- Interpersonal skills—are applicants personal or personable? Look for personable and friendly but still remaining in control of the conversation.

Self-Motivated, Self-Starter.   Since telemarketing, like most sales jobs, can be very frustrating and discouraging because of the resistance factor (more so for the inside salesperson compared to the outside salesperson), motivation of your applicant is crucial for ensuring long-term employment and increasing the synergy among TSRs working closely in the same environment. A telemarketing manager or supervisor can motivate and encourage, but it is easier and more consistent when the TSR has the desire within. When you are seeking your ideal applicant, you may want to ask applicants the following to determine their level of motivation:

- What are their goals and expectations?
- How do they perceive themselves, their attitude, and their enthusiasm?
- What is their work ethic and work history? Have they been consistent or inconsistent and why?

Other areas that you may want to consider when defining your ideal applicant are organizational skills, ability to negotiate, success stories at their previous jobs, and commuting distance to work. These are within your control and you have to decide what is most important to you. Ideally, you want to get the perfect match for all your needs—this is impossible! Therefore you need to determine your priorities and list them in order of preference. As you interview you can check off the list as the applicant is able to pass your standards for consideration.

The TSR Job Description

There are many benefits for having a job description: You'll increase your department sales and productivity from your TSRs, improve the TSRs' efficiency because they are more self-reliant, reduce employee grievances because everything is documented as to what is expected and who is accountable for particular job tasks, and overall develop a stronger department. The job description describes the tasks and responsibilities that are necessary to run an effective department efficiently. All job descriptions must meet your company's objectives.

What Does a Job Description Include?

A job description is a formal document that is 1 or 2 pages long. The following is a list of what you need to consider in developing your own job descriptions:

Date written

Job status (exempt or nonexempt, full-time or part-time)

Position or title

Immediate supervisor (to whom they report)

Job summary (a synopsis of job responsibilities)

Duties and procedures

Position requirements

Formal education requirements

Informal education required

The job description serves as an important guideline for hiring. Now you have a basis on which you can begin your search for TSRs.

The job description of a TSR greatly depends upon many factors. For example, if you are selecting TSRs to sell or generate appointments over the telephone, this would make a considerable difference in how your job description is written. If the TSR is prospecting business-to-business, business-to-consumer, and in-bound or out-bound, these are factors to consider when creating the job description, as is whether you are automated or on a manual system—perhaps data entry is not as important as the selling aspects of the job.

The following information is a sample job description to give you an idea of what you should look for when reviewing and selecting résumés for an interview. The sample below is a start. You don't necessarily use it entirely, create one on your own. However, it is important that you have a job description for everyone in your department and preferably throughout your entire company. Otherwise, how will your employees know what you expect of them?

Job Description for a Telemarketing Sales Representative

Position title: Telemarketing Sales/Service Representative (TSR)

Responsibilities/duties: Contacting existing and potential customers.

1. *Quality control:* Ensure existing customer base is satisfied with product and services.
2. *Cross-selling:* Expand existing accounts by selling other products customers are not using.
3. *Market research:* Contact target companies not doing business with company and qualify, establish wants, and create a need for company products and services. Profile each contact for future selling opportunities.
4. *Update database:* Contact existing customer base to update information.
5. *Prospect new customers:* Cold-call prospects to generate interest in company's products. Encourage prospects to participate in receiving information or sampling products.
6. *Suspense and follow up:* Mail and recontact those who received information or samples and close for product ordering, or make arrangements to have an outside sales representative meet with them personally for demonstration, presentation, and the like.

Skills required: Automation and data entry. Excellent communication. Professional language. Must have sales and customer service background.

Education: Second-year college or higher or equivalent of at least 5 years experience. Minimum 2 years experience.

Daily activities: Prospecting, selling, lead generation, market research, customer servicing, faxing, mailing, data entry, account managing, and reporting.

Ideally, you need to have your job description prior to interviewing and hiring your TSRs. In the event you did not have a job description when you hired your existing TSRs, it's not too late—you still have time to implement one and enforce it. However, you need to approach it differently.

Introducing the Job Description to Your Existing Employees

When implementing a job description after you've hired and trained your TSRs, you still have an opportunity to introduce the job description. How do you do this? By involving your TSRs during the development process. Begin by writing a job description of your own—one for yourself and other members of your staff.

Once you have completed your own job description, have a meeting introducing the idea and requesting that all participate in the development. You need to sell the idea and the importance of it to others on staff and to the company and be appreciative of their input. Your TSRs are able to better determine what they can and are contributing to their department and what more they can contribute . This also serves to motivate them and clear their own personal beliefs regarding how much they are really contributing. You'll be amazed at what they'll come up with!

After your staff has completed their own job descriptions, then you need to compile and review them. Compare their description with yours and try to come up with a couple of descriptions that best fit the one you had originally created. Have a meeting and pass out a copy of your final draft to discuss it openly. Read the entire job description and together discuss each issue. In discussing and negotiating the description, you will create one that all will agree upon.

When using this form of diplomacy, your staff won't be as resistant in honoring the new description. They are more likely to comply and meet with its requirements. To ensure that your TSRs are closely following the job description, provide them with target dates of when you will evaluate them. Upon evaluation if you have determine that they are not in compliance with the description, you can take the appropriate action to help them get back on track. Install an accountability factor so that everyone is expected to perform and follow through. Sometimes you may need to reposition some of your staff because they are not able to fulfill the requirements of the job description. You may opt to provide additional training for those who fall short of the description. In any event, having a job description will make your TSRs more accountable for their performance, and help obtain the results you're entitled to.

Recruiting

Using Your Local Community as a Resource

Nearly every community has a resource for recruiting TSRs at no charge to the employer. *Job service* facilities provide applicants, well qualified and pre-screened, who are available for interviewing. All you need to do is provide the services with a job description of what you're looking for and they will seek to fulfill that position. Of course, you will conduct the final interview process and make your own selection. The advantage of using this service is that you are talking only with candidates who fit most of your requirements. With some additional training, you may find your ideal TSRs at no recruiting costs to the company. Other programs that are run by the state and even federal programs may offer financial assistance to give you incentive to hire one of their applicants. These incentives are sometimes in the form of tax credits or co-op pay allowances, and even training dollars are provided so you would take the time to retrain individuals who may have the ability to perform the job but not enough training or on-the-job experience to compete with other more qualified applicants. Other areas for recruiting TSRs are your local colleges, universities, or technical schools. Better educated students are usually more disciplined in the area of dependability because they have good study habits and the maturity and eagerness to take on more responsibilities. If you are hiring part-time TSRs, student's schedules provide good opportunities, since students are ideal candidates for evening, weekend, and part-time day hours. This may be an opportunity for the student. Since telemarketing is a vastly growing industry, students may be able to get college credits. If they are able to get credits, they are more dedicated and committed to working for you, since they have something to gain not only in financial terms but in academic ones as well.

Existing Employees Are Good Referrals

Referrals are an excellent resource to find qualified applicants. In order to get referrals, you first need to establish a good reputation as a manager and as a company. When you develop a reputation that you care about your employees, you're supportive, you're reliable, pay well, and offer a positive and good working environment, you will have a constant internal referral base. However, be careful; sometimes problems arise when two friends are working together. Therefore, if you hire another TSR who happens to be one of your employee's friends, sit down and discuss openly what your concerns are prior to interviewing. This will clear the air of any unforeseen problems that may occur.

Promote from Within

Hiring within is an excellent source for candidates. They already know your company, the industry, your products and services. You have the ability to check their past performance, attitudes, work ethics, and so on. Continually communicate your needs internally and with other key management or personnel. Posting flyers to advertise the job opening will help you to gain candidates from within, especially those who feel its time for a change. You can often find your ideal TSR within the company by accidentally talking with employees during lunch, in a meeting, or on a walk to the parking lot. You may be impressed with someone you never noticed before. Always be in the recruiting mode and keep a look-out for ideal candidates. This includes keeping your eye out during your personal life. Recruiting is a continuous job. Even if you are not looking for anyone at the time, never close your eyes or mind to someone who is capable of meeting the job description. No firm is ever 100 percent satisfied with all its TSRs. There is always someone who can meet the description better than others. When you are hiring within, if you find someone to replace a nonproductive TSR, you may be able to reposition the latter into another department leaving an opening for a higher producer.

Know Your Competitor's Employees

Know who your competitor's employees are. This doesn't mean you dart after them and jerk them away from their desks. That is unethical. However, you can keep the communication going and make the most from your opportunities as they arise. Let your competitors know you are hiring and ask if they would keep their eyes and ears open for ideal applicants. A nonthreatening way of communicating your needs or expressing your desires to hire your competitor's employees is by inviting them to a job fair. In this way, they will decide for themselves whether they are interested enough to attend. Once they see what the opportunities are for them, they can stay and be interviewed. Otherwise, at a job fair they can opt to leave and no one feels embarrassed. If you really want an individual and are fearful of trying to approach them yourself, hire an employment agency and let its staff know who you have an interest in. The agency will approach the individual and determine the individual's interest without ever involving you.

Aggressive Measure for Recruiting Top Producers

If you are looking for a TSR that is a high-volume producer and you want a professional with little or no training required, place ads in trade journals or publications of local associations. There are employment agencies who specializes in seeking professional telemarketers and are able to seek TSRs willing to relocate for the right offer.

Write a press release. This is a way to get free publicity for your telemarketing program. High producers will take notice and be impressed with the publicity. You will get additional calls to inquire about the positions available. If your call center has been in existence for some time, then feature some of your top producers in the press release. This brings excitement into your department and shows appreciation for those who are extraordinary and possibly impresses and motivates other candidates to make inquiries.

Advertise with Newspaper Ads to Reach a Wide Audience

Your local newspaper classified ad section is the most popular resource for seeking applicants. It's fairly inexpensive and reaches a wider audience. The disadvantages are that most will not be qualified, and you are competing with so many others looking for the same ideal applicant. It is tougher to screen and weed out the nonqualified persons than to sell the position to those who are qualified. To minimize unproductive calls, you need to place your ad other than in the telemarketing section of the classifieds. A good place is the sales section, provided you are looking for inside sales. If you need an appointment setter or a market researcher, then you can still place ads in the sales section or in the clerical section. When placing ads in the telemarketing section, you will get too many calls because you will deal with those who have no or very little experience or who have a short-lived employment history from one job to the next. These are usually persons who job-hop and are not reliable. Should you have no other alternative but to place an ad in the telemarketing section, be sure to request a résumé to be sent as opposed to a phone call; this will minimize the unqualifieds. Those with résumés are more serious in seeking long-term employment opportunities and less likely to be wasting your valuable time.

Before you place your ad in the classified section of the newspaper, you need to develop a message that attracts the ideal applicant you're looking for. The message you use to attract an applicant should stress the benefits of the job and let applicants know in a few sentences why they should work for your company. You don't want your message to say everything, you only want to arouse interest and create enough curiosity to respond. Moreover, you only want to attract those who fit what you are ideally looking for; in this way you will have less weeding out to do. You don't want a larger volume of response; it's quality you're looking for. The following provides you with ideas of how to construct your message when recruiting TSRs.

How to Place an Effective Classified Ad for Recruiting Your TSRs

When placing any classified ads, several factors can help increase the response levels from your ad. The objective when placing your classified ads is to not only attract the right caliber of TSR but that the TSR job burn-out and turnover factor is decreased as much as possible. Here are some guidelines for telemarketing managers to follow in achieving their objectives in the recruitment process.

You want your add to have a professional style that is not flashy or unrealistic but noticeable in order to set your ad apart from your competitors. You need to know who your competitors are and what they are doing to advertise for their TSRs. There are two kinds of competitors: your primary competitors are a company similar to yours; your secondary competitors consist of anyone advertising in the same section of the paper as you.

Take a good look at the major newspapers in which you plan to advertise for a TSR position and notice how many other telemarketing and/or customer service ads are listed in the same section. Carefully view the ads and see what attracts your eye. Also, notice ads that discourage response. This will assist you in better preparing your ad and ensuring its superiority and professionalism over your competitors' ads. You want to stand out and set your ad apart from others but leave a positive and lasting impression. It may cost you more, but overall it's more cost-effective. You don't want to place an unattractive ad and not have enough good candidates and then need to place the ad again. This is too costly and nonproductive.

What to Look for in Your Competitors Ads.   Before placing an ad, scan the classifieds you're planning to place the ad in. Take a look at what others are saying to bring in potential applicants.

What salaries or pay plan are your competitors offering for the same position?

What benefits, incentives, and bonus programs are available?

How many hours are they requiring of the TSR?

How soon is the position available?

How long will the position last?

What type of products and/or services are to be marketed?

How many positions are open?

What size is the ad—is it small, medium, or large?

How and when is the TSR to apply for the position? (Does the ad have only a box to send a résumé to, or does it have an 800 number to call? What time of day can the TSR call, is the time flexible to make the call? Does the ad provide an address with no telephone number or perhaps a date already set for conducting the interviews.)

If you are unable to gain all this information from the ad, then you may want to make contact by calling the company directly to ask questions that will enable you to find out more detailed information and to determine how other telemarketing firms are handling their ad calls.

Why go to all this trouble? Telemarketing is a fast-growing industry, and professional TSRs tend to job-hop to different companies to find the ideal company that would best meet their employment objectives. A TSR's experience and value to a company also determine what the TSR is looking for when it comes to accepting employment with a particular company. Some of these qualities are longevity of the business, stability, how well it is capitalized, what has been the firm's track record, how profitable is the compensation plan, whether the plan offers benefits and how good the benefits are, and so on. Also, by calling other ads, you could determine how well other managers are handling their calls. This can help you to gain ideas for better approaches that you can implement. When contacting these ads, the following are some questions to ask yourself:

How personable was the manager?

How much information did the manager provide over the phone?

How professional did the manager sound? Did the manager present well?

How impressive was the manager's voice projection, what mental pictures did she or he paint in your mind?

Did you feel the manager knew what he or she was talking about?

How comfortable and positive did you feel after the conversation, was it impressive enough for you to want to be interviewed?

What areas impressed you the most, and what didn't impress you?

Take notes. Even go so far as to use an evaluation sheet and critique the phone interview. Compile the information and review your notes. This will assist you in becoming better at what you do when interviewing and hiring your TSRs.

Placing Your Ad to Attract the Ideal TSR for Your Call Center. Most telemarketing managers prefer to have the applicants call in. This allows the manager to start the interview process over the telephone. If the applicant doesn't qualify in the telephone interview, meaning the applicant doesn't project well, has a lack of experience or poor communication skills, then the telemarketing manager hasn't wasted too much time. However, this is not as effective as personal interrogating, and declining applicants over the telephone can be difficult. Instead, it is preferable to have applicants send in their résumé. Doing so may prove that the applicant is more serious about obtaining a long-term relationship, and having a résumé is more professional. Also, you can see applicants' experience by the information contained in the résumé—if they have had long-term employment, especially in the area of telemarketing, customer service, or sales. You can weed out inappropriate applicants faster by reviewing their résumés first and sending those that are out of the question a letter thanking them for applying and encouraging them to reapply another time.

For those résumés that you have selected, you can now contact them and conduct your interviews over the telephone. The telephone interview is discussed later in this chapter. Before this happens, you need to develop your *recruitment message* to lure in your ideal applicant. Figure 9-1 shows samples of ads that are cost-effective and will meet your recruiting objectives for your ad.

What to Avoid in Your Ad. Avoid ads that sound unrealistic, phrases that sound like overkill or are unprofessional (e.g., "earn $1000 a week (proof available)" or "CA$H PAID DAILY, Earn $15.00 per hour **GUARANTEED!**", "20 positions available no experience required, start today, rock-and-roll environment, flexible, relaxed, drink coffee, have fun") Your ad must be believable, and the words need to be carefully put together to motivate and encourage a professional telemarketer to call. Never use phrases that you're unable to validate during your interview time, or you lose credibility.

How Often Should You Run Your Ad? The length of time you keep the same ad running without any changes depends on the newspaper you place your ad with. Some newspapers provide discounts that offer incentives to keep

Sample Ads That Attract Your Ideal Applicants

Low-Cost Ads

SALES, INSIDE. 5 pt & ft positions. Up to $15 per hour guaranteed plus bon-incen. Exp. preferred. Co. will train. Resumes only: 1212 Successful Lane, CA 77777.

Medium-Cost Ads

Telemarketing, Appt. Setters, am/pm shifts avail. Up to $15 per hr. plus bonuses-incentives. Smoke-free office. Co. training. Résumés only: 1212 Successful Lane CA 77777.

High-Cost Ads

SALES MARKETING
Representatives. High Salaried for aggressive outgoing, enthusiastic candidates. Advancements, bonus plans and benefits. Min. 2 yrs exp. Customer service related. Co. training. Résumés only: 1212 Successful Lane CA 77777.

Sales, Inside. Aggressive co. seeks you for an immediate position. $2500/mo. average income min. 40 hrs a week. Increasing bonus and incentives. Résumés: 1212 Successful Lane CA 77777.

SALES, INSIDE. Immediate positions. Up to $15 per hr. Excellent bonus and incentives. Must have 2 yrs. exp. Co. training. Advancements. Résumés only: 1212 Successful Lane CA 77777.

Telemarketing, generate leads, all shifts. No selling, excellent pay plan with advancement opport. Bonus-Incentives, Benefits. Company training. Résumés only: 1212 Successful Lane CA 77777.

SALES REPRESENTATIVES. Inside sales for marketing firm. Training provided. Guaranteed paid plus Bonus-Incentives. Full- and part-time shifts. Advancements. Résumés only: 1212 Successful Lane CA 77777.

TELEMARKETING

If you are the following:

- Assertive
- High-energy
- Team leader
- Financially motivated
- Available full-time
- Experienced 2+ years

Send résumé with proof: 1212 Successful Lane CA 77777.

Figure 9-1. Sample ads.

the ad running longer. Others will give you an account if you run your ad 30 days in the month. You can get these ads at substantially lower prices.

It is recommended that you place the same ad for no longer than 14 days at a time without any changes. Sundays are the ideal time for starting and end-

Figure 9-1. Sample ads (*Continued*)

ing your ads. Most professionals will look at the Sunday classifieds to begin
their job search. They are able to prepare themselves for the following week
for scheduling interviews.

When placing your ads, establish a friendly relationship with your ad representative. By doing so, you may have more flexibility when asking for extra
service (e.g., placing your ads for 30 days every month ongoing with the ability to change that ad every 14 days and keep your cost down). This is the ideal
way to run your ads. It will take time and patience on your part to have your
representative work with you. Pay your bills on time, send flowers or a card
every so often, and ask for the same representative—in fact, insist on it! Soon
you will win your representative over to work with you and assist you in placing more cost-effective ads for your company.

Identifying and Qualifying the Applicant

Many companies are looking for the wrong traits for a TSR profile when interviewing. This is typically identified as "good phone skills, aggressive, self-
starting," and, although these are important, they are not complete. One of the
more accepted methods of screening possible TSRs is by focusing on job com-
petency. A company can identify the underlying skills and traits that determine a TSR's sales success and develop a means for selecting and improving
them. Rather than focusing on personality traits or phone skills, you can have
additional insights when interviewing applicants and be better equipped to
select the right candidates who will be more successful for your operation.

There are three areas of consideration:

Conceptual. Information analysis, decision-making, technical knowledge, planning, controlling, organizing, thoroughness, and written communication

Interactive. Oral communication, persuasiveness, flexibility, and personal sensitivity

Traits. Creativity, decisiveness, initiative, integrity, and determination

Training can improve the ability to write, organize, analyze, and acquire technical knowledge. But developing interactive skills is more difficult and is more time consuming to learn. Traits are gifts and not something that can necessarily be learned and, generally speaking, cannot be changed. Any screening process conducted should be focused on discovering the applicant's interactive skills and personal traits. For example, in the area of applicants' interactive skills, evaluate their phone presence and tone. This will immediately help you determine their oral communication abilities. If they don't pass this test they will probably not be successful. Second, how capable are applicants at expressing themselves, their thoughts, and ideas? Do they speak clearly and fluently? Is the presentation delivered in a concise manner? They need to have the ability to speak fluently and articulate effectively using appropriate vocabulary and grammar while presenting themselves in a professional manner. Also, applicants must have the ability to use their voices and project quality when communicating to others, especially when communicating over the telephone. They need to be able to think on their feet to give quick informed responses. Now that a determination of what to look for when conducting your interviews has been established, the following will assist you in screening applicants over the telephone.

How to Screen Applicants over the Telephone

Many companies believe that a good telemarketer only needs to be able to communicate well and have a reliable way to get to work. As you have learned earlier, this is far from reality. Other than a good script, the selection of a telemarketer is the most important aspect to achieving a successful telemarketing campaign. Earlier we discussed how to write ads to attract your ideal applicant and identify the quality applicant. Now you will learn how to conduct preinterviews over the telephone. This is the most important part of your interviewing process. The first personal contact you make with your applicants must be by telephone. This reduces wasted time spent interviewing unqualified applicants in person, and there is no better way to determine the applicants' abilities to communicate effectively over the telephone than by having them sell themselves to you during the preinterview.

Many managers simply talk at the candidate rather than ask the right questions. Interviews are easier when a list of questions are prepared in advance. (Create a *preinterview form* to guide you through the process.) The questions should draw out important information about the candidate. Try not to digress too much during the telephone interview, it's easier to measure one applicant against another on answers to the same questions. This method also shortens preparation time and reduces anxiety associated with not knowing what you want to ask or say.

When conducting a prequalifying interview, several things must be accomplished. The following is a guideline you can use when qualifying your applicants:

How did the applicants initially present themselves?

How do their voices sound? Is the applicant's voice crisp, nice to listen to, confident, assertive? Are you impressed?

How well does the applicant answer your questions?

Who is in control of the conversation?

How well does the applicant sell herself or himself over the telephone?

What was the applicant's rate of speed?

How well did the applicant modulate?

Did the applicant have a rhythm in their delivery?

Did the applicant enunciate words correctly?

Did the applicant project a positive self-image?

Could you hear enthusiasm in the applicant's voice?

How persuasive was the applicant?

Did the applicant stay on track?

Did the applicant speak logically yet professionally?

Was the applicant a good listener?

While going through the precall interview, ask yourself these questions and list the information on a form you have designed specifically for this purpose. After the call, you can collect this information and compare it with other applicants. If you feel that the applicant meets your precall requirements, schedule for a personal interview.

Your First Step in a Preinterview Call.   Before describing the position, you must first collect information from applicants to make sure they are qualified. Ask *open-ended* questions to draw out the information; this type of questioning encourages interaction and gives you a better opportunity to listen to how applicants respond. You will get statements from the applicant rather than a quick yes or no. Here are some examples of open-ended questions:

What motivated you to respond to our ad?

What made you choose telemarketing as a career?

How soon are you available to start work?

What type of training have you had?

Based on the training you've had, what would you have liked to see improved?

What jobs have you had that dealt with sales, public relations, or customer service?

What hours are you looking for?

How long do you plan to work for?

What were your reasons for leaving your last job?

When seeking employment, what do you look for?

Who, other than us, have you contacted regarding employment?

When asking these questions, be sure to use the screening guideline to evaluate the applicant's telephone voice. While you are asking questions, you can rate the responses by using a rating scale from 1 to 5, with 1 = unsatisfactory, 3 = satisfactory, and 5 = outstanding. What you want to spend more time on is evaluating how applicants present themselves, how well developed their oral communication skills are, whether they possess the elements for effective communication with regards to their responses, and whether they demonstrated effectiveness in their oral communication on previous jobs.

Figure 9-2 is a *preinterview evaluation form*. The questions will vary from one applicant to the next depending on their job function and previous experience. Also, you may choose to customize your own questions based upon your hiring objectives.

Once you have collected the information you need and feel comfortable with the applicant's response, proceed to educate the applicant about the job description.

How to Sell the Job Description

When selling the job description, keep in mind that the applicants who are calling in have contacted or will be contacting most of the other telemarketing ads in the same publication where you placed your ad. The applicant called your ad because it appealed in some way. First, you describe what your company is marketing. Describe the features and functions of the product or service, then proceed to list the implied and stated benefits the prospective employee will receive. This selling mode is similar to the presentation you would give to your prospects over the telephone. By following this method, you have accomplished two important steps:

1. You are selling the product or service to be marketed to the applicants so they see the value in it. This way you motivate the applicants' desire to come in for the interview because they are excited about what they will be marketing personally.

TELEPHONE INTERVIEW:
Interviewed By: _____ Date: _____ Time of Call: _____

APPLICANT INFORMATION:
Full Name: _____
Address: _____
City: _____ State: _____ Zip: _____
Phone: (____) _____
Yrs @ Present Address: _____
Present/Last Employer: _____ Job Title: _____
Responsibilities: _____
_____

INTERVIEW QUESTIONS:

1.   Describe your experience in Sales & Customer Service.
_____
_____

2.   Why are you leaving your present job?
_____
_____

3.   Why do you want this job? ...or Why Qualified?
_____
_____

4.   What motivated you to call our ad?
_____
_____

PROBING QUESTIONS:

1.   How long at last job?
          _____ less 6 mo? _____ 6 mo-1yr _____ 1-2 yr _____ 2+ yr
2.   How many employers last three years?
          _____ more than 3 _____ 2-3 _____ 1?
3.   Approximate annual earnings this/last job? _____
4.   How much do you expect to earn this job? _____
5.   Are you willing to work on commission (with a small base)? _____ No _____ Yes
6.   Average closing ratio? _____
7.   When available to start working?
          _____ over 1 mo _____ 2-4 wk _____ 1-2 wk _____ Immed.

EVALUATION

VOICE:	unacceptable	marginal	good	COMMUNICATION SKILL:	unacceptable	marginal	good
Speed	1	2	3	Usage of Language	1	2	3
Volume	1	2	3	Listens	1	2	3
Modulation	1	2	3	Logical	1	2	3
Rhythm	1	2	3	Descriptive	1	2	3
Enunciation	1	2	3	Persuasive	1	2	3
Overall	1	2	3	Stays "on track"	1	2	3
				Professional	1	2	3

SELF-IMAGE: _____ Low _____ Ave _____ Good _____ High   *SET UP IN-PERSON INTERVIEW?*
ENTHUSIASM: _____ Low _____ Ave _____ Good _____ High   Yes _____ No _____
COMMENTS: _____   Date: _____ Time: _____
_____   Reason: _____
_____   _____
_____   _____
_____   Signature: _____

Figure 9-2. Preinterview evaluation form.

2. You have gone through the presentation the applicants will be utilizing themselves, so now they have a better understanding of what is expected of them when working for your company.

Try not to discuss the compensation plan by briefly describing what type of plans you have to offer. It is better to let the applicant know that their desired earnings (information gained during your screening questions) from your compensation plan are greater than they are expecting. If your compensation plan is less, then either disqualify the applicant, or ask why he or she is worth more money. If you are impressed with the response, then you may request that the applicant come in for an interview and let the applicant know you would consider the possibility of negotiating the compensation. During the in-person interview, you will have greater control to sell your compensation plan or negotiate one that will meet both your objectives.

Once you have accomplished this step, "get a reaction" from applicants to see how they feel about the product or service to be marketed. If the response is positive, then ask if the applicant feels comfortable with the presentation you just gave. Ask if the applicant feels she or he could relate the same message to a prospect over the telephone. Once the applicant responds positively to your questions and you hear confidence and motivation in an applicant's voice, you have a good prospective applicant for your personal interview. The next step, if the applicant is prequalified and receptive to working for a company like yours, is to get him or her in for a personal interview.

The Personal Interview

Plan your personal interviews. Have folders ready for each applicant that have the following: the applicant's résumé, your preinterview screening evaluations, and your personal interview evaluation form. Provide each applicant with a folder that contains your company brochures, other marketing materials, your business card, and the compensation plan. This is very professional, and your applicants will be impressed with your efforts to provide them with all the information they need to make an educated decision about accepting employment with your company. Remember, when you have ideal applicants you're interviewing, it's a two-way street—you need to sell each other.

The personal interview evaluation form is designed to be attached to the preinterview telephone screening. The objective is to ask certain questions you asked over the telephone and see if they match what the applicant said during the personal interview. Also, you will be asking more aggressive questions in your personal interview that you did not ask in your telephone interview. Your form should also include a final rating system to assist you in your final selection process. Figure 9-3 is an interview evaluation form which you can use or modify for your personal interviewing process.

The following are steps for conducting the interview:

Step 1—Before You Meet with the Applicant.   Set your interviews 20 to 30 minutes apart. This way if one applicant doesn't show up you will not have unproductive time between interviews, and it's fine to have other applicants see a room full of other applicants—this heightens their interest and adds competi-

---

PERSONAL INTERVIEW:
Interviewed By: _____ Date: _____ Time of Interview: _____
APPLICANT NAME: _____

INTERVIEW QUESTIONS:

1. Other than college (or whatever), what seminars or other trainings have you attended to enhance your job skill?
_____
_____

2. Describe the worse call you ever made? _____
_____

3. How did you handle it?, and What would you have done differently? _____
_____

4. What bad experiences have you had on your last 2 years that really left you with a negative impression?
_____
_____

5. What do you enjoy most about your capabilities? _____
_____

6. In your previous job, what was your primary function? _____
_____

7. Describe the most skills or techniques you've learned? _____
_____

8. If we were to contact your previous employer, how would they describe your employment with them? _____
_____

9. What are your career objectives? _____
_____

10. How do you think this job will help you achieve your objectives? _____
_____

11. What are you expecting to earn within: _____ 30 days? _____ 90 days? _____ 1 yr. _____ 5-10 yrs.

12. If you could change anything about your present job to make you stay, what would that be? _____
_____

13. What are your greatest strengths? _____
    Weaknesses? _____

14. If you had to sell yourself and break it down into Features, Functions, & Benefits, what would they be? Starting with
you as a feature, what are the functions you can contribute?, and how can our company benefit? _____
_____
_____

CAPABILITIES: _____ Low _____ Avg _____ Good _____ High   *PROBABILITY IN HIRING?*
                                                                Yes _____ No _____

COMMENTS: _____   Reason: _____
_____   _____
_____   _____
_____   _____

Figure 9-3. Interview evaluation.

tiveness to the job. Have the receptionist greet each of the applicants and hand out your company's job application. Although you have their résumés, you should always have your own application for applicants to fill out. This gives you an opportunity to assess their writing skills. Writing skills are extremely important if applicants are to hand-write any documents, and this also enables you to see if they can spell correctly. When the first applicant is ready to be interviewed, the receptionist should either direct them to your office or conference area. It is preferable that you conduct your interviews away from your office, since it can be a distraction and slow down the interview process.

Step 2—Establish Rapport.   Establish a rapport with applicants to make them feel at ease with you. Shake their hands, offer them a seat, and don't start any serious questioning until you have built some rapport. You want the applicant to feel comfortable and talk openly with you. If applicants feel you are going to trap them, manipulate, or intimidate them, they are less likely to open up. Plan on asking some ice-breaking but productive questions, such as how long did it take for them get to the office, or did they find the location without any complications. Once you have opened the lines of communication, then you may begin setting the stage for how the interview will take place.

Step 3—Setting Up the Stage.   Describe to applicants the objective of the interview and why you have chosen them to be there. Walk them through your process so they have a clear understanding that they would not be there if they did not pass the first two phases: the résumé and the telephone interview. Tell the applicant about yourself and your personal objectives. Have your applicants know what the process is during their interviews and what the next steps are once the interviews are completed. You will never hire them on the spot, and they need to know that. This way they will continue to feel confident about their opportunities and be hopeful for the position.

Step 4—Probing Questions That Further Your Interview Process.
When probing your applicants, be sure to remain neutral. You don't want to give any indications or clues so that they give you responses that you might be looking for as opposed to what their own answers would be. Try to avoid facial expressions and other body language that could give you away. Remember, the applicant is also interviewing you! Another area you need to watch out for is leading your applicants by asking questions that answer themselves. For example: "You're not interested in part time are you?" "Don't you think that telemarketing requires a lot of patience?" "You're not going to stay in the business forever are you?" These type of questions are not very productive and are not neutral. Instead, you want to try and keep most of your questions open-ended. This gets applicants talking more freely and more descriptively. In addition, you can hear how well they are communicating with you. Whenever possible, instead of responding to your applicant's answers, try asking questions to probe deeper, this forces the applicant to keep talking and to provide you with more information.

Ask questions that will allow applicants to respond emotionally, such as, "What seminar have you been to that really impressed you?" "What was the worst call you ever made?" "What is the most memorable experience you can recall when prospecting?" "What bad experience have you had at your last two jobs that really left you with a negative impression?" These questions will not only help you sense the applicants' emotions but also will tell you a little more about them. The objective here is to make sure when you ask questions that they are always productive. You don't want to ask about the weather or golf, or things of that nature.

The following are progressive probes that relate to your hiring requirements.

What do you enjoy most about what you do?

In your previous job, what was your primary function?

When you have a prospect that curses at you, how do you deal with that?

What are the most important skills or techniques you've learned from your experiences?

If I were to contact your previous supervisor, how would she or he describe you?

What have you done in the past few years that you are really proud of?

What is your career objective?

How do you think this job will help you achieve your objective?

What steps are you taking to ensure you are meeting your objectives?

What are you expecting to earn in the first 30 days?

What are you expecting to earn in 90 days?

What are you expecting to earn this year?

Where do you see yourself in the next 5 years? 10 years?

If you could change anything in your present job to make you stay, what would that be?

If you had all the financial stability you needed, what would you do with your life?

If you had to sell yourself to me, as a product—a product intending to work for me—what are your most important features and functions, and why should I buy you?

What are your greatest strengths?

What are your greatest weaknesses?

In your previous job, what were the areas that you and your supervisor/manager disagreed on the most?

What did you agree on?

What kind of people do you enjoy working with the most?

What kind of people do you least like working with, and how do you handle them?

These questions are not meant for you to use in their entirety. Pick and choose the ones that best meet your requirements and add them to your personal interview evaluation form.

Step 5—The Bridge That Leads into the Compensation Plan. Once you are finished with the bulk of your interview process, ask applicants if they have any questions or concerns prior to getting into the compensation plan. If there are no further questions, proceed on to your next step. Now you must sell the compensation plan.

Step 6—Selling Your Compensation Plan. You have provided the applicant with a written form of your compensation plan. Earlier in the compensation chapter the different types of plans were discussed. Be sure you have provided several options for compensating your ideal applicants, because you want to ensure you get the best producers possible working for your company. The compensation plan offered will greatly affect your applicant's decision to work for you.

If you are providing your applicant with two income options, discuss the wage option first. Show applicants what they are going to bring home as a minimum and discuss the bonus and incentive programs last. Give examples of what others have earned with the plan you have and preferably show some validation of it so it is more realistic to the applicant. Many companies will "hype" their compensation plans to sound unbelievable, and if no validation is given to show proof, applicants may not accept employment who lack trust in the compensation figures given to them during the interview. Once you have gone through the first option, ask if there any questions, then proceed to go into the second option—commission. You need to show the minimum production figures that you know are achievable, never use average figures, and be sure to tell the applicant that you are using low figures so the figures are not overwhelming. Use a calculator if necessary to show income potential, and present validation that the figures are realistic.

Once you have completed selling the compensation plan, ask applicants if they have any further questions or concerns. Allow them to open up and give their feedback and opinions.

Step 7—Wrap Up the Interview. Thank applicants for their interest and mention that you will be checking their references. Ask them if they have any concerns about checking their references and be sure to note any such concerns on your evaluation form. If their concerns alarm you in any way, probe deeper and find out the particulars. In any case, you need to check their references, and if you are unable to do so because they are uncomfortable with the present job, let them know you need to check references and who would they recommend to contact. Applicants are always at their best in an interview, but once you check references you may find information that will be helpful to you in your final selection process. It's alarming how many companies do not check references and instead hire based on intuition.

Once you are completely finished, shake hands and let applicants know you will be in contact with them in a few days either by telephone or letter. Have your receptionist walk the applicant out and bring in your next applicant. And start this process all over again.

Checking References

A high number of résumés contain certain misrepresentations. You should check your ideal applicant's references. Your application requested references, the applicant gave them to you, so why are most companies not checking references? Possibly because it's time consuming and tedious, and many managers rely on their intuition to make their final decision. If you're really impressed with your applicant, why bother? Because applicants are always performing at their best during an interview, if you want to be sure they will continue to impress you, check their previous work history and whether they have been honest with you during their interview. By doing so, you can determine any inconsistencies between the applicant's statements and those from references.

Reference checking needs to be done carefully and legally. Many employers are reluctant to give negative references due to lawsuits that previous employees have filed. These law suits have been based on *character defamation*. However, an employer may welcome the employee's departure and not want to risk that employee's departure by giving information that would prevent another employer from wanting to hire the individual. Also, employers can avoid concerns with dealing with the unemployment issues by encouraging the employee to easily find another job.

If you are conducting the reference checking, you need to speak with the applicant's former supervisor. You need to be prepared to ask certain questions that are safe and legal to ask. List these questions in advance. Ask your local labor department for the types of questions it recommends to ask, so you are in compliance with any legal or ethical issues. Your objective is to determine applicants' individual work habits, their motivation and skills, employment dates, and the applicants' responsibilities. You also want to know when and why they are no longer working at their former jobs. If you are able, confirm the applicant's previous income and personal production history. Find out if the applicant had a good attendance record, how well the applicant worked under pressure, and whether the applicant got along with coworkers and supervisor. One final question to ask is whether the employer would rehire the applicant and, if not, why not.

If you're running into problems with getting previous employers to assist you in the reference checking, get a release form signed by the applicant. This form releases the former employee from all claims and any liabilities that may arise by releasing information you are requesting. In this way, the former employer will be more free to open up if necessary. This also says something about the applicants themselves. By signing a waiver, they are not in the least concerned about you checking their references. It shows they are confident and have been truthful in the information they've provided you.

If you are concerned whether applicants are being honest about financial income in order to sway you to pay them more than what they are accustomed to getting, there is an alternative. Try and verify through reference checking, but many previous employers may not be willing to give you this information or the information may not be accurate. You also can request applicants to furnish a copy of their most recent W-2 form. If you want to verify their education or technical training, have applicants bring in their school transcripts. This type of reference checking reduces your time spent making telephone contacts.

Once you have checked the applicant's references and are thoroughly convinced you have the ideal applicant, proceed to make contact to congratulate either by telephone or by letter. You can request the applicant come in again for one more final interview, and you would then inform the individual that she or he had been selected. The following are examples of these three different options. Choose the one that will best meet your hiring requirements.

Getting Your Ideal Applicant to Accept Your Offer

Once you have selected the applicants you want, you must contact them, and hopefully, they will accept your offers. At the time of the second interview with you, the applicant has probably been interviewed by several other prospective job opportunities, so you need to proceed with caution. Prepare your offer in advance. If you do not have a standard form to write your offer, then produce one. This simplifies the process. Be sure to have your form customized to enable you to personalize your offers according to each applicant you are hiring—leave plenty of room for information that addresses the motivations of each applicant.

Review your notes from previous interviews with the applicant. Prior to writing your offer, look for where the applicant stated goals, interests, and expectations. You want to incorporate these into your proposal. This lets applicants know you haven't forgotten what they wanted in their employment with you and that you want to incorporate such in the *employment agreement*. This is a mutual relationship. Your offer should project what you expect applicants to comply with. Also, your offer should indicate the employee's contribution. Although you may not be able to comply with all the wants and needs of each applicant, you should be able to present your offer to emphasize the benefits that are in the applicant's interest.

Figure 9-4 is a sample of the employment agreement. The basis of the agreement is get the hire date, job title, pay periods, and the compensation plan agreed to along with any incentive or bonus plans you're offering. The job description, the employee's requirements, and production expectations are all a vital part of the employment agreement.

Presenting Your Offer in Person

You can present your offer in a final interview. This is a more personal way of presenting it and allows you greater control of the process. Thank the applicant for his or her patience and the time it took to go through the selection process. Take your offer out and start going through it together. Never give applicants their own copy until you have presented the offer in full. Discuss the important facts of your offer, the position they have been accepted for,

Employee_____   Department_____
Hire Date_____   Supervisor_____

Job Title: TSR (Telemarketing Service Representative)

Pay Periods: 11th–27th paid on the 1st
                          28th–10th paid on the 15th

Compensation Plan: $10.00 per hour

Incentive Plan: $1.50 for every qualified appointment (verifi-
                          able, see definitions)

Bonus Plan: $40.00 for every 100 appointments set each
                          month

Job Description: Obtain qualified appointments by telephone for
                          field sales staff; data entry, mailing, faxing, and
                          tabulating daily call activities

Requirements: Work week—32 hours per week

Production: Minimum 15 qualified appointments per 32-
                          hour week

Position Outline

1. Production quota status will be reviewed with employee every 2 weeks.
   Reviews to be conducted by immediate supervisor. (Quotas will be
   adjusted to accommodate employee illness, vacation, and holidays.)

2. Entry-level quotas will be as follows:

   First 2-week period = 15 total appointments

   Second 2-week period = 25 total appointments

   The 15 qualified appointments per week minimum must be maintained
   from then on, as a job retention requirement.

Figure 9-4. Employee agreement form.

starting date, their compensation, and other benefits that pertain to their
employment. Remain professional and don't be overzealous, and then ask
applicants if they have any questions at that point.

  If the applicant wishes to think about your offer, ask how much time she or
he needs to make a final decision and agree to a time frame that is reasonable.
If applicants accept your offer, then prepare to give them an orientation packet to take with them to review and fill out prior to their orientation day. This
packet would include a copy of their offer. If the applicant declines your offer,
don't be defensive or behave badly, there could be a misunderstanding or

Other Requirements

1. Employee will be required to study all materials provided and participate in hands-on training as provided or requested by management.
2. Probationary period ends after 8 weeks, at which time employee has a choice of two options:
   a. The $10.00 per hour salary plan listed above
   b. Commission compensation plan @$15.00 per qualified appointment

Ethical Standards

Employees will to the best of their ability represent themselves as professionals with a high standard of ethics. Employee will get along with others within the company and customers outside the company. Should any problems arise, employee will try and resolve the problem using professional methods and good code of ethics. Should employee not be able to resolve the problem after making an attempt, then employee will schedule a meeting with the immediate supervisor and discuss the situation.

Termination Requirements

Employee's failure to obtain minimum qualified appointment quotas at any time during employment (probationary or permanent) will be considered failure to meet minimum job requirements and therefore reason for immediate termination of employment. In the event employment is terminated by company, all money due to employee will be paid at the time of termination. If termination is caused by a voluntary quit, then all money due will be paid on the regular scheduled pay period.

_____   _____
Employee   Date

_____   _____
Manager   Date

Figure 9-4. Employee agreement form. (*Continued*)

misconception and you need to uncover why your offer was declined. This would also help you in the future when presenting other offers. It may be that you need to adjust your compensation plan or benefit package. Therefore, ask the applicant why he or she declined and what it would take to have her or him reconsider. Do not immediately change your offer, this would give the applicant the upper-hand—never start off your relationship in this way. You may regret responding too quickly, if applicants are not worth what you thought they were. This does not mean that you don't comply, you just wait at least a day or two before you give your final approval. You need time to think about what is required, how that may effect your policies and other employees—especially your top producers. Once you have weighed the conditions and determined what effects an agreement would have in your department, and you still wish to hire this applicant, then write up another offer and discuss it over the telephone. You may be able to compromise. You can always negotiate a review after 90 days. Let applicants prove their abilities, with the understanding that if they can meet the production requirements and are consistent, you will reevaluate their compensation package. Should you fail to agree on an offer, thank the applicant for her or his interest and mention that you would like to keep the application on file in the event you are hiring another time. Also, let applicants know that you would like for them to keep in touch with you. Should they not be able to find suitable employment, they need to know that the door is always open for them to reapply. It will make your recruiting efforts easier and more cost-effective by keeping the door open in both directions. Recruiting is basically an ongoing process for you, so let them know that you would appreciate if they referred other possible applicants to you.

Mailing Your Offer

This is not as preferable as delivering an offer in person. However, it depends on how many applicants you may be hiring. Mailing your offer may be more time efficient. Be sure your package is neat, comprehensive, and professional in appearance. You need to enclose a personal letter congratulating applicants and welcoming them to your company. The letter should give a summary of the benefits your offer provides them; gear it to what you know would be more important to the applicant. Your final comments should state what the applicant's next step is with regards to communicating an acceptance of your offer. You may want applicants to contact you by telephone or sign the offer and mail it back to you. You can keep it either very professional or on a personable level. Once they have communicated their acceptance of employment, be sure to let them know when the orientation day is and that they should expect a packet to arrive in a few days. Always keep the communication flowing and never assume that they know what you expect them to do—tell them what you expect.

The Orientation Packet

Once the applicant has accepted your offer, send out an orientation packet. This saves everyone time and allows new employees to preview the information and research it. They have an opportunity in advance to list any questions or concerns they have prior to the first day or orientation. The packet gets them more prepared and geared up for their orientation day. This makes your orientation day run smoother and reduces conflicts or bad communication. You always want to project to your new employees that all the "cards are on the table" and that you are and will always be communicating well with them. Below is a list to guide you in developing this orientation package. You may want to delete or add to the packet. You need to decide what is important to you, the company, and to your new employees.

Personal letter

Job description

Compensation plan

Promotional literature (e.g., sales literature, brochures, articles, product, or service information)

Study materials (e.g., company history, company and department mission statements, policies and procedures)

Employee forms (e.g., W-2s, compensation agreement, conduct agreement)

You don't want to overwhelm your new employees with information and paperwork. This may cause them not to show up for orientation day. Your letter should explain that the information is for them to review prior to coming in as it will make them familiar with what is expected. Explain the benefits because this will make their orientation day run smoother. You are giving them an opportunity, prior to signing anything, to review and research the information provided them in advance. When you are up front with your new employees and keep the communication flowing, they feel more secure about the process.

Also, explain what they are to do next; give them the date of their orientation, what you need for proof of citizenship, and anything else that may pertain to your employment requirements.

How to Handle Rejected Applicants

Unfortunately, more applicants will be rejected—declined for employment— than hired. It is important that you handle these applicants with care. Although these applicants may not currently meet the qualifications of your recruiting requirements, they should be handled with respect. You don't want to cause ill feelings that may have these applicants discouraging others to apply for a position with your company. Instead, you want them to feel good about your company and your professionalism. These applicants may be future customers or an excellent resource for referrals! The following is a sample of a decline letter:

Dear_____,

   Thank you for your interest in applying for a position with our company. We considered your application very carefully but have decided to offer the position to someone else. However, we wish to keep your application on file, in the event that we reopen the position or a similar one that matches your qualifications.

   Please accept our best wishes as you seek a challenging and rewarding position.

Sincerely,

A Final Thought

Depending on how many TSRs you require, whether you are a start-up operation, what the level is of the TSR you are hiring, and the compensation you are willing to pay, you may need to consider hiring more TSRs than you actually need. It is almost certain that a few will not work out for you. They may not show up for their orientation day, or after a few days or weeks they will drop out. This happens when either the job is not what they had expected or they are not as productive as they claimed or projected they would be.

If you are engaged in a high-sales environment and you hired TSRs that are not experienced, you can expect an average turnover factor of 40 to 60 percent. This is why the recruitment process is very vital and requires careful thought and consideration. Never be in a rush to hire TSRs or to put them on staff soon after their initial interview. If they are unreliable or if another opportunity arises, by extending your offer and the orientation date, your chances are far greater of being able to weed out those who will not make it. You may be thinking of those you might lose because you did not hire them quickly. This is a possibility, however, in your interview you asked when they could start work and you communicated your process to them from the onset. The slower process is much wiser and will not have a negative effect on your recruitment process.

10

The Manager's Template

The manager's job is to plan for and allocate resources that get the maximum results from her or his department. The manager's job is not just to be the best telemarketer. It is to use expertise in the area of selling, objection handling, lead generation, and other phone skills with strategic planning to assist TSRs to be the best that they can be. A good telemarketing manager understands the needs of a TSR and what it takes to be successful. Many TSRs don't have the slightest clue—they've been too busy punching in numbers, reading their scripts and letting those numbers speak for themselves. A telemarketing manager realizes the necessity to have all the effective tools available to systematically run a department. These tools assist managers by enabling them to duplicate themselves to their TSRs. It also provides more consistency in how management runs its department.

Throughout this book, ideas have been provided to assist you in implementing and maintaining an effective call center. This chapter focuses on how to set up and conduct your new employees' orientation day and on using an instructor's lesson plan for training your TSRs. You will also learn how to monitor your TSRs' performance, measure their results, and perform live evaluations that will maximize their performance.

Unfortunately, turnover is inevitable for every company; however, in a telemarketing-inside sales environment, this turnover is much greater than in any other department. Learning how to reduce your turnover factor and retain positive and highly motivated TSRs is every manager's goal. The ideas presented in this chapter will help you achieve this goal and enable you to set the example for your TSRs. The examples that are provided will help you motivate them to continue performing in the way you initially taught them.

This chapter is full of information to make your job easier, more productive, and cost-efficient. You have been given a "template" that will guide you in your managerial duties thus making it easier for you to implement and instruct your TSRs. Following this template in the order that it has been written in the chapter gives you a step-by-step process for training new TSRs. This will help you to be more consistent and will save you time. Furthermore, you can use it throughout your managing career in the telemarketing industry. Let's begin by discussing the orientation day of newly hired TSRs.

Training and Orientation Day

You have selected your TSRs and sent them a preorientation packet to review (discussed in Chap. 9). Your next step is to plan for your orientation program. Your goal for orientation day is to help employees get off to a good start. Most new employees will quit during the first week to 10 days of starting their new job. The reasons are varied: you either made a hiring mistake, or perhaps they just didn't get along with your program. Most were not given the proper orientation prior to their first day on the job.

What exactly is an orientation? One definition is "determining one's position with reference to new ideas." In more specific terms, it's a day or two to introduce your TSRs to other employees of the company. The telemarketing staff should personally welcome your TSRs and any division managers. It is a day to discuss the company, the organization of the company, and departmental policies, procedures, and benefits. Your new employees should be given a tour of the facility, important departments, and organization members who are associated with the TSR's job function such as the shipping and receiving department, mail room, and marketing. Also, you need to show your new employees their workstations and give them time to sit there and fill out any pertinent paperwork required from personnel. Finally, it's a time to go over your new employee's job performance objectives and responsibilities. If your orientation day lasts at least 2 days, then it provides you time to conduct some training such as product knowledge, techniques, and/or software applications.

Once the orientation has been completed, give new employees a training agenda for the first 30 days along with homework assignments. You cannot require your employees to perform the homework assignments after company time—this is their option. However, you should give them a reasonable amount of designated paid time each day or week to study. Part of their qualifications to remain employed with your company can be to have them pass a test to ensure they have understood the assignments you've given them. This will satisfy personnel that they are making good use of their paid study time. Those who may require additional study time to pass the test can do so on their own time.

Getting the Most out of Your Training Agenda

Before you begin to set up your training agenda, you first need to understand that you cannot force your employees to learn. They must possess the DEW qualities:

Desire to grow

Eagerness to learn

Willingness to be taught

Hopefully during your interview process, you've selected individuals that have these qualities. Now you must cash in on these qualities and begin by training them.

A common mistake that trainers make is to assume that because someone attended a training session, that person has learned something. To train is simply to have educated, reared, or instructed, but that doesn't mean the trainee has learned anything. Therefore, your objective is not to train your employees to acquire knowledge or a skill; the objective is for your TSRs to *use* knowledge you have taught them—that makes the training program successful. You as a trainer need to focus your attention on having your TSRs learn behaviors that will make them more effective because this is more measurable than just insight or awareness.

You know when you've conducted a good training program when your employees are able to demonstrate desirable behaviors that they were not able to demonstrate before. To solidify the training and ensure your employees have learned what you intended, have them role-play scenarios such as getting through the secretary, selling the decision maker, handling rebuttals. Having them role-play presentations is essential. This is all part of the job function and determines how productive they will be if they understand and are able to follow through the process. It costs your company money when your employees are not learning the behaviors you want them to. Taking time to train, coach, reward, and reinforce are all essentials for an effective training agenda.

Determine what you're expecting from employees when setting up your training agenda. Keep in mind that everyone's skills are at different levels. You need to be sensitive to each employee you're instructing and individualize your training agenda to meet the needs of those you're training. Organize the subjects that you will cover during the training in the order that your employees need to know them.

Once you have selected the topics you are to teach, list the behavioral objectives for each topic. This will communicate to your employees what is expected of them when they are asked to apply what they're learning to their job function.

Always develop methods for measuring results, such as tabulation forms to monitor production, listening evaluations to monitor prospecting calls, and coaching during role plays. These methods can be duplicated to pass out to your employees and the originals placed in their *personal* employee file (not a *personnel* employee file). A personal employee file is what you as a manager should have on every TSR. This is where you will file production sheets, coaching results, behavioral reports, statistical analysis, and so on. The benefits of this type of file is that it's between you and the TSR. These files assist TSRs in improving their production, to measure results and reports from previous trainings or evaluations, and to determine future raises or advancement opportunities.

Prepare a Training Packet for Your TSRs

Be prepared to have a training packet for the first day of training. This should include a list of what's on the agenda. The following is a list you may want to consider:

Objectives of the training agenda

Schedule of the training day (e.g., topics, how much time spent on each topic, breaks, lunch)

Objectives of the telemarketing program and marketing strategies

Fulfillment procedures

Use of scripts, forms, equipment, database

Understanding of competition

Market needs, demographics, goals

Skills and techniques of the presentation

Common objections and answers

Role-play exercises

Hands-on evaluations

Homework assignments

Testing

Continuing education

Ongoing training

Setting Up Your Training Objectives

You need to determine your training objectives. As mentioned earlier, the most important benefits for training objectives is that they identify behavior to be performed by the TSR. Behaviors can range from complex skills such as probing and uncovering prospects' needs, selling the prospect your products or service, and/or analyzing call reports. Simpler forms of behavior are effectively reading from a script, using proper voice inflection and rates of speech, or filling out tabulation forms. The following is a list of training guidelines:

Focus on topic. Select a topic you want your TSRs to study.

Be task oriented. Provide assignments for each of the topics you are requiring your TSRs to learn about and implement in their job function.

Be specific. Give TSRs a list of what you want them to do in each of the assignments you've selected for them.

Quantify. Educate the TSRs about the assignments by showing them how you expect them to perform.

Specify a time frame. For each assignment given, tell TSRs when you want them to accomplish them and how long each of the assignments should take.

Provide prerequisites. Before TSRs start on a particular assignment, give them information, materials, books, and so on to reinforce their learning prior to implementation.

The following is an example of an effective training guide for *creating the need* in your prospect:

Topic. How to effectively ask probing questions of your prospect.

Task assignment. Create the need for your company's products and services so you can effectively sell them your offering.

Specifics. Select five questions that you would ask the prospect. List the responses that are positive. Then select three out of the five questions that your prospect may respond to negatively. Add additional probing questions to draw-out your prospect's wants and needs, then list the possible responses that will create the need for your offering.

Quantification. Your questions need to be open-ended. The first two questions are to qualify the prospects needs; questions three and four are to establish if they have any additional needs they are not presently getting; and the fifth question is to ask the prospect a question for which they do not have a viable answer. This is where you create doubt in their mind and that shows they may need your services. If you are unable to gain the kind of responses you're looking for, add additional questions to probe further and attempt to create a deeper need for your offering.

Time Frame. Take 30 minutes to complete the assignment. When you have finished, if you still have remaining time, clock the exact time it took you to finish the assignment. Go back through your assignment and recheck and make any adjustments. Log in any changes you've made and how long it took you to make the additional changes.

Prerequisites. Teach them the probing step, have them read again the information in their training manual, and do the self-tests listed at the end of the chapter.

Use this training guide for each and every job function they are expected to perform. This will ensure they have understood what you have taught them and they are able to perform and follow the process. Research proves that people remember only about 10 percent of what they read and 20 percent of what they hear, whereas they remember 90 percent of what they say and do—by application.

When instructing your TSRs, offer a variety of methods to train them. This will break up the monotony and add more diversification in their learning ability. Also, it's more fun! You have your lecture and most of it is conducted by you. However, it is recommended that you have other instructors or speakers, perhaps from another department or even an outside resource. This adds more positive interaction and helps to reinforce what you are instructing them. Having group discussions as a part of your training mix is very healthy because they allow for shared feedback, learning attitudes, and behaviors of those in the group.

Role playing is very essential for strengthening skills, giving employees the opportunity to perform without placing them on live calls when they are not ready. A role play is like a dress rehearsal, the more they practice the better and more confident they are when conducting live calls. Another method for training is putting your group into smaller groups. This is called a break-out session or round table. Let's say you have 20 students in your class; divide them into four smaller groups, now they are 5 to every group. Assign each group a particular task to role play, have those who are not participating in the role play observe and evaluate the players or have them all take part by taking sections of the task and breaking it further into smaller assignments. Give each group 10 to 15 minutes to complete the role plays and then have them move to the next table to role-play the task assigned to that table. You could have an easel at each table that lists the scenario that they are to role-play so they will know what is expected of them at each table. Also, you may want to include some of your TSRs who are already trained to be the head table master. They can supervise and coach each group's sessions.

Other training mixes are written exercises, activities, individual tutoring and coaching, reading assignments, viewing and listening to audio and video-tapes, observing others during live prospecting calls, and personal hands-on evaluations. You are the trainer and control what and how you want your training sessions to be conducted. The main objective is to have them planned out to ensure that you use a variety of methods and are able to effectively measure results!

Figure 10-1 is a trainer's presentation outline for CSR training. This provides a training overview. For step-by-step guidelines, however, you will use lesson plans.

Trainer's Lesson Plan for CSR Training

The following is the trainer's lesson plan for inbound training. The plan is broken down into four half-day sessions; however, if your training sessions are full days, then combine the two half-day sessions. This gives you 2 full days for training. If you need to reduce the training to 1 full day then you can modify some of the role-plays and incorporate them into the first day of the hands-on training.

Session 1

1. Introduce the program.
   a. Explain why customer service training is crucial.
   b. Explain what *bad* customer service does to a company's growth and how it prevents a company from maintaining existing customers.

1. Introduction
   a. Greeting
   b. Company/department name
   c. Request
 2. Establish rapport
   a. Exchange names
   b. First-name cue
   c. Reference
 3. Purpose of call—discern customer's call objective
 4. Approach
   a. Benefit statement
   b. Permission to ask questions
 5. Probing
   a. Qualifying customer's needs
   b. Establishing wants
   c. Creating a need
 6. Restate
   a. Summarize what customer said
   b. Get a confirmation
	7. Resolve—explain or describe what you plan to do
	 8. Get agreement—gain a positive response
	 9. Objections
	   a. Restate or agree and probe
	   b. Reflect
	   c. Feel, felt, and found
	   d. Ask customer for best solution
	   e. If I could, would you?
	 10. Close
	   a. Warm and friendly
	   b. Ask if there is anything else
	 11. Inform
	   a. Informing
	   b. Confirmation
	 12. Direct the call—connect the customer

Figure 10-1. CSR "12-Step" trainer's presentation outline.

   c. Describe the 12-step training concept and why a "step" process is vital for consistency throughout the company and easier for training purposes.

2. Open up discussion.

   a. Ask group members to share ways they were not serviced properly.

   b. How do they feel when receiving poor service?

   c. How have we ourselves not provided good customer servicing within the company?

   d. Have groups share ideas of what they could have done differently.

   e. Have one person in the group, from each department or function, role-play how they handle customers.

3. Review training materials.

   a. Discuss what you'll be training during each session.

   b. Explain the customization of the training for each department.

   c. Go over homework assignments and your expectations for such.

   d. Discuss students' commitment level and your commitment to them.

   e. Discuss the group's accountability factor.

   f. Go over forms. Explain each form and its benefits, and instruct how to use them.

4. Review 12-step outline.

   a. Explain the process.

   b. Explain to follow the steps and which areas *are* flexible and why. Also describe the areas that are *not* flexible and why.

5. Open up discussion.
    a. Allow for group interaction.
    b. Ask group specific questions to get them thinking.
    c. Provide feedback and solutions.
6. Set the stage.
    a. Explain why scripting is important.
    b. Discuss delivery styles and useful terminology.
    c. Teach style of delivery and voice communication.
7. Teach steps 1 to 4.
    a. Discuss the features, functions, and benefits of the steps and how each step will be taught.
    b. Teach steps 1 to 3; have group role-play in twos for 5 minutes. Circulate, evaluate, coach, and advise.
    c. Teach step 4, have the group role-play steps 1 to 4 in twos. Circulate, evaluate, coach, and advise.
    d. Select 2 people from the group, have them role-play out loud with you and the observers. Evaluate, coach, and advise.
8. Open up discussion.

Break time—15 minutes

9. Teach step 5.
    a. What type of questions?
    b. Teach the functions and benefits.
    c. Have group select questions from the examples that pertain to their department and/or job function.
    d. Role-play step 5 in twos and threes. Circulate, evaluate, coach, and advise.
10. Select and pass out scripts.
    a. Have group rewrite training script to match their job function.
    b. Role-play script in twos and threes.
    c. Circulate, evaluate, coach, and advise.
11. Role-play out loud.
    a. Select two people at a time in front of the group; use props and role play.
    b. Use stop and play (role-play) method. (Each time a person makes a mistake, stop role play and correct, then start over again.)
    c. Role-play script in twos and threes.
    d. Circulate, evaluate, coach, and advise.
12. Wrap up session.
    a. Review what the group learned.
    b. Discuss homework assignments.
    c. Encourage their commitment.
    d. Open for discussion and comments.

Session 2

1. Review homework.

   a. Identify who did their assignments and who didn't.
   b. Discuss and review any questions or concerns.
2. Review 5 steps.
   a. Test group's ability to remember each step, its function and benefits.
   b. Acknowledge how well they remembered.
   c. Open up discussion.
   d. Role-play the first 5 steps by pairs. Circulate, evaluate, coach, and advise.
3. Teach steps 6 to 8.
   a. Instruct on steps 6 to 8 and conduct role-play exercises.
   b. Customize examples for steps 7 and 8.
   c. Role-play in twos and threes. Circulate, evaluate, coach, and advise.
   d. Select two people to role-play steps 1 to 8. Have group observe and fill out their listening evaluation forms. You evaluate, coach, and advise the activity.
4. Open up discussion.
   a. Allow for group interaction.
   b. Ask group specific questions to get them thinking.
   c. Provide feedback and solutions.

Break time—15 minutes

5. Teach step 10, the close.
   a. Go into the tree different closing techniques.
   b. Discuss how they can combine their closing techniques.
   c. Have them write out which closing technique they will use according to their job function.
6. Open up discussion on steps 6 to 10.
7. Discuss steps 11 and 12.
   a. Explain to group how these two steps are used only when directing or passing the call.
   b. Go into benefits of informing.
   c. Point out the importance of the person who was informed and his or her role in restating the information back to the customer.
   d. Discuss both methods of directing the call.
8. Review steps 1 to 12 (except step 9).
   a. Explain benefits.
   b. Offer samples.
   c. Open up discussion.
9. Discuss homework assignments.
   a. Stress importance.
   b. Explain the necessity for completing the homework *prior to next session,* or they will complete it during the next session and participate in the next session.

Session 3

1. Review steps 1 to 12 (except step 9).
   a. Test group's ability to remember each step, its function and benefits.

    b. Acknowledge how well they remember.

    c. Open up discussion.

    d. Role-play in twos and threes all the steps using the scripts they've revised.

    e. Circulate, evaluate, coach, advise, and correct their scripts.

2. Teach step 9.

    a. Have group relate to the typical objections listed and discuss examples.

    b. Discuss the five techniques and customize as you teach each technique.

    c. Have group help participate in how to use each technique for their department or job function.

    d. Explain how to combine the techniques and offer examples.

    e. Review most common objections and answers.

    f. Role-play in twos and threes. Circulate, evaluate, coach, and advise.

    g. Select two people to role-play step 9. Have group observe and fill out their listening evaluation forms. You evaluate, coach, and advise the activity.

    h. Discuss group's homework assignment for step 9.

3. Stress for group to practice, practice, practice. Pass out 3×5 or 5×5 index cards and tell group to put the first five steps on the front side of card. Put steps 6, 7, 8, and 10 on the back side of the card and place them by their telephones.

4. Discuss emotion-packed words and negative words.

    a. Discuss good and bad words.

    b. Offer replacement words that are positive.

5. Discuss defusing irate customers.

    a. Address how to handle difficult customers.

    b. Discuss putting customers on hold.

    c. Discuss past calls.

6. Review customer service etiquette.

    a. Discuss and have group members write about situations where they didn't put the customer first.

    b. Describe situations to avoid.

    c. Do self-evaluation.

    d. Discuss achieving successful customer service relationship.

    e. Read "A Customer Is" out loud together as a group.

    f. Discuss an excellent versus poor customer service representative.

7. Stress importance of controlling the call.

    a. Discuss steps to accomplish.

    b. Identify disadvantages of losing control.

8. Exercise voices. Perform out loud as a group in a moderate tempo.

9. Open up final comments and discussion.

Session 4

1. Review homework.

    a. Identify who did and who didn't complete the work.

b. Set aside those who didn't and have them do it now.

c. Discuss and review any concerns.

2. Review steps 1 to 12.

 a. Test group's ability to remember each step, along with its function(s) and benefits.

 b. Acknowledge how well they remember.

 c. Open up discussion.

 d. Role-play in twos and threes all the steps using their revised scripts.

 e. Circulate, evaluate, coach, advise, and correct their scripts.

3. Have group role-play out loud with each department.

 a. Select two people from each department and have them role-play in front of group.

 b. Evaluate, advise, coach, and use the stop-and-go method.

4. Open up discussion. Make sure everyone has completed the homework assignments, if not, have them do so.

Break time—15 minutes

5. Teach about tabulating outbound activities.

 a. Discuss importance of tabulating.

 b. Teach them how to do it.

 c. Explain to group when to implement tabulation and what you plan to do with the information.

6. Wrap up program.

 a. Ask group to share what they've learned and how they will apply the information to their job function.

 b. Explain to group what they need to do to keep the information alive and fresh on a daily basis.

 c. Tell group what your continued role will be with them.

 d. Have group turn in their homework assignments.

 e. For those who didn't complete their homework, indicate a time frame in which you expect it to be turned in.

 f. Ask if they have any questions or concerns and thank them for their participation.

 g. Open up discussion.

7. Role play.

 a. In twos and threes, evaluate, coach, and advise.

 b. In front of group by department, have members evaluate by using their listening evaluations forms.

 c. Discuss role play as a group and offer advice.

8. Wrap up program.

 a. Ask group members to share what they learned and how they will apply the information.

 b. Explain to group what they need to do to keep the information alive and fresh on a daily basis.

 c. Tell group what your continued role will be with them.

d. Have group turn in their homework assignments.

e. Give those whose homework is not completed a day and time you expect it to be turned in.

f. Ask if they have any questions or concerns and thank them for their participation.

g. Open up discussion.

Testing.   Always have a test every time you train your employees. This should not be a test that purposely tricks them into not answering the questions correctly. Instead, make the test very direct and use plenty of multiple choices. If you make the test too difficult, it will demotivate people. The objective of testing is to ensure they have understood the information presented.

Discuss the objectives of the test and the rules for taking the test. Inform the group that they have 60 minutes for testing and that, once they've completed the test, to turn it in and take the balance of the day off. Ask if they have any questions or concerns. Pass out the test and put the timer on for 60 minutes, remaining in the room at all times.

Evaluate the Test Results.   To ensure that your CSRs have mastered the training you've provided them, you must evaluate their test results. Have your master test questions and answers available to use as a guide. Give those who scored less than 100 percent back their test, and allow them to research the information and retake the test the following day. There are no B, C, or D graduates. Insist on an A + each time you have your employees take a test. If they don't understand a process, then chances are they won't use it or do it correctly. It is a disservice to everyone when CSRs are not able to remember to perform everything you have taught them.

When you are insistent on your scoring requirements, your employees will take you seriously. They are more conscientious of their study habits and are better prepared to pass your testing requirements. It is not recommended that you make them aware of this in advance the first time around because you really want an opportunity to see who are the ones that take their job seriously. Also, you don't want to necessarily "stress out" anyone by being up front with your testing requirements. Some people are nervous about taking tests, particularly if they are aware of your difficult requirements. It may prevent them from doing their best. Also, you need to consider that some learn better by action—by having the ability to be on the telephones and learn with live calls. In this case, for those who passed over 80 percent of the test, allow them to spend time on the telephone and give them at least a week to study before retaking their test. If you have anyone that received 70 to 80 percent pass rate, they may need to evaluate their results and see where they were in error before retaking the test. They will be able to pass the next time. However, for those who were under 70 percent, they really don't understand what you expect them to do. You must provide additional training before they actually make live telephone calls.

1. Introduction
   a. Greeting
   b. Establish contact
   c. First-name cue
   d. Introduce self and company
   e. Landmark
2. Reference—how you acquired prospect's name
3. Request for time
   a. Respect for time
   b. Request for a call back
   c. Easy close
4. Purpose of the call
   a. Benefit statement
   b. Permission to ask questions
5. Probing
   a. Qualifying prospect
   b. Establishing wants
   c. Creating a need
6. Restate
   a. Summarize what prospect said
   b. Get confirmation from prospect
7. Features, functions, and benefits
   a. Features
   b. Functions
   c. Implied benefits
   d. Stated benefits
8. Get reaction—encourage positive response
9. Trial close
   a. Summarize benefits
   b. Ask for a commitment
10. Objections
    a. Defuse objections
       (1) What's the real issue
       (2) Solutions
       (3) Important points
       (4) Interpreting objections
    b. Six objection techniques
       (1) Restate or agree and probe
       (2) Keep selling
       (3) Reflect
       (4) Feel, felt, found
       (5) Prospect to sell themselves
       (6) If I could, would you?
       (7) Combining your techniques
11. Close—three popular closes and combinations thereof
    a. Assumptive
    b. Contained choice
    c. Direct
    d. Combining your techniques
12. Postclose
    a. Reassure prospect
    b. Request further information
    c. Post-close questions

Figure 10-2. TSR 12-step trainer's presentation training outline.

Trainer's Lesson Plan for TSR Training

Figure 10-2 is a TSR trainer's presentation outline. Again, for a step-by-step guide, you will need a lesson plan. The following is the trainer's lesson plan for outbound training. The plan is broken down into four half-day sessions. However, if your training sessions are full days, then combine the two half-day sessions. This gives you 2 full days for training. If you need to reduce the training to 1 full day then you can modify some of the role plays and incorporate them into the first day of the hands-on training.

Session 1

1. Introduce the training.
   a. Give an overview of the telemarketing industry and its expected growth.
   b. Explain why updating one's telemarketing approach is crucial.
   c. Explain what *bad* telemarketing does to a company's image and how it prevents a company from increasing their business opportunities.
   d. Describe the 12-step training concept and why a step process is vital for consistency throughout the company and easier for training purposes.
2. Open up discussion.
   a. Ask group to share ways they were approached and unimpressed by calls.
   b. How do they feel when receiving solicitation type calls?
   c. How, within their job function, have they not conducted themselves in a professional manner? How might prospects have misunderstood their approach?
   d. Have several in the group role-play their own or a typical telemarketing presentation they've recently heard.
3. Review training materials.
   a. Discuss what you'll be training during each session.
   b. Explain the customization of the training.
   c. Go over homework assignments and your expectations.
   d. Discuss commitment level from each TSR and your commitment to them.
   e. Discuss the accountability factor for each TSR and the department.
   f. Review the forms they are to use. Explain each form and its benefits and instruct how to use it.
4. Review the training outline.
   a. Explain the process.
   b. Explain how to follow the steps and which areas *are* flexible and why. Also identify the areas that are *not* flexible and explain why.
   c. Discuss the three fears prospects have when being marketed by telephone and how the 12 steps overcome these fears.
   d. Discuss the pie chart—the market share—and how the 12 steps clearly identify and address this market.
5. Open up discussion.
   a. Allow for group interaction.
   b. Ask group specific questions to get them thinking.
   c. Provide feedback and solutions.
6. Set the stage.
   a. Explain why use of a script is important.
   b. Discuss the importance of delivery styles and useful terminology.
   c. Teach style and delivery and voice communication.
7. Teach steps 1 to 4.
   a. Discuss the features, functions, and benefits of the steps and how each step will be taught.

     b. Teach steps 1 to 4.

     c. Have group role-play steps 1 to 4 in twos. Circulate, evaluate, coach, and advise.

     d. Select two people from group to role-play out loud while others observe. Discuss the role play as a group and define how you want them to perform.

  8. Open up discussion.

     a. Allow for group interaction.

     b. Ask group specific questions to get them thinking.

     c. Provide feedback and solutions.

Break time—15 minutes

  9. Discuss step 5 in detail.

     a. Discuss the value of open-ended versus closed-ended questions.

     b. Teach the functions and offer examples applicable to their prospecting.

     c. Have group select questions from the examples that pertain to their job function.

     d. Share ideas as a group.

10. Select scripts for each TSR's job function.

     a. Have group members rewrite the first five steps of their training scripts.

     b. Role-play script in twos and threes.

     c. Circulate, evaluate, coach, and advise.

11. Role-play out loud.

     a. Role-play script in twos and threes.

     b. Circulate, evaluate, coach, and advise.

     c. Select two people at a time in front of the group, use props and role-play.

     d. Use stop-and-play (role-play) method. (Each time a person makes a mistake, stop role play and correct, and start over.)

12. Wrap up session.

     a. Review what the group learned.

     b. Discuss homework assignments.

     c. Encourage their commitment.

     d. Open up discussion and comments.

Session 2

  1. Review homework.

     a. Identify who did their homework and who didn't.

     b. Discuss and review any questions or concerns.

  2. Review first five steps.

     a. Test group's ability to remember each step, its functions and benefits.

     b. Acknowledge how well they remembered.

     c. Open up discussion.

     d. Role-play the first five steps in pairs. Circulate, evaluate, coach, and advise.

3. Teach step 6.
   a. Instruct on step 6 and conduct role-play exercise.
   b. Instruct and do restate exercise together.
4. Teach step 7.
   a. Discuss and teach the four elements of step 7.
   b. Customize examples for step 7.
   c. Role-play in twos and threes.
   d. Select two people to role-play steps 1 to 7. Have group evaluate them.
   e. Discuss emotion-packed words and negative words.
   f. Offer replacement words that are positive and designed for the department.
5. Open up discussion.
   a. Allow for group interaction.
   b. Ask group specific questions to get them thinking.
   c. Provide feedback and solutions.

Break time—15 minutes

6. Teach steps 8 and 9.
   a. Offer examples of what they can say in steps 8 and 9.
   b. Demonstrate a few challenging trial closes.
   c. Divide group into twos and threes and have them role-play steps 7 to 9.
   d. Circulate, evaluate, coach, and advise.
7. Open up discussion on steps 7 to 11.
   a. Allow for group interaction.
   b. Ask group specific questions to get them thinking.
   c. Provide feedback and solutions.
8. Discuss steps 11 and 12
   a. Explain how the close is the simplest of all the steps.
   b. Go into the three different closing techniques.
   c. Discuss how they can combine their closing techniques.
   d. Have them write out which closing technique they will use according to their job function.
   e. Discuss step 12 and the benefits of post-closing.
   f. Go over the list of what they need to consider when using this step.
   g. Have them write out their own post-close that they will use in their job function.
9. Provide 12-step overview.
   a. Explain benefits.
   b. Offer examples.
   c. Open up discussion.
10. Discuss homework assignments.
    a. Stress importance of homework.
    b. Explain why they need to have homework completed *prior to the next session*. Otherwise, they will not be able to participate in the next session.
11. Stress for group to practice, practice, practice. Pass out 3 × 5 or 5 × 5 index cards and tell the group to write the first five steps on the front side of card.

Tell them to put steps 6, 7, 8, 9, 11, and 12 on back side of the card and place by their telephones.

12. Open up final comments and discussion.

Session 3

1. Review homework.
   a. Who did their homework and who didn't.
   b. Set aside those who didn't and have them complete it now.
   c. Discuss and review any concerns.
2. Review steps 1 to 12 (except step 10).
   a. Test group's ability to remember each step, its function, and benefits.
   b. Acknowledge how well they remember.
   c. Open up discussion.
   d. Role-play in twos and threes all the steps using the scripts they've revised.
   e. Circulate, evaluate, coach, advise, and correct their scripts.
3. Group to role-play out loud.
   a. Select two people and have them role-play in front of the group.
   b. Coach and critique them using stop-and-go method.
4. Open up discussion. Make sure people are finished with homework; if not, have them stop to complete it.

Break time—15 minutes

5. Train on step 10, objections.
   a. Have group openly discuss the typical objections they get when prospecting.
   b. When discussing the "Real Issue," get the TSRs to think about the three questions listed and open up discussion.
   c. Have the group narrow down all the objections they would ever receive into six categories. Don't allow TSRs to move to the page that lists them, see if they can narrow them down on their own. Once they feel like the six have been narrowed down, refer to the page that lists and interprets them.
   d. Discuss the six techniques of overcoming objections and customize as you teach each technique.
   e. Have group help participate in how to use each technique for members' job functions.
   f. Explain how to combine the techniques and offer examples.
   g. Review most common objections and answers.
6. Role-play.
   a. Divide group into twos and threes and have them role-play step 10.
   b. Circulate, evaluate, coach, and advise.
   c. Select two volunteers to role-play out loud and have others observe.
   d. Discuss the role play and advise the group.
   e. Keep role playing until your time is up.

7. Wrap up session.
   a. Review what the group learned.
   b. Discuss homework assignments for step 10.
   c. Encourage their commitment.
   d. Open up discussion and comments.

Session 4

1. Review what they have learned.
   a. Test the group openly on each of the steps they have learned.
   b. Discuss completion of their homework assignments.
   c. For those who did not complete their assignments, have them do so at this time.
2. Open up discussion.
   a. Allow for group interaction.
   b. Ask group specific questions to get them thinking.
   c. Provide feedback and solutions.
3. Role Play
   a. Use the stop-and-go method.
   b. Have observers fill out their listening evaluations forms.
   c. Discuss openly and advise.
   d. Keep doing this until everyone has had a chance to role-play.

Break time—15 minutes

4. Discuss tabulating outbound activities.
   a. Discuss importance.
   b. Teach how to do it.
   c. Explain when to implement the activities and what you plan to do with the information.
5. Wrap up program.
   a. Ask group members to share what they've learned and how they will apply the information to their job functions.
   b. Explain to the group what they need to do to keep the information alive and fresh on a daily basis.
   c. Tell group what your continued role will be with them.
   d. Have group members turn in their homework assignments.
   e. For those who didn't complete their homework, give a time frame in which you expect it to be turned in.
   f. Ask if they have any questions or concerns, and thank them for their participation.
   g. Open up discussion.

Training Materials Needed

Every trainer needs to have a check list of training materials, supplies, and equipment needed for each training session. It is easier and less time consuming to have a box or area that already has what you need for training. In this way you won't have to search around for what you need and you are prepared at any given moment to conduct a professional training session. You need to set up two types of training boxes. One is for the classroom itself, and the other is for any self-study materials that you will be requiring of your TSRs. Below are lists to consider for both boxes:

Classroom	*Self-Study Materials*
Study guide and workbook	Training manual
Instructor's guide	Reference manuals, materials
Worksheets, test	Worksheets, test
Student evaluation forms	Self-evaluation forms
Overheads, slides	Supervisor's guide
Flip charts	Learning cassette tapes
Learning cassette tapes	Videotapes
Videotapes	Sample scripts
Call center forms	Call center forms
Homework assignments	Homework assignments
Pens, highlighters, pencils, erasable markers, and the like	Highlighter, pencils, pens

Now that you have prepared for your training agenda, you're ready for day one training for your new employees.

First Day on the Job for New Employees

The first day of training should be intensive, mind provoking, and always motivational. Keep the training away from the department and telephone. This should be conducted in either a conference room or official training room, and if such is unavailable, depending on how many you are training at one time, rent out a hotel conference room. The objective here is to have an atmosphere that is formal and nondistracting. Don't ever train in your office or in the department itself. This is very distracting and unprofessional. By having a formal training setup, you communicate to your TSRs that the company is serious about telemarketing; this setup separates your firm from boiler-room environments that are typically unprofessional in their training and in their telemarketing approaches.

The length of the training depends on how many you are instructing at one time and the complexity of the behaviors to be learned. For most situations, two days is sufficient for training in a classroom environment. The balance of training is conducted in the call center itself—*hands-on training*. More training is required for TSRs that need to do more progressive selling, have to use highly developed organizational skills, or have more complex products and procedures.

Prior to the start of training be sure to inform the TSRs that you appreciate their interaction. If they have any questions or concerns write them down; periodically throughout each topic, ask if there are any questions at that time.

Encouraging your TSRs to be open and creative can be very positive and worthwhile as a general rule. There should be special times and places to allow for interaction. Your TSRs, especially your more experienced ones, probably can contribute to the training session; however, discourage them from doing so during all training sessions. You don't want them to confuse others as to what you expect of them. Therefore, prior to starting the training session, lay the ground rules of how you want the training to flow. Communicate to veteran TSRs that you encourage creative thinking and proven ideas, but the proper time to introduce them is once the TSRs have been on your program for a time. Let them know that there will be plenty of opportunities for their suggestions and you have an open mind to consider them when it's appropriate.

There is usually always one in the group who will try and control the training session, preventing you from completing your objectives and making your sessions fall behind schedule. Always remain in control. When someone gets out of hand, stop your session and take a break to discuss your concerns with the one interrupting. Suggest that the person take notes, and, once the training is completed, make a point to sit down with him or her privately and discuss anything the individual likes. If you don't "nip it in the bud" early on, you will have a more difficult time trying to do so later. This only causes unnecessary stress and friction among coworkers. Others in the group usually don't appreciate the interruption. They are annoyed at the one interrupting and become unmotivated quickly.

When conducting your training sessions, either stand up during the lectures and sit down during role plays, or, if you're uncomfortable standing for long periods, use a stool to sit on when you need to rest. The objective is as follows: When standing or sitting above the group's level, you project more confidence in your delivery and have control of your group. It shows you are more confident in your information. Also, when you sit down with them at a conference table, this tends to drag the session and individuals become easily bored since you are not moving your body around to help keep their attention. You even may find some who are dozing off!

Be careful when you take a lunch break. Your students may decide to eat food that is heavy and causes their digestive systems to work overtime. This decreases their energy, and they become very tired. It is better if you have control of what they eat by catering lunch into the training room or another designated area. Lunch should be salads, or light sandwiches with fruit and a variety of fresh vegetables. Do not eat Mexican, hamburgers, beef, pork, and the like. These foods take too much time to digest, and your students will not be as attentive.

Once you're first day of training is over, be sure to spend approximately 15 minutes to wrap up the session by going over what they have just learned. Ask them direst questions to determine whether they have learned anything. When they can answer quickly, this motivates them to continue because they truly believe they have learned. Remind them of their assignments and give them the date by which to have them completed. If your training continues on a second day, give them an idea of what they will be learning and recommend that they prepare by getting a restful night's sleep and eating a healthy light breakfast so they will be ready for the following day's agenda.

Monitoring and Coaching
Your TSRs

You have learned how to plan and conduct orientation for your new TSRs, what it takes to be a good trainer, how to design your training packets, determine the tools you and your TSRs will need for training, and ideas on how to conduct your first day of training. Now you need to monitor and measure results to ensure your TSRs are applying what they have learned.

Managers always want to give TSRs who report to them with problems or concerns regarding their production on-the-spot personal attention and periodic attention on a regular basis. Unfortunately, this is far from reality. It may be weeks before the manager can take time to offer proper feedback, and by then the TSR has developed bad habits that are hard to break. The manager not only must recognize other people's needs for coaching and counseling but must take the time to do it. Furthermore, the manager needs to schedule time each week to conduct hands-on evaluations. This will project a routine to others and make TSRs more accountable for improved performance. Addressing performance or attitude issues in a timely manner also helps increase motivation within the department. For most, good coaching is a skill that takes time and patience to learn. Those managers who think highly of themselves and their TSRs are usually the ones good at it.

Performance feedback can be given by the manager or delegated to a person who is in direct contact with the representatives. In either case, the manager and whoever else that assists in this activity must receive training on how to coach and counsel. The manager needs to be conscious of how and when positive coaching can take place.

The best coaches are those who learned from someone who modeled the behavior to them. For those few who are "born" with this ability their role model is probably the person who spent the most time raising and/or influencing them, or it could be a boss or peer who is really in touch with their staff and shows it. Also, a lot of coaching takes place in conjunction with call monitoring. Managers who do the monitoring need to know what to listen for, how to recognize when the correct skills are exhibited, and how to give constructive feedback to the TSR about the call. If someone else is doing the monitoring, then it's up to the center manager to train that person in the proper approach. Either way, managers have to know what they are doing or they lose their credibility and respect. The manager should learn good communication skills, how to motivate and use professional language, resolve conflicts, and negotiate.

Managers should either take the initiative to learn these skills on their own time or encourage the company to make the investment. If the company doesn't invest in it entirely, they may be willing to co-op the added education. There are plenty of half- or 1-day training seminars that will get you started. Of course, you only walk away with a synopsis of the information. Their objective is to promote their training materials. If you were impressed and felt it worthwhile, be prepared to purchase some of the products. You can either have your company pay for them, or you can negotiate!

Management Needs to Set the Example

Management doesn't have a clue of what it's like to prospect in many companies that I have personally consulted. In other situations, management hasn't prospected for many years and is not tuned into what is going on today. How many times has it been said by TSRs about their manager, "How do they know what it's like day-in and day-out; they never get on the telephone!" "Why don't they get on the telephone, I bet they can't do it either!" Therefore, when training and coaching your TSRs, especially your new employees, don't just put them on the telephone and tell them to "go get 'em, tiger." Although you've hired experienced TSRs, they are still uncertain as to how they are to handle their prospecting calls when all the information up in the head is still scrambled. Most TSRs, no matter their experience, are frightened to make that first phone call. It would make it easier for them if they could put it in perspective, with the help of the one who taught them.

Often, when management has completed training sessions with technical, product knowledge, and role plays, they expect their TSRs to get on the telephone and start prospecting. It is common knowledge that the TSR will have to prospect for a couple of days to "get their feet wet" in order to master their presentation. However, there is more to it than that. The manager needs to get on the telephone and demonstrate to their TSRs how it is done.

This will probably shock many of you who are reading this, but I truly believe that you will gain more respect from your TSRs when they know you can roll up your sleeves and pick up the telephone and make some of those calls yourself. It is essential for management to actually make live calls in order to fully demonstrate what is expected of TSRs. It's true when TSRs say, "How can they expect anyone else to do it if they are not willing to do it themselves?"

As a telemarketing consultant, it is my job to ensure that I provide the best quality training programs that are designed and acceptable for today's marketing. It doesn't matter that I have been doing this and training others how to all of my adult life. My philosophy is: "How can I confidently teach others to prospect, if I am not continually on the telephone prospecting myself?" This does not imply that I am on the telephone every day for 8 hours each day, but I do spend at least 20 percent of my time prospecting and demonstrating to others how to prospect.

When management is periodically prospecting and demonstrating to others how to do so, they keep their skills sharp. Should the scripts need to be modified or a determination has been made to incorporate something else that will work better, management has first-hand experience with it. This is very critical whenever you test scripts. Management should play a dedicated role to ensure that the verbiage and selection of questions are workable. Most call center managers will have their higher producers performing the test. These same top producers are also training the newly hired TSRs—management will have the new TSRs sit next to their top producers and listen to *their* presentation.

When management takes on some of this responsibility, they gain greater respect from their employees. Whenever management feels that they are "beyond" this, then it's time to reevaluate their job description and the selection of our call center managers. You need to define meaningful objectives for your department so that you have a foundation to stand on prior to motivating your TSRs to perform better when prospecting.

Motivational Techniques to Get Your TSRs Producing

It is the responsibility of the telemarketing manager to motivate their TSRs and keep them motivated. This is one of the elements of a good manager. Helping others get what they want ultimately helps you get what you want—highly productive and motivated TSRs. Showing that you care enough about your TSRs sums this up! This sincerity is unfortunately becoming obsolete because telemarketing has been primarily a discipline of numbers, numbers of dials, numbers of contacts, numbers of sales, and so on. This can get so out of control that there could be a tendency to start treating TSRs like numbers too. For example, when TSRs are recruited, a typical mind-set of a manager could be, "If my 20 TSRs made 40 new contacts each day, that's 4000 contacts every week, and with a minimum of 20 percent closing ratio, that's 800 new sales each week!" The numbers are very tempting and motivating to the manager, but to the TSR who has the responsibility to meet those numbers (without the proper training, motivation and ongoing coaching,) this could be deadly—*turnover!!!*

Don't treat your TSRs like numbers or productivity units if you want them to perform for you as they are able. Pushing numbers and rewarding them for the numbers and scolding them for not reaching the numbers is the old school of telemarketing. Telemarketing has come a long way, and many managers recognize the benefits of good coaching, encouraging TSRs to be more customer-service-oriented, and motivating TSRs other than through stressing the numbers. However, it's unfortunate that the numbers philosophy still exists. Of course, telemarketing is more profitable due to a steady flow of productivity, but without the proper training and management, it could be very costly.

How do you meet your department's productivity goals without pushing just the numbers? Just exactly that—don't *just* push the numbers! You can incorporate the numbers without pushing by giving them a specific goal or target to reach each day. For example, you can say before the day ends, "Today I would like for you to select 50 potential contacts that you will make for tomorrow." Your TSRs should be able to meet at least one daily requirement each day. When making any requirements, this should be made clear and understood by your TSRs. It's how you request your TSRs to achieve this requirement that will make a difference in their attitude in doing it. Instead of forcing them or making threats of job security, treat them professionally, ask for their input on what they could accomplish based on previous production. What would it take for them to meet the department goals? By getting them to participate, you will find less resistance to your requirements and more enthusiasm on the part of the telemarketer.

Developing Your Departmental Motivation Plan

One of the most important issues regarding developing your motivation plan is that the criteria for winning rewards are fair and attainable and that your plan helps achieve a greater objective for your campaign. You can begin by deciding what your campaign objectives are and when you want to reach them. If you have a particular campaign that is not meeting your department's objectives, and it's critical to meet them is in a short period, look at the problems that may have occurred. You certainly don't want to repeat the same mistakes. Therefore, if you trace your steps you may find out where the problem came from.

Once you have your objectives in perspective, determine the specific criteria that need to be met to grant whatever reward you are to offer. This will help you determine a way to implement a strategy whether it will be for a group or an individual. Also, you need to be clear on the time frame—when you will start and end the campaign and what is considered eligible or noneligible. Determine the rewards you will offer based on the difficulty of the campaign. Make sure the criteria for reward are measurable and that all have an opportunity to be successful. Your TSRs need to be reminded of how close they are in reaching their goals and if they are falling short of them—help them determine what is the problem and try to correct it. Do not isolate each TSR. Instead, publicize their results perhaps by using cardboard thermometers hung on a wall with each obtainable goal as measurements shown in red so it stands out. However, this can be intimidating if one or two of your TSRs are not performing well. You need to make the goals fair and obtainable. You will have those who are higher producers and you want to be sure that they are challenged. It's okay to have your thermometers set up to a degree to give others an opportunity to maximize their capabilities.

Finally, incorporate an accountability factor into your campaign. This means what, how, and when you will collect data and evaluate the results. Define the methods you will use to distribute rewards. This includes what role management will play and any fanfare planned.

Detecting TSR Burnout

Through the years, telemarketing operations have built the same reputation regarding high turnover as in the sales industry. However, the length of employment is much less for a telemarketer compared to the outside sales representative. According to national statistics, the average employment span of a telemarketer is approximately 3 to 6 months. The job of a TSR has some negative drawbacks that need to be addressed and solutions to help reduce this costly turnover factor. Think about the functions of TSRs: Their jobs are repetitive and stressful due to the pressures from management regarding meeting production quotas, and the resistance factor can be demotivating—especially when the TSR is fairly new and not familiar with product knowledge and the like. Also, think about the TSR stuck behind a desk all day, on the telephone with very little body movement. If the TSR is not kept motivated throughout the day, sitting itself can be a major contributor to high turnover.

Managers are often unaware of when their TSRs are burning out. This usually doesn't get noticed until they see a pattern of decline in production. In other situations, managers don't become aware of burnout until the TSR has already quit—then it's too late. Below is a list of TSR burnout signs. Knowing them can help you to take steps before burnout becomes a serious problem.

Rapid decline in performance

Increased time off or being late

Loss of competitiveness

Not motivated about their performance

Unattentiveness, not being helpful, and uncooperative with coworkers

Becoming hostile toward prospects

Complaining about the company or others

Challenging the authority of supervisors

Negative attitude

What techniques can managers implement to reduce turnover and to create career opportunities and challenges for their TSRs? Telemarketing managers need to find ways to motivate and retain TSRs. Also, managers need to offer promotions for TSRs who are high producers and have capabilities to contribute in other capacities that could be financially rewarding for them and the company. You don't want high producers feeling they have gone as far as they can and their only alternative is to find another job where they can advance themselves. You spent a great deal of time training and nurturing your TSRs and if they leave because you ignored their needs, it's the company who has far more to lose for the long haul.

It is imperative that your better producers are given more responsibilities and more pay. Losing them means losing revenue your company has been accustomed to, and trying to replace your better TSRs is more costly than finding ways to retain them. It is the same attitude that we have or should have with our customers. It costs a great deal of money to get them to be our customers and to lose them costs even more. The solution is to spend time and money to retain them. Doing so is more cost-effective and profitable.

The following information will provide you with steps to reduce turnover and challenge your TSRs to higher levels of achievement that will advance them up the ladder for greater career stability. This not only will help you to achieve higher levels of advancements but also will reduce your departmental cost and increase your company's bottom line.

Motivate Your TSRs Through Nonmonetary Incentives

Incentives and bonuses, discussed in Chap. 8, are designed to motivate your TSRs through monetary incentives that help meet and surpass quotas. You can also use nonmonetary incentives to motivate TSRs. This type of incentive helps reduce stress and overcome your TSRs' job burn. The following are just a few ideas to introduce nonmonetary incentives in your department; they don't necessarily require corporate approval, since money payouts are not involved.

On-the-Spot Praise.   Show appreciation to your TSRs for their work and their accomplishments. This is especially important when you are on a deadline and top management is pushing you to "get those numbers" in by Friday! When your TSRs have done their best, whether they achieved those numbers or not, thanking them for putting forth their best effort can be one of the greatest incentives that you can give.

Applause.   When TSRs perform exceptionally well, take time out to recognize it and applaud their efforts. This should be a standard for the entire department. For example, allow other TSRs to applaud their coworkers when one is having a tough time with a prospect and suddenly the TSR takes back control and is using the techniques designed to overcome this resistance. Another good way to applaud or give recognition is to have weekly meetings and discuss some positive encounters that the TSRs experienced; as a group, applaud their success. This peer recognition is invaluable for motivating others to perform at their best in order to gain applause in the next meeting!

Business Cards and Titles.   Each TSR should have her or his own business cards regardless of job function. This makes TSRs feel that they are important to the company. Moreover, select job titles that project stature within the company. Instead of putting *Telemarketing Sales Representative* put *Inside Sales, Account Executive, Sales Consultant,* or *Marketing Representative.* These titles make your TSRs feel their job function and contribution to your company are important. The job title you've given them affects their attitude, and they become more productive.

The Environment.   Telemarketing can be very stressful. Some days are very tedious. Offer frequent breaks that are only 5 to 10 minutes in length to reduce stress. Design a comfortable work space for them. They need to have a sense of privacy but not be totally hidden from others, which decreases production and loses the eye contact and high spirits gained by other TSRs. Posters, production charts, and cartoons can add to a more relaxed environment, just be sure to have a balance—you want to keep it more on the professional level. Lunch and/or break rooms can be designed where the TSRs feel more comfortable and relaxed. Some call centers have a punching bag to "let out steam" when a prospect behaves terribly. Everyone has a different way of reducing stress, but it should not affect others in the process!

Career Paths.   TSRs should know how they can advance themselves. This is not done only by verbally communicating it to them during the interview or orientation day—provide them with a written organizational chart that shows them the path that leads to other positions. Many companies use telemarketing or customer service positions as an entry level for new employees to learn more about the company, the industry, its products, and customer base. Based on the TSR's or CSR's ability, he or she can advance to sales and marketing or other positions such as lead person or confirmer dispatcher. You can also offer TSRs more responsibilities with their job functions. Of course, with more responsibilities comes more pay or incentives.

Job Diversification.   Diversity in a TSR's job function is more important than salary. TSRs look to the quality of their job for their own personal satisfaction. This can be a real challenge in telemarketing, where the job and campaigns can get tedious, especially if the company is not interested in expanding its telemarketing department to other telephone uses. For example, when you first hire TSRs, you place them at a level where they can learn in small increments such as having them conduct public relations for your existing client base. The TSR can contact previous clients and ask a series of questions to determine how well the company performed in each of its departments such as shipping, credit, and sales. This type of contact also allows the company to keep the relationship active by letting the customer know the company is still thinking about them. Most customers will leave because they feel ignored. A periodic call not only will impress the customer but also will serve to handle anything that may arise due to poor customer servicing.

Offer clear objectives each week of something new TSRs can spend a few hours a day on that is different from their day-to-day prospecting activities. One company would have their TSRs contact their customer base and ask for referrals or cross-sell a particular product or service that is on special and specifically designed for that purpose. Perhaps updating your database is another way to offer variety for their job function. There are endless opportunities for TSRs that not only increase business but keep business.

Weekly Meetings.   Every department should hold weekly meetings with its employees. This should be done at a designated time and day each week especially during a slow time of the day and/or week so as not to interrupt peak performance times. Each meeting agenda should be planned in advance. This will prevent sidetracking and not being able to meet your objectives. Set aside time in the meeting for open discussion, but also be clear on how much time will be used to discuss the issues. You may need to repeat the meeting two or three times in order to avoid pulling all your TSRs from the phone.

Never allow one or two individuals to control the meetings. The moderator is the manager of the department. The moderator should allow and encourage everyone to participate. The primary objective of these brief meetings is to motivate TSRs and stimulate ideas to increase the synergy of your department.

Stress Release Day.   This is a day when you set aside 1 hour of time in a quiet room with no more than four or five TSRs at a time. Each TSR would bring in a favorite pillow and blanket (the company could provide these). The TSRs would lay down on a floor mat in a low lighted room and listen to a 1-hour stress release CD tape.

This is very relaxing and soothing for them, and afterward, they feel like a million bucks. Be careful though, some are so relaxed that they want to go to sleep and you can't wake them up! Do this no more than once a month in the middle or towards the third week.

Employee Appreciation Day.   This is a day when management demonstrates to employees how appreciative it is. One way to do this is to have management provide an ice cream social. During break time, management would scoop ice cream and serve employees. Another way, is to have management bring in and serve lunch for employees. Or, after working hours go to a favorite coffee shop and have cappuccino or herbal tea together. Depending on how many TSRs are going to attend, be sure to make reservations so you are assured of getting a table.

Education Incentive.   Make a financial investment in your TSRs by encouraging them to take extra classes that would enhance their job function, such as a marketing, professional vocabulary and language skills, writing skills, and sales courses. Offer to pay 100 percent after they have graduated from the course by giving them a full reimbursement upon completion. You can opt to pay half up front and the balance upon completion. Everyone benefits when a company invests in the education of top producers and the producers make an investment of time and completion of the course.

Contribution.   Another outlook when motivating your TSRs is to reverse their roles by allowing your top producers to contribute their expertise to others by helping you train new TSRs, conducting role-play sessions, and doing listening evaluations with the results reported to you in written form.

Universities, adult schools, and city colleges are now integrating telemarketing into their marketing courses. Research how your top producers can participate as students or as guest lecturers who can contribute hands-on experience in the area of telemarketing business-to-business or to consumers in ways a professor cannot—especially if the professor never has been involved with the actual process.

In Conclusion.   There are many other things that you can do to reduce your TSRs' burnout and keep them motivated, productive, working, and working for you. Learn to be creative, to diversify, and, most important, *do something!!*

Terminating and Laying Off Your Employees

In today's economy, the words *termination, downsizing, early retirement, merger, bankrupt,* and *layoffs* are consistently seen or heard across the country. This forces us to discuss how to terminate or lay off employees. Most good managers are sensitive toward other people, and it can be painful and stressful to terminate individuals, especially if they have been with you for a period of time and you may have grown to like them personally.

Performing the Termination Interview

People are being released from jobs more than ever. This doesn't mean that companies are getting better at it. On the contrary, many companies are not aware of what they can or cannot do when it comes to letting go of their employees. Every state is different in how it regulates this procedure, and it is recommended that you contact your local labor board, get a pamphlet on the subject, and inquire what is expected of you as an employer. In the meantime, some common ground needs to be addressed to give managers a starting point to consider when performing this unpleasant and stressful task. Delivering bad news without offending or hurting anyone's feelings is very difficult to do. Terminations and layoffs must be conducted delicately and professionally so that you won't experience future problems with disgruntled employees. Otherwise, the employer could possibly experience legal headaches and future lawsuits. The following is a simple checklist that will guide you in setting up a standard method in your termination process.

The employee's direct supervisor or manager should conduct the termination interview. The exception occurs when the supervisor and the employee have a problem with each other or a poor relationship. In this case, the termination interview should be performed by the supervisor's manager—the human resource manager.

The termination interview should be conducted in the office of the person performing the termination. In all cases, it should be done privately away from possible interruptions and from others to preserve the employee's dignity.

It is best to terminate earlier in the week and toward the end of the day. This allows the terminated employee to clear out of the office without having to face other coworkers.

Discreetly supervise the clearing out of the terminated employee's belongings to ensure that no company property is removed.

If at all possible, avoid terminating employees during a major holiday—especially Christmas time or the New Year, or after an important event in the employee's life such as a birthday, wedding, or after the birth of a child.

Do not dismiss employees after they've just received a salary increase or after a positive performance evaluation.

Do not write a glowing letter of reference for the terminated employees unless they were laid-off or let go due to unforeseen circumstances beyond the company's control and not because of any direct fault of the employee.

Avoid offering emotional support during the termination interview. This can cause confusion in the message that is being delivered.

Have a third nonbiased party sit in on the termination interview to act as a recorder and witness should you need to utilize this information for a possible claim by the terminated employee.

Implement a standard practice for your company so employees won't feel isolated with this process should they be one of the unlucky ones to be terminated. This standard of practice should be discussed at the time of the employee's orientation with the guidelines written out and placed as a part of their employee packet.

Usually when employees hear about terminations they are in a state of shock, especially when they didn't have the slightest clue that they were going to be terminated. Once the initial shock and numbness wears off, the employee may start to feel anger and resentment, and the question will come up "why me?" This is the time people start to really dwell on what has just happened. They become disgruntled and several things occur.

The major concern to a company is when employees understand their rights and your company has not complied with the labor codes—this could cause expensive legal issues to arise. The employee gets free representation by the labor board, and you as the employer need to defend yourself or hire an attorney that specializes in protecting companies with these employee-employer labor issues. You're still out the cost of your own legal representation should you win—you're not entitled to any reimbursements for legal fees.

The second issue is that the disgruntled employee could cause a bad reputation for your company and the image you have been trying to protect since you've been in business. This could be very serious and have a negative impact on your business depending on how disgruntled the terminated employee is. He or she tells 30 people, then those people tell 30, and so on. What is the answer? How can you protect yourself from this? What's the best way to combat this? *Take steps for prevention.* The following are some steps you can take to help you conduct a positive and professional termination interview:

√ During the termination interview, try to make the employee feel as comfortable and as relaxed as possible.

√ The interview should be as short as possible—5 to 10 minutes would be ideal.

√ Be clear and concise in your delivery of the bad news and in the words you choose to convey the message.

√ Get to the point quickly and outline the main reasons for the termination.

√ If the employee starts to object, listen without responding. When the employee has finished, make it clear that the decision is final.

√ Follow this with the terms of the severance package and the signing of the release agreement, if you have one.

Following some of these examples will help you to address the issues and uncertainties when terminating employees. One last area that management has some difficulty with is informing others of the termination. Although most managers feel relieved once they have terminated the employee, they still need to deal with others within the department and any possible damage that might occur to employee morale and performance. The termination of an employee needs to be communicated delicately and honestly without making any kind of negative comments that reflect against the one terminated. This could be very damaging later, since the word does eventually "get around." The following is a list that is indirect yet beneficial when communicating a termination to others within the same department.

√ Management should take proactive steps toward any fears others may have about their job security.

√ Show a positive perspective for this change and how everyone can eventually benefit by it.

√ Be honest without stepping over the boundaries of confidentiality.

√ Advise employees how they will share the work load.

√ Instruct employees and the receptionist of what to say when callers request to speak with the terminated employee.

√ Decide to whom those in-bound calls should be directed.

These suggestions are starting points for you to begin implementing standard procedures in your termination process. The objective is to have something that is concrete, that works within your company objectives, and meets with the labor laws that are within your state. Having everything documented and communicated will ensure a more harmonious employee-employer relationship that will have a long-term benefit for the entire company.

The following information is a tracking system that helps to support the training provided to TSRs. You can better determine their strengths and weaknesses when you know how well they are performing on a daily, weekly, and monthly basis. Also, this tracking method validates your department's effort and who your star performers are.

A Support System That Keeps Top Management Informed

Peak management performance occurs when the company supports the manager's ongoing development and provides support for the call center from the top. This includes providing up-to-date information on the corporate revenue goals and how they will be realized. This permits telemarketing managers to be clear on what their departments need to do to support company goals. The telemarketing manager needs to provide a strong and positive reporting system that keeps top management informed on the department's progress. These reports may actually justify the telemarketing center's existence, especially when a company may be streamlining its budgets. The center's existence at its current operating budget should be justified, or it should be granted a higher one.

Prepared for:_____   **Date:**_____

Regarding: Telemarketing Contact and Production
                              For the period of _____through_____
                              Total 5 days.

Prepared by: _____

This analysis is based on the data provided by each individual and pertains to
a staff of (_____) TSRs.

Basic Dial Statistics

  Total number of phone hours by the group = _____
  Average number of dials per hour, per individual* = _____

Problem Areas

Tabulations:_____

_____

_____

_____

_____

_____

_____

The provided grand totals are as follows:
(_____) hours (_____) dials (_____) contacts.

The actual totals by groups are:
(___) call backs + (___) not interested + (___) hang-ups + (___) not ready + (___)
appts/sales/market research = (___)

Contacts

The contact total should be: (___) not (___)

To provide status, you will use the actual totals of (___). Contact number is for
calculation purposes.

  *National average per individual (manual dials) for businesses is 20 to 30 dials per hour and
for residences is 30 to 50 dials per hour.

Figure 10-3. Group statistical analysis.

Comments:_____

_____

_____

_____

Phone Hours:

Total number of phone hours by group (___)

Average number of dials per hour per individual (___)

Comments: _____

_____

_____

_____

Group Activity Status (during the 5 tabulated days)

Contact with decision maker obtained: (___)% of dials

Prequalified appointments obtained: (___)% of decision makers

Recontact base with potential buyers (call backs) established: (___)% of decision makers

Remainder of decision maker responses:

(___)% not interested

(___)% not ready or no money

(___)% hung up

Additional information re group activity status:

- _____
_____
_____
- _____
_____
_____
- _____
_____
_____
- _____
_____
_____

Figure 10-3. Group statistical analysis. (*Continued*)

Close Ratios:

- _____
  _____
  _____

- _____
  _____
  _____

- _____
  _____
  _____

- _____
  _____
  _____

Percentages on an Individual Basis:

<u>TSR name</u>. 10 hrs. = (___) dials = (___) decision maker contacts

(_____) dials per hr.

Of the (___) contacts:

(___)% = appointments (___)   (___)% = call backs (___)

(___)% = not interested (___)   (___)% = not ready/no money (___)

(___)% = hung up (___)

_____ - 10 hrs. = (___) dials = (___) decision maker contacts

(_____)dials per hr.

Of the (___) contacts:

(___)% = appointments (___)   (___)% = call backs (___)

(___)% = not interested (___)   (___)% = not ready/no money (___)

(___)% = hung up (___)

_____ - 10 hrs. = (___) dials = (___) decision maker contacts

(_____)dials per hr.

Of the (___) contacts:

(___)% = appointments (___)   (___)% = call backs (___)

(___)% = not interested (___)   (___)% = not ready/no money (___)

(___)% = hung up (___)

Reviewed by:_____

Figure 10-3. Group statistical analysis. (*Continued*)

Name_____   Date:_____

Status overview_____
_____
_____
_____
_____

Comments_____
_____
_____
_____
_____

Recommendations_____
_____
_____
_____
_____

Strengths_____
_____
_____
_____
_____

Weaknesses_____
_____
_____
_____
_____

Figure 10-4. Individual instruction on tracking program.

The manager must always stay within or above the company's objectives regarding profits and cost containment. You don't want to wait until the end of the quarter to find out whether you met those objectives or fell short of them. To assist you in keeping track of your TSRs' performance and to identify whether they are meeting their personal production requirements, you need to conduct daily tabulations, and from the information that was tabulated, run a weekly statistical analysis. This type of tracking will help your department remain on track.

Should one or more of your TSRs not meet the goals you know they need to reach in order to be cost effective, you can catch this in its early stages. This gives you time to correct the problem and concentrate on strengthening the areas that need improvement. The objective is to get your low producers back on track again. However, if you find a TSR who is way off track in meeting production requirements and you have tried to work with the individual and the reports still show that he or she is not cost-efficient, you have the report for validation to take any action that may be necessary such as replacing the TSR or transferring her or him to another department.

Figure 10-3 will give you an idea of how to effectively report each TSR's performance to determine individual production. If you have teams or different shifts, you can also run the report by each group. Keep in mind that you still need to have your TSRs tabulate. If you're automated, your software will do this for you. In any case, tabulate first, then run your report based on the information gained from the tabulation. Figure 10-4 is a report form to document your follow-up with TSRs on their production results.

11

Forms

The following sample forms give you an idea of what you can use when designing or enhancing your telemarketing center. Many companies use these forms with very few modifications. However, when a telemarketing center is completely automated, some of the forms are not necessary, since the telemarketing software already provides them. Not everyone is automated, especially the company just starting out with a telemarketing call center. Having these forms is another means of providing all the tools necessary for running an organized and profitable telemarketing center.

Appointment Form

This form (Fig. 11-1) is designed for a manual operation: However, should you have an automated call center, you can customize the appointment form accordingly. If you are prospecting residences, then you would need to eliminate the company name, contact person, and title.

The TSR's discussion and information is designed for five key questions you will be asking during the probing step (step 5) of your presentation (these questions are discussed in Chapter 10). Remember as a rule of thumb, you will be asking five questions. The first two are *qualifiers* (Q); questions three and four, *establish wants* (W); and the fifth question, *creates need* (C). If you make the form two-sided, you'll provide more space for any additional comments the TSR can contribute along with any suspense dates or other future activity with the prospect or salesperson.

Market Research Form

The market research form (Fig. 11-2) is designed for conducting outbound lead generation. The suspense information is for keeping track of any follow-up calls that need to be conducted once the initial contact has been made. The form can be used for either residential or business prospecting. If your compa-

Today's date ____-____-____   TSR _____
                                            Date of appt. _____
                                            Time of appt. _____

Company :_____
Address: _____   Salesperson _____
City, zip: _____
Phone: (____)_____
Contact:_____
Title: _____

Directions & cross street:

_____
_____

TSR's discussion and information:

Q. _____
_____

Q. _____
_____

W. _____
_____

W. _____
_____

C._____
_____

Sales rep's. results/comments:

_____
_____
_____
_____
_____
_____
_____

Figure 11-1. Appointment form.

ny does both types of prospecting, it is better to use one form for both activities. It makes it too confusing for the TSRs when the forms are closely related.

The form can be utilized in a two-sided format when conducting a survey-type questionnaire or using a two-call close (call first, create the need, send information, and follow up to close). When conducting a two-call close, you need to have more room to show the follow-up activity. It is good to put the follow-up information on the back of the form and title the back side *Follow-Up Form*; doing so indicates this was a two-call close. After conducting the

TSR _____   Today's date_____/_____/_____

SUSPENSE INFORMATION

_____
_____
_____

Please send packet of information to:

COMPANY: _____
NAME: _____ TITLE:_____
ADDRESS: _____
CITY, ST, ZIP: _____
PHONE: (   ) _____ FAX: (   )_____

Notes:

_____
_____
_____
_____

Discussion and information:

Q _____
_____

Q _____
_____

W _____
_____

W _____
_____

C _____
_____

Results/comments

_____
_____
_____
_____
_____
_____
_____

Figure 11-2. Market research form.

market research, if you are going to send your information you can list what you sent in the front side of the form where "notes" is listed.

Additional space for more questions is necessary when conducting a survey. Also, be sure to specify and list the questions that were asked of the prospect. When conducting a survey, your questions are carefully selected from a combination of multiple-choice questions with closed-ended questions along with open-ended questions. Be sure you have the different type of questions segmented so you are asking them in sequence, which is easier for the prospect who is participating in the survey.

Inbound Product Sale Form

The inbound product sale form is slightly crowded in order to keep it on a single page (Fig. 11-3). It is important to make reference to when the product was sent and purchased. This provides information you can refer to when conducting any follow-up calls. If you need to send information first, there is a space to place your call-back date and time. It is critical for you to always follow-up

PRODUCT SENT_____   **PRODUCT PAID** _____

Today's date:_____/_____/_____   **CSR** _____

NAME _____ **TITLE** _____

COMPANY _____

ADDRESS _____

CITY _____ **STATE** _____ **ZIP** _____

TELEPHONE _____ **FAX** _____

| **CALL BACK:**   **DAY** _____ **DATE** _____ **TIME** _____ |

QUESTIONS

Q. _____
_____

Q. _____
_____

W. _____
_____

W. _____
_____

C. _____
_____

Additional comments:
_____
_____
_____

Sales results:
_____
_____
_____

Figure 11-3. Inbound product sale form.

on your mailings within a 3- to 5-day time frame. If the CSR does not conduct the follow-up call, then it is very important to ensure that the CSR clearly communicates the information gained from the caller and any additional information that gives the one conducting the follow-up call some insight about the prospect. Such information will increase the chances of a successful close.

Call-Back Form

The call-back form (Fig. 11-4) is to be used in conjunction with the suspense form (Fig. 11-5). This is only for a manual system. When you're automated, the process is already included with the software application. The call-back form is designed to be cut into four separate forms that are small enough to fit into a file card box. It is only necessary to use this form when you do not have a market research or appointment form already filled out. For example, when you are trying to reach a certain individual and you've been given a call-back date for recontact.

Another time to use this form is when you have contacted a decision maker and for some reason or another you have not gone into your probing step (step 5). Rather than wasting your other forms (that are more costly to use), you should use the call-back form until you have completed at least the probing step and you consider the prospect a viable candidate for your products and services.

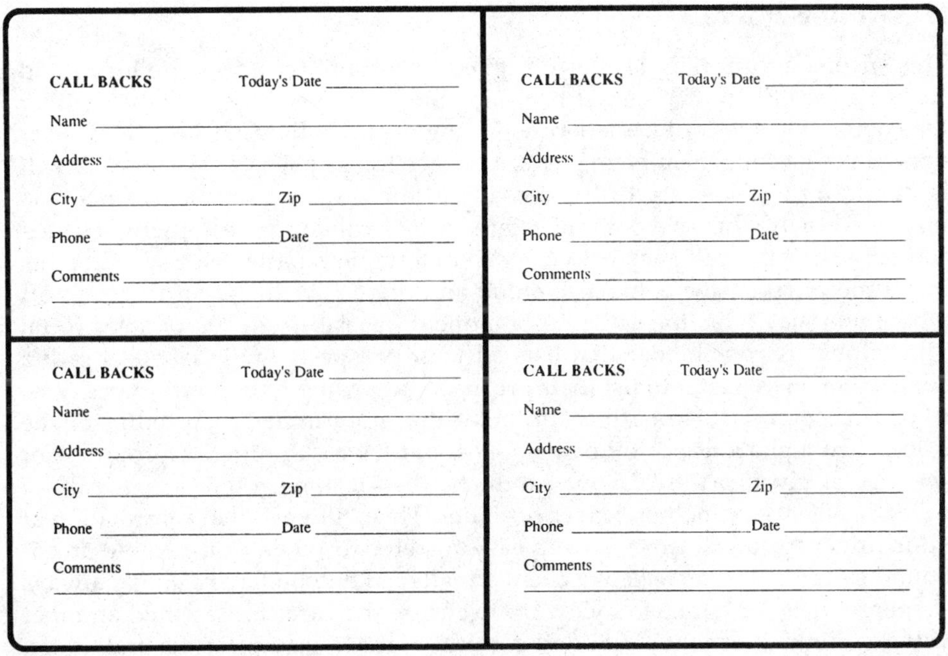

CALL BACKS Today's Date ________
Name ________
Address ________
City ________ Zip ________
Phone ________ Date ________
Comments ________

CALL BACKS Today's Date ________
Name ________
Address ________
City ________ Zip ________
Phone ________ Date ________
Comments ________

CALL BACKS Today's Date ________
Name ________
Address ________
City ________ Zip ________
Phone ________ Date ________
Comments ________

CALL BACKS Today's Date ________
Name ________
Address ________
City ________ Zip ________
Phone ________ Date ________
Comments ________

Figure 11-4. Call-back form.

ACCOUNT _____

DATES TO CALL BACK_____
_____
_____
_____
_____

___Alpha   ___Pending   ___Sold

ACCOUNT _____

DATES TO CALL BACK_____
_____
_____
_____
_____

___Alpha   ___Pending   ___Sold

ACCOUNT _____
DATES TO CALL BACK_____
_____
_____
_____
_____

___Alpha   ___Pending   ___Sold

ACCOUNT _____
DATES TO CALL BACK_____
_____
_____
_____
_____

___Alpha   ___Pending   ___Sold

Figure 11-5. Suspense form.

Suspense Form

This suspense form (Fig. 11-5) is designed to cut into four separate forms and fit into a card file box. Where it lists "account," you need to place there either the company name for business prospecting or the individual's name for residential prospecting. You have plenty of space to list your call-back activity. It is important to list every call you made to the prospect or client, since you may need to use this as a point of reference and validation. Another good reason for listing the call-back activity is to determine a pattern for which is the best time to reach the contact. Include an area below the form to check off where you may have the actual appointment, market research, or sales form. The "alpha" is your binder that lists all your prospects in alphabetical order. Some companies prefer to list their prospects according to industry types or A, B, or C accounts (this is a measurement that determines the quality of the lead), then alphabetically by name. Once you have submitted a proposal for services or given prices of your products, then it is wise to segregate those potential clients in another binder or folder. This will keep that information at your fingertips at all times and is easy to refer to when you receive an inbound call from the prospective client. Finally, when you have a client, always suspense them for a time to follow up to ensure they are still satisfied and that you are thinking of them. You will earn the right to gain referrals and added business when you stay in touch.

Ideally, if you are automated, then these forms are not required. When you automate your call center and understand the process, it simplifies your telemarketing activities and saves a tremendous amount of time each day.

Appointment Log Form

The appointment log form (Fig. 11-6) can also be used as a sales log form and should be kept by the TSR at all times. Each TSR needs to be responsible for keeping track of her or his own activities. This is especially true for those who are on commission or an incentive program that rewards TSRs for their own production. This also saves time when clarifying payroll; there is a double entry for validation. At the end of each pay period, you may wish to have your TSRs make copies of the completed forms and give them to their managers to submit for payroll purposes. When something is in doubt, personnel can refer to the manager for this information and not impose on the TSR. If there is ever any confusion or questions concerning the TSR's production, it is better not to approach the TSR until you have no other alternative. The

APPOINTMENT LOG

PAY PERIOD _____   TSR _____

	COMPANY NAME	TODAY'S DATE	CONTACT	M.R	APPT DATE	RESULTS
1.						
2.						
3.						
4.						
5.						
6.						
7.						
8.						
9.						
10.						
11.						
12.						
13.						
14.						

Figure 11-6. Appointment log form.

appointment log form will serve as a secondary confirmation for payroll and production analysis.

Place the form in an area that can be seen by anyone walking by. This serves a dual purpose: performance-wise it is a motivator for the TSR and their colleagues to see each others' production and for management to offer training assistance should the production be under the quota. Suggest to your TSRs to keep the forms after payroll so they can go back 6 months to a year later and see their own progress.

Final Report Form

This form (Fig. 11-7) is for the manager or supervisor to complete and distribute to the TSR either on a weekly, semiweekly, or monthly basis. List the name of each prospect that the TSR made a positive contact with and attempted to sell your company's products or service to, or made an appointment for the outside salesperson. Mark in the appointment or proposal date. The *P* stands for pending. This means that the TSR or the outside salesperson hasn't sold anything yet and there still is an opportunity to do so. The *DNS* means "demo

FINAL REPORT

SALES REP _____

NAME	DATE	$	P	DNS	N/G	N/S	R/S	COMMENTS

Figure 11-7. Final report form.

no sale." This is when the outside salesperson or the TSR demonstrated or presented the offering and no sale or close occurred. For prospects who say they are not interested at the end of the presentation, then you would mark it as a DNS. The *N/G* stands for "no good." Whenever you have approached a prospect and they either are not qualified or something out of your control stands in the way of making a final close, then this constitutes "no good." The *N/S* means that there has been "no status" given yet on that lead. Therefore either the TSR needs to report the status, if he or she is responsible, or the outside salesperson must do so. The next report should reflect this status. If not, then this would "red flag" the lead, and it should be communicated to whoever is ultimately responsible for giving final reports. The *R/S* stands for "reset." If there is a date placed in the box, this indicates when it was reset for, and the TSR should make a notation on the appointment log form. If no date was listed and there is a check mark, then this tells the TSR that he or she needs to reschedule the appointment.

Be sure that whoever is filling out the final report form always puts something in the comments section of the report. This thoroughly communicates to TSRs exactly what happened on their leads and can be used as a learning or coaching tool providing that the comments are constructive and offer positive feedback.

Outbound Tabulation Form

The benefits of tabulating are discussed elsewhere. Again, when you are automated, the software is designed to tabulate your prospecting activities. When tabulating manually, this form (Fig. 11-8) has four slots to tabulate each hour of prospecting up to 4 hours. If your TSRs are prospecting more than 4 hours, make this form two-sided. Have your TSRs place "tic" marks in groups of five for every dial they make and every decision maker they are in contact with. Based on the contact, the TSR would place one additional mark in another category to best describe what happened during the phone conversation. The headings for each category can be changed to whatever you wish to tabulate. It is best to leave at least one blank category so the TSR can specifically tabulate an area they are having difficulty with. The total "Appts." (appointments) can be changed to reflect your specific telemarketing activities such as total "sales," "surveys," or "market research." When configuring the grand totals, be sure to offer some statistics to the TSRs closing percentage. This will help them to stay on track with your department objectives.

Also, this form is used to conduct the "bottom line tracking" program discussed in Chapter 10. It is wise to keep these forms in your employee's production file for further reference—for example, whenever there is a dispute when terminating a TSR due to lack of production—or to show a quarterly, semiannual, or annual review. After each year you can discard the tabulation forms to allow more room for the following year's tabulation forms.

OUTBOUND TABULATIONS

NAME: DATE:

Hours	30-50 Res. Dials 20-30 Bus.	20-30 Res. Contacts 5-15 Bus.	Call Backs 5-7	Not Interested	Not Qualified	Not Ready		Total APPTS
Total								
Total								
Total								
Total								
Grand Total								

Figure 11-8. Outbound tabulation form.

Customer Service Tabulation Form

This form (Fig. 11-9) is deliberately designed differently from the outbound tabulation form so as to not confuse the form in your internal operations. The benefits of this form are discussed in Chap. 18. You would handle this form in the same way as the outbound form with the exception that the CSR is tabulating all inbound activities and measuring the effectiveness of the company's advertisements. The key is to determine where your peak hours are so you

Hours	Inbound Calls	Transferred	Advertisement	Referral				
Total								
Total								
Total								
Total								
Grand Total								

CSR Name _____   Date _____

Figure 11-9. Customer service tabulation form.

have adequate staffing to handle those calls and to ensure that the company is spending its marketing dollars wisely.

The four category areas that are blank are for you to tabulate specific areas that you wish to monitor depending upon what departments you want to tabulate and the job function of the CSR. For example, if the CSR is responsible for selling products, then you would want to tabulate how many sales each hour there were, and if no sale was made you need to tabulate why. This will

HOTLINE CALLS

Call date_____   Response time returned _____
Call time_____   Manager _____

Name of TSR/CSR _____

How long with department? _____

Recommendations given: _____
_____
_____
_____
_____

RECOMMENDATIONS GIVEN: _____
_____
_____
_____
_____
_____
_____
_____
_____
_____
_____
_____
_____

Figure 11-10. Hotline call form.

help you to offer additional training whenever you see a slack in production. Another category you could tabulate, if a customer is calling in and has a complaint, is the fault of a particular department. When this is detected, then you can clearly communicate this to the supervisor of the department that is causing the problem. This gives the department an opportunity to rectify the situation before it gets out of hand. If you are rewarding your CSRs for troubleshooting or handling certain types of calls or making a percentage of sales, the tabulation will help you to validate the reward when human resource is requesting the source.

Hot-line Calls Form

This form (Fig. 11-10) is specifically designed to assist your TSRs and CSRs with problems they are facing that they need additional information about. The TSR or CSR needs to fill in the top portion of the form with the exception of the response time and manager's name that the hot line was assigned to. The TSR or CSR needs to describe precisely what occurred in a brief format. Based on the information given, the manager could write in recommendations about how to handle it the next time, or better yet, to prevent the situation from occurring altogether. The benefits of this form are to give the TSR or CSR time to think of what occurred and to vent out on paper objectively. I call this "therapy."

In addition, the manager has an opportunity to consider the options and offer constructive advice. This also saves time. It takes less time to offer this type of training, as opposed to discussing it openly, or to sit down and provide one-on-one coaching. Whenever you have your weekly or monthly meetings, select at least three hot-line calls, don't mention any names, and share the problems and recommendations with the group. Others will benefit by this activity, and it encourages those who are not participating in the hot-line program to do so.

12
Setting the Stage

Market Share

Before learning the 12 steps to successful telemarketing in the following chapter, you need to understand your market share. There are prospects who say *no*, those who say *yes*, and the ones who *would*, providing you *create the need* and deliver your message well. Figure 12-1 will give you an idea of your market share when prospecting.

As you can see, 10 percent of the contacts you will make will say *no*. These prospects say no to *everything*. They have decided, even if you give your product away, they will have nothing to do with your offer. Don't take it personally. It's a statistical reality. This isn't because they are not in the market at this time, it is simply because they will never do business over the telephone. Do you

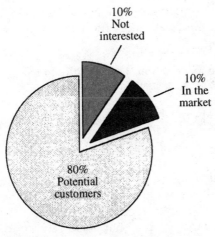

Figure 12-1 Market share.

recall ever getting a no prospect on the telephone? They usually will tell you within the first 30 seconds of your presentation. Their resistance, expressed in the beginning stages of your presentation, is silence and guttural utterances. When you get this no prospect, you must understand that they really do exist as part of your day-to-day prospecting activities, or they could ruin your day!

How do you really determine that this is a typical no prospect so that you will not close the door prematurely? Is *no* just a smoke screen, or is your prospect just having a bad day? You need to qualify the *no* person by using the easy close. For example, you are seconds into your presentation and barely have introduced yourself when suddenly your prospect says, "I'm not interested." The easy close will allow you to gracefully back off and attempt to test your prospect's response in order to determine whether the prospect *really* means no, or instead, that the no is just a smoke screen. If it is a smoke screen, the easy close will allow you to keep the door open for a future contact. The following is an example of an easy close:

I respect that. If I could send you information about (*offer some examples of what you could send*) **that you would have an interest in, what would that be?** (*Use an assumptive statement.*)

Offering examples will allow you to plug in what you are marketing while describing to your prospect the diversification of the products and/or services your company has to offer. Most important, this allows your prospects to tell you what *they* have an interest in.

As you may have noticed, there is a period at the end of the sentence instead of a question mark—this indicates that you need to use proper voice inflection to project an *assumptive statement* request. By using the statement effect, you are projecting to your prospect the assumption that they have an interest in something. Because of this assumption, the prospect will usually respond with a positive answer, thereby enabling you to keep the communication door open.

The hook to determine whether your prospect is *really* interested in the information or just gracefully "blowing you off the telephone" is to qualify whether the prospect is going to review the information or ignore it and throw it away. How do you qualify this? By saying:

Once you've the opportunity to review the information, I would like to gain your feedback. Does that sound fair enough? (*Use an assumptive statement.*)

Again, using the assumptive statement approach. If your prospect is truly interested in receiving the information, he or she will agree to your follow-up call; if the prospect is not interested, she or he will simply say, "That's okay, I'll call you."

What you have accomplished is the *weeding out* process of your list. The 10 percent who say no either will have not allowed you to continue this far or will not want you to conduct a follow-up call upon receiving your information. Are you going to send your information anyway? That is entirely up to you. However the statistics have shown that the prospects who say, "I'll call you," will never call you back. You may be wasting money on postage and brochure costs and wasting your time.

Just as there are the 10 percent who say no, there are also the 10 percent who say yes. This 10 percent is "in the market." You happen to be calling at the right time and with the right product or service. These prospects support the "numbers game," which is based upon the idea that if you make enough calls you'll ultimately reach enough prospects in that 10 percent category to do business with.

Although there is some statistical validity to the numbers game approach, it is a time-consuming, tedious, and inefficient way to prospect in today's sophisticated market. It is true that even some of the weakest closers will get a percentage of the 10 percent prospects that readily say yes. Be careful of those who do say yes too easily, since sometimes it's the unreliable yes because the prospects don't know how to say no! Therefore, you should still take the time to prequalify them, since you don't want to waste anyone's time unnecessarily, and, most of all, you don't want to experience a high cancellation factor because *you did not take the time to prequalify*. Even though it will be tempting to close too quickly, take the time to qualify *all* your prospects and walk them through the process within your presentation. During step 5 (probing) of the 12 steps, you will have the opportunity to qualify.

When looking at the pie chart, you will notice that the 80 percent of those you are in contact with present a better marketing opportunity for you. These people are rarely prospected in the right way. What this means is that most TSRs don't take the time within their presentation to establish their prospects' wants and try to create the need for their products or service. Instead, they are too busy selling and closing too quickly (going after the numbers game) rather than servicing and consulting with their prospects. The main reason for this is that many presentations are not designed to service the prospect into the sale or appointment but to close, close, close.

As mentioned earlier, many presentations are designed to captivate the 10 percent who readily say yes as opposed to going after the 80 percent of the prospects who would close provided you took the time to create the need for what you have to offer. The objective in a telemarketing operation is to contact as many prospects per hour as possible; this is due to the stringent quotas set by the manager. If TSRs have to spend too much time with prospects on the telephone, then it will be more difficult for them to meet their quota.

Based on the pie chart, the vast majority of the market to concentrate on when prospecting are those who are not sitting by their telephone anticipating your call. Let's face it, if you think about it, you are in business to take your competition's business away, correct? Most of your prospects are probably participating in a service or using a product you have to offer. Your objective is to convince your prospects they need what *you* have rather than what your competition has. When you think about it, it's very simple. If you walk in with the attitude that your prospects already see value in what you have to offer, then the challenge you need to face is convincing them they need to get it from you! But this requires a more skillful presentation, which is addressed in the training chapters ahead.

Before you begin learning how to generate additional selling opportunities or appointments with the 80 percent, you first need to learn techniques that will help you to deliver your message better. This will help you to further set yourself apart from your competition. The competition is not only your direct competitors, it is *anyone* who is using the telephone as a marketing tool. Your prospects receive many calls each day with someone vying for their business. Because your prospects are so accustomed to getting inundated by telemarketing calls, they have developed their own scripts or presentations to identify you quickly in order for you to lose interest in them. That is why your style of delivery is so vital in assisting you to separate yourself from other telephone sales calls.

Style of Delivery and Some Useful Terminology

Approximately 60 percent of communication is lost over the telephone due to lack of eye contact, gestures, facial expressions, and so on. You have only your voice to work with. Properly used, your voice can be communicative and persuasive. It is important to learn ways to enhance communication skills by using methods other than facial expressions and body language. Style of delivery is very crucial when reading from a script. There are tips that performers, television, and radio broadcasters use to make their scripts sound less "canned." Incorporating this style of delivery will set yourself further apart from a solicitation phone call.

Let's take a moment to paint a scenario in your mind. Pretend you are the prospect, and three separate companies approached you. These three companies are offering the same product, price, service, and guarantee.

Everything across the board is precisely the same. Now, what would be one area, singling out the other two companies that would finally help you in choosing which of the three you would end up doing business with? Of course, the one that impressed you the most. The one that delivered its message the best. The one you liked!

This is what differentiates within a company's telemarketing department the high closer from the poor closer. Both have been equally trained on product knowledge, skills, and techniques. Each TSR is offering the same products and services and pricing structure and using the same presentation script. However, the one with the higher closing percentage is usually the one who is concentrating on delivering the message better. Having a great product or service and a good compensation plan is not the answer to increasing production. Providing you made a good selection in your recruiting process, what is typically lacking within the telemarketing department is either a good script (for which we will discuss scripting techniques in another chapter) or in many cases, an effective delivery. The delivery of a TSR's presentation is usually the cause for a telemarketing department's peaks and valleys within its overall production.

Study the following techniques and implement them into your presentation. Later in Chap. 16 you will notice that each of the scripts already has symbols and indications for style of delivery. Whenever you rewrite or develop scripts, also write these symbols and indications appropriately. Otherwise, they will be forgotten and not used as a part of the delivery.

Strategic Pause

A strategic pause is indicated in the sample scripts with the symbol:

...>

The strategic pause allows you to gain an extra few seconds of your prospect's attention. Utilize a strategic pause when you are about to give a benefit statement or at other points in your presentation when it is important that you keep your prospect focused. What, specifically, is a strategic pause? It is a purposeful interruption of a sentence that suspends your prospect's attention and promotes active listening. It is a verbal speed bump which helps to intensify your prospect's involvement in your presentation. *Slowing down* after the pause is essential to place needed emphasis on your next statement. Here's how to use a strategic pause to enhance your presentation:

I recommend you have a consultation. This will provide you with...>increased awareness." (*slow down*)
My company requested...> I contact you personally. (*slow down*)

When you use a strategic pause, the prospect's natural inclination is to finish the sentence you've begun. Our minds tend toward maintaining continuity in speech (think of your natural inclination to "help" someone with a severe speech impairment). Your prospects are no different. They will want to fill in the pauses. This usually happens on a subconscious level. It is a very subtle anticipation, but the use of strategic pauses is a very effective way of capturing their attention. For example:

My company requested...>(*during the strategic pause your prospect's silent question will be, "requested what?"*) **I contact you personally.**

Strategic pauses can be used very effectively at different points in your presentation. Properly employed, they keep your prospect actively listening, help you to move into your next step, and help maintain the momentum you need to reach your final objective—the close.

Voice Inflection

When reading from a script it is important to vary the quality and tone of your voice. There is nothing more distracting for a presentation than a flat, monotonous voice. How can you impress your prospective client and generate enthusiasm when there is a distinct lack of it in your own presentation? You can't! You need to add a human dimension to the 2-dimensional page. How do you do this? By voice inflection! Just as actors read a script and project emotions to an audience, you must also convey a sense of enthusiasm, and perhaps even excitement to each of your contacts. By raising or *modulating* your voice, you generate emotion. People pay as much attention to emotion as they do to the actual words being spoken. For example:

And we're *lo*cated...

The italics indicate a rise in inflection. Say it aloud and listen to the difference when you exaggerate the rise in inflection on the first syllable in "*locat-ed*." It adds emphasis and excitement to your statement.

Volume

Volume is also an important consideration. One way to increase the effectiveness of your communication is to increase the volume. Turn it up! This will project greater confidence in your voice, and your prospect will be able to hear this confidence. Therefore, for those who are soft-spoken, try to speak approximately 25 percent louder than you normally would. If you're in a small or confined environment, don't concern yourself whether you would be distracting others by raising your volume. This would only be a distraction if the conversation taking place had nothing to do with business. ("Small talk" within a confined environment can be extremely distracting, since the other ear wants to listen in on the second-hand conversation rather than listening to what is being said to or from the prospect.) For those who already have a strong voice projection, just use your natural volume.

Rate of Speech

Pacing will always play an important role in your presentation. By using variable speeds you will avoid the monotonous drone which so often typifies prospecting. When using a variable-speed approach, you will verbally shift gears. You can speed up when you want to get quickly through a part of your sentence. You can also slow down when you want to gain your prospect's full, focused attention (this is usually during a benefit statement or after a strategic pause). Try to indicate in your scripts where you would like to slow down. One way is to underline in your written scripts the phrases or sentences in which you should take notice to slow down. Remember, writing your scripts in the way you want to deliver your message will help you to the read scripts without sounding canned. Use the following exercise to practice this variable-speed technique:

Information will be provided to compare ... >the *existing* programs you have in place. In this way, when you're *ready to upgrade,* this will give you peace of

mind by having a *better understanding of what you're needs are*, thereby ... >helping you when making your final selection.

Notice, the strategic pause, voice inflection, and now the variable speed for your pacing are used. Try the exercise again without the voice techniques you just learned and hear the difference they make in your style of delivery. In order to master this example, keep practicing it until you feel comfortable with the way it sounds.

Pitch

Many people breath incorrectly with the exception of athletes, singers, actresses, e.g., those who have gone through professional training that teaches them to use their voice or breathing apparatus efficiently. The following example demonstrates this further.

By the count of three, take a deep breath. Pretend you are about to dive into a pool of water, and you are going to be under for a few minutes. Don't worry, you won't have to hold it for that long, but let's just pretend for the sake of proving this point. Okay, let's begin—1, 2, 3, and take a deep breath. Now let it out. When you took that deep breath, what was moving? For many of you, it was your chest and shoulders. If that is what you did, then you're breathing incorrectly.

Consider this, how does a baby breath ? When you see a baby lying on it's back, what is moving? The stomach. Somehow, when we grow up we use the upper part of our chest area to breath as opposed to that part of our anatomy that we were born to breath from, i.e., through our diaphragm (the muscular partition between the chest and abdominal cavities). Try the same exercise, but this time use your diaphragm. For some of you, this will take some practice and concentration, especially if you have not used this muscle for quite sometime. Just remember where your diaphragm is located and try expanding that muscle area outwards as opposed to holding your stomach in!

What is the importance of this? Your diaphragm will help you to better control the variations in your pitch, and will either benefit or detract from your presentation. A deep, low voice can be a distraction, especially if your voice sounds "froggy." A high-pitched voice can sound nasal, squeaky, or mousy. None of these enhance your prospecting. It is desirable to control your pitch at or about a level which makes for easy listening. An appealing, pleasant voice can soothe and disarm and is a valuable tool for those who market over the telephone. An unattractive voice can be a detriment.

Practice different pitches and record your voice to get a better idea of how you sound. A good technique for this is to lay flat on your back, take a deep breath, and speak slowly from the diaphragm. Repeat the alphabet or make vowel sounds (A-E-I-O-U) while letting your breath out slowly. This will help you exercise your diaphragm and will aid in altering your pitch. This technique also increases your endurance while reducing your stress level and exhaustion at the end of each day. You will prospect longer with a strong and durable voice.

Smile!

Realizing you've heard it before, and because of it's importance, it's worth mentioning again—smile! It is important to smile as often as you can while prospecting on the telephone. Wouldn't you smile if you were in a face-to-face presentation? Of course! Smiling when using the telephone projects a pleasant and friendly voice. You create a *positive* mental picture of yourself in your prospect's mind.

Let's try a simple exercise. Without smiling say, "You're really going to like it." Listen to how it sounds. Now, *smile!* (If you don't feel like smiling, "fake it." As long as your mouth curves up, the effect of smiling will be there.) Okay, let's try it: "You're really going to like it!"

Can you hear the difference in your voice projection? Doesn't it sound pleasant? If you are unable to hear it, then do it in front of someone and ask for their feedback or record yourself and then listen carefully. You can hear it! So, as the saying goes—"smile and dial!!"

Keys to Good Listening

An important skill is *listening*. During the probing step in the training chapters you will be asking open-ended questions which allow your prospect to communicate with you. By listening effectively, you can determine how you want to individualize your presentation, avoiding a canned or robotic style of presentation and allowing you flexibility in presenting your products and services. This is your opportunity to *customize your presentation* based on your prospect's response. The following are some tips that will increase your listening skills:

- *Let your prospect talk 80 percent of the time.* Limit your own talking to 20 percent. (This is achieved during step 5, the probing step.)

- *Identify with your prospects.* Place yourself in their position. Their problems and needs are important. You can better understand your prospects if you keep their point of view in mind.

- *Ask questions if you do not understand something.* You may be missing a very important point. Asking shows your prospect that you are listening. Be sure your questions are open-ended.

- *Do not interrupt.* Listen for a pause—that's your cue to interject.

- *Concentrate!* Be on top of the subject at all times.

- *Take notes.* Write down important points that can be helpful to your prospect. Be aware of the phrases that recur during the prospect's comments. Later, bringing up certain comments made by prospects will let them know you were listening.

- *Listen for attitude.* You can learn a lot about your prospects' attitudes and feelings by listening to their tone of voice. This awareness will help you overcome any objections that may surface later in your presentation.

- *Do not respond to your own questions.* Let your prospect do all the talking. When you respond, your prospect then knows what your emotions are. This will have an adverse effect on your presentation. However, you may respond to your prospect's answers with another open-ended question.

- *Turn off your personal problems.* This can greatly affect your prospect's attitude toward you. Your prospect can sense your problems and worries through your voice projection.

- *Prepare yourself.* Know your product and competitors. This will allow you to deal with objections effectively and confidently.

- *Have empathy and understanding.* Feel for your prospects, even if they seem irritable. Do not let their emotions affect your attitude toward them, and do not take it personally. Consider it a challenge to get on their good side.

- *Avoid making any assumptions about what your prospect is about to say.* That is, allow your prospects to complete their sentences. You may find yourself creating unnecessary objections in the process!

- *Listen for mental pictures painted within your mind.* This is a key indicator that the picture is an important issue. In effect, your prospect is telling you, "This is important to me!"

- *Listen to what has not been said, especially if your prospect is negative.* This is your opportunity to point out some positive reactions and statements. If it is during an objection-handling process, then your prospect may not always want to reveal the real reasons for objecting or disconnecting. Probe and find what the real issue is and outweigh it.

- *Practice listening during conversations.* Use your friends, family, or coworkers—anyone you come in contact with! Use these encounters as an opportunity to improve your listening skills in order to sharpen your ear.

Effective listening strengthens your understanding of your prospect's needs and personal desires. Properly developed listening skills can enable you to determine what you want to sell and how it relates to your prospect's needs. You can overcome many possible objections that may never surface but that nevertheless exist. Remember to put yourself in the prospect's position. If you know that your needs are being met and that someone has a clear understanding of what those needs are, then you will be more receptive and listen to their ideas!

Key Points

A word about using absolute or overwhelming statements—when entering into the selling step of your presentation, be careful of speaking in absolute statements or using statements that seem too good to be true. These are identified as *overwhelming statements.* Instead, preface your statements with reasonable qualifiers, such as:

It seems to me that...
Many others have found...
Most of the time this will...

These types of statements will keep the lines of communication open, honest, and sincere between you and your prospect. Follow these guides:

- *Establish prospect's needs.* Buyers don't purchase products or services. They are investing in what the products or services will do for them. Which leads into the next point.

- *Many people think about themselves a great deal of the time.* A skilled salesperson will satisfy a prospect's personal desires with successful sales techniques combined with effective listening.

Okay, now you're ready to begin your *first step* on the road to more productive and profitable prospecting!

13
The TSR Presentation

The Three Fears

A great deal of thought and research have gone into developing an effective presentation that meets today's market. Telemarketing has been around for centuries, and this high-tech, rapidly growing industry will be around for many centuries to come. The good news is that those who have made a career out of it will be around for a while, and the bad news is that consumers and businesses alike will be hearing more presentations over the telephone. Therefore, not only must we hire the right individuals to telemarket, we must also concentrate more time on how to conduct a professional and effective presentation. You do not want your presentation to sound canned to your prospects, like the last six calls they received earlier that day. That is why I have developed a *12-step method* that guides a telemarketer step by step from introduction to postclose without the presentation sounding too familiar. That familiarity could turn off your prospect within a few seconds into the presentation and prevent the TSR from making the sale or an appointment!

Thought and research, however, are only a part of the 12-step method. The techniques contained in this chapter have been applied repeatedly, resulting in increased productivity for thousands in a variety of industries, such as telemarketing, real estate, insurance, computers, investments, and consumer to business products. The skills presented in this chapter will provide the most up-to-date and innovative approaches available in today's sophisticated market. The verbiage contained within the steps, in certain areas, is very precise and will further set your presentation apart from others. This program has made a difference for many large corporate and *Fortune* 500 companies and it will do the same for you!

The 12 steps offer rookie and veteran TSRs alike a complete step-by-step method that takes the guesswork out of prospecting for inside and outside sales departments. It is specifically designed for *today's* market, which is inundated with "solicitation," whether by telephone, direct mail, or door-to-door sales. With so many different approaches in the market, whether you are a manager and/or a trainer of a telemarketing department or a TSR, you must develop techniques that distinguish you not only from other competing TSRs within your industry but also from others aggressively vying for your prospect's time and money.

The 12 steps use the unique approach of customizing and individualizing your sales and servicing efforts to the prospect. *The approach is not the typical frontal assault employed in most types of prospecting.* You do not immediately attempt to sell to your prospects but rather initiate a "rapport" that will *assist you in the prospecting process.*

The 12 steps originated from the idea that the key to prospecting is the relationship we develop with our contacts. Part of this relationship is understanding that prospects have three primary *fear points* that need to be overcome in order for your telemarketing efforts to be successful. These three fears exist in the face-to-face selling arena for which professional outside salespeople spend more than half their careers learning how to conduct effective face-to-face presentations that overcome these fears.

The inside salesperson (TSR) should take on the same attitude. In amazement, I find many TSRs within a variety of companies who are not motivated to take the extra time, on their own, to learn new techniques that would further enhance their presentation. Again, this falls back partly onto the recruiting and hiring process and the compensation plan. However, if the TSR is aware of the fears prospects have when being approached on the telephone, and TSRs have the skills to overcome these fears, TSRs are more motivated. They will spend the time to learn what it would take to have a successful encounter when prospecting. The three primary fear points are:

1. *The Approach.* "What does this salesperson want from me?"

2. *Prepurchase Insecurity.* "What if I make a decision and later regret it?"

3. *Postpurchase Remorse.* "What have I done now?"

Each of the 12 steps in this chapter will help to overcome these fear points *before they emerge as objections.* That is, principally, what the 12 steps are all about—satisfying and overcoming potential objections *before* they surface. Many companies are spending too much time and training dollars teaching their TSRs how to overcome an objection. This is contrary to how the 12 steps are designed. What is an *objection?* It's not an opportunity to sell, and it's not raised because your prospect needs more information. *An objection is an indicator you have not done an effective presentation!* When you make your primary objective to conduct an effective presentation, you will have a better opportunity to effectively sell your prospect. This is accomplished by the information you provide in your selling step. However, in the event the TSR is unable to overcome objections, the 12 steps will teach how to outweigh objections as they occur.

Let's take the first fear, *the Approach*—steps 1 to 4 overcome this fear. Within the first 30 seconds of your presentation, you will tell the prospect who you are, the company you represent, where you're located, how you got the prospect's name, that you'll respect his or her time, and what the purpose of your call is. Think about it. If you were the prospect, would you want to know this information? So do your prospects. In fact, many will interrupt a TSR's presentation and ask, "How did you get my name?" "What's this all about?" or, during the middle of your presentation, "I'm busy now!"

The second fear is *Prepurchase insecurity*; steps 5 to 9 overcome this fear. This is where you begin to qualify your prospects, establish their wants, and create the need for your products or services. Once you have achieved that, you will fulfill their needs and attempt to trial close. This is the bulk of your presentation and, besides getting through the first initial barriers, the most critical.

The third and final fear is *Postpurchase remorse*; step 12 overcomes this fear. By incorporating this step into your presentation you will reduce your cancellation factors tremendously. Most TSRs are trained to hurry up, close, get off the telephone, and move on to the next call before prospects change their minds. Because a Postclose was not incorporated into their presentation, once the call is terminated, prospects will begin to talk themselves out of the sale or the appointment. This is why companies experience cancellations as high as 60 percent!

As you may have noticed, steps 10 and 11 are not included when addressing and overcoming the three fears. Step 10 is the objection step, and an objection is an indicator that you have not done an effective presentation. Therefore, since the presentation is designed to overcome your prospect's fear, objections typically do not occur. Sounds too good to be true doesn't it! It is the very reason that the 12 steps have been designed to overcome resistance *before it occurs*. This will enable you to conduct an effective presentation and have a positive encounter with your prospect. If you could accomplish this, how valuable would it be for you to start using the 12 steps and increase your selling opportunities immediately?

Step 11, *the Close*, is also not included in addressing the three fears because this is a very natural transition based upon your successfully following the previous steps. According to the national statistics, most salespeople do not know how to close. The three possible reasons for this are, they don't close, they don't know when to close, or they don't know what to say when closing. In this step you will know who to close (you will not close everyone), and you will know exactly when to close and what to say when closing. This step is the simplest part of your presentation. What is incredible about it is that you will never get objections in your close step.

As you can see, the 12 steps do address your prospects' three fears, and you will take approximately 3 to 5 minutes (depending on how long the prospect takes to respond to your questions), to successfully complete a presentation. By following this method, you will have the tools to be in complete *control* of your presentation. Nowhere within your presentation will you ever give up your control. As you study and practice the steps and implement them into your telemarketing operation, you will be impressed with the results. What is more important, your prospects will be even more impressed!

While learning the 12-step program, keep in mind that each of the 12 steps has different *features, functions,* and *benefits.* Whenever you are selling to your prospect, you must describe what it is you are selling (the feature), what your product *does* (the specifications, size, performance of what the feature is; this is the function), and finally, what good your prospect gains by the product (this is the benefit). These elements within your sales presentation are important to persuade your prospect to buy into your offering. The same selling method within your sales presentation is used within this training chapter. It is important that you understand the *benefits* that each of the 12 steps and each of the functions have to offer, otherwise you will not be sold on the step method. The information contained in this chapter is designed to be used as a constant resource. It is a reference guide to your new prospecting skills. If you are responsible for training others, the 12 steps are designed to make it easier for you to train your TSRs. It will give you more continuity in your training efforts and you will experience a higher level of consistency in production.

I want to hear from you and assist you with your success when using the 12 steps! Please share with me how you're doing: Call 1-800-STEPS 4 U.

How to Conduct Effective Market Research

For many years companies have concentrated their telemarketing efforts by conducting a *one-call close.* Today, due to the inundation of calls by telemarketing, not only is it necessary to approach prospects differently, it is equally important to slow the selling process down by conducting a *two-call close.* You don't always have to close your prospect on the first contact. The following are several ways in which you can accomplish this; however, you need to decide which method is going to maximize your prospecting efforts in the most cost-effective way. Each company may choose differently depending on its objectives and budget.

The primary way many companies are doing a two-call close has been, for many years, by direct mail. Usually this is accomplished by sending an inexpensive mail piece to a particular targeted market. This may get some attention. In reality, depending upon your mail piece and who your targeted market is, you may average only a half of a percent response. It could be higher, such as 3 percent, even as high as 10 percent. This depends greatly on where, to whom, and what you are mailing. The question is, how many pieces of literature do you need to mail to give you a profitable return on your investment? In the thousands! When considering the up-front costs and then factoring the rate of return, is this the way in which you want to expand your market share?

One way to ensure a higher level of response is to follow up within a few days after your prospect has received your information. You will encounter some level of resistance from your prospects, and the following are typical responses:

Please keep in mind that there are certain areas within the steps where there is no flexibility. It will be pointed out to you where you have flexibility and where you do not.

Consider a scripted presentation in two fashions. One, it is a road map. If you have never driven to a faraway place before, you would take a road map. You would probably take this road map many times until you finally learned the way. Once you have learned the way, you may still have the map near you just in case you get lost. Second, your scripted presentation is like a recipe. You need to follow the basis of the recipe verbatim, especially in certain areas, since you don't want to change the texture or the flavor too much. Otherwise, your dish would not turn out the way it was intended.

The 12-step method is similar to the road map and recipe examples. This method is not meant to be picked apart-where you take a little from the 12 steps and another from some other training program and intermingle different ideas and concepts. When doing so, you are mixing the outcome of the results. The 12 steps are written precisely to be used in its entirety.

Take quality time to learn and practice the steps. Also, take a fair amount of time in implementing the steps. Remember, you have been using your presentation a certain way, and for those who are veterans at prospecting, it will take time to unlearn what you have already internalized. Be patient, it will be worth it! Monitor your results before, during, and after; in this way, you will see a marked improvement in production and attitude and less turnover and burnout in your telemarketing department!

Step 1: Introduction

The opening statement of a call is one of the most crucial parts of your presentation. With only seconds to create a favorable impression, the opening statement must captivate your prospect and must proclaim, *"Here is a reason to listen to me!"* In the first 30 seconds, bridges must be built and crossed. The right introduction will get you beyond your salutation. The wrong introduction is likely to get you nothing more than an abrupt end to your prospecting. You must impress your prospective client with your courtesy and your patience, while maintaining *control* of your presentation.

What is the most effective opening? How do you optimize your chances for completing your presentation in these critical seconds? It all begins with the proper introduction.

By following a few general principles, you should be able to establish a positive rapport. To increase your chances of success, it is essential that your introduction contain the following information:

√ *Who* you are

√ *What* company you represent

√ *Where* you are located

I don't remember receiving your information, why don't you send another.

Or

I threw that in the trash with all my other junk mail.

Does this sound familiar? How much money was lost in your brochures, your time, and mailing costs? Be careful not to send too many brochures out at one time. If you don't follow up within a few days of your prospects' receiving the information, they will simply have put it out of their mind. Your effort along with the financial investment is wasted.

I'm not suggesting you never conduct a direct-mail campaign. On the contrary, direct mail can be extremely profitable providing you are targeting your primary market and prepared to send out a substantial amount of information at one time. The benefits to you include a bulk mail rate discount and captivated prospects who are calling you and fall into the 10 percent who *are in the market* (see Chap. 12). Should you conduct a direct-mail campaign, be sure to have enough incoming lines and the appropriate staffing of customer service representatives (CSRs) to support it.

A more cost-effective and profitable way of accomplishing a two-call close is to conduct market research. This increases closing percentages as much as 80 percent. The concept is to first contact your prospect, establish rapport, qualify the prospect, determine your prospect's needs, and create the need for your products and services. Once you have completed this process, you can conclude your presentation, close off, and request to send your information with permission to conduct a follow-up call after the prospect has had the opportunity to review it.

Understandably this is a slower process, and you don't necessarily have to conduct a market research. The idea is to purposely slow the selling process down so you have more time to conduct your precall objective planning when you conduct your follow-up call. Also, sending your information after you have spoken with your prospect serves to lay the "red carpet" down prior to your selling steps. Not only will this increase your selling opportunities, your prospect will be impressed with your attitude toward customer service. You have projected that you're someone who cares more about going the extra mile to service as opposed to trying to close the sale or the appointment. The two-call close will serve to further set yourself apart from your competition.

The average closing percentage is much higher conducting a two-call close as opposed to a one-call close. The only drawback is having to wait a few extra days to get your commitment. This is to your advantage, since according to the recent statistics, it can take up to five contacts (approaching your prospect), before you can convert a prospect into a customer. If you narrow down your personal contacts to each of your prospects to only one call, you increase the odds of closing the door permanently, losing the sale altogether.

The following five steps are designed for a two-call close or for market research. Try and follow the steps precisely the way they are written and or ad-lib or be creative with the ideas once you have internalized the proc

Offering these three pieces of information will improve communication with your prospect in a number of ways. First, by openly giving out information, you are anticipating and satisfying your prospect's curiosity, which often emerges in the opening stages of communication as an objection. Second, you are distinguishing yourself from other sales representatives by being deliberately up-front with your prospects. This information helps disarm objections that tend to appear in these early stages.

Why should you take this approach? Remember the *first fear point: "What does this salesperson want from me?"* Put yourself in your prospects' places. Do they want to embark on a potentially long telephone conversation with an anonymous voice without knowing some basic details? A prospect's first inclination is to detach from the call, to withdraw and to be a little bit defensive and skeptical. Giving your prospect some of this basic information will decrease the likelihood of a defensive response.

By offering a greeting containing *WHO you are, WHAT company you represent,* and *WHERE you are located,* you begin to take shape in your prospect's mind. You are no longer just a disembodied voice over the telephone. Your name, your company, and your location are clarified, and as you begin to present a picture of yourself, your prospect becomes preoccupied with trying to visualize you. Creating an objection at this point becomes less likely.

The following are the *five functions* that must be contained in step 1.

Greeting

Greet your prospect with "Good morning," "Good afternoon," or "Good evening." This is the first stage in developing rapport with your prospect.

Why? Look at it this way. Modern technology has made it convenient and cost-effective for almost anyone with a product or service to utilize the telephone as a marketing tool. As a result, your prospects are, on a daily basis, inundated with unprofessional solicitation calls. These calls usually begin with, "Hi," "Hello," "How are you doing," and the like. Haven't you received some of those calls yourself? A *formal greeting* serves to set you apart from those annoying solicitation calls and helps to project a *positive professional image.*

Establishing Contact

Have you ever made the mistake of assuming someone's gender over the telephone just because, due to the tonality of the person's voice, you believed you were talking to Mr. Smith when you were, in fact, talking to his wife? Do you think you succeeded in partially alienating Mr. Smith by committing that error? Or have you ever asked, "Is your mommy home?" and received an icy reply, "This is the mommy."

Making mistakes in assuming a person's gender or age is quite common in telemarketing, but it is also unnecessary. You should never assume that the person answering the telephone is male or female, adult or child, simply by the sound of the person's voice. Below are some examples of how to establish contact for residential and business-to-business prospecting.

Residential Prospecting.   In residential prospecting, it is best to specifically ask for your prospect, using a statement such as, **"I need ... > to speak with Mr. or Mrs. Phillips, please."** Notice **"I need ... >"** was used rather than "May I." The benefit of using **"I need ... >"** is to remain in control and to show a sense of urgency in your call. (By asking, "May I," you give up your control, encouraging your prospect to begin playing "20 questions.")

Your prospect might answer, **"This is Mrs. Phillips,"** or **"This is Mr. Phillips."** If you're dealing with a single person or a divorcee, a typical response is, **"This is Ms. Phillips,"** or **"There is no Mrs. Phillips, but this is Mr. Phillips."** In some instances, the marital status may not be clarified here. In such a case, it will then be identified in step 11 (the close).

Notice that a strategic pause (... >) was used after the word *need*. Remember, a strategic pause encourages active listening. Your prospect will be actively thinking, "You need what?"

Business-to-Business Prospecting.   In business-to-business prospecting, establishing contact is handled differently. Most of you have gone through secretarial screens. After crossing this barrier, hopefully you are transferred to your prospect. Sometimes you are facilitated to the wrong department or individual. One way of determining such an error is when your prospects answer the telephone. They may identify themselves and even their department voluntarily: **"This is John Smith,"** or **"Marketing department, this is John."** If your prospects identify themselves, then there is no need to verify further. You can then proceed to your next function. If your prospect answers with "Hello" only, then you need to verify your contact. Do so by stating: **"Good morning, I need ... > to speak with Mr. Smith, please."** Be sure to ascertain your prospect's gender in advance when doing business-to-business prospecting. This information may be available from your *lead list* or can be obtained during the secretarial screening process (see Chapter 16).

By keeping your statement neutral, you allow your prospects to tell you who they are. By remaining neutral, you avoid the potential embarrassment of making an erroneous assumption or assuming you have the correct person when actually you were misdirected.

One of the more effective ways of ensuring that your call gets transferred quickly and to show a sense of urgency is to employ a tone that implies you *expect* to be transferred to the right person: **"I need ... > to speak with."** *I need* is more effective than *May I please speak with* because it conveys to the person answering the telephone that you expect that your contact is in and will want to talk to you. **"I need ... >"** imparts a sense of urgency to your request. Use a softer voice inflection to prevent your prospect from feeling intimidated. Raise your voice inflection on the word *I* and don't emphasize the word *need*. Also, you do not want to ask for permission to speak with your prospect. When you ask permission, you give up your control.

You must maintain control of the call during the 12-step process. Take notice of the word *with* when saying "to speak *with*." Phrased differently, "to speak to," is too directive. The verbiage is very precise to ensure that you have a continued flow of positive communication with your prospect. Certain words and phrases can irritate and create a negative image of you within your prospect's mind.

Whenever there is a difficult last name to pronounce, either of two things happen: TSRs will skip over it and move on to the next prospect (rarely do these prospects get contacted), or TSRs try to sound it out and will end up mispronouncing the prospect's last name anyway. If you are not well versed in other languages and with their vowel constructions, more than likely a difficult last name will not be pronounced correctly.

Mispronouncing names is not only a common mistake in prospecting but it is extremely unprofessional. This irritates prospects and creates a new barrier for a TSR to overcome. What should you do? Use the humbling technique by simply giving up your control but in a way that the prospect will be impressed and make it easier for you to continue with your presentation. The humbling technique is,

> **Good morning, this is Susan Garner and I am having a difficult time in pronouncing your last name. Would you please help me.** (*Use the assumptive statement request.*)

More often than not, your prospects will assist you in pronouncing their last names. Also, this serves to break the barriers and freely move on to the your next function.

First-Name Cue

This function allows you to determine whether you should proceed on a first-name basis with your prospect. Never assume just because your prospect sounds friendly that it would be all right to call the prospect by her or his first name; it is important that your prospect gives you a cue before you attempt to be on a first-name basis.

Provided you have the first name of your prospect, your next statement will be to simply repeat and emphasize the first name, as if you are verifying your information:

> **Ms. *Mary* Smith?** (*Voice inflection on the first name.*)

Your prospect will respond with:

> **Yes, this is Mary, or Yes, this is Mary Smith, or Yes, this is Ms. Smith, or Yes.**

If your prospect responds with a first name only, this is your *only* cue to proceed on a first-name basis. If the prospect responds in any other way, you must proceed on a last-name basis.

Why is it so important to establish a first-name cue? Your entire objective within the 12 steps is to break down barriers. If you approach your prospect and use improper or unprofessional tactics, you run the risk of irritating your prospect and kindling an objection. Assuming an attitude of familiarity too quickly in your conversations may alienate your prospects at a very early stage. They may feel uncomfortable if a person they don't know quickly assumes this level of intimacy. For some, prematurely communicating on a first-name basis becomes an immediate "turn-off." This is one trap you should be careful to avoid.

Another good reason for using the first-name cue is that you may easily compound the error by using an informal name that is simply the wrong one. For example, if you call a prospect named Robert, "Bob" (in the interest of establishing rapport, of course), and he has been called, "Rob" since he was a boy, you have only succeeded in increasing the distance between you and your prospect.

Establishing a positive rapport afterward will be that much more difficult. The objective at this point is to address your prospects in a manner with which *they* feel comfortable. Remember, selling your products or services involves selling yourself first. Our goal, in the early stages, is to establish an atmosphere in which to do business.

Keep in mind that not all your prospects answer their telephone in the same way. Effective listening will help you when applying the steps and their functions. For example, if your prospect answers the telephone immediately by saying, **"Hello, this is Betty."** You would not say, **"Good evening, I need ... > to speak with Mr. or Mrs. Phillips please,"** if your prospect had just identified herself as one of the two you were wishing to speak with. What is more important, taking this same scenario, you would not continue to say, **"Mrs. Betty Phillips?"** when in fact your prospect has already identified that you made the right contact, her gender, and she has given you indirect permission to use their first name.

The steps and their functions are designed to guide you smoothly throughout your presentation. If your prospects are ahead of you, then follow the next step or function that would be more appropriate.

Introduce Yourself and Company

When introducing yourself and your company, it is best to offer your full name, even though your prospect has given you permission to proceed on a first-name basis. This tells your prospect a little more about who you are. You begin to acquire an *identity*. To your prospect, you are no longer a nameless voice. Should you feel uncomfortable using your full name, especially if you also have a difficult last name, then it would be appropriate to use a "stage name." Many TSRs use a stage name. Somehow it gives them a separate identity. Whenever a prospect is difficult, the TSR doesn't feel personally affected. Be sure to use the same name throughout your employment and make sure that others internally are aware of your stage name. Failure to do so could raise some problems should a prospect wish to speak with you.

Now that you have greeted the prospect professionally, you may use the word *hello* to begin the process of building rapport. Your statement should be as follows:

Hello, Ms. Smith, this is Carol Roberts and I represent ABC Company.

Be sure to say, "This is" rather than, "My name is," which just reinforces the fact you do not know each other. Your goal is to gradually increase the level of rapport, not create further distance. Careful, thoughtful selection of effective words is vital to successful prospecting. Remember, you don't want to sound like a typical solicitation call!

Landmark or Location

Giving your company's location and/or landmark is essential. The intention is to create a mental picture of the location or landmark in the prospect's mind, thereby offering a familiar point of reference. Your prospect's attempt to visualize a positive and familiar image will help to engage his or her mind and keep the prospect actively listening.

What is the benefit of promoting a mental image by offering a location or a landmark? Consider what typically happens when you give your company name—your prospect gets a "warning signal." This signal in most situations may not always be positive, depending on the nature of your products or services and your prospect's experiences. Let's face it, your prospects are not sitting by the telephone anticipating your phone call. When they hear your company name, especially if it identifies what your call objective is (e.g., XYZ Insurance Company or ABC Computer) pausing after your company name will allow the prospect to conjure up an objection. In other situations where the name of your company doesn't identify at all what your call objective is, you may arouse too much curiosity and encourage unnecessary objections or resistance. This is why many TSRs fail in the first 15 seconds of their introduction. The prospect's objection preempts their presentation. During the first few seconds into the presentation you stand weak with the prospect. This lessens the chance of overcoming any resistance and spending too much time dealing with the resistance factors as opposed to conducting an effective presentation.

By using a location or landmark, prospects are presented with something tangible, something they can relate to, something to mentally focus on, thus diverting the thought process that would create the objection. Your prospect's familiarity with this landmark will make it easier to visualize you and your company.

Proper use of *voice inflection* and *strategic pauses* are crucial throughout your presentation but extremely beneficial during this function. Using the proper voice inflection with strategic pauses helps set the stage for painting a clear mental picture in your prospect's mind. Remember, you want to *engage* prospects. You do not want to give them time to conjure up objections. The following is an example of the *fifth function* in your introduction:

Hello Ms. Smith, this is Carol Roberts. I represent XYZ Company, and we're lo**cated … > near City Hall.**

Or, if you're calling out of the local area:

Hello Ms. Smith, this is Carol Roberts. I represent XYZ Company and we're lo**cated … > off highway 99 and Benson.**

Or, if you're calling out of state or into an area that is outside your immediate location:

Hello Ms. Smith, this is Carol Roberts. I'm *with* **ABC Company, and I repre-** *sent* **… > the west coast region.**

Notice the bold italics. For effective emphasis, be sure to raise your voice inflection on the italicized syllables.

The *fifth function* tells your prospects a little more than just your name and the company's name, while keeping their minds engaged in active listening, thus preventing premature objections from surfacing. It isn't important they know where you are located, the concept is, voice inflection with a strategic pause. The objective is, to keep their mind actively engaged in your presentation and off your company name.

You have completed the five functions of step 1. Now, move on to step 2.

Step 2: Reference

There is only *one function* in reference. Your prospects will want to know **how you got their names.** Your prospects either interrupt you by asking you this question, or they are no longer actively listening—they have shut down because they are thinking of how you got their name. You do not have to specifically tell them *where* you acquired their names, but you must satisfy their curiosity about why you are calling into *their* homes or businesses, or you run the risk of creating an unnecessary barrier. Remember, barriers prevent active listening.

The reference statement you use will depend on the type of calling you're doing and your call objective. The idea is to keep it simple, brief, and non-threatening, i.e., nonselling. The following are just some of the possible reference statements that may be suitable for your company:

My company requested … > I contact you personally. (*This reference is very effective for cold calling.*)
I recently sent you information.
You requested … > I contact you personally. (*From a bingo or reply card.*)
(*Name of referral*) **requested … > I contact you personally.**
I understand you recently had a baby. Congratulations!
I understand you recently purchased a new home. Congratulations!

My company is actively advertising in this area.
I specialize in this area (or) business.
We spoke some time ago (*give date or event*).

These are just a few of the types of reference statements you can choose from. You can also create your own. The objective is to *not* use a selling statement or spend too much time explaining or detailing your reference. You want to sound professional, without being too specific, in order to satisfy the prospect's curiosity *for the moment*. This will allow you to confidently move into your next step.

Step 3: Request for Time

It is important to convey to your prospects your awareness of their time and that you *respect* that time. In today's busy world, time is a valued commodity. How do you get prospects to share some of their time with you without allowing them a "way out" of the phone presentation?

There are *two functions* in step 3, both of which are uniquely designed to give your prospect a feeling of control. You can do this without actually surrendering control of the call yourself. The key is **how** you ask for their time. Your request can be made in such a way as to encourage a positive response from your prospect, such as, **"Sure, go ahead!"**

How would this response affect your attitude to continue with your phone presentation? Would this response increase your confidence level? Would this response help you present your products and services better, knowing that your prospect has given you permission to continue? Of course!

Although there are many ways to request for time, virtually all encourage negative responses and give up your control. The *assumptive statement request* has proved to be more effective in eliciting positive responses. What is an assumptive statement request? An example may help to clarify this concept:

I hope ... > I haven't caught you at a bad time, *have* **I.**

Notice there is no question mark! The assumption on your part is that "now is a good time to talk," but this assumption must be phrased delicately. The prospect is most likely perceiving the statement as a question, but it is also an *answered question.* Let's break this statement into four components.

The first is the phrase *I hope.* This softens the perception of the assumptive statement request, making it sound less aggressive and threatening. Using a *strategic pause* after saying *I hope* serves to keep your prospect's mind actively listening and thinking, "You hope what?" This allows you to get to the more vital aspects of your communication.

The second component is the word *caught.* This is used instead of the word *called.* In prospects' minds, TSRs are always calling at bad times, especially if prospects know we are selling something. What I want to know is whether I caught them at a bad time, such as during the dinner hour, an important meeting, or feeding the baby.

The third component is the word *bad*. This is used to reinforce the word *caught*. Again, in the prospect's mind TSRs are always calling at an inconvenient time, but did I catch the prospect at a bad time? Most prospects will allow you to continue because of the selection of words.

The fourth component is the way you use your voice inflection when you say, "*... have* I." This is critical here! You *must not* ask this as a question. When phrased as a question, you allow your prospect to make the decision to terminate the conversation, and you're reinforcing the possibility that you may have caught them at a bad time. Try this right now. ... Say the request for time aloud as a question, with a raised inflection on the *I* (as opposed to a statement), and listen to how it sounds.

I hope ... > I haven't caught you at a bad time, have *I*?

Now, say it again and lower the inflection on the final *I*. Practice until you can hear and control the difference. *You don't want to ask permission for prospects' time.* (Remember, when you ask permission you give up your control!) By lowering the pitch of your voice on the *I* you will make a *statement*, not ask a question.

Hint: If you are having difficulty lowering the inflection on *I*, try concentrating on raising the inflection on *have*. The *I* should naturally follow as a lower note. Better yet, use the word *rabbi* to hear the proper voice inflection. Make *have I*, one word with two syllables:

I hope ... > I haven't caught you at a bad time, *have* I.

Although you will often receive the **"Sure, go ahead"** response, you will also receive other responses when requesting for time, and you should know how to respond to them. If this is truly an inconvenient time to talk, your prospect has an opportunity to tell you so.

The **second function** is used only when your prospect doesn't answer with a positive response. For example, your prospect might say,

> **I'm busy right now.**
> **I have someone in my office.**
> **I was just leaving.**
> **I'm right in the middle of something.**

Prospects who claim to be busy fall into two categories, and we need to be able to separate them. The first type of prospect is truly busy, and we need to respect that and call back at a more convenient time. In return, your time will be respected when you recontact the prospect. This type of call-back has a high probability of success because so far you have established positive communication with your prospect.

The second type of prospect is not busy but is trying to use your request for time as a way out of the conversation. You can distinguish between the two by using another assumptive statement request:

Why don't I call you back in about an hour. Would that be all right *with* you.
(*Again, note that there is no question mark.*)

You are assuming that if your prospect is truly busy that an hour from now will be an appropriate time to recontact him or her. Remember not to give a questioning lift to your voice at the end of the request. We are not asking for permission. Instead, we are making a statement.

If your prospect responds with, **"No, I don't want to be called back,"** or should your prospect interrupt and cut you off at any time during the first four steps of your presentation by saying, **"I'm not interested,"** or **"I don't like solicitation phone calls,"** then use the **"Easy Close"** by saying,

> **I respect that. If I could *send* you information about** (*describe what you can send*) **you would have an interest in, what would that be.** (*Assumptive.*)

Or,

> **I respect that. I would like to *send* you information about our services. Would that be all right *with* you.** (*Assumptive.*)

When prospects agree to your sending information, then you must qualify whether they truly have an interest in the information (some really do) or they are gracefully "blowing" you off the telephone. Qualify their interest by saying,

> **Once you've had the *opportunity* to review the information, I would like to gain your feedback. Does that sound fair enough.** (*Assumptive.*)

It's only fair that if you send information your prospect will allow you to recontact her or him at a future date. Amazingly you will find many prospects who will allow you to conduct a follow-up call. No longer are you sending information to be thrown away and never looked at. More important, you have a *healthy call-back.* Using the 12-step method can increase your healthy call-backs into appointments and/or sales as much as 80 percent!

The closing statement keeps the door open for future contact. The close also tests your prospects to determine whether they are in the 10 percent "no" category or are simply not in the mood at the time. Remember, about 10 percent of the market will have no interest in being prospected. Expect that, and don't be dismayed. It is not a rejection, but rather a statistical reality. Actually, you have just weeded out, in fewer than 30 seconds, someone with whom you don't want to waste additional time.

The prospect who is *truly busy* will agree with your proposal or suggest a better time to call back. The prospect who only claims to be busy will use the request for time as a *way out of the presentation* and will not want you to call back. Their response will be along the lines of **"What is this all about?"** or **"What are you selling?"** In this instance, you should be aware that your prospect may be trying to catch you off-guard, to disrupt your presentation. Your next step would be to go to the next step.

By following the 12 steps you will not be sidetracked by such responses. When your prospect gives you immediate permission to continue or asks you, **"What is this all about?"** you will be prepared to answer, because your next step has already been planned. This will keep you in control and help you remain confident throughout your presentation. Regardless if you receive a positive response to your initial request for time *or* you have to use the second function, you simply proceed to your next step.

Step 4: Purpose of Call

The importance of letting your prospects know the purpose of the telephone call (without being too specific) is to release any negative curiosity or doubts in their minds. As in step 2, you need to use an approach and hook or an interesting catchy statement without sounding too pushy or too selling. Your objective is to arouse interest so you can keep prospects' minds actively listening.

There are *two functions* in step 4:

1. Benefit statement
2. Permission to ask questions

The *benefit statement* gives the prospect a reason that you need to ask questions. If prospects have a clear understanding of why you need information, they are more free to participate in your *probing step* and give you the response you're looking for to continue on with your presentation.

The *purpose* leads you right into step 5, which is your main objective from the beginning. Step 5 is the time to get to know your prospects better, to qualify them, find out what their motivation factors are, and create a need for you, your products, and your services. Step 5 is your first target goal—your halfway point to a successful presentation. Below are some examples of stating a purpose. (Refer to Chap. 16 for additional examples.)

> *Function 1:* **I'm following up on the information I personally sent you. In order for this information to be more** *effective* ...
> *Function 2:* **I need ... > to ask you** *just* **a couple of** *quick* **questions, if you don't mind.**
>
> **My company wants to get a better feel of the market. In order for us to** *continue* **providing a better** *service,* **I need ... > to ask you** *just* **a couple of** *quick* **questions, if you don't mind.**
>
> **I have several clients in your industry who have expressed an interest in our services, and in order for me to** *continue* **providing a better** *service,* **I need ... > to ask you** *just* **a couple of** *quick* **questions, if you don't mind.**
>
> **Our company concentrates its advertising in this area. In order for us to determine ... > how** *effective* **it is, I need ... > to ask you** *just* **a couple of** *quick* **questions, if you don't mind.**

The *benefit statement* is purposely used as a lead-in to asking questions. As you have noticed, **"I need ... > to ask you** *just* **a couple of** *quick* **questions, if you don't mind,"** is *always* used in the *purpose*. This second function *never changes*. Use it exactly as written. **"I need"** shows a sense of urgency. The strategic pause after **"I need ... >"** will have your prospects unconsciously asking themselves, "You need what?" Proper use of voice inflection (a rise in tone) when you emphasize the words *just* and *quick* tells prospects you will not take up much of their time. They need to know that!

The phrase **"if you don't mind,"** makes the statement less threatening and serves to show respect. If they do mind, then you would go back to your easy close and try another time. Be sure *not* to make the phrase **"if you don't mind,"** a question by raising your voice inflection on the word *mind*. If you do, you will weaken the effect of the purpose and encourage a negative response, because you give up your control when you ask permission. Also, be sure to *smile* when you say, **"if you don't mind."** It makes a big difference in your voice projection and softens the approach slightly.

Using both functions (benefit statement and permission to ask questions) will avoid prompting your prospects into being cautious of your request for information. They will be more receptive to participating in your next step.

Step 5: Probing Questions

All the preceding steps are vital for effective prospecting because they allow you to reach the point where you can begin to uncover your prospect's wants and needs. Step 5 is the open-ended question-and-answer time, or *probing* time. In this phase, your prospects can communicate their personal wants and needs to you. Aside from eliciting needs, you will be able to create wants and needs for your prospects, while qualifying them in the process. Later on, you will learn how to adapt this step to take control of your prospect and narrow down any objections that may arise.

Effective Probing

By probing you will obtain information that will enable you to better determine the specific needs of your prospect. Thus, you will be able to promote your ideas and information in a manner that will appear to be tailor-made.

In probing a prospect, you must ask *open-ended questions* and be ready to offer *solutions or answers* quickly (during step 7, the selling step), being careful not to take up too much of the prospect's time. Do not ask closed-ended questions, since these only offer two responses—yes or no. You cannot communicate effectively if you do not create opportunities for your prospect to speak freely. The closed-ended approach also sounds like an interrogation process. The prospect can become irritated quickly. A closed-ended question might be: **"Do you provide your people with training?"** An open-ended question might be: **"What type of training do you provide for your people?"**

The answer to the open-ended question will be more than a simple yes or no. You will gather information from your prospect's response that allows you to highlight the individual's concerns and needs in your notes. You can sell your prospects' own ideas back to them when you begin to promote your products or services. Keep in mind that an open-ended question is not always also a very productive question, and it could also be threatening. For example,

"**How did you like the product?**" Your prospect's response may be, "**It's okay.**" Instead you would ask, "**Please** *describe* **what you liked about the product?**" A threatening question would be, "**Why are you not interested?**" Your prospect could respond with, "**Because I'm not!**" A more positive way of asking this question and drawing the information out from your prospect is to say, "**Please** *share* **me some of your concerns?**" or, "*What* **are some of your concerns?**" The art of asking questions doesn't come easy, but now that you are more aware of it, you will be more careful in your selection process.

How many questions are too many to ask? Your initial call objective, whether you are conducting market research, sending information, or conducting a one-call close (generating an appointment or a sale in the first contact), will determine how many questions you ask.

A good rule-of-thumb is to ask *five questions*, designed to lead you into your features and benefits (covered in step 7). Asking a prospect more than five questions increases the risk of irritating them and creating further barriers, especially if you are trying to close on your first contact.

If, however, you are conducting market research (asking survey questions) or calling with the intent of just sending information, you can ask up to 10 questions, provided that your purpose (step 4) indicates that intent. Use your listening skills to better determine your prospect's patience level.

An "open-ended" question contains one of the following: who, what, where, why, when, how, explain, describe, or share. Open-ended questions allow your prospects to do most of the talking, which gratifies their egos (who doesn't like talking about themselves?), satisfies an important need to express their wants, and helps to break through the three fear points that tend to develop during the course of prospecting.

Probing, using open-ended questions, helps you to learn about your prospect, which will help to customize your descriptions of features, functions, and benefits (found in step 7) to the prospect's needs. In short, if you allow prospects to tell you what *they* have an interest in, you will know precisely what products or services to promote in order to address their needs later on in your presentation.

By asking probing questions, you are accomplishing *three functions:*

1. Qualifying (Q) your prospects; you will ask two qualifying questions.

2. Establishing their wants (W); you will ask two want questions.

3. Creating a need (for your product or service) (C); you will ask one question, and it will be your last question.

The first two of these five questions in your probing steps are qualifying questions. (See Chap. 16 for more examples). What are *qualifying* questions? Here are some examples:

What are your company's primary methods of marketing your products and services?

Please share with me whether your company has a customer service and inside sales department?

How many employees do you have?
Where do you order your products from?
How long have they been servicing you?

In the *qualifying process,* the prospect's status is identified, and a determination is made whether the prospect is a candidate for your products and services. Based on the prospect's response, you can determine what your next question will be. This strategic planning individualizes each presentation. The next two probing questions are designed to *establish their wants.*

Establishing wants is essential to determine the level of motivation of your prospect. This will give you the ammunition you need to fulfill the needs of your prospects in step 7, features and benefits. You establish wants with probing questions. Here are some examples:

How effective is your telemarketing department, and what would you like to see improved?
What *motivated* you to select that particular training method?
Now that they have been servicing you for some time, how do you feel about their products, their service, and their rates *today*, compared to when you first acquired them?

Once you have firmly established your prospect's wants, you now need to strategically plan your *final probing question, creating a need,* that will direct your presentation into step 6 and allow you to continue with the balance of your presentation.

When creating a need, you're offering prospects something they haven't yet considered. You *can* create a need simply by asking the right qualifying and establishing-their-wants questions. It is more effective, however, to ask a creating-a-need question that cannot be answered by your prospect. This serves to arouse interest and make your prospects look at their situations in a different light.

Another perspective, perhaps a perspective the prospects themselves might have missed, just might be the incentive they need to redirect their thinking in a way that is beneficial to you and your company. (See Chap. 16 for further examples). For example:

When was the *last* time you evaluated your current production to determine ... > if you're *maximizing* its potential?
When have you *recently* examined other *successful* training programs to ensure ... > that you are developing your training methods in a way designed for *today's* market?
What steps have you taken to evaluate your *current* supplier to determine ... > that you're getting the quality you are *entitled* to and at the most *competitive* rate?

Remember, choose only one creating-a-need question, and it *must* be your final question. Be sure to ask the questions in this order: qualify, establish wants, and then create a need. You will not be able to create the need without establishing their wants, and you can not establish their wants unless you've qualified your prospects. Creating-a-need questions are lengthy; however, with proper pacing, voice inflection, and strategic pauses, they are very powerful questions. The power of this question is one reason that you want to save it for last. If you are *unable to create a need*, it will be difficult to continue with the balance of your steps. You have other possible choices, such as sending information and then following up to try again and create a need. You may also determine that your prospect may not be a viable candidate for your product or service.

It is possible that your prospect may respond to your create-a-need question in a negative manner, such as: **"I just evaluated our training department this week."** Or, **"We just finished conducting an analysis of our production methods."** How do you approach this response? This is an opportunity to try to *create a deeper need* for your product or service. Do this by continuing to ask probing questions. The concept is to first *qualify* the prospect's answer then ask another *creating-a-need question* for which the prospect may not have a viable answer, such as:

> TSR: **What were the *results* of your evaluation?**
>
> PROSPECT: **We determined that our department was functioning just fine.**

Now, you continue to ask a question for which they may *not* have an answer:

> TSR: **What steps have you taken to secure ... > a *second* opinion by our company that would offer you *additional* information, from a *fresh* perspective, to ensure ... > that you are *maximizing* your efforts in the most profitable way possible?**

Your prospects are now most likely to respond with,

> PROSPECT: **"I haven't."**

This approach serves to *reinforce* the need for your service, allowing you to continue with your presentation.

During step 5, you will need to decide where you want to take your prospect. The following can help you during your probing stage:

Four Steps of the Probing Process

1. Ask open-ended questions that *qualify* your prospect. *Establish wants* and *create needs.*

2. Listen to and mentally paraphrase all points. Write them down! (Use the listening exercise techniques).

3. Assure prospects that you want to help them select the right product or service by the type of questions you ask.

4. Identify dominant wants or needs. Later, get the prospect's agreement (discussed in step 6).

The following are some important ideas to keep in mind for effective probing:

People buy what can satisfy their own needs, not what you want for them.

Selling is determining and satisfying needs, fulfilling wants, and offering solutions.

Focus on the prospect's needs, not your own.

Probe with open-ended questions, containing the words *who, what, where, why, when, how, explain, describe,* or *share.*

During the probing step, let your prospect talk approximately 80 percent of the time. Spend 20 percent of the time asking open-ended questions. Remember, the prospect's problems and needs are the keys to your success.

Do not act or react as a salesperson by responding to your prospect's answers. This is crucial! Respond *only* with another probing question. Use this time to get to know your prospect by actively listening. Later on, prospects will get to know you (this is discussed in step 7).

There is no need to persuade your prospects to buy your product or services. By using probing open-ended questions, they will talk themselves into it!

Never begin *selling, telling,* or *demonstrating* your product or service until your prospects have *adequately established their needs.*

One very crucial guideline is that you cannot continue past step 5 unless you create a need for what you have to offer. Continuing on with your presentation will encourage unnecessary objections and reduce the likelihood of an opportunity to close down the road. Remember, prospecting is not only generating immediate revenue, it's planting seeds for a future harvest. Once you've planted a seed, keep in touch by watering it, feeding it, and eventually you'll reap the fruits of your labor!

There are so many questions you could ask, just remember as long as you use, at the beginning of your questions, the words: *who, what, where, why, when, how, explain, describe,* or *share,* and your questions are nonthreatening, your questions will be productive. Base your questions on your prospect's responses. Being able to think quickly on your feet is a tremendous advantage when prospecting. Asking the *right questions* at the *right time* is a skill. Like most skills, the ability to probe effectively must be learned. Once you are aware of the differences between open and closed-ended questions, you will have taken a significant step.

Knowing the difference between open versus closed-ended questions and implementing that knowledge are not the same. Now you need to make a point of practicing using open-ended questions. It will be helpful to evaluate others, listen to the types of questions they use, and analyze their techniques. Try to revise their closed-ended questions into open-ended ones. You will benefit from this form of exercise.

You've asked open-ended questions and have received information that qualifies your prospects and establishes their wants. You've created a need for your products and services. Now, what do you do with that information? You could go to the next step, *restate,* or close off and conduct a two-call close. Remember when you slow the process down, this impresses your prospects;

they are taken back that you didn't "pounce" on them, or, "go for the throat" as many TSRs and salespeople have done and are still doing. Your close at this point is similar to the easy close discussed during step 3, the request for time. Here is an example:

> **Thank you for sharing this information with me. I would like to** *send* **you information about our company and the products and services we offer. Would that be all right** *with* **you.** (*Assumptive statement.*)

Once your prospect has agreed to receiving your information, then qualify their interest level by saying:

> **Once you have had the** *opportunity* **to review the information, I would like to gain your feedback. Does that sound fair enough.** (*Assumptive statement.*)

When your prospect agrees to receiving a follow-up call by you, now you have a "healthy" call-back. You have increased your opportunities in closing for a sale or an appointment on your next call. Should you encounter the 10 percent who are in the market and they wondered why you didn't call yesterday, then you wouldn't want to use a two-call close. It's obvious that if they are in the market now and expressed this to you during your probing step that you wouldn't say, "I can't sell you anything today, I have to send you some information first." Conducting a two-call close is a judgment call on the TSRs part, and the decision is usually based on how the prospect responds during the probing step.

If you are to conduct a follow-up call, you need to do a postclose in order to further stabilize your prospect's agreement to receive your information and establish his or her willingness to allow you to conduct a follow-up call. Your postclose is:

> **To** *ensure* **that your information gets to you in a timely manner, I need to verify my information. Your mailing address is 1212 Step Lane, is that correct? What is your fax number? Who, other than yourself, should I make this information attention to? Thank you for the additional information. You should be receiving this by Tuesday, would Thursday be a good day for me to follow up and gain your feedback? Would you prefer I contact you during the morning or afternoon? Is 9:00 a.m. good, or would 10:00 a.m. be better? I have that on my calendar for Thursday at 10:00 a.m. In the meantime, are there any other questions or concerns you have at this time? Again, thank you for taking my call, and I look forward to gaining your feedback on Thursday at 10:00 a.m. You have a good day!**

As you can see, this is a really healthy call-back. The prospect is fully aware of your intent, but you have allowed her or him to preview you in bite-size pieces. Some may argue that prospects will eventually talk themselves out of the follow-up call, because of the postpurchase remorse (what did I just do now?). However, because you have prequalified your prospects, and you have successfully established their wants and created a need for what you have to offer, it is highly unlikely that you will lose them. Actually, you have increased your opportunities by retaining greater control of the selling process. You have more ammunition, you stand much stronger with your prospect, and, should you encounter resistance in your follow-up call, you will have an easier time overcoming this resistance! This is validated in the following steps.

Before moving on to the remainder of the 12 steps, take a look at what you have learned so far. The following is a self-test to assist you in the internalization process of the steps you have just learned. You can also provide this test when teaching others on this program.

Self-Test

1. How many fears does your prospect have?
2. What are they?
3. Which steps overcome the first fear?
4. Which steps overcome the second fear?
5. Which steps overcome the third fear?
6. Step 1 is called?
7. How many functions are in step 1?
8. What are the benefits of using a landmark or location?
9. In step 2, reference, are you to tell prospects where you got their names or how you got their names?
10. What is step 3?
11. What kind of a statement are you to use in step 3?
12. Should your prospects say they are not interested and cut you off prior to step 5, the probing step, what are you to do?
13. How do you qualify that your prospect is interested in receiving your information?
14. In step 4, purpose of call, how many functions are there?
15. What is a strategic pause?
16. How does your script indicate using voice inflection?
17. What is step 5?
18. How many questions, as a rule of thumb, should you ask?
19. How many functions are in step 5, and what are they?
20. If you did not create the need in your five questions, what are you to do next?
21. If you are unable to create the need altogether, then what should you do?
22. What is a two-call close?
23. What is the benefit of a two-call close?

24. If you wanted to conduct a one-call close, could you?

25. How do you know when a one-call close is appropriate?

If you have not been able to successfully complete the self-test, do not move on until you go back through the chapter and read the steps you need more information on. If you are in a learning mode, the disadvantage of continuing on is that you will miss essential areas within the first five steps that will assist you in successfully completing the remainder of the 12 steps.

Providing you have completed the self-test, go back through the chapter and check your answers. By doing so, you will strengthen your comprehension of the 12-step training concepts and help yourself to internalize the process. This will give you greater confidence when conducting your live presentations.

Step 6: Restating

The Bridge That Leads to the Selling Step

During step 5, probing, your prospect is actively answering your questions. Once you have completed probing, prospects don't remember exactly what they had said. Therefore, in the *restate* step you need to summarize the prospect's responses, emphasize the important ideas he or she gave you, and reflect them back to the prospect in a more dynamic way—thus prospects can see their own expressed wants and needs from a fresh and objective perspective. This puts your prospects on the out circle looking into their needs, and, later in your presentation during the trial close, should they respond negatively, you can reflect back to the restate step and make them more accountable.

By *restating* the information your prospect shared with you, your words reinforce the prospect's own sense of what is important. Prospects will agree with points you found most valuable to them. From this information, you will be able to begin determining what direction you should take during the next step (step 7—features and benefits).

There are two functions in step 6. The first is to *summarize* what the prospect just said, but in a more positive way. The second function is to get a *confirmation* from your prospect. This will give you a "yes" response, which you may need later during the objection-handling process—this is how accountability comes into play. Below are examples of restating:

> **Based on what you've said, Ms. Smith, your company sees the *value* of XYZ product. Unfortunately, you have not been given the *opportunity* to conduct a competitive analysis to *determine* ... > the cost-effectiveness of your current supplier. That comparison would give your company a better *competitive* edge in the marketplace. Is that correct?**
>
> **I want to be sure I have the information correct. You're currently working with XYZ company, and you were *motivated* to select that company because of its competitive rates. However, you expressed a concern that you haven't**

heard from your representative for some time, and the firm's rates are not as good as when you initially acquired service. Customer service and quality are *important* to you, yet you have not made a recent comparison to *determine* ... > how you can get the service you're entitled to while still meeting your needs cost-effectively. Is that correct?

As you can see, the restatement qualifies and summarizes the information your prospect has given you during your probing step. By enhancing the information, you encourage your prospect to agree with what you've just said. This is called *indirect selling*. Be careful not to overexaggerate your restatement, it must be closely correlated to what your prospect said, but your rendition should give an even more positive emphasis of the prospect's views.

Make it a priority to get good at restating! It is a crucial part of prospecting, it allows you to remain in control, and it will prove extremely effective in handling objections.

Restate Exercise

Before you begin this exercise, it is important to clarify what is meant by *positive* and *negative* responses. A positive response is in your favor. If your prospect responds in a way that indicates a need for your product or service, this is the positive response you are looking for.

An indication that a prospect doesn't need your product or service is considered a negative response. When this happens, you *must keep probing* to get a positive response to create a need for your products or services. Remember that in step 5, probing, this was called *creating a deeper need*. Should you not be able to create the need from your fifth to seventh question, you need to conclude your presentation. Use your easy close, offer to send information, and try again later. Now is not the time to sell your prospect. The following are examples of positive and negative responses from your prospect and how you should respond with questions to try to create a deeper need and to successfully conduct your restate step:

> *Positive:* I'm unhappy with the service. *Responding probe:* What would you like to see improved?
> *Negative:* I'm very happy with the service. *Responding probe:* What is it that keeps you a satisfied customer?

The goal here is to try and find out what your prospect is unhappy about, so that you can fulfill needs in your selling step. If prospects are happy with whom they do business with, you have less opportunity to continue with your presentation. Therefore, you want to try to find out what keeps a prospect a satisfied customer. Why is that so important? This will enable you to try to provide the same service or product. Your objective is to add more value compared to what the prospect currently has. You want to develop some type of an incentive for the prospect to do business with you.

You now have an understanding of the difference between positive and negative answers. You have learned how to probe deeper to create a deeper need for your products or services. Now go ahead and try the following exercise so you can get good at restating.

List the five key open-ended questions you plan to use when prospecting. Be sure to use two *qualifiers*, two *establishing wants*, and one *creating a need* as your last question. Your key open-ended questions are:

1. _____

2. _____

3. _____

4. _____

5. _____

Now list the possible responses your prospect might give you. Try to give just the positive ones first. We'll work on the negatives later.

1. _____

2. _____

3. _____

4. _____

5. _____

On the basis of your prospect's response, how would you restate? Take a look at the previous examples to give you an idea of what you could say.
Let's take three of your prospect's responses from the five and turn them into negatives.

1. _____

2. _____

3. _____

On the basis of your prospect's response, what questions could you ask? Keep in mind that you need to turn those negative responses into positive ones. Your objective is to be able to create a deeper need to conduct your restating successfully.

1. _____

2. _____

3. _____

If you are able to gain a positive response and have created a need for you to continue on with your presentation, go ahead and conduct your restating.

Restating takes some practice to sound smooth and confident. Concentrate on asking the right questions to gain the kind of responses you're looking for. This will give you the bridge that leads you into your next step, which is to start selling your products, your services, or the appointment.

Step 7: Selling

Features, Functions, and Benefits

Below are *four functions* necessary for an effective selling presentation. Learning and customizing them to your prospect's specific needs will greatly enhance your success with the *12-step* method. It is important that *all four functions* are implemented. It is common, during many sales presentations, to bypass one or two of these functions. Doing so makes the presentation incomplete and increases the risk of an unsuccessful close.

One of the following functions is eliminated during most presentations. As you read on, try to determine which function is most often neglected.

Feature. What product or service you want to promote.

Function. What the product or service does.

Implied benefits. What your prospect is going to get out of the product or service.

Stated benefits. How much money or time is made or saved by using the product or service.

Features.   Introducing features is the *first approach* in promoting a product or a service. Step 5 of the 12 steps helped you to identify your prospect's needs. The features in this step tell your prospect which specific product or service will be promoted. This will assist you in customizing your presentation to meet the individual needs of your prospect. Example of feature words include:

Consultation, ABC company, XYZ services, competitive analysis, telemarketing training, evaluation, 123 computer

Function.   Describing the *function* will help you to pinpoint your prospect's needs prior to describing the benefits. The function is what the product does, how it works, and what different needs it will address. You will want to identify which functions are the most important to your prospect by evaluating the responses you get from your open-ended questions (step 5). Examples of function phrases include:

Provide information, 20 years in the business, provide a second opinion, offers objection handling training, ideas are provided to ..., define financial needs, analyze existing programs, 480 megabytes of memory, 24 hours service

Implied Benefits.   Prospects do not purchase a product based on its features or its functions. Their decisions are based more upon the benefits they receive from the features and functions. The *implied benefits* tell your prospect what "good" they will derive by using the product or the service. There is a tendency to pass over this all-important function, but it should not be ignored. If this benefit is not included with the other elements of your presentation, you may end up losing the prospect altogether. The implied benefits will enhance the "push" of your prospect's "hot buttons," because this function appeals to the emotional aspect of the sales process. The implied benefits are what justify the cost! Words and phrases associated with implied benefits include:

Confidence, success, satisfaction, self-improvement, increased knowledge, peace of mind, improved performance, quality control, customer-oriented

Stated Benefits.   The *stated benefits* are the bottom line. Most likely, your prospect will be thinking about this throughout your presentation. The stated benefits relate to *money* or *time* made or saved by using the product or service. However, all too often, this step is overemphasized. Many salespeople believe that the money issue is *all* the prospect wants to hear, and so this benefit is expressed by the salesperson throughout the presentation. The stated benefit *is* essential, it's important to use it when you're trying to accomplish the primary objective, which may be to bring the prospect in, send a representative out, place the order today, or create a favorable enough impression so that your prospect will remember you and your company based solely on your conversation. However, remember that the implied benefit is what "justifies" the cost. Words and phrases associated with stated benefits include:

Profitable, cost-effective, productive, time-saving, faster speed, reduces down-time, affordable, increased value, lowers overhead, increased income.

In *"Stated Benefits"* you are telling the prospect how they will earn or save their time and/or money by saying "yes."

Key Points in Features and Benefits

The prospect buys *benefits*, not features. It is important that you identify and continue to evaluate the differences between features and benefits. There is a tendency to become absorbed in stressing the features of a product over the benefits a prospect will receive. This can be very detrimental when you try to *get reaction* in step 8 and *trial-close* in step 9. Time spent talking about size, weight, shape, durability, and performance detract from the overall objective of the call, which is to sell the benefits, not the features. It is important to translate the features of your product or service into the benefits your prospect will receive.

Translating Features into Benefits

Now you've learned the four functions that must be used, in specific order, to make step 7 effective. The following is a model to use. Simply fill in the blanks with information related to your products or services.

Mr./s. Prospect, from what you have told me I recommend (features). I recommend this because (functions). What this will do for you is (implied benefits) and, more important, ... > you can (stated benefits)."

In actual use, it might sound more like this:

> **I recommend ... > a consultation. I recommend this because it will provide you with <u>information about other services</u> you're *entitled* to. What this will do for you is ... > update your information and provide you with <u>more diversifi-cation to choose from.</u> This information will *increase* your knowledge and awareness to give you the *confidence* when you're ready to upgrade. More important, ... > you will <u>save the time of</u> *researching* <u>the information</u> on your own and can reduce your overhead.**

While you are describing the features, the prospect may be thinking "Why should I buy this product?" or "Why should I make an appointment?" Directing prospects' attention to the benefits they have to gain will enable them to answer these questions themselves. As a rule, people don't want to be sold—but they will eagerly help sell themselves.

Always describe your features, functions, implied benefits and stated benefits strict-ly in this order. By doing so, you will stress your selling points in an order your prospect will be able to recall. Don't mix them up, since this will confuse your prospect. Limit yourself to *two features* in step 7. Otherwise, you run the risk of overselling your prospect.

Remember, one of these four functions is neglected during most presenta-tions. Which one do you think it is? The one function that is passed over dur-ing most presentations is implied benefits. Implied benefits appeal to the emo-tional side of the sale. They are the "sizzle" in your presentation. Without them, you are only addressing issues related to money or time, that is, the stat-ed benefits. Why do you think consumers patronize higher-priced stores when the same products can be obtained elsewhere for less money? Because of the implied benefits!! They'll outweigh the cost issue almost every time.

Below is an important list to bring to your attention. When constructing your features, functions, and benefits, think about the reasons that prospects will say yes to your products or services. This list will help you to formulate your own customized list:

Reasons That Prospects Buy Products or Services

1. Desire wealth
2. Desire health
3. Image, admiration, status
4. Satisfy desire
5. Amusement
6. Safety and security for self or family
7. Perceived usefulness or value
8. Self-improvement
9. Desire to save time
10. Comfort

11. Potential to be trouble- or worry-free

Which of the above apply to implied benefits and which to stated benefits? Note that the decision to purchase is influenced only *partially* by financial considerations. Stress those implied benefits!

Features, Function, and Benefit Examples

The accompanying table is an example of features, functions, and benefits for various products and services (Customize your own to tailor them to your products and services):

> I recommend <u>the 12-step training program</u>. I recommend this because it provides you and your TSRs a <u>step-by-step process that guides you from your introduction to your postclose</u>. It is also designed to <u>overcome the three fears your prospects have</u> when vying for their business. This offers you <u>greater control of your presentation</u>. Also you will <u>reduce burnout</u> that is typical in most telemarketing applications due to high prospect-resistance factors. The step concept will make it <u>easier to teach</u> others thereby offering <u>more continuity</u> in your telemarketing operation. More important, ... > the 12 steps can <u>increase closing percentages</u> as high as 80 percent! Thereby gaining a <u>greater profitability</u> in your bottom line.

By carefully selecting the feature, function, and benefits statements, you can be creative with step 7 and make it come alive in your prospect's mind. Tell prospects what *they* want to hear! You will have the confidence to do that, because they told you what it was they wanted to hear in the probing step and you reinforced this in the restating step.

Features (I recommend)	Functions (I recommend this because)	Implied Benefits (What this means)	Stated Benefits (More important)
XYZ Computer	280 megs memory	Advanced technology	Increase speed
Our training	20 years of research	Motivate new ideas	More business
ABC Dry Cleaning	24-hour service	Customer satisfaction	Saves you time
Life insurance	Funds in case of death	Secure, safe, reliable	Affordable
Our company	In business for 15 years	Reliable, diverse products	Cost-effective
A consultation	Provides information	Increase your knowledge	More value
Evaluation	Second opinion	Informed decision	Saves time
This seminar	Selling skills	Advanced techniques	Higher closing

The following is an exercise that will help you to practice translating features into benefits. Be creative with your own verbiage and style of delivery! Try creating your own features, functions, and benefits that are customized for your company's products or services in the accompanying blank table. If you are making an appointment, try selling the appointment. Be careful not to recommend an appointment as your feature word. It's too strong at this point, wait for the close. Instead, use the word consultation or evaluation. Remember to use translating features into benefits to lead you from one function to the next, as in this series: "I recommend," "I recommend this because," "What this means to you is," "More important, this will."

Features	Functions	Implied Benefits	Stated Benefits

Effective Selling Tips

Here is a checklist of selling ideas to remember when entering into steps 7, 8, and 9.

√ *Appeal to* as many of your prospect's senses as possible (i.e., taste, touch, sight, hearing, and smell).

√ *Allow your prospect* a feeling of control without surrendering total control yourself.

√ *Prospects do not care about features* as much as they want to hear the *benefits.* Stress benefits!

√ *Most purchases are guided* by emotion rather than logic. Use emotion-packed words to stimulate interest.

√ *Get your prospect's reaction by asking:* "How important is this to you?" or "How valuable would this service be to you?"

√ *Answer premature price questions* with a request for information: "I know price is important to you and that you want the best price possible. Before I can offer any figures, I need...> a little more information from you." Begin taking your control back by asking open-ended questions.

√ *When an objection occurs,* probe the prospect (ask open-ended questions). Then offer recommendations with features and benefits and get the prospect's reaction. If the reaction is negative, probe again, and pursue other methods of handling objections (see step 10, objections)

√ *Paint word pictures in your prospect's mind* when describing features, functions, implied and stated benefits.

√ *Name-drop or use testimonials* from other satisfied customers as additional selling points.

√ *Use strategic pauses* to enhance the dynamics of your benefits. This will gain a few additional seconds of your prospect's attention.

Validating Your Claims

Before you can expect a prospect to do business with you, your prospect must *believe the claims you make* during your presentation. It is not enough for *you* to believe these claims. Your prospect must also believe in them. To do this you must validate your claims. Validation occurs when you:

√ *Portray* yourself as educated and knowledgeable.

√ *Project* a professional and positive image of your company (establishing company credibility and company history).

√ *Advertise* satisfaction in your products or services (testimonials by others, names of satisfied customers).

√ *Stress* the benefits to validate how effective the features and functions are.

√ *Validate* your claims from the beginning to the end of your presentation.

√ *Create* a positive image of you and your company in your prospect's mind. Many salespeople try to negotiate and close before they have validated their claims. Failure to validate usually results in an unsuccessful presentation. *Validation must take place before closing.*

√ Don't speak in absolute terms. Preface your statements with qualifiers: **"It seems to me that," "Others have found," "Most of the time this will."**

Buyers are sensitive to unreasonable statements and claims. *You must validate, not exaggerate!*

You must continue to motivate your prospect during step 7. Help prospects choose a particular product, brand, or service. Below are three elements to emphasize during this step:

√ Product or service will do what it claims to do.

√ Availability will meet the prospect's needs or situation.

√ Product or service will last or satisfy future needs.

The following are some points to remember:

■ Once people place their trust in you, they will believe what you say.

■ Do not exaggerate or make unjustified claims. Make your points believable. You must preserve your credibility.

- Price is *not* the most important factor in a sale. The prospect is looking for *value!*

Step 8: Getting Reaction

Once you have completed step 7, you need to encourage a positive response. This is accomplished in *step 8, getting reaction*. This serves to test whether you have successfully satisfied your prospects' needs—did you tell them what they wanted to hear? Your prospects' responses enable you to encourage and motivate them into responding positively to the benefits. This positive response will also help you confidently move on to your next step, which is trial closing, step 9.

Getting a positive response assists you should your prospect offer resistance when entering into step 10, objections. You can refer to the positive things your prospect said during step 8. This technique is called *keep selling*. Getting your prospects to agree with you in this step is crucial to successfully completing your presentation. Step 8 must not ask for a commitment, since that would ensure a negative response. For a positive response, here are some examples of good questions:

> **How important is this information?** (*when setting an appointment*).
> **How valuable is this product or service?** (*when selling over the telephone*).

These examples are generalized; however, you can create your own. When doing so, keep the get-reaction question open-ended and nonthreatening. Don't push your prospect. You can have confidence that your prospects will interact and put themselves in a position to sell themselves provided you have fulfilled their needs in step 7 (tell them what *they want to hear*). How do you know what their needs are? In step 5, your probing step, you established their wants and created a need. By successfully performing in step 5, you were able to continue on with your presentation. If you hadn't accomplished getting positive responses during step 5, you wouldn't have been able to get this far.

The open-ended question in step 8 is designed to elicit the positive response you need to get to continue onto step 9, the trial close. A positive response in step 8 will lessen the chances of your receiving an objection during your trial close.

If you should get a negative response in step 8, refer to the "reflect" method in the objection handling in step 10. This will teach you how to effectively overcome the negative response. Whenever you receive a negative response in step 8, such as, **"No it's not important,"** this is an indicator that you did not create a need during step 5, probing. Instead, you chose to continue on with your presentation with a prospect who really wasn't interested. However, if you felt you did create a need, then you had no impact in your selling step, step 7. You need to work on your voice inflection, strategic pausing, your variable speeds, and your selection on emotionally charged words. Otherwise, assuming you have gained a positive response during step 8, you now may proceed to your next step, the trial close.

Step 9: Trial Close

The *trial close* has two functions. The first allows you to summarize the product or service benefits for the prospect. The second function asks for a commitment; this is called a *trial-closing question*. This question must be closed-ended. You want either a yes or a no response. A trial-closing question allows your prospect to inquire about any missing pieces.

If you follow the 12 steps precisely, you should not receive objections until the trial close, which is a time that will encourage objections. If objections are to arise, you want to address them during the trial close rather than in your close. An outstanding presentation (steps 1 to 8) should elicit a *positive response* during trial close, preventing objections from surfacing (eliminating the need for step 10) and making the close (step 11) the simplest of your 12 steps. Here are some examples of a trial close:

> **This gives me an *opportunity* to introduce myself and demonstrate the services I provide my clients. When you're ready to *enhance* the benefits and services you're entitled to, my *intention* is that you would *consider* my services. Does that sound fair enough.** (*Make this an assumptive.*)

If you are selling your products or services, then your trial close would sound much different:

> **Our Objection Hotline membership will allow you <u>unlimited training support</u> over the telephone. Our <u>trained consultants</u> will coach and role play with you while offering words of encouragement to keep you *motivated*. In this way ... > you will have *greater* success in *achieving* the <u>results you are anticipating</u>. Your membership investment is only $1299.00 per year, and each call you make on the hot line is *completely* <u>toll free to you</u>. If you could *increase* your production each month by a *minimum* of 10 percent, would the Objection Hotline pay for itself."** (*Assumptive.*)

The following two trial closes are very aggressive and should not be used as a first option, except whenever you're faced with a prospect who has a bottom-line or a controlling personality. These trial closes are also very effective, especially, when used after certain objections and you need to trial-close again.

> **We have a *challenge* offer for our prospective clients. Try our products once and allow us the *opportunity* <u>to serve you at our best</u>. If we are *unable to impress* you with your first order, we <u>simply don't</u> *deserve* <u>any of your</u> *continued* business. Does that sound fair enough.** (*Assumptive.*)

> **I realize your time is valuable. Allow me 15 minutes. If I'm unable to *impress* you with our products or services within <u>the first 15 minutes of our time together</u>, I won't take up any more of *your* time. I <u>simply don't</u> *deserve* <u>your future business</u>. Does that sound fair enough.** (*Assumptive.*)

Whether you are closing for an appointment or a sale and what your product or services are will greatly affect what type of trial close you use. The rule-of-thumb is to *summarize* your benefits and ask for an attempt to close. If your prospect is receptive and her or his needs have been satisfied, you should be ready to close. Otherwise, objections may surface. When objections do surface, you should be prepared to handle them.

Remember, in many scenarios, *an objection during trial close may be an indication that your presentation needs further improvement.* You need to review how you executed each of the previous steps and where you need to strengthen the process. However, some prospects will interject an objection only to test your persistence, to see how far you're willing to go to get their business.

Should your prospect object during your trial close, you would go directly to step 10, objections. This step is discussed in Chap. 15.

However, let's assume your prospect gives you a positive response in your trial close; your next step then is to "close." This is step 11.

Step 11: Close

An effective *close* is the natural conclusion to all the previous steps. Whether you do close, however, will depend on how successfully the preceding steps were performed. You should have confidence in your close, provided you received yes responses in getting reaction during step 8 and in your trial close in step 9.

By avoiding tricky, slick, or fast-talking techniques, the close should simply come down to asking prospects to buy or to make a commitment to see you. (Research reveals that the majority of sales calls end without ever asking the prospect to say yes!). *Learning when to close is very important.* The right time to ask is when you think prospects will say yes! You will know when a prospect is ready to say yes by asking a trial-closing question in step 9. For example, **"Does that sound fair enough,"** or **"Would that be all right *with* you."** (Remember to use the assumptive approach in your trial closing question.)

The 12 steps guided you through your presentation while increasing your ability to effectively close. Once you have created the need for your products or services in probing in step 5, the balance of your presentation is pretty much on automatic pilot. However, don't be overzealous. You still need to fulfill their needs in your selling step, gain their reactions in step 8, then trial-close in step 9. Although these steps don't require as much thought process as your probing step, you still need to incorporate them precisely as instructed into your presentation. All the steps work uniquely together and bypassing one or more of the steps would hinder you from a smooth close.

Four Action Guides

Here are *four action guides* to a successful close:

1. Get opinions and a positive response during step 8:

   How valuable would that be for you?

2. *Summarize the benefits* and give a positive reinforcement, Ask a trial-closing question to get a yes or no response:

Would that be all right *with* you.
Does that sound fair enough.

3. If you receive a no response in your trial close, narrow down the real issues and *outweigh them with benefits* that will overcome any issues your prospect may have; be sure to get a positive yes response before closing (see dealing with objections in step 10).

4. Reinforce your prospect's commitment in the close, step 11; then pause, wait patiently for a reply.

Whenever you are unable to close effectively, it means you did not complete a prior step—something went wrong in your presentation. Be sure that you have done the following in the order listed below:

Establish rapport (*steps 1 to 4*). Earn the right to conduct your presentation.

Probe (*step 5*). Create the need for what you are offering.

Restate (*step 6*). Reinforce your prospect's needs.

Sell (*step 7*). Fulfill your prospect's needs through discussion of features, functions, and benefits.

Get reaction (*step 8*). Encourage a positive response.

Trial-close (*step 9*). Summarize and ask for a positive commitment.

Handle objections (*step 10*). Negotiate and outweigh your prospect's resistance and aim to get a positive response.

Close (*step 11*). Assume your position.

Do your postclose (*step 12*). Finalize the order or appointment.

The following are points to remember:

- A trial-closing question asks for a commitment; a close reinforces the decision.

- You should begin asking a trial-closing question after you summarize the features and benefits.

- Ask a closing question only after you receive two or more positive answers during restating in step 6, getting reaction in step 8, or trial-closing in step 9.

- Help prospects make decisions by pointing out how the benefits outweigh the costs. This occurs during the first function in your trial close, when you summarize the benefits.

- When you close, expect prospects to say yes! Anticipate a positive response. Use proper voice inflection, to create increased confidence in your projection. Assume your close will be positive.

- When you ask prospects to commit, be quiet until they respond.

Once you have accomplished these action guides successfully, use one of the following closes that best fits your closing objectives.

Three Popular Closes

As you have discovered, by step 11, the close, now *is* the right time to close. You probably have heard that there are over a hundred ways to close. In reality there are only three closing techniques to remember. There may be many different ways to express it, and that is a choice you can make on your own. The important issue is to *close!*

The examples below offer ideas for you to be creative with your own style of close. Choose a close that not only feels comfortable to you but that also correlates with whom you are prospecting. For example, you would not want to use the direct close with someone who is an easy-going prospect; the direct close would be more useful with strong personality types.

The Assumptive Close. Ask for a decision, assuming your prospect will make an affirmative, major buying commitment. For example:

In addition to the benefits that we've discussed, is there anything else we need to consider before we schedule delivery?

In addition to the benefits that we've discussed, is there anything else we need to consider prior to our meeting?

The Contained-Choice Close. Ask your prospect to select one or two proposed delivery or appointment dates:

What about a delivery on the first, or would the fifteenth be better for you?
I can schedule an appointment for you on Tuesday, or would Thursday be better?
What time of the day is better for you and Mr./s. Green, during the morning, afternoon, or evening?

Direct Close. Simply ask prospect to take the appropriate closing action. You do not ask prospects to buy, but you specifically ask them to take a closing action. For example:

Who, other than yourself, do we need to OK the agreement?
How much down-payment can you provide today?
I need a requisition from you so I can get a purchase order.
How would you like to process this?
A letter of agreement would expedite your order today!
I would like to schedule delivery for you. Would Friday meet your needs?

Be creative! Combine your closes. A combined close, for instance, could be an *assumptive contained choice* or a *direct and contained choice.* An example of an assumptive and contained choice close might be:

I'm going to process your order today. How would you like the product delivered, COD or credit?

A direct and contained choice might be:

Who other than yourself, do we need to consider when scheduling our appointment? Would you prefer mornings or afternoons?

Step 12: Postclose

Eliminate the Prospect's Postpurchase Remorse

Once you have received a commitment from your prospect, you need to reinforce or strengthen that commitment with a *postclose*. Many TSRs are instructed, "Close and get off quickly." In reality, what they're being told is, "Close and get off quickly, before prospects change their mind!" You do not need to be concerned, provided you have followed your presentation as instructed. If you have received a yes response in step 6, step 8, and step 9 and you were able to close effectively, remaining on the telephone and gaining additional information is just a part of your presentation, and your prospects will continue to be receptive.

The postclose step will decrease cancellation, rescheduling, or no-shows. Postclose serves to overcome the third fear point ("What have I done?"). Wouldn't you rather have this surface now as opposed to later when you no longer have control? The following is a checklist of what you need to do in your postclose:

- Highlight points that are in prospect's best interest.
- Offer motivating words of encouragement to bring excitement to the idea.
- Ensure that all decision makers will be present for the appointment.
- Ask open-ended questions that will further your direct presentation.
- Remind prospects of their commitment to you.
- Go over scheduled appointments or delivery dates.
- To end your conversation, add any other ending in your close that would fit in at this point.
- Thank prospects for their time and consideration.
- Never hang up first.

The following is an example of a postclose:

To save you time and allow me to *personalize* **the information, I need ... > a little more information from you.**

1. **How many inside sales representatives do you have?**
2. **What is the percentage of turnover you've been experiencing within the past year?**
3. **How motivated are your people when it comes to learning new training concepts?**

4. Other than yourself, who do we need to include in our meeting that would have a part in selecting a training program for your company?

Thank you for the additional information. I'm looking forward to meeting with you personally on Tuesday, the 5th at 2:00 p.m. What other concerns can I address before our meeting? Have a good day!

A selling example of a postclose would be:

Thank you for your order. To ensure that your product arrives to you in a timely manner, I need ... > a little more information.

1. Who, other than yourself, should I make this attention to?
2. What is the correct spelling of your last name?
3. What department should I have this directed to?
4. What is your billing number?

Thank you for the additional information. I will be processing your order today, and you should expect your package within the next 3 weeks. Should you have any questions or concerns, ask for me, Debbie Smith, and I will be happy to assist you. Is there anything else we need to consider before I finalize your order? Have a good day!

The Confirmation

When you are generating appointments, postclose will help you to *strengthen* your *confirmation.* You've completed your presentation. The following is an example that will give you an idea of how to confirm your prospect's commitment without creating a negative response.

Good afternoon, I need ... > to speak with Mrs. Bennett, please. This is Gregg Davis with ABC Company. I just called to let you know that I have the information prepared as *promised,* and I am looking forward to meeting with you and Mr. Bennett tomorrow afternoon at 3:00 p.m.! Thank you.

Notice that the word *promised* is emphasized. Its use reinforces the idea that you have followed through for your prospects and have already begun to provide service to them even before meeting them. Be sure to request prospects who originally made appointments with you so that, should prospects tell you that their partners are not as interested in appointments as the prospects are, you have greater control of turning possible cancellations back into confirmed appointments (see objections and answers in step 10). Note that if there is more than one decision maker, you need to include them all in your confirmation statement, as shown in the example above.

Always confirm the day *before* your meeting. Never confirm the same day; this will increase your cancellation ratio. Many salespeople will try to confirm by saying, "I just called to say I'm on my way." Most people will try to renege their commitment at the last minute, and the response is usually, "I'm glad you called, we have to reschedule." Others will not confirm and just show up.

When that happens on a residential appointment, the lights gradually turn off as you drive up, or they don't answer their door.

When it's business to business, the secretary typically says, "I'm sorry he is in an important meeting, and I am instructed not to disturb him," or "Ms. Green had an emergency and is not able to be here, but she requested that you leave your information with her assistant." Have you ever had that happen? Anything could happen between the time you made the appointment and the time you are to meet with your prospects. Of course, provided you have done an effective presentation, this is unlikely to occur. However, one of the most common reasons for cancellations is that there is another partner involved who could change the quality of your appointment.

When you confirm the day before, your prospects do not feel pressured. This will help you to remind your prospects of their commitment to you. Should there be a need to reschedule, you can plan your day more productively. It's important, however, that you do not, at the time you make appointments, tell prospects that you will call the day before to confirm or offer to give your phone number unless asked. Otherwise, you imply that the appointment is flexible and that it's not necessarily a firm commitment. That implication increases the chance of having the appointment rescheduled and having "something else come up."

12-Step Overview

Congratulations! You have completed the 12 steps! Spend time daily on studying, learning, and applying each of the 12 steps. You will notice within 30 days of a committed effort a marked improvement in your prospecting and selling efforts. Don't just be interested in the information but make a strong commitment to get good at using the steps on the telephone. It is the most valued tool you have, besides your voice! *To your success!*

To master this step-by-step concept you *must* apply the information learned. The following are some helpful tips to make this learning process easier: Memorize the 12 steps. Know what each of the steps are. Once you have memorized each of the steps, now memorize the *functions* of each step. For example, step 1, introduction, has five functions:

1. *Greeting:* "Good morning."
2. *Establish contact:* "I need ... > to speak with Mr. or Mrs. Jones, please."
3. *First name cue:* "Mr. *John* Jones?"
4. *Introduce yourself and company:* "Hello Mr. Jones this is Jennifer Smith, I represent ABC company."
5. *Give your location or landmark:* "... and we're *located* ... > near City Hall on 10th and Palm."

Memorize the benefits of using each step and the benefits of each function. For example:

Greeting is to professionalize my introduction and set myself apart from a solicitation or personal call.

Establish contact is to ensure that I'm speaking with the correct person without making assumptions (assuming it's Mr. Jones when it may be Mrs. Jones with a low-sounding voice). Also, in residential prospecting, I keep my statement general such as, **"I need ... > to speak with Mr. or Mrs. Jones, please."**

"I need" with a strategic pause (... >) expresses a sense of urgency and helps me remain in control while keeping the prospect's mind actively listening. Also, this statement may elicit useful information about the prospect's marital status (single, widowed, divorced, separated)

Be able to do this for *all steps and functions.* If you understand the benefits and you understand why each function is used, you'll have greater confidence in your presentation.

Rewrite your sample scripts to fit your personality and style of delivery. Use verbiage you're comfortable with. *Practice* with the 12 steps on the telephone by making real contacts for at least 2 hours nonstop, without interruptions (coffee breaks, personal calls, other business, and so on). *Tabulate* your prospecting efforts to determine areas in which you need improvement. *Record* your live prospecting calls. Play them back and listen to your delivery and style. *Ask yourself:*

√ Are you enthusiastic about your product or service?

√ Do you project a positive, confident image?

√ How well are you following the 12 steps?

√ Would you be impressed with you?

This can be an *extremely valuable* exercise, and its usefulness never diminishes. Get into the routine of recording yourself at regular intervals so you'll always be sharp and at your best! Be aware that you'll probably be your won toughest critic, so don't be too hard on yourself. It also helps to get an opinion from others who you trust to offer honest, constructive advice.

14

The Customer Service Representative Presentation

The customer service representative (CSR) presentation is similar to the 12-steps outbound prospecting chapter in the use of step method. However, the information here is directed to handling in-bound call activities. Due to the rising number of infomercials on television, along with an increase in mail orders and 800 numbers, the volume of incoming calls has increased dramatically, with the typical response being the "numbers game." This chapter addresses how to handle the greater number of incoming calls while constantly meeting the objectives of customer servicing and quickly closing the sale. Furthermore, this chapter addresses issues pertaining to call handling by the switchboard operator, the receptionist, and the secretary. Some issues of call handling include how to properly get information and take a message without sounding like an interrogation is being conducted, how to properly put a customer "on hold" when directing the call to another department, and how to prevent your customer from getting the runaround.

This chapter offers the rookie and the veteran CSR alike a complete step-by-step training course that takes the guesswork out of your customer-servicing departments. It is specifically designed for today's market in which consumers are desperately awaiting major improvements in how companies approach and handle their customers. With so much customer servicing of poor quality in today's market, you, as a CSR, must develop techniques that will distinguish you from competing industries.

The 12 steps for the CSR use the unique service approach that is both customized and individualized to your servicing efforts. The approach is not the typical frontal assault employed by many customer service representatives, who are pressured in handling volumes of calls ever minute, 6 to 8 hours a day. This 12-step method allows you to immediately attempt to establish a rapport and be personable but not personal. The approach also projects a more professional image of you and your company while offering that extra customer service. By accomplishing all the above, you will reap a harvest of long-lasting, repeating business and even gain referrals!

No longer are we just handling in-bound activity to "take the order." These people calling into your company *want service*. Many commercials and direct forms of advertisement are bringing the calls in, but those in-bound calls are not always the easy sale we've been accustomed to in years' past. Because of our highly competitive marketplace, consumers are very cautious as to their product selection and the company that will stand behind the warranty, not to mention the consumer's own pocketbook! Money is not the primary issue of why a consumer will buy from you. On the contrary, consumers are buying value, so don't start lowering your prices!

Many surveys and studies have proved that consumers won't mind spending more for a product or service as long as they feel they are getting *good value for their investment.* To validate this observation further, consider why consumers shop at a higher-priced store to purchase a particular item when they can get it elsewhere for a much lower cost? Perhaps it is the return policy or the guarantee, or maybe they just prefer the ambiance. In any case, not all consumers will shop at higher-priced stores, it all depends on their budget, their motivation, and their awareness.

Place yourself in the position of a consumer for a moment. If you could financially afford to buy that new exercise machine you just viewed on television, you were in the market for one, you knew it would give you results within 30 days, and if you were not completely satisfied you had a money-back guarantee, would you invest in it yourself? Of course you would. Let's break that question apart: financially afford it = *budget*, you are in the market = *motivation*, 30-day money-back guarantee = *awareness*.

Infomercials (30-minute commercials) are extremely profitable for companies who can afford the up-front cost to produce them. The benefit to a company is the extra time it has to demonstrate its products or services in order to captivate their audience. Instead of airing a commercial in 30- or 60-second segments sporadically throughout the day for 352 days out of the year, an infomercial can have a company's spot on television only once a week for 30 minutes. This can generate thousands of calls with potentially motivated buyers. As you may have noticed, I said "potentially" motivated buyers. The infomercial definitely attracts the 10 percent who are in the market. The commercial aired at the right time and the right place will bring in the easy sale. However, most of the calls that the CSR will get are from those for whom the commercial sparked only an interest, although enough of an interest to encourage the in-bound caller to seek additional information. This is where many inside salespeople, who are considered CSRs or have been trained as such, fall short. Their training has been more concentrated in taking the order as opposed to making the sale.

This chapter teaches you how to determine which are the calls where one can simply take the order and how to identify those prospects who need more selling. In reality, the CSR doesn't have much time to spend with each caller. However, if the company wants to increase sales to surpass the 10 percent in the market who readily say yes, then it is necessary to incorporate selling skills into the CSR environment. Having more CSRs who are capable of selling, rather than just taking the order, is something we are going to see more of.

Depending on how many CSRs are on the floor handling the in-bound call activity and taking into consideration peak call times. You may want to have the CSR offer to send information in response to a particular call. Within a few days of mailing your product or service information, the outbound department elects a telemarketing sales representative (TSR) to conduct the follow-up call to attempt to close the sale. Having both the in-bound and out-bound departments working and communicating together will further increase your company's bottom line.

The CSR needs to learn how to handle the volume of calls swiftly, efficiently, and professionally while using more progressive selling approaches that are customer-service-oriented. Just as important, CSRs need to learn how to handle and facilitate "bad-willed" customers while keeping a positive attitude throughout the day.

This focus on the 12 steps to successful customer service does not imply that you use all 12 steps. Depending on one's job function and each call one receives, one would determine which steps to use and at what point in the presentation the steps would be best utilized. The idea of the step method is to guide CSRs through the process and assist them in handling every situation. Regardless of the call or what mood the customer is in at the time of the call, you should be able to handle most situations with a positive, professional, and persuasive attitude. By using the step method, you will feel better at the end of each day knowing that you have done your job well!

Step 1: Introduction

The opening statement of an in-bound call is the front cover of your company's image. With only seconds to make an impression, the opening statement says to your customer, "This is a company I want or would like to do business with!" Within seconds, your customers can determine if the call will be a positive encounter. To increase your company's professional image and create a positive transaction, the opening statement should contain the following *three functions.*

Greeting. Many CSRs are busy handling a vast amount of calls throughout the day. The tendency is to *rush* the customers and not take time to develop rapport. For example, the CSR's introduction usually sounds like this, **"ABC Company, this is Jennifer, may I help you?** (*with a rushing voice*)." Sometimes they leave out **"... may I help you?"** It's important that your customers feel welcomed by a friendly greeting. This sets the stage for building rapport. Greet your customer with a **"Good morning, afternoon, or evening."** This is the beginning stage of developing good rapport. This also sets the mood for your customer. If they are not having a good day, then you are wishing them one. The only way this will work effectively is to *say it with meaning.* Using the proper voice inflection with a smile and not rushing through it will make a big impression on your customer. In most situations when you have greeted prospects in a friendly manner, if they are not in a good mood, they tend not to take it out on you personally. This will help you when you need to either facilitate their call or assist them.

Company/Department Name.   How many times have you called a company and been facilitated to the wrong department? After giving full explanation of the purpose of your call, you realized that you were not directed to the correct department? This happens more often then it should; because it is extremely annoying to your customer, customers feel more at ease when you identify your company or department name right after your greeting. In the event that they have been misdirected, it will save both you and your customers time.

State your full company or department name by saying. **"Good morning, ABC Company."** Or, **"Good morning, Customer Service Department."** Again, it's important that you don't rush through your statement; rushing conjures a rude image of you in your customer's mind.

Request.   The third function is to show that you want to help your customers. Use an open-ended question that will allow your customers to express their wants such as, **"How may I help you?"** or, **"Where may I direct your call?"** Many times CSRs use the wrong statements such as, "Can I help you?" or, "May I help you?" or, "How may I direct your call?" These statements will not encourage customer participation. The customer's mind will be actively thinking, "I don't know, can you help me?" or, "Of course you can help me." When a CSR or a receptionist says, "How may I direct your call?" I am tempted to say, "You should know how to direct my call, by pressing a button!" Although your customers may not be making comments, they may be mentally saying them, as I do every time I hear bad CSR statements.

These statements only reinforce in your customers' minds that you "may" or "possibly" can service them, and you have painted a negative mental picture that you are incompetent or inexperienced. This weakens your request and puts your customer in a position of power. You want to let your customers know you are *prepared* and *willing* to help them. Presenting oneself with sincerity, confidence, and a smile tells your customers that you are interested in their needs and want to service them.

Step 2: Establishing Rapport

During this step you want to project to your customers that you're interested in them and that you want them to feel more comfortable with you. There are three functions in step 2. However, depending on your job function and what type of calls you are handling, you may not use all the functions.

Exchanging Names

The first function is essential: Make the effort to exchange names with your customer. In order for you to gain your customer's name, you must first provide your name. Just as if exchanging business cards, for you to receive, first you must give. This also serves to personalize your contacts with your customer, making them feel important, comfortable, and special. In order for you to reinforce who you are in contact with, use a statement like, **"This is Debbie Johnson and who am I speaking with?"** or, **"This is Debbie Johnson and your name is?"** Notice use of the words "This is" as opposed to "My name is." You want to simply state who you are by saying, "My name is," but this method only reinforces that your customer doesn't know who you are and creates further distance between the two of you. During the first few seconds with your customers, you want to establish rapport and get closer to them. By doing so, you will project that you are personable while remaining in control by keeping your relationship on a professional level.

It is important that you offer your first and last name. By doing so, you will encourage customers to give their first and last names. Also, because you have freely offered your first and last name, your customer feels you have made yourself more accountable to her or him. Should your customer call back, he or she would know who to make reference to rather than simply Mary or John, especially when there are more than one or two of you.

For most in-bound calls, particularly when you don't know the caller, using the caller's last name is much wiser. Names are a private, prized possession. Contrary to the feeling that starting off on a first-name basis establishes a friendly rapport, many people are offended by such. It's always much safer to remain on a last-name basis until your customer gives you permission to use a first name. The following will let you know where you stand with your customer—on a first-name or a last-name basis.

First-Name Cue

It is important that your customer gives you a "cue" before you attempt to call him or her by a first name. Provided you have the first name of your customer, your next statement will be to simply repeat and emphasize that first name, as if you are verifying your information. Use proper voice inflection on the first name: *"Mr. John Smith?"* Your customer will respond with either, **"Yes, this is John,"** or, **"Yes, this is Mr. John Smith,"** or, **"Yes, this is Mr. Smith,"** or, **"Yes."** If your customer responds with a first name only, this is your *only* "cue" to proceed on a first-name basis. If the customer responds in any other way, you must proceed on a last-name basis.

Should the customer respond from the beginning with a first name only, then the first-name cue is not important to do, just skip over it. Remember, the main objective in doing this is to determine what your customer feels comfortable being called by. If you could refer to your customer on a first-name basis, would you feel more at ease? Of course you would. This added benefit is another reason for using the first-name cue.

So far, your introduction sounds like this:

> CSR: **"Good morning, ABC Company, how may I help you?"**
>
> CUSTOMER: **"I need some information about your product lines."**
>
> CSR: **"This is Cindy Johnson, and who am I speaking with?"**
>
> CUSTOMER: **"This is Bob Allen."**
>
> CSR: **"Mr.** *Bob Allen?"*
>
> CUSTOMER: **"Yes, this is Bob."**

The following are important points to remember:

Properly greet your customer.

Be sure to give the name of your company or department.

Use an open-ended question to begin servicing your customers.

Ensure a prompt exchange of names.

Use a first-name cue whenever possible.

Don't rush your statements.

Use proper voice inflection.

Smile at all times.

Don't allow past situations to affect your delivery.

Remain professional and personable at all times.

Reference

This third function is used only when it's a first-time customer. You need to find how the customer came to know your company. This helps to determine the cost-effectiveness of your advertising efforts. This also serves to help you know to which department you may need to direct incoming calls. When collecting the reference, use open-ended questions such as: **"How did you hear about our company?"** or, **"Who referred you to our company?"** or, **"What advertisement did you see our company participate in?"**

If you have an automated call center, it should provide a function to tabulate all in-bound activities and measure the type and results of each call. If you are on a manual system, you should keep a tabulation of all incoming calls by using a tabulation form (see Chapter 11). The tabulation will report all the in-bound activities. Furthermore, it will help you to determine the strength of your advertising efforts and the peaks and valleys of the volume of calls coming in, and it will enable your company to see how you handled them. When your company wants to evaluate how you are handling your customers, this is not meant to intimidate you or to place your position at risk; rather evaluation is used primarily to continue training you to be at your best!

Step 3: Purpose of Call

If your customer did not make you aware of the purpose of the call in the beginning of your introduction or if you need to discern the customer's call objective prior to directing her or him to the appropriate department or individual, then, you need to screen the caller by including this step. This is also helpful in providing a better, more productive service. Quickly you will be able to address a customer's concerns or situation or to determine the placement of the in-bound call. Asking for the purpose of the call, in a nonthreatening manner, will help your customers by saving them time and making them feel you are concerned about their needs. Use the following examples that are appropriate to each type of call: **"How can I help you?"** or, **"What can I do for you?"** or, **"What shall I say to Mr. Benson this is regarding?"**

Getting the purpose of the call from your customers help to lay the groundwork for any further qualifying action, to direct the call or to handle the call personally. If the call is to be directed at this point, skip the remainder of the steps and go immediately to step 8, get agreement. Otherwise, continue on into step 4, approach.

Step 4: Approach

Prior to asking your customers questions, you need to give them a clear understanding of why you need to know the information. This will free up the lines of communication and the customer will be more willing to participate in the call. However, if your customer is upset or has a complaint, this step will reinforce that you are prepared to help. It is a bridge that leads you to gather your information and resolve the situation. There are two functions in the approach step:

1. Benefit statement

2. Permission to ask questions.

Some examples of an approach include:

In order for me to assist you better, I need ... > to ask you *just* **a couple of** *quick* **questions if you don't mind.**

To save you time, I want to ensure that I will direct you to the correct department. To accomplish this, I need ... > to ask you *just* **a couple of** *quick* **questions, if you don't mind.**

To determine the best way to handle this, I need ... > to ask you *just* **a couple of** *quick* **questions, if you don't mind.**

I want to help. In order for me to evaluate the situation clearly, I need ... > to ask you *just* **a couple of** *quick* **questions, if you don't mind.**

The benefit statement is purposely used as a lead-in to asking questions. As you have probably noticed the second function, **"I need ... > to ask you** *just* **a couple of** *quick* **questions if you don't mind,"** is always used in the approach. This function never changes. Use it exactly as written. *I need,* shows a sense of urgency. The strategic pause after *I need* ... > will have your customers unconsciously asking themselves, "You need what?" Proper use of voice inflection (change of tone) when you emphasize the words *just* and *quick* tells your customers you will not take up much of their time. They need to know that!

The phrase, *if you don't mind* makes the statement less threatening. Be sure not to turn the phrase into a question. You can avoid this by lowering your voice inflection on the word *mind.* If you don't, you will weaken the effect of the approach and encourage a negative response because you have given up your control when you ask permission. Also be sure to smile when you say **"if you don't mind."** It makes a big difference in your voice projection and softens the approach slightly.

Using both functions (the benefit statement and permission to ask questions) will avoid prompting your customers into being cautious of your request for information. They will be more receptive to participating in your next step.

If your job function is to conduct more of a selling presentation style of delivery, then at this point stop here and refer to Chapter 13 and continue on from step 5. If you are more on a customer service level when handling in-bound calls, then you can proceed to the next step.

Step 5: Probing

This step is the open-ended question-and-answer time, or probing. Depending on the type of in-bound call received, you need to accomplish up to three functions. First qualify your customers or their concerns. This will help you determine the direction you should take the conversation. Next, you need to let your customer communicate his or her personal wants and needs to you. This is important if you are to overcome a problem or concern your customer may have. It also assists you when selling your products or services. The third function is creating a need for your products or services. When dealing with irate customers or objections, you can use this function in greater depth.

Here are four steps used in the probing process:

1. Ask open-ended questions that will draw out information to serve your customer better.

2. Listen and mentally paraphrase all points. Write them down!

3. Identify dominant wants or needs. Later, get the customer's agreement that you understand the customer's position and that you are handling the situation to her or his satisfaction.

4. Assure customers that you want to assist them. Direct the call or offer solutions.

These are important guidelines for probing:

- People will do business with you only if you can meet *their* criteria of a solution to their needs, rather than *yours.*
- Focus on your customer's need. Show sincerity and a willingness to help.
- Open-ended questions always contain the words *who, what, where, why, when, how, explain, describe,* and *share.*
- Listen to your customers 80 percent of the time. Spend 20 percent of the time talking.
- Make sure your questions are sincere.

Probing serves to gather additional information enabling you to find out more about your customer needs. In addition, probing makes your customers feel that their needs are being addressed and that they therefore can express themselves more clearly. When directing calls or placing customers on hold for a time, open-ended questions allow your customers to feel that they have accomplished something productive during the first few seconds of the call.

Ask questions. Find answers and solutions quickly. Try not to take much of their time. Time spent unnecessarily with one customer allows less time for others needing your assistance. Try to spread yourself evenly.

Many times an in-bound call can be dealt with very quickly. Probing will help you accomplish this and allow more productive time for other in-bound calls. Too many questions will irritate your customers and make them feel like you're interrogating them. Use carefully designed questions that quickly gain the most productive answers.

The tendency is to ask closed-ended questions. This returns only two types of responses: yes or no. Closed-ended questions typically have the words: *have you, would you, could you, did you, are you, can you, is that,* and so on. Using these type of questions decreases the communication level between you and your customer. You need to open the lines of communication freely. There are several areas that you need to focus on when asking open-ended questions. Remember that you have up to three functions in your probing step; these functions are:

- Qualify the customers' needs and get them to open up.
- Establish their wants and determine customers' direction, enabling you to service them better.
- Create a need whenever possible (this depends on your job function) to discover potential interest in your products and services.

Probing Questions

Ensure that all your questions are nonthreatening questions and that you use probing questions to help narrow your customer's concerns. Below are some examples of probing questions you could ask in step 5. Try to choose the ones that would be best suited for your particular in-bound calls. Rephrase and customize them for your company.

Qualifiers

What can I do for you today?

Who did you speak with before?

When did you place your last order?

What are some of your concerns?

How did you arrive at that conclusion?

How did you arrive at that price?

Who, other than us, have you talked with about this product?

Who is handling your account at this time?

When did you receive the information?

What is your account number?

When did you send in your check?

What is the correct spelling of your last name?

Who handles your accounts payable?

Other than today, what steps haveyou taken to communicate your needs to us?

Please describe exactly what happened?

Where can you be reached at if I should require additional information?

How can I assist you?

When did you process the payment and send it to us?

What was your method of payment?

Who, other than yourself, is handling this situation?

Other than this department, what other departments were you directed to?

Other than yourself, whose attention should this be sent or addressed to?

Establish Wants

How do you feel about the service we provided, and what would you like to see improved?

When would you like to receive it?

Describe some of the areas that you feel strongly about?

How important is that information to you?

How valuable is that service to you?

What would you like to see improved?

What can I do to help you see the benefits?

What would you recommend if you were in my position?

What concerns have you had with your account, and what would you like to see changed?

What originally motivated you to choose us to service your needs?

What can I do, within our guidelines, to be sure your needs are being met?

I want to help you. You mentioned many areas you're unhappy about. What are the major concerns you have that I can assist you with today?

Other than (*describe*), what other concerns do you have?

On the basis of your current situation, how much can we count on today, to bring your account up to date?

What else do we need to consider before I finalize this?

What motivated you to select XYZ competitor as your major wholesaler?

What are your plans if we're unable to provide all that you are requesting?

What would be some of your requirements?

What about the information interested you the most?

Now that you've had an opportunity to use our products for sometime, how do you feel about them today compared to when you first acquired them?

What other products are you using that we are not providing you?

What can we do to regain your faith and the opportunity to service you better?

Create a Need

What steps have you taken to allow us the opportunity to service all your needs?

How often has your representative followed through or contacted you to ensure that you're getting a quality product and the best service you're entitled to?

When was the last time you evaluated your progress, and what were the results of that evaluation?

How confident are you that you're getting the best product at the most competitive rates?

When do you plan to reevaluate your supplier, and what other suppliers would you be considering when making this evaluation?

How cost-effective and flexible is your current distributor in comparison to others available?

What steps has your representative taken to research that for you, ensuring you're getting the lowest cost available?

The last time you placed an order was on (*state*), what can I do for you today to ensure you're adequately stocked?

What other resources does XYZ company have that we are not able to provide you?

How cost-effective are your current methods and procedures to determine whether you're maximizing your production?

Share with me if anyone has described the additional benefits you're entitled to?

Self-Test

Below are some questions to ask your customers. Decide whether each of the questions is an open-ended or closed-ended question. If it is a closed-ended question, rewrite it to make it an open-ended question.

Are you happy with the products and services you have now?

What are your plans to increase your order in the near future?

Can you tell me some of your concerns?

Are you planning to send in your payment?

Can you tell me the person you spoke with before?

What other information can I help you with today?

Tell me if you are paying by COD or credit?

The following are some possible answers to the self-test questions:

How happy are you with the products and services you have now?

What are some of your concerns?

When do you plan to send in your payment?

Who was the person that you spoke with before?

What will be your method of payment?

These are not the only possible questions. As long as you use, at the beginning of your questions, the words: *Who, What, Where, Why, When, How, Explain, Describe,* or *Share,* and your questions are nonthreatening, you will be productive.

Do not respond with your own comments or opinions but with another question to gain additional information. This is more productive. Continue to practice creating and asking open-ended questions on a daily basis. Being able to think quickly on your feet is a tremendous advantage when communicating with your customers. Asking the right questions at the right time is a skill. Like most skills, the ability to probe effectively must be learned. Once you are aware of the differences between open-ended and closed-ended questions, you will have taken a significant step.

Knowing the difference and implementing that knowledge, however, are not the same. Now you need to make a point of practicing using open-ended questions. It will be helpful to evaluate others, listen to the types of questions they use, and analyze their techniques. Try to revise their closed-ended questions into open-ended ones. By doing so, you will benefit from this form of exercise.

Once you've asked open-ended questions, received information that qualifies your customers, and established their wants and you've attempted to create a need for your products and services (create a need is only applicable to certain departments), now what do you do with the information? Your job function and the type of call that you are handling would determine what you need to do next. For example, if your job is to take the order and time doesn't allow you to conduct a thorough presentation, then you would skip the remainder of your steps and go to the close step. However, if you need to assist your customer in resolving a certain situation, you would proceed to the next step, i.e., restating. Customer servicing and selling are essentially the same in regards to having common sense and being able to think quickly. Good CSRs are able to handle most situations under pressure without feeling overwrought. Overall, this process provides the prospect and the customer with a positive encounter while improving your company's image!

Step 6: Restating

In step 6 you reaffirm the customer's needs through restating. Also, this step will help lead in to a resolve step. In step 6 you need to summarize customers' responses, emphasize the important ideas, and reflect them to the customers in a dynamic way so they can see their own expressed wants and needs from a fresh prospective. This step will help you place your customer's remarks in a more concise format. This tells your customer you were listening effectively and are preparing to resolve the situation. Your objective is to restate your customer's responses to the open-ended questions in a better and more positive outlook. Your customer will agree with you and demonstrate better cooperation. From the information gained in the probing step, you will be able to begin determining what direction you should take during the resolving step. With the confirmation you gain from your customer in the restating step, you will have greater confidence during the balance of your presentation.

There are two functions in step 6. The first is to *summarize* what the customer has said in a more positive way. The second function is to get a *confirmation* from your customer. This will give you a yes response which you may need later during the objection-handling process. The following are examples of restating:

> **I want to be sure that I have this information correct. You are responding to our direct-mail advertisement, and you would like information about our advanced product line, XYZ. You would also like to gain additional information regarding** (*describe*). **Is that correct?**

> **... You're Mr. Allen's customer, and you would like to speak with him about a concern you have regarding your purchase agreement, and you can be reached at 555-1212 within the next 30 minutes, is that correct?**

... You want to speak with our department manager regarding service that may not have been provided. You also feel that the sales representative was too aggressive, and you would like to receive a reimbursement. Is that correct?

I want to be sure that I will forward this information correctly. You wish to speak with Ms. Greenly and this is of a personal nature. Therefore she will know ... > what this is in regard to. Is that correct?

As you can see, the restatement qualifies and summarizes the information your customer has given you. By being more positive with the information, you are not only attempting to reassure your customers, you are also encouraging them to agree with what you say. Also, if you are screening a call for your manager, you will make the caller accountable for what she or he has just said. In this way, if the caller is not being truthful and is using a tricky maneuver to get through to the decision maker, the caller may want to add to your restatement to prevent greater resistance from your manager. Should the caller agree with your restatement, the caller is accountable for any statements that may not have been honest or straightforward.

The restatement should be closely correlated to what your customers said, but your rendition should give a more positive emphasis to their views. Practice restating by role-playing different scenarios that you would encounter on an in-bound situation. You can use an exercise similar to the restatement exercise in Chap. 13. Your main objective is to practice asking the right questions to gain the necessary information you need in order to resolve your customer's needs and restate them in a more positive manner. Restating is a crucial part of handling your customers because it allows you to remain in control and is extremely effective in handling objections.

Step 7: Resolving

In step 7, you resolve, sell, or take the order. Resolving will let your customers know exactly what you plan to do with them. You have previously restated your customer's responses to your probing questions, signalling your clear understanding of the issues. Depending on your job function, you now have the responsibility of deciding to do one of the following:

Direct the call

Handle concerns

Offer solutions

Take a message

Pass the call

Provide information

The resolve step will perform one of these services. However, at this point you must also determine how far you need to go into the remainder of the steps. This greatly depends on the type of customers calling in, the nature of their business, and your job function. To keep the flow of the 12 steps, continue reading the steps in order.

As a CSR, you must always keep the customer's objectives in mind while offering that *extra service* to give customer satisfaction. Handling the resolution step personably, professionally, ethically, and morally will win your customer's confidence in both you and your company. Failing to keep the customer's confidence in mind will allow a poor customer service representative to damage a company's image.

When you resolve, clearly explain or describe what you plan to do so your customer feels confident that the call will be handled properly. Below are some examples:

> **Mr. Johnson, Mary Hartsfield is the sales representative you should be speaking with, and she would have the information on the product line you're inquiring about. Just one moment please, while I inform her of what your needs are.**

> **Mr. Johnson, Mr. Allen is unavailable at this time. However, he is expected to return by 2:00 p.m. I can have him return your call or if you prefer, I can have Ben Phillips, his assistant, help you immediately.**

> **Mr. Johnson, Ms. Greenly is in a meeting for the next hour or so and is scheduled for an appointment immediately afterward. I can have Peter Smith discuss this issue with you. Should he be unable to fully take care of the situation, I will personally see to it that Ms. Greenly or myself contact you before the day ends to determine how we can proceed.**

> **Mr. Johnson, the product you're inquiring about is available. The features have (*describe*) and the benefits are (*describe*). Based on the volume you wanted, I can get that out to you at a cost factor of (*describe*).**

These examples may not always address every type of call that a CSR encounters. The concept is to use professional language skills with a friendly and sincere voice projection. It is equally important to offer either a permanent or temporary solution. Resolve the customer's needs! This will make your customers feel you are wanting to do your best to help them. Once you have accomplished the resolve step, you proceed to the get agreement step.

Step 8: Get Agreement

In step 8, you get agreement before closing. This step allows your customer to have input in your offerings or solutions in the resolve step. It's important that your customer feels some control of the situation without your giving up your control. Your customers will feel that their needs are being satisfied and that they retain some options for meeting their needs. Examples based on the resolve step are as follows:

... Just one moment please, while I inform her of what your needs are. <u>Would that be all right</u> *with* <u>you</u>.

... I can have him return your call, or, if you prefer, I can have Ben Phillips, his assistant, help you immediately. <u>What would you prefer</u>.

... Should he be unable to fully take care of the situation, I will personally see to it that Ms. Greenly or myself contact you before the day ends to determine how we can proceed. <u>What would be more helpful to you</u>."

... Based on the volume you wanted, I can get that out to you at a cost factor of (*describe*). <u>Would that meet your needs today</u>."

Notice, there are no question marks after the close of these sentences. Use the assumptive statement approach. Remember to go down on your voice inflection—make a statement, don't pose a question.

Providing you have fulfilled your customer's needs in the resolve step, the get agreement step is designed to ease the transition to the close step by eliciting a positive response from the customer which allows you to easily continue. If you should get a negative response in the get agreement step, then you need to go to the next step, this is step 9—objections. This step is discussed in Chapter 15. Assuming your customer will agree, let's continue on to the close step.

Step 10: Closing

In step 10, you sign off while keeping the door open. An effective close is the natural conclusion to all the previous steps. Make your close sound warm and friendly, giving your customer the feeling of a successful encounter. You want your customers to know that they can count on you for assistance again. Also, calling your company is not an interruption of your day—serving the customer is the *purpose* of your company! The following are examples of how you can close effectively:

Thank you for calling. Please feel free to call again if I can be of further assistance.

It was my pleasure to help you. If you should have any further questions, just ask for Chris Lane, and I will be happy to help you.

I'm confident that you will be satisfied with your purchase. Is there anything else I can do for you today?

Step 11: Informing and Confirming

Step 11 covers how to pass the call and inform; there are two functions to the inform step. The first is to inform the person you're directing the customer to. The second function is to have the person you directed the customer to inform the customer that he or she understands the purpose of the customer's call.

Informing

The time to inform is when you direct the customer to a specific person or department. Inform the person in that department of the name of the customer on hold, the nature of the customer's call, and any other relevant information. Many times a customer will explain the purpose of the call to the customer service representative, who will then direct the call without relaying the information. Inevitably, the customer is placed on hold for long periods, has to reexplain the purpose of the call, and naturally, becomes frustrated at how the call is handled.

Informing prevents customer irritation and provides *extra customer service* to satisfy and impress your customers. This step should not take up much time. It must be precise and clear without any personal comments that reflect your emotions or reactions. A professional customer service representative will be objective and resourceful and will allow the person informed to make her or his own judgments of the customer. Examples of informing are as follows:

> **Good morning, Mr. Allen, this is Sheila Hansen. I have Mr. Johnson on line one who is calling about your direct mail advertisement. He would like information about your advanced product line, and he also wanted to speak with the purchasing department.**
> **Good afternoon, Mr. Campbell, this is Sheila Hansen. I have Mr. Johnson on line one. He purchased your product line from Mr. Allen and has some concerns about service that may not have been provided as promised. He requested to talk with you personally for assistance."**

Be sure to properly and professionally greet the internal employees when approaching them. This keeps your image professional, wins respect from others, and sets a positive mood in your conversation.

The person who was informed is eventually going to handle the customer. Therefore, the person needs to quickly personalize the contact by restating the relayed information to the customer. For example:

> **Good morning, Mr. Johnson. This is Mr. Allen. I understand that you are interested in our advanced product line and would like some additional information. You also would like to speak with our purchasing department, is that correct?**
> **Good afternoon, Mr. Johnson, this is Mr. Campbell. Sheila Hansen explained to me your concern about service that may not have been provided as promised, and you would like some assistance in this matter, is that correct?**

This proves to your customer that you want to help and that your company is communicating well internally and with its customers. A professional, long-lasting image of your company will be painted in your customer's mind. Customers will tell their friends, who will tell their friends, and so on. That's the essence of building your company on a referral system while lowering the attrition rate of bad-willed customers.

Confirming

This is the second function of the inform step. You must receive a confirmation from the person you are informing. Once you have informed that particular person or department regarding the details of the situation, you need to validate that your customer will be taken care of by the use of *confirmation*. This is a small step requiring a brief statement such as:

> **... He would like information about your advanced product line. You *would* be able to assist Mr. Johnson?**

> **... He requested to talk with you personally for assistance. Mr. Campbell, should I direct the call to you?**

This will surely give you the self-gratification that your customers' needs are being met. The positive feelings now gained about your company and the service they provide enable you to have a positive and enthusiastic attitude toward your company, yourself, and future customers! This will also lower your burnout so that you will continue to have energy to help your customers throughout the day.

Step 12: Directing the Call

There are two ways to effectively direct your customers to a person or department. The first technique is not as personable as the second. The first is designed only when you need to quickly direct the call because your in-coming lines are too busy. After receiving a confirmation from the person you've informed, simply *connect your customer*.

The second way is much better for the customer. Once you have received a confirmation from the informed person or department, the procedure is to get back to your customers and let them know you have informed the person or department and you will be directing them. In addition, let customers know who they will be speaking with.

Directing the call greatly depends on the type of telephone system available and how sophisticated your office procedures are. The volume of in-bound activities a CSR receives on a minute-to-minute basis affects this procedure as well. If in-bound call activities are frequent, you should probably use the first alternative. If time allows, your customer would benefit from the second alternative, thus giving your company a more professional image with quality and that *extra* customer service! Below is an example of this procedure:

> **Mr. Campbell, I will let Mr. Johnson know you will be with him in a moment. Hello, Mr. Johnson? This is Sheila Hansen, thank you for your patience. I just informed Mr. Campbell of your concerns, and he will be with you in just one moment. Or, ... and I am going to direct you to Mr. Campbell right now. Just one moment please.**

12-Step Overview

Congratulations! Now you have completed the 12 steps to successful customer service. You must apply the information learned to master this step-by-step method. Continue reading and study the 12-step overview, then put it into practice.

The following are some helpful tips to make this learning process easier: Memorize the 12 steps. Know what each of the steps is. Once you have memorized each step, then memorize the functions of each step. For example, step 1, the introduction, has three functions:

1. Greeting—**"Good morning."**
2. Company or department name—"... **ABC company** ..." "... **marketing department** ..."
3. Request—**"How may I help you?" "Where may I direct your call?"**

Memorize the benefits of using each step and the benefits of each function. For example:

> The *greeting* makes my customer feel welcomed, builds rapport, and creates a positive encounter with my customer.
>
> Giving the *company or department name* lets my customers know they have reached the right company or department.
>
> **"How may I help you?"** tells my customer I am prepared and willing to help them.

You must be able to do all the above steps and functions. If you understand the benefits and understand why you use each function, then you'll have greater confidence in your presentation.

Write and rewrite your scripts to fit your personality and style of delivery. Use verbiage you're comfortable with.

Practice with the 12 steps as often as possible. Take time to role-play, and spend quality time, nonstop, to get to know the steps and be comfortable with your delivery.

Tabulate your in-bound calls to determine the areas where you need improvement.

Record your live in-bound calls. Play them back and listen to your delivery and style. Ask yourself, "Do I sound enthusiastic about my job, my company, and about my customer?" "Do I project a positive and confident image?" "How well am I following the 12 steps?" "Would I be impressed with me?"

This can be an extremely valuable exercise, and its usefulness never diminishes. Get into the routine of recording yourself at regular intervals so you'll always be sharp and at your best! Be aware that you'll probably be your own toughest critic, so don't be too hard on yourself. It also helps to get colleagues you trust to offer honest and constructive advice.

15

Interpreting, Narrowing, and Overcoming Objections

Objection Handling for the Out-bound TSR

An objection during step 9, the trial close, is *not* a rejection. At this point you stand strong with your prospect. In most cases, an objection is telling you, "I need more information, more facts ..." Assume objections will surface during some of your presentations. Provided that you have followed the 12 steps closely, the objections will typically occur during your trial close, so be prepared to handle them. Objections give you an opportunity to continue strengthening your relationship with your prospect: selling your products, services, company, and your ideas. It is a time to listen, probe, and to understand and fulfill your prospect's needs. There should not be any feelings of personal rejection. Your prospect's objections are not necessarily directed at you personally. Do not be defensive or react negatively. More important, don't attack the objection immediately with more selling. This is a time to remain in control and impress your prospects with your persistence and professionalism.

Early in your presentation, prior to step 5, when prospects sound or behave in a negative way, it usually results from a problem they had prior to your contact with them. If your prospect seems rude during the beginning of your presentation, try to release barriers. Ask, **"What are some of your concerns?"** This statement serves to clear the air, your prospect is more likely to open up and tell you what the real issue is. If this is unsuccessful, conclude your presentation by using the easy close. Try approaching your prospect at another time. Don't allow your prospect's resistance to affect your prospecting activities. Instead, remain confident and continue with your prospecting efforts. Resistance may indicate that your prospects are not ready at this time. Your best option is to use the easy close technique discussed in Chap. 13. The easy close will give you another opportunity in the future.

Whenever you get objections, the following provides you with ways in which you can take your control back and effectively close (depending on where you are at within your presentation).

How to Defuse a Negative Statement

Acknowledging and agreeing with your prospects is one effective way to get on their good side, especially if your prospect is angry or upset. Defusing your prospect's anger will increase the likelihood of a successful presentation. You can defuse many negative situations with statements such as:

> **I understand your concerns.**
> **I know price is important to you.**
> **Of course you need to think it over.**
> **I'd be happy to send you information.**
> **Thank you for making me aware of that.**
> **I appreciate your concerns.**
> **I respect that.**

In any case, when objections surface during step 9, your first step when your prospects object is to interpret what they are trying to say to you. Determine what the real issues are that you're dealing with.

The following information will help you to make the necessary determination. When you are faced with objections, you need to establish precisely what your prospect is really saying. For example, **"I'm not interested,"** "Call me back in 6 months," **"I'm not ready now,"** are not real objections—their disinterest may be superficial and may mask another problem that lurks just below the surface. By narrowing what their real concerns are, you will be better able to overcome the objections. When receiving objections, ask yourself three questions:

1. Where, exactly, do you stand with your prospect?

2. Was your prospect listening to your ideas?

3. What is your prospect really trying to tell you?

Where do you stand with your prospect?   Let's look at the first question. Analyzing at what point in your 12 steps the objections arise will help you to know where you stand with your prospect. Below are numbers one through twelve:

1 2 3 4 5 6 7 8 9 10 11 12

These numbers simulate each of the 12 steps. When you get objections using the 12-step method, where would you ordinarily receive them? Take a moment and think about it first. It's not where you would expect it to occur. When using the 12 steps precisely as instructed, objections would most likely surface during the trial close. Therefore, you stand strong with your prospect, correct? Of course! In step 9, you have completed most of your presentation.

Think about what you have accomplished so far. You established rapport in the first four steps by stating who you are, the company you represent, and your location. You have told your prospects how you acquired their name, respected their time, and gave them the purpose for your call. Then you qualified your prospects, established what their wants were, and you created a need for your products or services. Your prospects confirmed those needs when you restated their needs in step 6, and then you fulfilled their needs (told them what they wanted to hear). In step 8, you got a reaction, you gained a positive yes response confirming that you fulfilled their needs. Therefore, by the time you entered into your trial close in step 9, you were in a very strong position. You just need to learn how to gain your control back as you have throughout your presentation.

Without the 12 steps, where do objections usually occur? They occur early on, within seconds of your presentation. Now where do you stand with your prospect? Extremely weak. That is primarily the reason for the first four steps. Each step is designed to eliminate your prospect's resistance before it occurs. In this way your position is stronger when you enter into the trial close. You now have more ammunition to outweigh and overcome your prospect's objection.

If the objection occurs within the first four steps, you know that your rapport building process was not effective and the objection is superficial, e.g., **"I'm not interested"** or **"What are you selling?"** At this stage in your presentation you are in a weak position with your prospect. To determine what went wrong, you need to analyze what step you were in when receiving your prospect's objection.

Remember, approximately 10 percent of your prospects will say no to everything, and that is not any fault of your own; unfortunately it is a statistical reality. Should you get more than 10 percent resistance early on within your presentation, prior to step 5, then it is because the steps are not being properly implemented. Unless you record yourself and evaluate your presentation, it will be difficult to determine what went wrong and where you need to improve. For example, if you get resistance in step 3, your request for time, then you are probably going high on the *I* in *"have I."* If resistance is occurring after you have introduced your company name, you are pausing too long instead of quickly going into your fifth function, the landmark or location. You need to say, **"and we're *located* ... >."** Be sure to use the word **and** immediately after you state your company name; this will help you not to *pause*. Pausing at an inappropriate place will allow the prospect an opportunity to interrupt your presentation. Interruptions usually end on negative notes rather than positive ones.

When objections occur in step 9, the trial close, you have greater confidence in overcoming them, since at this point, you have built up rapport and credibility, and you stand firm with your prospect. The objection occurring in step 9 indicates that your prospect needs additional information. This information should have been provided in your selling step. Just consider this objection as an opportunity to progress in your selling efforts.

Was your prospect listening?   You will have assurance that your prospect was listening to your ideas in one of the steps prior to your trial close (step 9). Can you remember where this step is? Where did you receive a yes response after you expressed your ideas? You encouraged this yes response when you got reaction in step 8 (**"How valuable is this to you?"**). Your prospects are not going to readily say yes unless they were truly listening to what you just said. Therefore, when you get an objection during trial close, you have confidence that your prospect was listening. This second issue is not the problem.

Should you get a no response during step 8, then any one of the following might have occurred:

√ You did not satisfy your prospect's needs in step 7, selling features and benefits.

√ Your prospect wasn't listening to your ideas during step 7. This indicates that your prospect was *not* impressed.

√ You did not create the need in step 5, probing, and yet you continued on with your presentation.

The solution is to ask the right questions and listen to your prospect's responses during your probing step so that when you enter into your selling step you will ensure that you touch the prospect's "hot buttons." Once you have accomplished this successfully, you will be able to encourage a yes response in step 8, when you get reaction. This is extremely important, since *you cannot move on to your next step until this has happened.*

If you have completed all the steps, and you *still* receive a no response during trial close, then you need to determine what the real issue is.

Consider the following important points when entering into step 10, handling objections:

√ Attempt to determine if the objection is the result of a preexisting problem or a misunderstanding of the product's features and benefits.

√ When you hear an objection, consider it an invitation to provide additional selling points!

√ Draw out your prospects. Try to understand their needs. You will find the best approaches in the "Six Methods of Handling Objections" later in this chapter.

When your position is strong with your prospect and he or she was listening to your ideas, then your only alternative is to answer the third question.

What is your prospect really trying to tell you?   First, when faced with an objection, you need to go through an interpretation of the objection. *What is* *your prospect really trying to say?* For example, when the objection is about price, your prospect might say, **"It's too much money,"** or, **"I can't afford it!"** You don't want to agree with your prospect's objection, nor do you want to assume that this is exactly what the prospect means. Agreeing with the objection will *decrease* your opportunity to sell your products and services. What you must do first is interpret the objection. You should be thinking, "There must be a misunderstanding or a misconception about the products or services."

Second, you need to assess what that *misunderstanding* or *misconception* is. If you were to gather all the objections you would ever receive from your prospect and put them into six categories, what would they be? Below are the categories, and there are no others. When you really think about all the objections you could get, they would fit into one of the six listed. Using one of the *six methods* for handling objections will enable you to interpret the objection more clearly so that you can customize your rebuttals to your prospect's specific needs.

Again, all the objections your prospects may have are classified into one of the six categories below. Next to each objection is an example of the prospect's expression of that objection and how you should interpret that expression.

Objection	Prospect's Expression	Interpretation
Money	"Too much money" "Not enough money"	There is a misunderstanding or misconception of the cost.
Time	"Not now, call back." "Call me in the spring."	There is a condition standing in the way.
Information	"Send me information." "I have to talk it over with my partner."	Confirm it! Is prospect interested or not? Qualify this! Lack of information.
Competition	"I know someone in the business." "I like ABC company."	Prospect needs to be educated.
Customer service	"I don't like salespeople." "I never do business over the telephone."	Prospect had a bad situation or experience.
Silence or guttural utterances	"Yes," "No," "I don't know," "Don't care," "Maybe" (not participating, hung up)	You're losing control, you need to break through undetermined barriers. You need to take control of the situation, to get the prospect to open up.

Once you have categorized and interpreted your prospect's objections, the next step is to narrow down the **"real issues"** and begin overcoming or outweighing the objections. Your interpretation enables you to select the most effective objection-handling method.

Six Objection Methods

Below are *six methods* to narrow, overcome, and outweigh objections. Pick the ones you feel comfortable with and that are appropriate for objections you may get from your prospect.

1. Restate or agree, and probe.

2. Keep selling.

3. Reflect.

4. Feel-felt-found method.

5. Ask prospect for best solution.

6. "If I could..., would you. ..."

These six objection methods are in order of preference. The key is to use a method that is not continually used by your competitors or that is not typical in a sales environment. This helps to set you apart and impress your prospect with your unique style of presentation.

Restate or Agree and Probe.   You can find the real issue by *restating or agreeing, and probing.* However, this strategy is only effective if the objection can be restated in a positive way. You are not going to do all three. You will either restate and probe or agree and probe. For example, a restatement might go like this:

Objection: **I have no money.**
Restatement: **What you're saying is that if it were cost-effective and profitable, you would consider it. Is that correct.** (*Make this an assumptive.*)

An example of agreeing would be:

Objection: **Send me information.**
Agree: **I would be happy to. ...**

A probing question would be:

Objection: **I'm not interested.**
Probe: **What are some of your concerns?**

By using the *restating* method, you can get a confirmation from your prospect. This narrows down the real issue quickly. You can then proceed to your probing questions. Otherwise, skip over restating and immediately *agree and probe* to draw out real issues. Agreeing is used to help defuse the objection quickly so your prospect will actively listen and respond to your probing questions more openly. Let's put together the two examples and demonstrate how they work together.

Restate and probe: **What you're saying is that if it were cost-effective and profitable, you would consider it. Is that correct.** (*Make this an assumptive.*) **Other than the affordability factor, what other concerns do you have?**

Agree and probe: **I would be happy to send you information. What information would be most valuable to you?**

Once you have either restated and probed or agreed and probed, then you must outweigh the objection with features and benefits, get reaction, and, if your prospect's response is positive, then you close.

Figure 15-1 is a flow chart of the restate or agree, and probe strategy. This will direct your objection process more clearly. The first method is the ideal

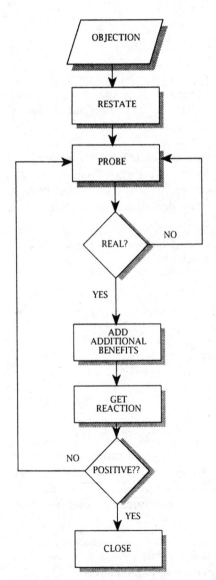

Figure 15-1. Restate or agree, and probe.

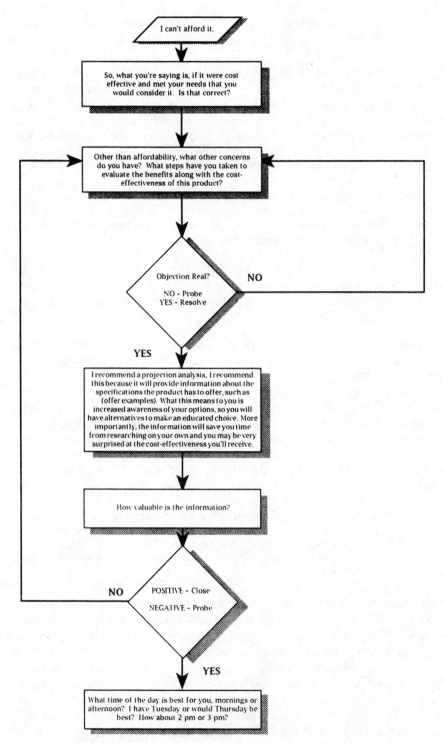

Figure 15-1. *(Continued).*

process to use, since it quickly identifies the real issues and guides you through additional selling.

Keep Selling.   Your second method of handling objections is *keep selling*. This is ideally used when you have previously received a yes response. You can refer to the yes response your prospect offered when you get reaction in step 8. Using this technique makes your prospects accountable for what they have agreed to earlier in your presentations, when you asked: **"How valuable would this be for you?"** You need to remind them of their positive reaction. Below is a format to follow. Just fill in the blanks to fit what the prospect said.

> I understand, Mr./s. Prospect. We talked about *many* benefits. You liked the fact that _____ , and the idea that we can give you _____ . One of the areas we haven't talked much about is _____ . Mr./s. Prospect, how *important* is that to you? *(or)* How *valuable* is this to your company?

This gives you an opportunity to do additional selling. However, there is some flexibility when using this technique. If you don't want to go into something else and risk pushing another hot button, then you can change this format slightly by saying:

> I understand, Mr./s. Prospect. We talked about *many* benefits. You liked that _____ , and the idea that we can give you _____ . What other concerns do you have in allowing me the opportunity to validate this further?"

Reflect.   The *reflect* method is similar to the second strategy—keep selling. The only difference is that you do not add additional selling points or get reaction. This is more readily used when you get a no response when you get reaction in step 8. You need to refer to what your prospect said yes to in your restatement in step 6. This will remind the prospect of what her or his needs are. For example:

> We talked about many issues. You mentioned that your company sees the *value* of _____ , and you have a concern with _____ , and you feel that conducting a competitive analysis would help you to *determine* ... > the cost-effectiveness of your *current* product. What other concerns do you have about *receiving* this information?

Feel, Felt, Found.   This technique is another excellent method for handling objections, especially if your prospect is skeptical, unsure, or sounds irritable. Defuse the objections with the *feel, felt, found* statements, and then offer solutions with your features and benefits. One drawback when using this method is that many salespeople tend to use it, and it may sound too familiar to the prospect, which could cause a negative reaction. Therefore, when using this technique, be sure to use verbiage that is unique and unfamiliar—do not say, "I understand how you feel, and others have felt the same way until they found out that...." Below, are some alternatives to the feel, felt, and found words to help you be a little more creative.

Feel

Empathy   Put yourself in your prospect's place:

I respect what you're saying.
I appreciate your concern.
Thank you for letting me know that.

Felt

Relate   Make them understand that their concerns are not unique:

Many people I speak with share the same concerns.
It's not uncommon today

Found

Offer solutions.   Give your prospect objective answers:

Until they discovered ...
Until they had an opportunity to ...

Try not to sound *canned.* You must be sincere and genuine so the method literally comes across naturally. Again, you do not necessarily have to use the words *feel, felt,* and *found.* Instead, be more creative in your statements by using some of the variations offered above, or create some of your own. To put this into a better perspective, the following is an example of using the feel-felt-found technique.

I appreciate your concerns for the cost factors, and it's *not* uncommon in *today's* market. It's *unfortunate* that for a company such as yours, that wishes to *upgrade,* and what usually is standing in the way, is the financial *affordability.* Once a company has an *opportunity* to evaluate and *compare* us and our competitiveness in the marketplace and compare our *guarantee* and pricing structure, we have been able ... > to *reduce* their bottom line by 30 percent. If you could accomplish this same savings, how *important* would that be to you and your company?

Ask Prospect for Best Solution.   This is beneficial when you have done *everything* possible to overcome your prospect's objection and this is the last rabbit out of your hat. It's not recommended for the first two rounds. However, you have nothing to lose when you use this as your final resort. This method is known as the *bottom-line objection technique.* When you really want prospects to see your position, this helps put them in the position of *selling themselves.*

What would you suggest?
What can I do that will help you see the benefits?
What would you recommend?
What would be of interest to you?
What can I do to validate this further?
What would it take to earn the right to do business with you today?

"If I Could ... , Would You ... "   This method is very popular with many salespeople (which is why it is the last on the list here). That is why it is used the least in these examples. Even though it is used extensively, this method can be extremely effective when used with the proper verbiage so it sounds more original:

> **I appreciate what you're saying. If I could show you how we can** (*describe*)**, would you agree that this would be** *valuable* **information?** (or) **Would you allow us the opportunity to service your needs?**

Note that these are *closed-ended trial-closing* questions. You can also use an open-ended approach, such as, **"How valuable is this information?"**

Use the *six objection-handling methods* as your models when entering into step 10. Choose the method that is best suited for the type of objection you received. By first interpreting the objection, you will be able to select the most appropriate means of handling it. *Remember:* Always outweigh the objection with *benefits,* then *get reaction*—"How valuable would this be for you"—and then *close.*

Combined Objection-Handling Methods

You can also combine the methods to be more creative in overcoming the objections. For example:

> **I** *understand* **your concerns, Mr. Smith. I know that price is important to you, and that you want the** *best* **price possible. I recommend a consultation. This would enable you to clearly understand and** *justify* **the price. For example, you will** *increase* **your employees' confidence and motivation and** *enhance* **your company image. More important ... > you will** *reduce* **your production overhead and** *increase* **your company's profitability. If I can show you a way to gain the** *benefits* **I've just described, would you allow me the** *opportunity* **to meet with you personally so that I can validate this further?"** (or) **"Would you allow us the** *opportunity* **to validate this further by using the program for 30 days. If you're not** *completely* **satisfied, we will refund your investment back 100 percent. Does that sound fair enough."** (*Assumptive.*)

Which objection techniques were used? Yes, the **"feel, felt, found"** and **"If I could ... , would you ... "** methods. Now, *you* practice combining the methods to create your own style of delivery!

Never Say Never

Never give up on an objection until you try to overcome or outweigh it at *least three times.* The *first objection* may be telling you, **"I wasn't listening."** The *second objection* is saying, **"You haven't given me enough information."** The *third objection* is letting you know, **"I still need more information; you haven't pushed my 'hot button' yet."** If you still have not been successful after the third round, be sure to leave the door open for future contact by using your easy close:

> **Thank you for your time and for sharing the information with me. If I could** *send* **information you** *would* **have an interest in, what would that be.** (*Make an assumptive statement.*)

Be sure to get your prospect to commit to your follow-up call, to encourage a healthy call back, and ensure the prospect's interest in receiving the information. Maybe now is not the right time for your prospect, but if he or she has gone this far with you, there is still an interest. You may need a few more contacts to establish rapport. The key here is to *establish and build up a relationship*. Do not create unintentional bad-will by being overly insistent. Perhaps now is not the time to sell. It doesn't mean, however, that you can't begin a rapport that will develop into a future sale or even a referral!

A Positive Outlook

A prospect's complaints are sometimes based on a *previous bad experience*. An objection can be viewed as a concern of the prospect. Once you have gone through the objection process, narrowed down the objection to the real issue, and determined that you can do nothing more to offer solutions that will satisfy your prospect, you should not have any negative feelings about your contact. You've done your job to the best of your ability. Remember, you can always keep the line of communication open by using the *easy close.* There are still plenty of prospects out there! Knowing that you have followed what you were instructed to do helps you to remain *confident* and *positive* for your next prospect.

Earlier in this chapter, we discussed the benefits of having your presentation in a script format (your road map); your prospects' most common objections with your appropriate answers also needs to be scripted. In an automation environment, this is accomplished by placing it into the software. However, when you are in a manual environment, these objections and answers should be readily available.

Ideally, what you want to eventually accomplish is to internalize your rebuttals. The best way to do this is by practicing through role playing, understanding how the objection techniques function, and using them daily. Included in this book, you will find the most common objections and answers. Rewrite them to fit your particular company's needs and start role-playing!

Objection Handling for the In-bound CSR

An objection received by a CSR is not a rejection. In most cases an objection is telling you, "I'm not happy," "I need that extra customer service," or "I want you to just hear me out." Whenever you are representing your company, always expect to receive resistance or irate customers. Your job is to *defuse* the situation quickly before the customer gets out of hand and you lose control. If you "pass" or direct the call to someone else, try to leave a positive impression with your customer. Doing so will make things much easier for the person who will eventually handle the customer. You will not feel badly because you will know that you did your best. You will then be able to move on and effectively service your next customer with a positive and professional attitude.

When customers sound or behave negatively, it is usually the result of a problem they've had prior to your contact with them. If your customer seems rude during your contact, then try placing the blame on yourself just to release some barriers and allow your customer to cool down. Ask the customer, **"What happened?,"** or **"Have I said anything to cause you to feel this way?"** Make sure you express yourself by using proper voice inflection—sound as if you meant it! These questions will serve to clear the air, and the customer will be more likely to open up and tell you what the real issue is. Acknowledging and agreeing with your customers is an effective way to get on their good side, thereby increasing your success in developing rapport and establishing confidence with them.

What Is the Real Issue?

When you are faced with an objection, you need to define what the customer is really trying to tell you. Statements such as, "I don't want to be on hold!," or, "I want to talk with your manager now!," don't represent the real issues at hand—something else is behind these statements. Narrowing the objections will help you to determine the best solutions to defuse the situation. Before trying to overcome your customer's concerns or make any assumptions of what you think is the problem, analyze the following criteria: *What relationship does your customer have with you and your company? What is your customer really trying to tell you?* The following objections are typical in a customer service environment. You may have faced many of these at one time or another. I'm positive you can also relate from your own *personal* experiences. Think about it, how did you feel and react when *you* received these objections from one of your own customers? How did you react or respond?

> I don't have the time.
> Forget it! I'll call back.
> I have a problem.
> I don't want to be on hold!
> I want to talk with your manager *now!*
> Who is *his boss!?*
> I'm tired of getting the runaround!
> You people are all alike, you don't care!
> I'm really upset!
> I don't want to talk with you.
> I want to talk with someone right now!
> Who is your boss?
> I called before and didn't like the way I was treated.
> You disconnected me!
> Your person referred me to the wrong store or individual.
> I was placed on hold too long!
> You said I could get service by Monday, and it wasn't ready. ...
> I am being overcharged!
> I want some answers *now!*
> You blankety blank blank!

The list could go on and on. The point is to never allow these types of objections or resistance to surface. You need to take the right steps to prevent them altogether. Following the 12 steps will help you to achieve this goal. However, these objections do occur, what do you do? The following information will be of assistance in professionally overcoming these common objections. Study the techniques, role-play with them, and then apply them in your customer service environment. By doing so, you will have greater control of each situation while your customer will feel their needs are being taken care of properly.

Five Objection Methods

Below are five methods you can use to narrow, overcome, and outweigh your customer's objections or resistance. Pick the ones you feel comfortable with and that are appropriate for the response you may get from your customer.

1. Restate or agree, and probe
2. Reflect
3. Feel-felt-found method
4. Ask customer for best solution.
5. If I could … , would you … ?

Restate or Agree, and Probe.   You can find the real issue by restating or agreeing, and probing. You will not use all three individually. Instead, you will either restate and probe or agree and probe. However, restating and probing is only effective if the objection can be restated in a positive way. The following is an example of a restatement:

> Objection: **I have no money to pay on this account.**
> Restatement: **What you're saying is that you agree you need to pay on this account, however your concern is, you have no funds available to do so at this time. Is that correct?**

Here is an example of agreeing:

> Objection: **I want to talk with your supervisor.**
> Agreement: **I would be happy to direct you to Mr. Campbell.**

This is an example of probing:

> Objection: **I'm really upset!**
> Probe: **What are some of your concerns?**

By using the restate method, you can get a confirmation from your customer. This narrows down the real issue quickly. You can then proceed to your probing questions. Otherwise, skip over restating and immediately agree and probe to draw out real issues. *Agreeing* is used to help defuse the objection quickly so your prospect will actively listen and respond to your probing questions more openly.

Figure 15-2 is a flow chart of this technique of restate or agree, and probe. This will direct your objection process more clearly. This first method is the ideal process to use, since it quickly identifies the real issues and guides you through additional selling.

Reflect.   The reflect method is an opportunity to use the information your customer has previously given you and make him or her accountable for it. This is very effective especially when you have already received a prior commitment from customers and they are planning to renege. This method is important because it helps you remain both position and confident.

> **I understand, Mr. Johnson. You mentioned quite a few concerns. You mentioned** (*reflect*)**, the idea that** (*reflect*)**, and you also want to** (*reflect*)**. One of the areas that I did not hear you talk about is the fact that we can** (*describe*)**. Mr. Johnson how important is that to you?" or, Would you agree that this would be more beneficial to you?**

Feel, Felt, Found.   Put yourself in your customer's place. When using this technique, try not to sound canned. You must be sincere and genuine so the method comes across naturally. You do not necessarily have to use the words *feel, felt,* and *found.* Instead, be more creative in your statements by using some of the variations offered earlier in the chapter or create some of your own. Below are some other examples:

Feel (empathize):	**I understand how you** *feel.*
	I respect what you're saying.
	I appreciate your letting me know that.

Once you have empathized with a customer's situation, make the customer understand that there are no unique concerns. In this way, a person will not feel that her or his situation is uncommon or that you are not capable of handling or overcoming it. For example:

Felt (relate):	**I would have** *felt* **the same way.**
	I would to be concerned.
	I'm sure it's a concern for others.

You may not always have the answers your customers are looking for, but you can offer some solutions they have not yet considered or provide a temporary solution until you can research it further. Give your customer objective answers by offering solutions:

Found (resolve):	**Until they** *found* **that ...**
	Until they discovered ...
	Until we had the opportunity ...

Ask Customer for Best Solution.   This is beneficial when you really want your customer to see your position. This helps put customers in the position of

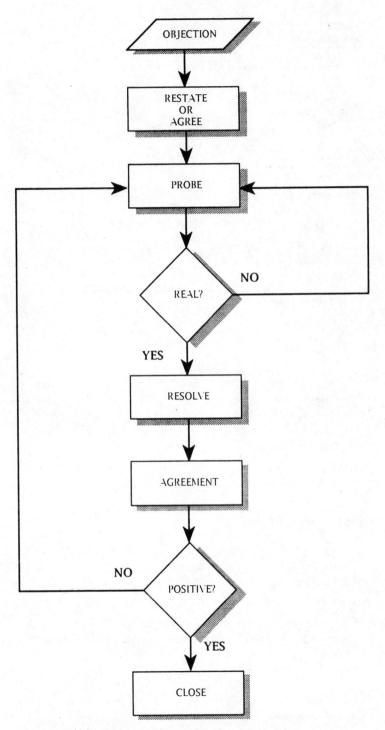

Figure 15-2. Restate or agree, and probe.

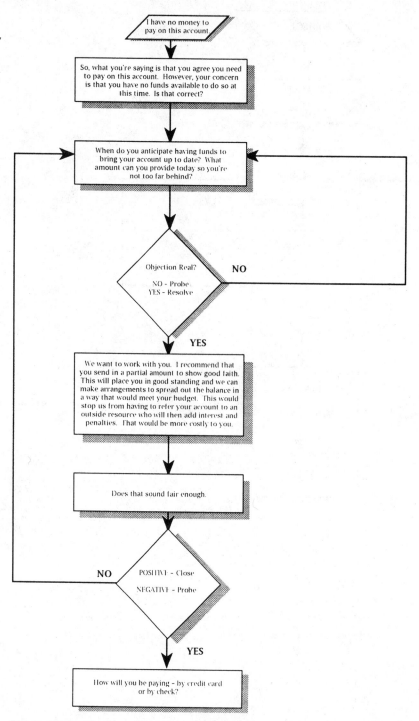

Figure 15-2. (Continued).

helping themselves and finding their own solutions if they are not allowing you to help them.

> **What would you suggest if you were in my position?**
> **What can I do that will help you while still meeting the company guidelines?**
> **What would you recommend?**
> **What would satisfy your needs while meeting our company's objectives?**
> **What would it take to allow me the opportunity to assist you better?**

"If I Could...,Would You...?"   This method is very popular with many customer service representatives. Even though it is used extensively, this method can be extremely effective when used with the proper verbiage so it sounds more original.

> **I appreciate what you're saying. If I can provide you with** (*describe*)**, would you agree to the terms that were originally set up when you first contacted us? or, Would you allow me the opportunity to get the final approval from my supervisor? or, Would that be all right *with* you.**

Note: These are closed-ended questions. You can also use an open-ended approach such as, **"How would that meet your needs?"**

Remember to use the five objection-handling methods as your models when entering step 9, handling objections, of your CSR presentation. Choose the method that is best suited for the type of objection you received. Plan out in advance the objections you are getting and decide which method is best and script out how you will be overcoming them.

Combined Objection-Handling Methods

You can also combine the methods to be more creative in overcoming the objections. For example:

> **I appreciate your concerns, Mr. Johnson. I know this has placed you at an inconvenience, and you want some answers immediately. I recommend that I get as much information as possible, then I will proceed to research it and do my best to get you what you're looking for. If I can accomplish this today, would you allow me the opportunity to try?**

Which objection techniques were used? Yes, the feel, felt, found and "If I could ... , would you?" Now, *you* practice combining the methods to create your own style of delivery!

The Points to Remember for Objection Handling

Bring objections into the open so you clearly understand them.

Do not be defensive when faced with an objection.

Develop the habit of listening carefully to objections.

Remember, people do not always say what they mean.

Treat objections as attention getters or customers asking for more information.

Keep ego and pride out of the way. Do not let your emotions take over.

Decide whether you want to make a customer happy or win arguments!

In general, people can't be talked into changing their minds, but they can be "listened" into changing their minds. It all depends on the approach.

Many people will be receptive to your ideas if they feel you are really trying to understand their needs.

Put the ball in the other person's court. Let him or her tell you how to best solve the objection.

After overcoming objections, take control by getting the customer's reaction such as: **"How does that sound?"** or **"Would that be all right *with* you."** (*Use an assumptive.*)

Be direct, if necessary, by asking your customer, **"What are some of your concerns?"** Or, **"Other than the shipping cost, what else is preventing you from keeping the product?"**

Welcome objections by letting customers know that you understand their feelings.

Identify specific objections by asking your customer if they have any other concerns not yet discussed.

Discuss possible solutions by asking for your customer's opinion as to the best solution. Put customers in a position to sell themselves.

Never Say Never

Never give up on an objection until you try to overcome or outweigh it at least *three times*. The first objection may be telling you, "I'm angry." Your reaction is to *cool the customer down*. The second objection is saying, "I wasn't listening." Now you try to explain by *offering solutions*. The third objection is letting you know, "I'm not going to listen, I want it my way." Now it's probably best to *pass the call* on to someone else with a different voice and with a new perspective.

Most Common Objections and Answers

There are common objections you will hear repeatedly. It is essential that you learn how to overcome them. Here are some answers to help you until you have the opportunity to work the objections out on your own. Try to identify which methods are used in each example. This will help you gain a better understanding of how to use them proficiently.

Objection: *Forget it! I'll call back.*

Answer: **Certainly you may call back Mr. Johnson, however, I would be more than happy to try to assist you personally, or if you like, direct you to someone else who can try and service you better than I can. How would you prefer that I handle this Mr. Johnson?**

Objection: *I don't want to be on hold!*

Answer: **I can appreciate that Mr. Johnson; however, I do have another customer waiting before you who is just as *important* as you are. If you feel I should have my customer wait longer, I would like to let my other customer know, so he or she won't feel I have abandoned them? Would that be all right with you.** (*Use an assumptive.*)

Objection: *I'm tired of getting the runaround!*

Answer: **I certainly can understand and appreciate your frustration, Mr. Johnson. Share with me what has happened so I can make sure you won't experience this again?**

Objection: *I got disconnected.*

Answer: **I apologize, Mr. Johnson. It was my fault. Whom do you wish to speak with, and I'll make sure you are directed properly.**

Objection: *I was put on hold for too long.*

Answer: **I apologize that you have been inconvenienced, Mr. Johnson. I would be more than happy to assist you, where may I direct your call?**

Objection: *You said I could get service by Monday, and I didn't.*

Answer: **I apoligize for the inconvenience, Mr. Johnson. In order to determine what happened and to help correct it, I need ... > to ask you *just* a couple of *quick* questions if you don't mind. Who was the person you placed your order with? When was the order taken? What was your order?** (*Restate answers.*) **Let me see what I can do. This may take some time for me to investigate; however, I will take it upon myself to do this personally, and if I am unable to service your needs I will direct this matter to my supervisor who will. Would that be all right *with* you, or, Does that sound fair enough.** (*Use an assumptive.*)

A Prospective Outlook

Your customers' complaints are sometimes based on bad experiences they have had. An objection can be viewed as a concern of the customer. Once you have gone through the objection process, narrowed the objection to the real issue, and determined that you, as a customer service representative, can do nothing more to offer solutions that will satisfy your customer, you should not have negative feelings about your contact. You've done your job to the best of your ability. Remember you can always pass the call and let someone else deal with the situation, if you've done all you can. There are plenty more customers out there who need you! Remain *confident* and *positive* for your next customer.

Handling Difficult Customers

Handling difficult customers is not easy for anyone, but this very vital task needs to be given attention. Your customers have mood swings along with good and bad days. Don't respond to a difficult customer by flaring up at bad manners or rudeness. Instead, try to reverse the situation through extra attention. Turn your negative customer into a positive one. You'll really show your professionalism and skill as a customer service representative! Accept this customer as a challenge. Don't behave as your customer does. If you do, the end result will be a dissatisfied customer, an upset customer service representative, and a potential loss in revenue for your company. Here is an example of how to *defuse* your customer and try to *cool* him or her down:

I'm really sorry you feel that way, Mr. Johnson. What can I do to help you?

Mr. Johnson, my job is to assist you. If there are any concerns you're unhappy about, I would like to help you in any way I can. If I'm unable to you, I'll find someone who can. Does that sound fair enough. (*Use an assumptive.*)

Using a feel, felt, found attitude can also be very effective. Sympathize with your customer. Make the customer feel that you're on her or his side until the opportunity arises to cool down. You won't be able to deal with the customer objectively until then. Remember, the *feel* is an *empathy statement*. The following are some examples:

I can appreciate that, Mr. Johnson. ...
I understand, I want to help you. ...
I'm sorry you feel that way, Mr. Johnson. ...
Thank you for letting me know that. ...
I respect what you're saying. ...
It's important that you are happy with our service. ...
I understand your concerns. ...

Results depend on each situation, but the idea is to be a sympathetic listener *first*, then try to present a solution to the problem. You play an extremely important role as a representative of your company. You must be able to deal effectively with any difficult situation. It will impress your customers and nurture their confidence in you, your ability to assist them, and your company as a whole. The best position is to be willing to hear them out—to be a solution not an obstacle. The true test of *full customer satisfaction* lies in how well a company can deal with problems, and it all starts with the first phone contact—which is you!

16
Scripts

Chapter 16 provides 30 scripting samples covering both business-to-business and residential prospecting. They serve as blueprints when using the inbound and outbound 12-step training programs from the previous chapters. You are provided with several scripting examples that can be easily applied to your own prospecting efforts including, "Cold Calling," "Cross-Selling Existing Accounts," "Catalog Order," "The Receptionist Script," and much more.

Secretarial screen scripts are included to give you ideas on how to get through the gatekeeper when outbound prospecting business-to-business. The contact ratio is much lower when prospecting the business market, therefore it is critical when prospecting this market that you make contact with a decision maker; each hour of prospecting will increase your opportunities to make your offer. Without a good presentation to cut through the secretary's barrier, the likelihood is less that you will get through. Also, the higher the level of your decision maker's position, the more difficult it will be to get through. The telemarketer needs to learn *how* to get through the gatekeeper to be fully equipped for successful prospecting. The techniques taught in this script are quite different. The ideas provided are uniquely designed to react to the *gatekeeper's instincts*. When the decision maker is unavailable, the telemarketer uses this script to obtain the information needed to get through on the second contact, yet the telemarketer gives the secretary the feeling of being in control.

When reviewing the various scripts, keep in mind they are training scripts. You do not use them verbatim. Instead, you pick what you are comfortable with in regard to verbiage and style. I encourage you to be creative and unique in your delivery. The importance is that you follow the concept of the 12 steps. Do not change these concepts. Otherwise, they will not work as effectively.

Each script is written in a general format. This ensures that it can be applied to anyone's telemarketing operation. Remember, when you rewrite these scripts, you must place the symbols for strategic pauses and voice inflection and identify the use of variable speeds in your pacing in the correct places. When making notations in your scripts as to when variable speeds are used, you can do so by highlighting or underlining the points where you slow down.

After reviewing the scripts, if you are not happy with the way they are written, then at least take the idea along with the concepts of the 12 steps and try to create your own. You can create a script that fits your telemarketing campaign, but be sure to test it out on the telephone to ensure that it sounds the way you want your prospect to hear it. When you are testing scripts, it is best to record yourself. This helps you hear how you are delivering your presentation, where you need to add voice inflection, and, based on your prospect's response, what you need to do to "tweek" it! This testing period could take several hours or a couple of days to get your script to the point where you really feel comfortable with it. You may end up making changes after several weeks—even months.

When you are more experienced with the steps and are making live prospecting calls, the creativity starts to really kick in, and you realize your options and flexibility. When this happens, prospecting becomes more creative, challenging, and interesting. Be sure not to allow yourself to get so creative that you recreate the steps method and lose its concept.

Outbound Scripts

Business-to-Business Prospecting

The following two examples show how a prospect may answer an incoming line once you have gone through the initial secretary screening process. Use the one that best fits your prospecting call. If your prospects clearly identify themselves, use this first approach:

STEP 1   Introduction

PROSPECT: Hello, this is Ms. Williams.

TELEMARKETER: Good morning, Ms. *Jane* Williams?

PROSPECT: Yes.

When you are directed to the person you wish to speak with but that person answers the telephone in a way that really doesn't indicate if you were directed correctly, you need to establish your contact person:

STEP 1   Introduction

PROSPECT: Hello.

TELEMARKETER: Good morning, I need ... > to speak with Ms. Williams, please.

PROSPECT: Yes, this is she.

TELEMARKETER: Ms. *Jane* Williams?

PROSPECT: Yes, this is Jane.

TELEMARKETER: Hello, Jane, this is Jim Larson, I'm with XYZ Manufacturer and we're *located* ... > (or) I repre*sent* ... > (**give landmark, territory, or location**).

STEP 2   Reference

TELEMARKETER: My company requested ... > that I contact you personally.

STEP 3   Request for Time

TELEMARKETER: I hope ... > I haven't caught you at a bad time, *have* I. (*Assumptive*)

PROSPECT: I'm busy right now.

TELEMARKETER: Why don't I call you back in about an hour, would that be all right *with* you. (*Assumptive*)

PROSPECT: What is this all about?

TELEMARKETER: I have several clients in your industry who have expressed an *interest* in our products, and in order for me to be of better *service*, I need ... > to ask you *just* a couple of *quick* questions, if you don't mind. (*Assumptive*)

STEP 5   Probing

For Step 5 and throughout the chapter the following abbreviations are used.

Q   Qualify

W   Establish wants

C   Create a need

Q: Who is currently handling your sales account at this time?

Q: What is your monthly volume?

W: What *motivated* you to select XYZ Competitor as your major wholesaler?

W: What are some of your specifications?

C: What have you compared *recently* to ensure ... > that you are maximizing your *potential* cost-effectively? (*Remember, you must be able to create a need for your services with this final question. You can try and create a deeper need, otherwise you will not be able to continue.*)

STEP 6   Restate

I want to be sure that I have the information correct. Your company is currently doing business with XYZ Competitor, and you were impressed with the benefits the product has to offer, especially the features that save you time and operating costs. However, you expressed a *concern* about not receiving the quality assurance you once had, and you have not heard from your representative for quite sometime. You have not had an *opportunity* to conduct a competitive analysis to determine ... > whether you can still gain many of the features you're happy with and to *ensure* you are receiving ... > the most *competitive* cost that you are *entitled* to. Is that correct? (*Wait for response; you must get a positive response. Otherwise, restate again correctly.*)

STEP 7   Features and Benefits

I recommend an evaluation. This will offer you *additional* information about our products and services compared with XYZ competitor. Our deluxe line will offer you the same specification you require along with the quality assurance you look forward to and are not receiving at this time. More important ... > we can offer you a 10 percent discount which is approximately a 15 percent reduction of your current overhead.

STEP 8   Get Reaction

How profitable would this be for you and your company? (*Wait for response. If the response is positive, go to step 9, otherwise go to step 10.*)

STEP 9   Trial Close

We would like the *opportunity* to introduce ourselves, our products and the services that set us apart from others. Try our products once, if you're not impressed with your first order, we simply don't deserve the right to have your continued business. Does that sound fair enough. (*Assumptive.*) (*If the response is positive, simply close. Otherwise, you can refer to the objection chapter. Find which method is best suited to overcome the negative response.*)

STEP 10   Objections

See Chapter 15.

STEP 11   Close

I can place your order by COD or credit, which would you prefer?

STEP 12   Postclose

In order to save time and process your order faster, I need a little more information.

1. Who, other than yourself, should I make this attention to?

2. How many units do you usually order each month?

3. What type of account system do you currently have with XYZ competitor?

Thank you for your order. You should expect delivery within the next 3 days. Should you have any questions or concerns, please contact me personally. Ask for Jim Larson, my extension is 123. Is there anything else I can do for you before I process your order? Have a good day! (*Wait for prospect to hang up first!*)

Cross-Selling Existing Clients

STEP 1   Introduction

Good_____, I need ... > to speak with Mr. (**last name**) please? (*Use first name cue if rapport has been previously established.*) Hello (**first or last name**), this is (**your full name**) with (**your company name**) and we're located ... > (**territory, landmark, or location**).

STEP 2   Reference

My company requested ... > I contact you personally. (Or) I'm contacting our distributor's customers to help keep their inventory up-to-date. (Or) I'm updating our distributor's accounts.

STEP 3   Request for Time

I hope ... > I haven't caught you at a bad time *have* I. (*Assumptive.*)
Why don't I call you back in about an hour, would that be all right *with* you. (*Assumptive*)

STEP 4   Purpose of Call

We are reviewing our distributor's customer base and in order for us to *continue* offering the best products on the market, I need ... > to ask you *just* a couple of *quick* questions, if you don't mind. (*Assumptive*) (Or) As I mentioned earlier, I'm updating our distributor's customer inventory (**or**) accounts and, in order to *ensure* you are getting the best service you're entitled to, I need ... > to ask you *just* a couple of *quick* questions, if you don't mind. (*Assumptive*)

STEP 5   Probing

Q: How familiar are you with the variety of (*describe*) products we manufacture?

Q: Other than (*describe*), what other products do you offer your customers?

Q: What is your most popular product line?

Q: What is your least favored product line?

Q: Who do you order your (*describe*) from?

Q: Since you serve (*describe*), who do you order your (*describe*) from?

W: What motivated you to choose XYZ competitor?

C: When was the last time you evaluated and cost compared *ensuring* you offer the best products while maximizing your profits?

C: Regarding (*describe*), what have you compared recently to determine ... > the best (*describe*) available for your customers?

Easy Close

I respect that. (Or) Thank you for sharing the information with me. If I could *send* you information about (*describe*) you would have an interest in, what would that be. (*Assumptive*) Once you have had the **opportunity** to review the information, I would like to gain your feedback. Does that sound fair enough. (*Assumptive*)

STEP 6   Restate

I want to be sure I have the information correct (*restate their answers*). Is that correct?

STEP 7   Features and Benefits

Based on the information I have on your account, I recommend you try using (*describe the feature you are selling*). Our (*describe the functions of the product*). How this benefits your customers (*describe the implied benefits*). More important, ... > This offers continuity in customer ordering and increases your sales.

STEP 8   Get Reaction

How important would that increase be to your bottom line? (Or) How valuable would that be to your customers?

STEP 9   Trial Close

Great! I recommend that you try (*describe*). Start out with a test order, and see what kind of response you receive. Your distributors will check back within a couple of weeks to see how you are doing to ensure ... > you don't run out of stock.

Does that sound fair enough. (*Assumptive*) (Or) Based on your current orders, I recommend (*describe*) to start out with, and if your distributor doesn't hear from you by (*offer time frame*), I will check back with you to see if we need to make any adjustments to your order. What else do we need to consider before I process your order?

STEP 10   Objections

See Chapter 15.

STEP 11   Close

I will expedite your order today, and your distributor will be able to get that out to you by (*offer time frame*). Does that meet within your time frame?

STEP 12   Postclose

To process your order more efficiently, I need to go over the information to be sure I have everything correct. (*Go over your order form.*) Thank you for your order. We will be looking forward to gaining your feedback!

Direct Mail Follow-Up

STEP 1   Introduction

Good_____, I need ... > to speak with Mr/s. (**first or last name**), please. Hello, this is (**your full name**) with (**company name**).

STEP 2   Reference

You requested that we contact you personally. (Or) You expressed an interest in (*describe*). (Or) I'm following up on the information you requested.

STEP 3   Request for Time

I hope ... > I haven't caught you at a bad time, *have* I. (*Assumptive*)
Why don't I call you back in about an hour, would that be all right *with* you. (*Assumptive*)

STEP 4   Purpose

I'm following up on your request regarding (*explain*). In order for me to provide you with all the information you are most interested in, I need ... > to ask you *just* a couple of *quick* questions, if you don't mind. (*Assumptive*)

STEP 5   Probing

   Q: What about the information interested you?

   Q: Who, other than us, have you requested information from regarding (*describe*)?

   Q: Who is currently providing your (*describe*)?

W: What areas would you like to see improved?

W: Other than affordability, what other concerns do you have?

C: When was the last time you evaluated your options to **determine** ... >
what steps are available to (*describe*)?

STEP 6   Restate

I want to be sure that I have the information correct (*restate their answers*). Is
that correct?

STEP 7   Features and Benefits

I recommend that you acquire a second **opinion** regarding (*describe*). You will
be provided with information regarding (*describe*). You will have peace of
mind knowing you have alternatives to your (*describe*). More important, ... >
you may be able to increase the value of your current (*describe*).

STEP 8   Get Reaction

How important is this information to you?

STEP 9   Trial Close

If I'm unable to offer ideas that will help you achieve what you're looking for
within the first 30 minutes of our time together, I won't take up any more of
your **valuable** time. I simply don't **deserve** your future business. Does that
sound fair enough. (*Assumptive*)

STEP 10   Objections

See Chapter 15.

STEP 11   Close

Great! What time of the day are you and **(partner or spouse)** available, during
the mornings, afternoons, or are evenings better? I have **(day)** or would you
prefer **(day)**? How about **(time)** or **(time)**? Which is better for the both of you?

STEP 12   Postclose

In order for me to save you time and allow me to personalize the information,
I need a little more information. (*Ask up to four additional questions to do your
preliminary profiles.*)

Thank you for the additional information. I look forward to seeing you and **(partner or spouse)** on **(day, date, and time of appointment)**. In the meantime are there any questions or concerns you have that I can address at this time? Thank you for your time and consideration. You have a good day!

Dissatisfied Clients

STEP 1   Introduction

Good_____ , I need … > to speak with Mr. or Mrs. **(last name)**, please. Mr/s. (**First** **and last name**)? (*Wait for response.*) Hello, this is **(your full name)**, I represent **(client's name)** and we're *lo*cated … > **(landmark/location)**.

STEP 2   Reference

I'm updating our customer's information. (Or) My company requested … > I contact you personally. (Or) I've been given the opportunity to review [(or) service] **(previous TSR's name)** customers.

STEP 3   Request for Time

I hope … > I haven't caught you at a bad time, *have* I. (*Assumptive*)
Why don't I call you back in about an hour, would that be all right *with* you. (*Assumptive*)

STEP 4   Purpose

I'm updating our customer's information and in order for **(company's name)** to *continue* to service you at our best, I need … > to ask you *just* a couple of *quick* questions, if you don't mind. (*Assumptive*)

(Or)

I'm contacting **(previous TSR's)** clients and in order to *ensure* your needs are being adequately met, I need … > to ask you *just* a couple of *quick* questions, if you don't mind. (*Assumptive*)

(Or)

I want to get a better *understanding* of the service we've provided and in order to accomplish this effectively, I need … > to ask you *just* a couple of *quick* questions, if you don't mind.

(Or)

I have been with **(company's name)** for quite sometime, and I am actively reviewing many of our customer's service and (*describe*) needs. In order to *ensure* your needs have been taken care of properly and to your satisfaction, I need … > to ask you *just* a couple of *quick* questions if you don't mind. (*Assumptive*)

STEP 5   Probing (Pick and Choose)

Q: When was the last time you were contacted by our company?

Q: What were the results of your last servicing and how do you feel about the way you were treated?

W: So far, based on how we have serviced you, what *improvements* would you recommend, with regards to ... > how we can meet your needs *better*?

W: What *motivated* you to select XYZ company to service your needs?

W: Now that they have been servicing you for sometime, how do you feel about the service and the price you're getting *today*, compared to when you *first* acquired them?

W/C: What concerns do you have in allowing us the *opportunity* to offer you a *second* opinion, to determine ... > whether we can offer you *better* servicing at a more *competitive* price?

C: When did you *last* make a comparison to determine ... > whether you're getting the *maximum* benefits at the most competitive cost?

C: What steps have you taken to allow us an *opportunity* to conduct a thorough review of your (*describe*), to confidently assure you that your needs are being *fully* taken care of?

Easy Close

I respect that. (Or) Thank you for sharing the information with me. I would like the opportunity to *send* you updated information about other services that may benefit you. Would that be all right *with* you. (*Assumptive*) (Or) I respect that. (Or) Thank you for sharing the information with me. If I could *send* you information about (*offer examples*) you would have an interest in, what *would* that be. (*Assumptive*) Once you've had an *opportunity* to review the information, I would like your feedback. Does that sound fair enough. (*Assumptive*)

STEP 6   Restate

Based on what you said.... Is that correct?

STEP 7   Features and Benefits

I recommend that you allow us an *opportunity* to service your needs once again. We have made many internal changes within our company such as (*describe*). Also, we have increased our product line by adding (*describe the features and functions and benefits*). How this benefits you is (**implied benefits**) and more importantly ... > you will (or) can (**stated benefits**).

STEP 8   Get Reaction

How important is this to you? (Or) How valuable is this to you?

STEP 9   Trial Close

This gives me an *opportunity* to personally meet with you and show you what I specialize in and to continue … > keeping you informed of the services you're *entitled* to regarding your (*describe*). Does that sound fair enough. (Or) Would that be all right *with* you. (*Assumptive*)

(Or)

I would like the opportunity … > to *send* you a sample of the (*describe*). In this way you will be able to evaluate the difference between the quality of our product and that of (**XYZ company**). You may be surprised to know how we are more *superior* than others and the fact that we can offer you more *competitive* prices. Does that sound fair enough. (*Assumptive*)

STEP 11   Close

What time of the day are you and (**partner or spouse**) available, during the morning, afternoon, or evening? I have (**day**) or would you prefer (**day**)? How about (**time**) or (**time**). Which is better for you and (**partner or spouse**)? (Or) I will send you the information [or product] (*describe*) within the next 24 hours. Who, other than yourself, should I make this attention to?

STEP 12   Postclose

In order for me to save you time and allow me to *personalize* the information. I need … > *just* a little more information. (*Ask additional questions to do your preliminary profile.*)

Infomercials Follow-up

STEP 1   Introduction

Good_____, I need … > to speak with Mr/s. (**last name**) please? Mr/s. (**first and last name**)? Hello (**first or last name**). This is (**your full name**). I represent (**company name**), and we're *located* … > (**landmark/location**).

STEP 2   Reference

My company [or marketing department] requested … > I contact you personally. (Or) We recently sent you information that you requested. (Or) You recently viewed one of our infomercials on television about (*describe*). (Or) You requested … > that we contact you personally. (Or) You expressed an interest in our (*describe*).

STEP 3 Request for Time

I hope ... > I haven't caught you at a bad time, *have* I.
Why don't I call you back in about an hour. Would that be all right *with* you.
(*Assumptive*)

STEP 4 Purpose

We specialize in (*describe*). In order for us to **continue** providing better programs [or products], I need ... > to ask you *just* a couple of *quick* questions, if you don't mind.

(Or)

I'm following up on the information we sent you. In order for us to provide you with **additional** information you may have an interest in, I need ... > to ask you *just* a couple of *quick* questions, if you don't mind.

(Or)

According to my records you recently requested information about (*describe*). In order for me, [or us] to **ensure** that you have all the information you're looking for, I need ... > to ask you *just* a couple of *quick* questions, if you don't mind.

(Or)

We're updating our information. In order for us to **continue** providing **quality** products to consumers, I need ... > to ask you *just* a couple of *quick* questions, if you don't mind.

(Or)

We're contacting people who learned about (*describe*) on our television commercials. In order to determine ... > how we can **continue** providing the best programs/products available, I need ... > to ask you *just* a couple of *quick* questions, if you don't mind.

STEP 5 Probing (Pick and Choose)

Q/W: When did you receive the information, and what interested you the most?

Q: When did you first learn about (*describe*), and what impressed you about our (*describe*)?

Q/W: What concerns do you have that I can address at this time?

W: What is your opinion about (*describe*), and what would you like to see different or **improved** that would help you to create a **greater** interest in the program?

W: What originally motivated you to respond to our commercials?

W: Now that you know more about our products, what price did you have in mind for a program such as this?

C: If you could receive this today, providing it met your expectations, how valuable would this be for you to have?

STEP 6   Restate

Based on what you said.... Is that correct?

STEP 7   Features and Benefits

I recommend (**feature**). I recommend this because of (**function**). This will provide (**implied benefits**), and more important ... > you can/will (**stated benefits**).

STEP 8   Get Reaction

How important is this to you? (Or) How valuable would this be to you?

STEP 9   Trial Close

I suggest you try (**product name**) for 30 days. If you're not *absolutely* satisfied with the results and the *increased* (*describe*) you're anticipating, simply return the program [or product] for a *complete* refund within that 30 day time frame. We simply don't deserve the right to have your *continued* business. Does that sound fair enough. (*Assumptive*)

STEP 10   Objections

See Chapter 15.

STEP 11   Close

Assumptive Close
In addition to the benefits that we've discussed, is there anything else we need to consider before I process your order?

Direct Close Contained Choice Close
I can accept your Visa or MasterCard, which do you prefer?

Contained Choice Close
Which card do you prefer, Visa or MasterCard?

STEP 12   Postclose

I have your address at (**state**)?

What is the card number and expiration date?

What name would you want the product registered under?

I can have this shipped to you within 24 hours, and you should expect it within the next 7 to 10 days. Is there any other information you need at this time?

We appreciate your business. Should you need any further assistance, please don't hesitate to call, we would be happy to help you. Again, this is **(your name)** and you have a nice day! (*Smile*)

Market Research Business to Business

STEP 1   Introduction

Good_____, I need … > to speak with Mr/s. **(last name)**, please. Mr/s. **(first and last name)**? Hello, this is **(your full name)** with **(company name)** and we're located … > **(landmark or location)** (Or) I represent … > **(territory)**.

STEP 2   Reference

My company requested … > I contact you personally. (Or) I recently sent you information. (Or) We specialize in servicing your industry (*be specific*).

STEP 3   Request for Time

I hope … > I haven't caught you at a bad time, *have* I. (*Assumptive*)
Why don't I call you back in about an hour, would that be all right *with* you. (*Assumptive*)

STEP 4   Purpose

We are currently expanding, and in order for us to service the market better, I need … > to ask you *just* a couple of *quick* questions, if you don't mind. (*Assumptive*)

(Or)

I'm following up on the information I personally sent you. In order for this information to be more effective, I need … > to ask you *just* a couple of *quick* questions, if you don't mind. (*Assumptive*)

(Or)

My company wants to get a better understanding of the needs within your industry (*be specific*). In order for us to meet with demands of this market, I need … > to ask you *just* a couple of *quick* questions, if you don't mind.

(Or)

I have several clients within your industry who have expressed an interest in our service. In order to determine whether we can meet your needs, I need

... > to ask you *just* a couple of *quick* questions, if you don't mind. (*Assumptive*)

(Or)

We specialize in servicing (*describe*) and in order for us to be more effective, I need ... > to ask you *just* a couple of *quick* questions, if you don't mind. (*Assumptive*)

STEP 5 Probing

Q: How familiar are you with our company and the products/services we have to offer?

Q: What best describes your type of business—corporation, sole proprietor, or a franchise?

Q/W: In the areas of (*describe*), who are you currently doing business with and how long have you been with them?

W: What *motivated* you to choose XYZ company?

W: How often does your representative follow up, *ensuring* your needs are taken care of?

C: When was the last time you *compared* (*describe*), and what did you do with that comparison?

C: When do you plan to reevaluate your (*describe*) and what other companies would you be considering when making this evaluation?

C: When was the last time anyone *determined* the cost-effectiveness and quality of your (*describe*) and if they are still meeting your specifications?

Easy Close

Thank you for sharing the information. If I could provide you information about the difference between our company compared to XYZ company that you would have an interest in, what *would* that be. (*Assumptive*)

(Or)

I would like to *send* you some information about our company. This will give you insight on what is available and the features and benefits you will receive in *comparison* to what you currently use. Would that be all right *with* you. (*Assumptive*)

(Or)

I'd like to have the opportunity to *send* you some information about our products and the services we provide. This will help you to evaluate what sets us apart from our competitors. Would that be all right *with* you. (*Assumptive*)

Once you've had the *opportunity* to review the information, I will contact you personally in a few days to gain your feedback. I'll be prepared to address any questions you may have. Does that sound fair enough. (*Assumptive*)

Business Market Research Follow-up

STEP 1   Introduction

Hello, Mr/s. (**first or last name**)? This is (**full name**) with (**your company name**).

STEP 2   Reference

We spoke on (**give date**), and I sent the literature you requested. (Or) You requested ... > I contact you personally.

STEP 3   Request for Time

I hope ... > I haven't caught you at a bad time, *have* I. (*Assumptive*)
Why don't I call you back in about an hour, would that be all right *with* you.

STEP 4   Purpose

Now that you've had an *opportunity* to review the materials, I need ... > to ask you *just* a couple of *quick* questions, if you don't mind. (*Assumptive*)

STEP 5   Probing (Pick up to Three Questions)

- *Q:* When did you receive the information?
- *Q:* What price range are you looking for?
- *W:* What about the information interested you the most?
- *W:* What is your opinion about the diversity of products we offer and the services we provide?
- *W:* What exactly are you looking for when it comes to meeting your companies' needs?
- *W:* What are some of your concerns?

STEP 6   Restate

Based on what you just said ... (*Restate the answers from the first and second contact. Make it sound positive and encouraging—this helps you to lead into your features and benefits.*) Is that correct? (Or) When we spoke before you said.... Is that correct?

(The following is an example of a restatement:)
Last time we spoke you said that you see the value of *(describe)* for your business. Unfortunately, you have not been given the **opportunity** to conduct a competitive analysis, to determine ... > how cost-effective your **current** products are. That comparison would give you a **greater** competitive edge on your overhead costs. Is that correct? *(Restate the answers and make them sound positive and encouraging, this helps you to lead into your features and benefits.)*

STEP 7 Features and Benefits

Mr/s. **(first or last name)** our company offers a full range of products and services that meet what your company is looking for. I recommend *(describe a product or service)*. This will *(describe the particular functions and specifications of your product and/or service you are promoting)*. We are highly competitive and reliable. Furthermore, *(describe product or service)* is designed for today's market. Our *(describe)* provides you with diversification and high performance. We offer after-purchase support and guarantee the service available. This assurance allows our customers to use our services without having to worry about being dissatisfied with cost or quality of service. More important ... > this will **maximize** your savings from 30 to 60 percent over the other major competitors. Our services [or products] offer premium benefits and are cost-effective for all our customers compared to others on the market.

STEP 8 Get Reaction

How important are the benefits I've just described to you? (Or) How valuable is this to you and your company?

STEP 9 Trial Close

My recommendations are, to allow our company the **opportunity** to validate what our *(name the product or service)* will do to increase the quality of *(describe)*. This will also give you an opportunity to evaluate us, compare our aggressiveness in the marketplace, and to know why our customers have confidence in us. Would you agree that your company can benefit from some of the areas I just described. *(Assumptive)* (Or) Does that sound fair enough. *(Assumptive)* (Or) Would that be all right **with** you. *(Assumptive)*

STEP 10 Objection

See Chapter 15.

STEP 11   Assumptive Close

I will have one of our representatives give you a call, and he or she can set the appointment in order to meet both your calendars. (Or) My representative is available to meet with you during the mornings or afternoons. Which is better for you? I have **(date)** or would you prefer **(date)**? How about **(time)**, or is **(time)** better? (Or) I can expedite this today for a minimal fee of $_____. What would you prefer, COD or 10-day net?

STEP 12   Postclose

In order for met to ensure that I have all the correct information, I need ... > to ask you *just* a few more *quick* questions, if you don't mind. (*Ask any questions that would help you to further your appointment or processing of the order.*)

Residential Market Research

STEP 1   Introduction

Good morning/afternoon, I need ... > to speak with Mr/s. **(last name)**? Mr/s. **(first and last name)**? Hello, this is **(your full name)** with **(your company name)** and I repre*sent* the **(territory calling into)**.

STEP 2   Reference

My company requested ... > I contact you personally.

STEP 3   Request for Time

I hope ... > I haven't caught you at a bad time, *have* I. (*Assumptive*)
Why don't I call you back in about an hour, would that be all right *with* you. (*Assumptive*)

STEP 4   Purpose

We're updating information for your industry *regarding* (*describe*). In order for our efforts to be successful in providing quality service and product development, I need ... > to ask *just* a couple of *quick* questions, if you don't mind. (*Assumptive*)

STEP 5   Probing

Q: Who other than yourself handles the (*describe*)?

Q: What type of (*describe*) and who do you get them from?

Q: In reference to (*explain*) how *competitive* are their rates in comparison to the service and performance?

Q/W: How often do you review, and what are you generally looking for?

W: Other than (*describe*), what is your *primary* method of (*describe*)?

W: What would you like to see improved?

C/Q: When did you last review your current system, and/or what were the results of that comparison?

C/W: How receptive is your department in gaining a second opinion to *determine* whether you can improve on the quality while keeping your overhead cost down?

C: When was the *last* time you researched other (*describe*), so you're *confident* your getting what you're entitled to?

Easy Close

I respect that. Thank you for sharing that information with me. If I could *send* you information about (*describe*) you would have an interest in, what *would* that be. (*Assumptive*) Once you've had an *opportunity* to review the information, I would like to gain your feedback. Does that sound fair enough. (*Assumptive*)

Sending Information Postclose

In order to save you time and allow me to *personalize* the information, I need … > a little more information from you.

1. I have your mailing address at (**state**).
2. Whose attention, other than yours, should I send this to?

You should be receiving the information by (**date**); if you have your calendar handy, I would like to follow up on (**date**), would you prefer mornings or afternoons? I have (**time**), or is (**time**) better? Do you have that on your calendar? Terrific! I look forward to talking with you again on (**day, date, and time**). Are there any other questions or concerns that I can address at this time? Thank you for your time and consideration. Have a good day!

Prospecting Your Network for Market Research

STEP 1 Introduction

Good_____, I need … > to speak with Mr/s. (**name**), please. Mr/s. (**first and last name**)? (*Wait for response.*) (*First-name cue is optional if you are already on a first-name basis.*) Hello, this is (**your full name**) with (**company name**) and we're located … > (**location or landmark**). (*Keeping prospect's mind actively listening.*) (*This is optional if they don't know where you are located.*)

STEP 2   Reference

I'm actively conducting business with those I network with. (Or) I am contacting those from the **(organization or club they are affiliated with)**. (Or) We met at the **(organization or club they are affiliated with)**.

STEP 3   Request for Time

I hope ... > I haven't caught you at a bad time, *have* I. (*Assumptive*)
Why don't I call you back in about an hour, would that be all right *with* you. (*Assumptive*)

STEP 4   Purpose

When we spoke **(state the date or event)**, you said that (*describe*). I am following up on our discussion, and in order for me to determine your needs *better*, I need ... > to ask you *just* a couple of *quick* questions if you don't mind. (*Assumptive*) (Or) I wanted to have an *opportunity* to *increase* my knowledge of your area of expertise and others within my network to whom I can refer my clients. In order for me to be confident in providing *reliable* information to my clients, I need ... > to ask you *just* a couple of *quick* questions if you don't mind. (*Assumptive*)

STEP 5   Probing

- *Q:* How long have you been in the (*describe*) business?
- *Q:* What can you tell met about this area that would *motivate* my clients in utilizing your services?
- *W:* What arrangements do you require in order for me to introduce my clients to you?
- *W:* What would I say to my clients that would get them interested in what you do?
- *C:* What steps are you taking to network with other professionals such as yourself to do business with, and how do you *determine* who will provide the quality and *dependable* service [or products] you're *entitled* to while keeping a personable and *professional* relationship?

(You can close to request they send information to you or proceed to step 6.)

Close

Thank you for sharing that information with me. I would like for you to *send* me information about your services and your company so that I may have an opportunity to become more knowledgeable when I recommend my clients to you. Would that be all right *with* you. (*Assumptive*)

Once I have had the *opportunity* to review the information, I would like to either get together to discuss our two companies further and how we can work together to help *expand* our businesses. Does that sound fair enough. (*Assumptive*) I look forward to talking with you in a few days.

Follow-up for Prospecting Your Network

STEP 1   Introduction

Good_____, I need ... > to speak with Mr/s. (**name**), please. Hello, this is (**your full name**) with (**company name**).

STEP 2   Reference

I'm following up on the information you sent me.

STEP 3   Request for Time

I hope ... > I haven't caught you at a bad time, *have* I. (*Assumptive*)
Why don't I call you back in about an hour, would that be all right *with* you. (*Assumptive*)

STEP 6   Restate

I appreciate the information you sent me, it was well put together and very informative. When we spoke before, you said (*restate prospects' previous answers to your probing questions*). Is that correct?

STEP 7   Features and Benefits

I recommend that you and I have an opportunity to get together. We can share *important* information about each other's services to determine how we can benefit from each other's clients, such as (*describe*). We can both determine our *options* in the services that are available to each other and how our clients can benefit. This may help to expand our business. More important, ... > our networking may be able to quickly expand our market share while *generating* additional income for each other.

STEP 8   Get Reaction

How valuable would this be for you?

STEP 9   Trial Close

This will give us an *opportunity* to know each other better professionally. When you and I have clients we can provide quality service to, in the area of our expertise, we will have a *resource* we can depend on. Does that sound fair enough. (*Assumptive*)

STEP 10   Objections

See Chapter 15.

STEP 11   Close

Great! What time of the day are you available, during the morning, afternoon, or are evenings better? I have **(day)** or would you prefer **(day)**? How about **(time)** or **(time)**. Which is better for you?

STEP 12   Postclose

(*Get additional information on meeting place and go over day, date, and time of your appointment.*)

Promotion of Existing Clients

STEP 1   Introduction

Good afternoon, I need ... > to speak with Mr/s. **(last name)** please? Mr/s. **(first and last name)**? Hello, this is **(your full name)**. I represent **(your company name)** and we're *lo*cated ... > **(landmark or location)**.

STEP 2   Reference

My company requested ... > I contact you personally.

STEP 3   Request for Time

I hope ... > I haven't caught you at a bad time, *have* I. (*Assumptive*)
Why don't I call you back in about an hour. Would that be all right *with* you. (*Assumptive*)

STEP 4   Purpose of Call

We have a special promotion this month, and in order to *determine* if this would benefit you, I need ... > to ask you *just* a couple of *quick* questions if you don't mind. (*Assumptive*)

STEP 5   Probing

  Q: The last time you ordered **(product)** was on **(date)**, how many are you needing at this time?

Q: I notice we are not providing you with **(product)**, where do you ordinarily receive them from?

Q: How long have they been servicing you, and how often do you reorder from them?

W: What *motivated* you to choose **(XYZ company)** to service your needs, as opposed to our company?

W: Now that they have been servicing you for sometime, how do you feel about the products, the service, and the rates *today*, compared to when you first acquired them?

C: What steps have you taken to allow us to determine ... > whether we can provide you with the same product, while offering you the service you're *entitled* to at a more *competitive* rate?

STEP 6   Restate

Based on what you've said, you are currently in need of **(product)** and you also are currently using **(product)** from another resource. You like using (*describe*), however, you expressed a concern about whether you were getting the best service and at the most competitive rate. Is that correct?

STEP 7   Features and Benefits

We offer a similar product that we feel is a more superior and reliable product. Currently, we have a special with that particular line. You will receive the exact same features and functions such as (*offer examples*). The benefit to you is that you will receive them from us and will only have to work with one vender as opposed to two. In this way we can service all your needs and still give you the kind of service you are accustomed to. More important, ... > because you are a preferred customer, you will receive a special discount which will make our product a lot more affordable for you.

STEP 8   Get reaction

How valuable would that be to you?

STEP 9   Trial Close

I can get you **(product)** today and I recommend you start out with **(quantity)** which will give you even a greater discount at a total of only (*offer discount figure*). Does that sound fair enough. (*Assumptive*)

STEP 10   Objections

See Chapter 15.

STEP 11   Close

How would you like to pay for this—by COD or credit?

STEP 12   Postclose

In order to *ensure* that your order gets to you in a timely manner, I need a little more information from you. (*Ask postclose questions regarding shipping, billing, and updating your data.*)

Prospecting People You Know

STEP 1   Introduction

Good_____, I need ... > to speak with (<u>name</u>) please. Hello, this is (<u>your name</u>).

STEP 2   Reference

I'm actively calling people I know. (Or) I'm *updating* my information.

STEP 3   Request for Time

I hope ... > I haven't caught you at a bad time, *have* I. (*Assumptive*)
Why don't I call you back in about an hour, would that be all right *with* you. (*Assumptive*)

STEP 4   Purpose

I want to *ensure* that I am providing up-to-date information regarding what I do, and in order for me to *continue* giving *reliable* information and quality service to my friends and family, I need ... > to ask you *just* a couple of *quick* questions, if you don't mind. (*Assumptive*) (Or) I'm contacting my friends and relatives to promote my services. In order for me to determine...> how I can service your needs *better*, I need ... > to ask you *just* a couple of *quick* questions, if you don't mind. (*Assumptive*)

STEP 5   Probing (Pick and Choose)

Q: As you know I am in the (*describe*) business, how much do you know about (*describe*)?

Q: Where are you getting your (*describe*) from, and how long have they been servicing you?

Q: What price are you getting it at?

W: What concerns do you have about (*describe*) that I can offer you additional information?

W: If you had *two* options to *enhance* the quality of service and performance, what would they be. (*Assumptive*)

W: What *motivated* you to choose XYZ to service your needs?

W: Now that you have had them for sometime, how do you feel about the products, the service, and the price today *compared* to when you *first* acquired them?

C: When was the last time you discussed your (*describe*) to determine ... > what areas you need to consider *today* to ensure ... > you are getting what you're entitled to and at the most competitive [or affordable] pricing?

(You can close to send information or proceed to step 6.)

Close

I appreciate you answering my questions. This helps me to be aware of my friends' [or relatives'] (*describe*) needs and how I can offer important and up-to-date information. I would like to *send* you information regarding (*describe*). Would that be all right *with* you. (*Assumptive*) I'll research that for you and send it off right away. I'll be talking to you soon.

STEP 6   Restate

I want to be sure I have the information correct (*restate their answers to your probing questions*). Is that correct?

STEP 7   Features and Benefits

I recommend (**features**). I recommend this because it will offer (**functions**). What this provides to you are *alternatives* that will help you to know what your options are. You may be very *surprised* to know what our company can do that will (**implied benefits**). More important, ... > (**stated benefits**).

STEP 8   Get Reaction

How valuable is this information?

STEP 9   Trial Close

This gives me an *opportunity* to service your needs on a professional and personable level. Should I be able to provide you with a *better* product or service compared to what you have now, my intention is that you would *consider* doing business with me. Does that sound fair enough. (*Assumptive*)

STEP 10   Objections

See Chapter 15.

STEP 11   Close

Great! What time of the day are you available, during the mornings, afternoons, or are evenings better? I have **(day)** or would you prefer **(day)**? How about **(time)** or **(time)**, which is better for you?

STEP 12   Postclose

In order for me to save you time and allow me to *personalize* the information, I need ... > just a little more information. (*Ask additional questions to do your preliminary profile.*)

Prospecting for Referrals

STEP Step 1   Introduction

Good_____, I need ... > to speak with Mr. or Mrs. **(first or last name)**, please. Hello, this is **(your full name)** with **(company name)**.

STEP 2   Reference

I'm expanding my business. (Or) I'm actively contacting my clients.

STEP 3   Request for Time

I hope ... > I haven't caught you at a bad time, *have* I. (*Assumptive*)
Why don't I call you back in about an hour, would that be all right *with* you. (*Assumptive*)

STEP 4   Purpose

I'm following up on clients I've serviced, and, in order for me to expand my business opportunities and *continue* providing *good*, reliable, and quality service, I need ... > to ask you *just* a couple of *quick* questions if you don't mind. (*Assumptive*)

STEP 5   Probing

Q: How do you feel about the service I provided you, and share with me whether I was able to address all your concerns?

Q/W: Now that you've had the (*describe*) for some time, how do you feel about it today compared to when you first acquired it?

W: If there was anything you *would* have liked to see improved, what would that be. (*Assumptive*)

C: Who do you know that has a *desire* to receive the same kind of services/products you have invested in?

STEP 6   Restate

So, based on what you said.... Is that correct?

STEP 7   Features and Benefits

I'd like to recommend that you refer my services to people you know who have a need for (*describe*). My services will enable your friends and relatives to receive opportunities as you have enjoyed. You will be providing them with *options* to (*describe*). More important, ... > they can (**stated benefits**).

STEP 8   Get Reaction

How valuable would this information be for people you know?

STEP 9   Trial Close

When the *opportunity* arises, I would like to introduce my services and to tell people you know about the type of work I specialize in. Would that be all right *with* you. (*Assumptive*)

STEP 10   Objections

See Chapter 15.

STEP 11   Close

Who did you have in mind that I can contact and introduce my services to?

STEP 12   Postclose

Thank you very much for your time, and I appreciate your business and support. Is there anything I can do for you at this time? You have a good day!

Receptionist

STEP 1   Introduction

Good morning, (**your company name**), where may I direct your call (*in a friendly nonrushing voice*)?

STEP 2   Establish Rapport

This is (**your first and last name**) and who am I speaking with?
   Mr/s. (**first and last name**)?
   What is the correct spelling of your last name please? (*Optional*)
   What company are you with?
   How did you come to know our company? (*Sales calls only*)

STEP 3   Purpose of Call

Mr/s. (**first or last name**), what shall I say this is in regards to?

STEP 4   Approach

In order to direct you to the right person who can provide you with the information you're looking for, I need … > to ask you *just* a couple of *quick* questions if you don't mind. (*Assumptive*) (Or) Just one moment please, and I'll be right with you. (*Do not go to step 5.*)

STEP 5   Probing (Optional)

Ask open-ended questions to determine the direction of your customer's call. This is only necessary when you do not know where to facilitate your customer. Otherwise, skip step 5 and step 6 and proceed to step 7.

STEP 6   Restate

I want to be sure I have the information correct. … Is that correct?

STEP 7   Resolve

Thank you for the information. (**Person's name**) who is our (**title or position**) is currently with another customer. I expect her to be able to return your call shortly, or, if you prefer, if you wouldn't mind waiting, as soon as (**person's name**) is finished with her customer, she can assist you with the information you're looking for.

STEP 8   Get Agreement

What would be more helpful to you?

STEP 9   Objections

I appreciate your concern (**first or last name**), and I want to help you. (**Person's name**) is the one who is more qualified to give you the information you're looking for. However, if you prefer to talk with someone else, I can have her assistant (**assistant's name**) help you, while we're waiting for (**person's name**) to finish servicing his/her customer who was before your call. What would you prefer?

STEP 10   Close

I apologize for the inconvenience. In the meantime, is there anything I can do while we're waiting for (**person's name**)?

STEP 11   Inform

Good morning (**person's name**). This is (**your name**), I have (**customer's name**) on line 1, he has been waiting for some time. He is wanting information about (*describe*). The information I gathered was (*explain*), and he needs to speak with you immediately. I informed him that you were with another customer before him. Would you be able to assist him now?

STEP 12   Direct the Call

I'll inform (**customer's name**) you will be with him in just a moment. Hello (**customer's name**), this is (**your name**) and I informed (**person's name**) that you've been patiently waiting. He's ready to assist you. Thank you for your patience. Just one moment and I'll direct your call.

Residential Prospecting

STEP 1   Introduction

Good morning, I need ... > to speak with Mr. or Mrs. (**last name**) please. Mr/s. (*first* **and last name**)? hello, (**first or last name**) this is (**your full name**). I'm with (**your company name**) and we're *lo*cated ... > (Or) and I repre*sent* ... > (**landmark, location, or territory**).

STEP 2   Reference

My company requested ... > that I contact you personally.

STEP 3   Request for Time

I hope ... > I haven't caught you at a bad time, *have* I. (*Assumptive*)
Why don't I call you back in about an hour, would that be all right with you. (*Assumptive*)

STEP 4   Purpose

My company would like to get a better understanding of the market, and in order for us to provide better service, I need ... > to ask you *just* a couple of *quick* questions, if you don't mind. (*Assumptive*)

STEP 5   Probing

Q: How long have you lived in the area?

Q: Who is currently handling your (*describe*)?

W: What motivated you to select XYZ competitor?

W: What would you like to see improved?

C: When was the last time you made a *comparison* to determine ... > that your needs are still being met cost-effectively?

STEP 6   Restate

So, basically, you are currently working with XYZ company. You chose them because of price. You have been with them for two years and like the representative; however, you feel the *quality* of their service needs improvement. You also said that you have not had an *opportunity* to compare what other alternatives are available to you that may be more cost-effective while giving you the *quality* of service you're entitled to. Is that correct?

STEP 7   Features and Benefits

I recommend that you evaluate (*describe*). This will provide you with valuable information to determine ... > what steps are needed to *increase* the quality of service you expect at the price you're looking for. You may be very *surprised* to know the difference between our products and quality of service *compared* to XYZ competitor. This will help you to *increase* the value of your investment and *maximize* its cost-effectiveness.

STEP 8   Get Reaction

How important is this information?

STEP 9   Trial Close

I would like the *opportunity* to introduce myself and show you the type of work I provide. This is complimentary. When you're ready to reevaluate your (*describe*), my *intention* is to have you *consider* my services. Does that sound fair enough. (*Assumptive*) (Or) Would that be all right *with* you. (*Assumptive*)

STEP 10   Objections

See Chapter 15.

STEP 11   Close

What time of the day is better for you and **(partner or spouse)** to provide this information for you, would you prefer mornings, afternoons, or evenings?

What day is better for you and **(partner or spouse)**, Tuesday or Thursday? I have 6:00 p.m., or would you prefer 8:00 p.m.?

STEP 12   Postclose

In order to save time and to allow me the opportunity to *personalize* the information, I need … > a little more information.

1. What are some of the features you currently enjoy?
2. What is the rate of return to you?
3. What are some of your other concerns about the product?

Thank you for the additional information. This will help me provide you with a more realistic evaluation. Our appointment is on Tuesday the 8th at 8:00 p.m. Please jot our appointment down on your calendar. Have a good day!

Confirmation

Good evening, I need … > to speak with **(prospect's name)**, please? Hello, this is **(your name)** with XYZ Company.

I just called to let you know that I have the information prepared as *promised*, and I look forward to meeting you and **(partner or spouse)** tomorrow at 8:00 a.m.

Reviving Lost Accounts

STEP 1   Introduction

Good_____, I need … > to speak with Mr/s. **(last name)**, please. (*Do not use first-name cue if rapport has been established.*) Hello, this is **(your full name)** with **(company name)** and we're *lo*cated … > **(location or landmark)**. (*Keep prospect actively listening.*)

STEP 2   Reference

We spoke (or) met some time ago (*offer dates*).

STEP 3   Request for Time

I hope … > I haven't caught you at a bad time *have* I. (*Assumptive*)
Why don't I call you back in about an hour, would that be all right *with* you. (*Assumptive*)

STEP 4   Purpose

I would like to get a better *understanding* of how I service my customers. In order for me to *continue* providing the best service possible, I need … > to ask you *just* a couple of *quick* questions, if you don't mind. (*Assumptive*)

STEP 5   Probing (Pick and Choose)

Q: Share with me if you are still (*describe*)?

Q: Share with me if you are still *motivated* to (*describe*)?

Q: Who are you *currently* using now to service your needs?

Q/W: What was your opinion about how I serviced you, which caused you not to continue?

W: What originally *motivated* you to use my services?

W: What was your deciding factor to choose XYZ company to service your needs?

W: Now that you have used their services for sometime, how do you feel about them compared to when you first acquired them?

W: What would you have liked to see happen differently that would provide you with the service you're looking for?

W: What can I do *further* to make *positive* steps to regain your faith in my *ability* to meet your needs once again?

C: What steps have you taken to reevaluate your (*describe*) to determine ... > whether we *can* meet your needs more cost-effectively while giving you the service you're entitled to?

STEP 6   Restate

Based on what you said.... Is that correct?

STEP 7   Features and Benefits

I have made rapid *changes* that are directed to meet my clients' needs. I have kept my database *sophisticated* to provide faster and more *reliable* service. I provide myself with professional training to offer more customer service satisfaction. My fees are *highly* competitive, and I have added more *diversification* to my (*describe*). This gives my clients peace of mind and *reliability* of services. More important, ... > you'll receive quality and fast service.

STEP 8   Get Reaction

How valuable is this service to you?

STEP 9   Trial Close

I recommend you allow me an *opportunity* to service your needs once again. If I'm unable to live up to your expectations and *impress* you with my personalized and professional approach, I simply don't deserve your *continued* business. Does that sound fair enough. (*Assumptive*)

STEP 10   Objections

See Chapter 15.

STEP 11   Close

Great! What time of the day are you and Mr/s. (**spouse**) available, during the mornings, afternoons, or are evenings better? I have (**day***)* or would you prefer (**day**)? How about (**time**) or (**time**). Which is better for the both of you?

STEP 12   Postclose

In order for me to save you time and allow me to *personalize* the information, I need … > just a little more information. (*Ask additional questions to do your preliminary profile. Make sure clients jot down the appointment on their calendars. Thank them for their time and tell them that you look forward to meeting them personally!*)

Reviving Pending Accounts

STEP 1   Introduction

Good morning [or afternoon], I need … > to speak with Mr/s. (**last name**) please. Mr/s. (*first and last name*)? Hello, this is (**your full name**), I represent (**your company name**).

STEP 2   Reference

Our customer service [or marketing] department requested … > I contact you personally.

STEP 3   Request for Time

I hope … > I haven't caught you at a bad time, *have* I. (*Assumptive*)
Why don't I call you back in about an hour, would that be all right *with* you. (*Assumptive*)

STEP 4   Purpose

(**Rep's name**) met (or) spoke with you on (**offer date**) and presented our (*describe*). In order to determine … > the effectiveness of our program, I need … > to ask you *just* a couple of *quick* questions, if you don't mind. (*Assumptive*)

STEP 5   Probing

Q: What was your opinion of our (*describe*)?

Q: How did you see this being implemented into your company?

Q: When we presented our company to you and our (*describe*) program, what was your opinion of our presentation?

W: We service many companies who are currently experiencing **tremendous** increases in their business activities by implementing our (*describe*) program. What could we have done **differently** to present it better that **would** meet **your** objectives when it comes to offering a quality (*describe*)?

C: What **are** your plans to **enhance** your (*describe*), so you can **increase** the level of business that you're entitled to?

Create a Deeper Need

Q: What was the main reason that you chose not to take advantage of our program [or service]?

C: What can we do, to earn the **opportunity** to present it better to you and other key individuals within your company—in this way, all of you can **evaluate** your options together?

Business Is Slow / No Money

Q: Other than cost, what other concerns do you have?

W/C: How much of an increase in your business would it take, within the next 30 days, for this to pay for itself?

W/C: What are your plans within the next few months, to **ensure** that you have a more **profitable** year and that you will not experience the same uncertainties next year?

C: With your current production, how **confident** are you that your company [or department] will remain (*describe*) to give you the production you **need** so that you can ensure a more profitable year?

STEP 6   Restate

I want to be sure I have the information correct …. Is that correct?

STEP 7   Features and Benefits

Thank you for sharing the information with me. I would like the **opportunity** to have (**name of other rep**) give you a call/contact you, she [or he] is better qualified to offer you information that would give you greater insight as to how your company can benefit by us. By gaining a **different** perspective, you may find that we are just what you're looking for in the area of quality, servicing, and price. Also, we have resources to assist you with the investment factor, to *ensure* that you are able to fully take advantage of our offer while remaining *within* your budget.

STEP 8   Get Reaction

How valuable would that second opinion be for you to have?

STEP 9   Trial Close

Thank you for reconsidering! This will give us an *opportunity* to *ensure* we have done *everything* possible to meet your needs prior to your making a final decision. In the meantime, are there any other questions or concerns I can address at this time?

STEP 11   Close

What time is better for you and **(rep's name)** to get together. I have **(day)** or would you prefer **(day)**. How about **(time)** or **(time)**.

STEP 12   Postclose

In order to save you time and *ensure* your meeting is productive, I need a little more information from you.

1. (*Confirm address.*)
2. (*Get cross street.*)
3. Who, other than yourself, would need this information to determine whether you will implement this within your company?

Secretarial Screen

Depending on the kind of telemarketing you are doing, you may find yourself in the position of having to get past a "gatekeeper," a guardian secretary, to reach your decision maker. Here are some ideas:

√ If your prospecting list does not provide the information, find out who the decision maker is (first and last name) and his or her title or position from the secretary. This may require a special call. Do not identify yourself or the reason for your call unless asked to do so. Never try to "sell" this individual.

√ Try answering all questions you get with a question. For example, if you are asked, **"Who's calling, please?"** you would respond with, **"This is Terry Connors, and who am I speaking with?"** This will keep you in control of the conversation.

√ If you have been leaving messages that have not been returned or if you keep missing the decision maker, tell the secretary: **"Please do me a favor. It's very important that I speak to Mr. Jensen today. When is the best time to call?"** (Or) **"I need your help. Would you see to it that my message reaches Mr. Jensen today please."** (*Assumptive*)

√ When you reach a secretarial screen, immediately adopt a tone that projects assertiveness and a "personable relationship" with your prospect. For example: **"I need ... > to speak with Kelly Johnson, I'll wait while you direct my call. Thank You."** This will let you through a good percentage of the time. Don't ask it as a question ("Can you direct me?"). Make it a statement. Try using your prospect's first and last names as in the previous example, or first name along with the department. For example: **"I need ... > to speak with Kelly in purchasing, please. I'll wait while you direct my call. Thank You."** Say it with a confidence that infers there is a personable relationship.

√ If you are asked, **"Who is this?"** give *only* your name. Do not volunteer the reason for your call or the name of your company. If you are asked, give a valid, slightly vague non-sales-related answer such as, **"I'm calling for information based on our last conversation"** (Or) **"I'm calling in reference to a purchase"** (Or) **"I made a commitment to call today."** If all else fails, use the objection-handling skills you have developed to make a statement that will engage the secretary's interest in assisting you by appealing to the power of her position. For example, **"I need your help. I appreciate that it's your responsibility to qualify Mr. Jensen's calls. The information I have is very important to Mr. Jensen, and I need to speak with him briefly today or tomorrow. What would *you* recommend?"**

√ Remember, once you have answered their question, *ask* a question, such as, **"She *is* in, isn't she?"**

The following "secretarial screen" script is designed for an initial contact with a company you are calling. It's very representative of a typical scenario.

Secretary Screen First Call

SECRETARY: Good morning, ABC Company. How can I help you?

TELEMARKETER: Good morning, I need ... > to speak with John Smith please. I'll wait while you direct my call—thank you. (Or) Good morning, I need ... > to speak with the head of purchasing, who would that be. (*Assumptive*)

SECRETARY: May I ask what this is concerning?

TELEMARKETER: Certainly. I made a commitment to call Mr. Smith. He is in today. (*Assumptive*) (Or) Sure you can. This is concerning a purchase. He is in today. (*Assumptive*) (Or) I'll wait while you direct my call. Thank you.

SECRETARY: I'll check, and your name is?

TELEMARKETER: This is Kathy Roberts, and your name is? (*Answer question with a question.*)

SECRETARY: My name is Chris, I'll see if he is in.

TELEMARKETER: I appreciate that, Chris.

SECRETARY: Mr. Smith is not in. May I take a message?

TELEMARKETER: Sure you can, Chris! When do you expect that Mr. Smith will be in, later this morning, or would this afternoon be better?

Note that "sure you can" or "certainly" is a defusing mechanism. The secretary is momentarily thinking you'll leave a message. This gives you the control so you can gain more information you need for your call-back. However you will not leave a message, you would only be red flagging yourself to be officially screened on all your future calls.

SECRETARY: Afternoon is usually better.

TELEMARKETER: It's important that I reach Mr. Smith today. I will call back this afternoon. Would you say around 3:00 p.m. is a good time?

SECRETARY: You can try.

TELEMARKETER: Thank you Chris. Have a good day!

Secretary Screen Second Call

Use this script when you have already contacted the company and have gone through the initial secretarial screening process.

SECRETARY: Good afternoon, ABC Company. How can I help you?

TELEMARKETER: Good afternoon, is this Chris?

SECRETARY: Yes.

TELEMARKETER: Hello Chris, this is Kathy Roberts, I need…> to speak with John Smith. I'll wait while you direct my call Thank you.

SECRETARY: I'll check to see if Mr. Smith is available, what is this regarding?

TELEMARKETER: I spoke with you earlier, Chris (**offer time frame you called**) and you said Mr. Smith would be in. He is in, isn't he. (*Assumptive with a concerned tone*).

SECRETARY: Just one moment please.

Surveying Existing Clients

STEP 1 Introduction

Good_____, I need … > to speak with Mr./s. (**last name**) please. (*Use first name only if it's appropriate.*) Mr./s. (***first* and last name**)? Hello Mr./s. Prospect, this is (**your full name**), I'm with (**your company name**).

STEP 2 Reference

I'm updating our client records.

STEP 3   Request for Time

I hope ... > I haven't caught you at a bad time *have* I. (*Assumptive*)
Why don't I call you back in about an hour, would that be all right *with* you. (*Assumptive*)

STEP 4   Purpose

My company wants to get a better *understanding* of the needs of our customers. In order for us to continue to provide a better service, I need ... > to ask you *just* a couple of *quick* questions if you don't mind. (*Assumptive*)

STEP 5   Probing

Q: Other than (*describe*), what other related supply products are you currently using?

Q: Who do you order **(product)** from, and how long have they been servicing you?

Q: What motivated you to choose XYZ competitor to service you as opposed to us?

Q: How often do you order these products, and how fast is the delivery?

Q/W: How many other venders do you use, and how do you feel about using one company to service your needs?

W: I noticed you have been using our (*describe*) for (*state*) years, how satisfied are you with it?

W: What would you like to see improved?

C: How often do you reevaluate your supplier to ensure you are getting quality products at cost-effective pricing?

Q: What were the results of your last evaluation?

C: How familiar are you with the diversity of products we market now?

Close

Thank you for sharing that information with me. Are there any final comments, questions, or concerns you have at this time? Have a good day!

Survey New Accounts

STEP 1   Introduction

Good_____, I need to speak with Mr./s. **(last name)** please. Mr./s. (*first* **and last name**)? (*Wait for response.*) Hello, this is **(your full name)**, I represent **(your company name)** and we're *located* ... > **(your location, landmark, or territory)**.

STEP 2   Reference

My company requested ... > that I contact you personally. (Or) My company is conducting a nationwide survey in your industry.

STEP 3   Request for Time

I hope ... > I haven't caught you at a bad time, *have* I. (*Assumptive*)
Why don't I call you back in about an hour, would that be all right *with* you. (*Assumptive*)

STEP 4   Purpose

My company wants to keep current in today's market. In order for our survey to be successful, I need ... > to ask you *just* a couple of *quick* questions if you don't mind. (*Assumptive*) (Or) My company wants to get a better understanding of the needs within your department. In order for us to provide a better service, I need ... > to ask you *just* a couple of *quick* questions if you don't mind.

STEP 5   Probing

Q: Who do you currently order your (*describe*) from, and how long have they been servicing you?

Q: Other than (*describe*), what (*describe*) related products are you using?

Q: How often do you order these products, and how fast is the delivery?

Q: How many other venders do you use, and how do you feel about using *one* company to service all your needs?

W: Now that you have used their products and services for some time, how do you feel about it today in *comparison* to when you first acquired them?

W: What would you like to see improved?

W: What *originally* motivated you to choose your current (*describe*)?

C: How often do you reevaluate your supplier to *ensure* you are getting quality products at the most cost-effective price?

Q/C: What were the results of your last evaluation?

C: How familiar are you with our company and the products we market?

Close

Thank you very much for participating in our survey. (Or) Thank you for sharing that information with me.

Upgrade

STEP 1   Introduction

Good_____, I need ... > to speak with Mr./s. (**first or last name**), please.
Hello, this is (**your full name**) with (**company name**).

STEP 2   Reference

We spoke on (**date**) and you requested ... > I contact you personally (Or) I'm
following up on our last conversation. (Or) I'm following up on the information you requested. (Or) I'm contacting our clients to update our information.

STEP 3   Request for Time

I hope ... > I haven't caught you at a bad time, *have* I. (*Assumptive*)
Why don't I call you back in about an hour, would that be all right *with* you.
(*Assumptive*)

STEP 4   Purpose

I'm following up on the information you requested. In order to *ensure* the
information I have is what you're looking for, I need ... > to ask you *just* a
couple of *quick* questions, if you don't mind. (*Assumptive*) (Or) I'm contacting
our customers who have been with us for (*state how long*). In order for us to
continue providing reliable information with quality service, I need ... > to ask
you *just* a couple of *quick* questions, if you don't mind.

STEP 5   Probing (Pick and Choose)

Q: When did you receive the information?

Q: What about the information interested you?

Q/W: How do you feel about the way we have serviced you, and what
        would you like to see improved?

Q/C: How aware are you of our (*describe*)?

W: When do you see yourself (*describe*)?

W: What factors will be important in determining an upgrade?

W: Other than affordability, what other concerns do you have?

W/C: Other than (*describe*), what else did you have in mind to meet your needs
        in a more affordable way?

C: When was the last time you had an *opportunity* to discuss your options to
        determine ... > what steps can be taken to use the *remaining* equity you
        may have in your (*describe*), to afford you the opportunity to upgrade?

STEP 6   Restate

I want to be sure I have this information correct. (*Restate their answers in a more positive way*). Is that correct?

STEP 7   Features and Benefits

I recommend that you acquire a second *opinion* on (*describe*). This information will be important to help you determine the steps you need to *consider*. This will enable you to achieve what you want and in the time frame you're hoping for. You will know when the best time to (*describe*), and by understanding your options more clearly, you will have peace of mind knowing that you're not depreciating your investment too quickly. Otherwise, you could be left with little or no value with which to conduct a profitable trade. Based on your personal needs and the type of model you *really* desire and have your mind set on, I *can* demonstrate what approaches would be most *advantageous*. More important, … > I will *evaluate* your current situation, enabling you to *secure* an upgrade into (*describe*) that would prove to be more financially affordable for you as opposed to waiting for a later time. (Or) I recommend we evaluate the current investment of your (*describe*). I recommend this because you will have necessary information on the fair market value and the depreciation that may have occurred since you first acquired it. This benefits you because it will help you determine the best time to trade in and step up into what you *really* want and need for yourself. Having more equity will give you *greater* control of the negotiation process. More important, … > you may find that it would prove to be more *profitable* to take care of this today as opposed to waiting later for an unknown market.

STEP 8   Get Reaction

How important would it be to have this information early on?

STEP 9   Trial Close

If I'm unable to *impress* you with my knowledge, expertise, and negotiation skills to help you get what you're looking for within the first 30 minutes of our time together, I won't take up any more of your *valuable* time. I simply don't *deserve* your future business. Does that sound fair enough. (Or) Does that seem reasonable. (*Assumptive*)

(Or)

Allow me the opportunity to appraise your (*describe*) and present an offering. If I'm unable to provide you with a reasonable offer, I simply don't *deserve* your business. Does that sound fair enough. (*Assumptive*)

STEP 10   Objections

See Chapter 15.

STEP 11   Close

Great! What time of the day are you available, during the mornings, after-noons, or are evenings better? I have **(day)** or would you prefer **(day)**? how about **(time)** or **(time)**. Which is better for you? (Or) Whose attention, other than yourself, do I need to make my proposal to?

STEP 12   Postclose

To save you time and allow me to *personalize* the information prior to our meeting, I need a little more information. (Or) To save you time and to *ensure* my proposal is fair, I need a little more information. (*Ask additional questions to do your preliminary profile.*)

Inbound Scripts

Catalog Order Department

STEP 1   Introduction

Good_____, **(your company name)**, where may I direct your call? (Or) How can I help you?

STEP 2   Establish Rapport

I would be happy to help you, this is **(your first and last name)**, and who am I speaking with? (Or) and your name is? (*Wait for a response, be sure to get the correct spelling.*) And the correct spelling of your last name is? What company are you with? (*Optional, on business sales only.*)

STEP 3   Reference

How did you hear about us?

STEP 4   Approach

In order to provide you with the information that you're most interested in, I need ... > to ask you *just* a couple of *quick* questions, if you don't mind. (*Assumptive*)

STEP 5 Probing

Q: Who are you currently getting your (*describe*) from?

W: What particular products do you have more of an interest in?

W: What are some of your specifications?

C: What have you compared with so you're **confident** that you are getting the most competitive price with the volume you currently are ordering?

STEP 6 Restate

I want to be sure I have the information correct. (*Restate their answers.*) Is that correct?

STEP 7 Features and Benefits

I recommend we send you our catalog which lists our complete line of products. This will give you a better idea of our diversity of (*describe*). Also, this will help you to compare our prices with your current distributor. (Or) The (*describe*) is (*go into features, functions, and benefits*).

STEP 8 Get Agreement

Would that meet your needs? (Or) Is that something you are looking for?

STEP 9 Trial Close

Great! Once you have had the chance to review the catalog, I would like to have one of our representatives follow up and gain your feedback. Would that be all right **with** you. (*Assumptive*) (Or) I can get that out to you for (*state cost*) and you should receive it by (*state when*).

STEP 10 Objection

See Chapter 15.

STEP 11 Close

I will process your catalog today. You will have it within the next few days. (Or) To whose attention should I address this shipment to?

STEP 12 Postclose

To process this more efficiently, I need ... > to go over the information to ensure I have everything correct. (*Ask questions you need to process the order.*) (Or) What else do we need to consider before I finalize this for you? Thank you and you have a good day. (Or) I will expedite your order today and you should receive it by (*state*). Is there anything else I can do for you?

Inbound Cross-Selling Appointments

STEP 1   Introduction

> TSR: Good_____, (*company name*). Where may I direct your call? (Or) How may I help you?
>
> CUSTOMER: I need some information about my (_____).

STEP 2   Establish Rapport

> TSR: I would be happy to help you, this is **(your name)**, and who am I speaking with (or) and your name is?

There is no need to perform steps 3 and 4. This is an existing customer just requesting some information. The objective of this type of call is to quickly service the customer and then attempt to update their account and create the need for an appointment.

STEP 5   Probing

> Q: What information can I help you with? (*Ask whatever you need and assist them with the information they are looking for. Proceed to next step.*)

STEP 4   Purpose

While I have you on the phone, I would like to update our information so that we can continue to provide you with good service. In order to accomplish this, I need … > to ask you *just* a couple of *quick* questions if you don't mind. (*Assumptive*)

STEP 5   Probing

> Q: I have here that we are providing you with (*describe*). Who is currently servicing you with your (*describe*)?
>
> Q: How long have they been servicing you?
>
> W: What *motivated* you to choose **(XYZ company)** as opposed to our company to determine … > whether we can service your needs better?
>
> W: Now that XYZ company has been servicing you for sometime, what would you like to see improved in the areas of service, quality, and pricing?
>
> C: What concerns do you have in allowing us to offer you a second opinion

to determine … > whether you're getting the quality you're entitled to at the most affordable price?

C: How aware are you of other programs we have to offer that would further enhance your current (*describe*) while gaining the service you expect?

STEP 6 Restate

I want to be sure I have the information correct…. Is that correct?

STEP 7 Features and Benefits

I recommend … > you evaluate your (*describe*) along with the other programs we offer. You will be able to have a better **understanding** of what your current plan/program provides you and whether you are getting the **maximum** benefits you're entitled to. This enables you to (*describe*) and offers you peace of mind because you **know** your needs are **fully** taken care of. You will increase your knowledge of the different products/services that are available, while tailoring your (*describe*) to be more cost-effective for you.

STEP 8 Get Reaction

How important is this information to you? (Or) How valuable is this information?

STEP 9 Trial Close

This will give us an **opportunity** to continue to service you at our best. Should we be able to provide you with a better program, our intentions are for you to consider us for all your needs. Does that sound fair enough. (*Assumptive*) (Or) This gives us an opportunity to **continue** providing the service you're looking for and ensuring that your needs are fully being met. Does that sound fair enough. (*Assumptive*)

STEP 11 Close

We can get together with you and **(spouse)** either at your home, or if you like, we can meet here at the office, which do you prefer? I have mornings, afternoons, or evenings available, what time of the day is better for the both of you? How about **(time)** or would you prefer **(time)**?

STEP 12 Postclose

In order for me to **ensure** our time together is spent more productively, I need a little more information. (*Ask whatever questions you may need to assist you with your direct presentation. Thank them for their time and say that you will look forward to meeting with them on date, day, and time of appointment.*)

Cross-Selling Inbound Clients

Once you have assisted your clients with their initial "call objectives," then proceed to the following steps.

STEP 4   Purpose

While I have you on the telephone, I would like to update our records. In order for us to *continue* providing you with quality service, I need ... > to ask you *just* a couple of *quick* questions if you don't mind. (*Assumptive*)

STEP 5   Probing

Q: So far how do you feel about the service we've provided you and what would you like to see improved?

Q: I notice you only receive our (*describe*), what other (*describe*) do you use and who do you ordinarily get them from?

Q: How long have they been servicing you?

W: What motivated you to choose that supplier?

W: How often were you out of product between deliveries?

W: Now that they have been servicing you for sometime, how do you feel about the products, the service, and the price today, *compared* to when you *first* started with them?

C: When have you compared *recently* to determine ... > what else is available that would meet your needs better and offer you a more *competitive* price?

STEP 6   Restate

Based on what you just said. ... (*Restate the answers and make your restatement positive and encouraging, helping you to lead into your features and benefits.*) Is that correct?

The following is an example of a restatement:

I want to be sure that I have the information correct. You feel we have provided you with good service. You currently are using XYZ supplier to service you with your (*describe*) **needs, and you also use** (*describe*)**. It has been quite some time since you have made a *recent* comparison to determine ... > the cost effectiveness of** (*describe*)**. Is that correct?**

STEP 7   Features and Benefits

Since we are providing you (*describe*), and you are satisfied with our ability to meet your needs, I recommend **(feature)**. I recommend this because of **(functions)**. Our (*describe*) will provide you with **(implied benefit)**. More important,

... > because you are a client of ours and we want you to *continue* doing business with us, this (*describe*) will **(stated benefits)**.

STEP 8   Get Reaction

How does that meet your needs?

STEP 9   Trial Close

Great! Why don't we try (*describe*) at a cost factor of (*state*). In approximately 30 days I will check back with you to *ensure* you have what you need and whether I can provide further assistance. Does that sound fair enough. (Or) Would that be all right *with* you. (*Assumptive*)

STEP 10   Objections

See Chapter 15.

STEP 11   Close

I will expedite your order today and you will receive it by **(date)**. Is that the time frame you are looking for?

STEP 12   Postclose

To process your order more efficiently, I need ... > to go over the information to be sure I have everything correct. (*Go over your order form*). What else do we need to consider before I finalize your order? Thank you for your order. I look forward to talking with you soon!

Cross-Selling Inbound Accounts

STEP 1   Introduction

Good morning **(name of company/department)**. How may I help you?

STEP 2   Establish Rapport

I would be happy to assist/help you, this is **(your first and last name)**, and who am I speaking with? (or) and your name is? Mr./s. **(first and last name?)** And the correct spelling of your last name is? How did you hear about us? (Or) Who is your parts representative?

STEP 3   Purpose of Call

How can I help you? (Or) What shall I tell **(person's name)** is the purpose of your call? (Or) What can I do for you?

STEP 4   Approach

I would be happy to take your order. To speed up the process, I need ... > to ask you *just* a couple of *quick* questions if you don't mind. (*Assumptive*)

STEP 5   Probing (Example)

> Q: What part do you need information on?
>
> Q: What is the number on the part?
>
> W: When do you need it?
>
> W: What model and year is it?
>
> C: What about the associated areas, how do they look?

STEP 6   Restate

I want to be sure I have the information correct.... Is that correct?

STEP 7   Resolve

I'm going to check my stock and see what I have available. Just one moment and I'll get back with you. Yes, I have that available, and I can get it to you at (**price**).

STEP 8   Get Agreement

Is that agreeable *with* you. (*Assumptive*)

STEP 10   Close

I can have it shipped out to you by (*state when*) or if you prefer, you can pick it up any time today. Which do you prefer?

STEP 4   Purpose

While I have you on the phone, I would like to update our records. In order for us to *continue* providing you with quality service, I need ... > to ask you *just* a couple of *quick* questions, if you don't mind. (*Assumptive*)

STEP 5   Probing

> Q: So far, how do you feel about the service we've provided you and what would you like to see improved?

Q: I notice you only receive our (*describe*). What other parts do you use, and who do you ordinarily get them from?

Q: How long have they been servicing you?

W: What motivated you to choose that particular supplier?

W: How often were you out of (*describe*) between deliveries?

W: Now that they have been servicing you for sometime, how do you feel about the products, the service, and the price today, *compared* to when you first ordered with them?

C: When have you compared recently to determine...> what else is available that would meet your needs better and offer you a more competitive price?

STEP 6   Restate

Based on what you just said...Is that correct? I want to be sure that I have the information correct. You feel we have provided you with good service. You currently are using XYZ supplier to service you with your (*describe*) needs and you also use (*describe*). You have not made a *recent* comparison to determine ... > the cost-effectiveness of that product. Is that correct?

STEP 7   Features and Benefits

I recommend **(feature)**. I recommend this because of **(functions)**. What this will provide you is **(implied benefit)** and, more important, ... > you can **(stated benefits)**. (*Note: Go into specific features and benefits that are directed to the customer's wants and needs, such as products, services, and compatibility of usage.*)

STEP 8   Get Reaction

How important is this to you? (Or) How valuable is this to you and your customers?

STEP 9   Trial Close

Great! Why don't we try (*describe*) and in a month or so, I will check back with you to make sure if you need anything else and how we can continue to service you better. Does that sound fair enough. (Or) Would that be all right *with* you. (*Assumptive*)

STEP 10   Objection

See Chapter 15.

STEP 11   Close

I will expedite your order today and you will receive it by (*state when*). Is that the time frame you are looking for?

STEP 12   Postclose

To process your order more efficiently, I need ... > to go over the information to make sure I have everything correct. (*Go over your order form.*) What else do we need to consider before I finalize your order? Thank you for your order. I look forward to talking with you soon!

Customer Discontinuing Service

STEP 1   Introduction

Good_____, I need ... > to speak with Mr./s. **(last name)**, please. Mr./s. **(first and last name)**? (*Wait for response.*) Hello, this is **(your full name)**, I represent **(company name)** and we're *lo*cated ... > **(landmark or location)**.

STEP 2   Reference

I'm updating our client information (Or) My company requested ... > I contact you personally (Or) I've been given the opportunity to review [or service] **(previous telemarketer's)** clients.

STEP 3   Request for Time

I hope ... > I haven't caught you at a bad time, *have* I. (*Assumptive*)
Why don't I call you back in about an hour, would that be all right *with* you. (*Assumptive*)

STEP 4   Purpose

I'm updating our clients information and in order for **(company name)** to service you at our best, I need ... > to ask you *just* a couple of *quick* questions, if you don't mind. (*Assumptive*) (Or) I'm contacting **(previous telemarketer's)** clients and in order to *ensure* your needs are adequately being met, I need ... > to ask you *just* a couple of *quick* questions, if you don't mind. (Or) I want to get a better understanding of the products [or services] **(telemarketer's name)** recommended and in order to accomplish this effectively, I need ... > to ask you *just* a couple of *quick* questions, if you don't mind. (Or) I have been with **(company name)** for quite some time, and I am actively reviewing many of our client's (*describe*). In order to *ensure* your needs have been taken care of properly (to your satisfaction), I need ... > to ask you *just* a couple of *quick* questions, if you don't mind. (*Assumptive*)

STEP 5 Probing (Pick and Choose)

Q: When was the last time you were contacted by our office?

Q: What (*describe*) did (**previous telemarketer**) recommend the last time she/he contacted you?

Q: Other than your present product, what other products [or programs] are you using? (*Offer examples if necessary.*)

W: So far, based on how we have serviced you, what *improvements* would you like to recommend as to how we can meet your needs *better*?

W: What *motivated* you to select XYZ company to service your other (*describe*) needs?

W: Now that they have been servicing you for sometime, how do you feel about the products, the services and the price you're getting *today* in *comparison* ... > to when you first acquired them?

W/C: What concerns do you have in allowing us the *opportunity* to offer you a second opinion, to see if we can provide you with a better program at a more competitive rate?

C: When did you *last* make a comparison of your (*describe*) to determine ... > if you're getting the *maximum* benefits at the most competitive price?

C: What steps have you taken to allow us an *opportunity* to conduct a thorough review so you are *confident* that you are getting what you're entitled to?

Close

Thank you for sharing this information with me. I would like the opportunity to *send* you information on other products and services we offer and that you may be able to benefit by. Would that be all right *with* you. (*Assumptive*) (Or) Thank you for sharing the information with me. If I could *send* you information about (*offer examples*) that you would have an interest in, what *would* that be? Once you've had an *opportunity* to review the information, I would like to gain your feedback. Does that sound fair enough. (*Assumptive*)

STEP 6 Restate

Based on what you said (*restate their answers*). Is that correct?

STEP 7 Features and Benefits

I recommend reviewing [or updating] your (*describe*). I recommend this because it will provide information about your current programs that were recommended and other options available to you that may *prove* to be more beneficial and would meet your current situation. You will *increase* your knowledge and awareness of the benefits you now have and give you the *confidence* that your (*describe*) are being met. This also gives me an opportunity ... > to become more familiar with your needs, so you'll *continue* to get the best service you're entitled to. More important, ... > you may be able to *increase* the value of your current programs.

STEP 8   Get Reaction

How important is this information to you? (Or) How valuable is this information?

STEP 9   Trial Close

This gives me an opportunity to meet you personally and show you what I specialize in. In addition, I will continue keeping you informed of the services you're entitled to. Does that sound fair enough. (*Assumptive*) (Or) Would that be all right *with* you. (*Assumptive*) (Or) This gives me an *opportunity* to ensure that you are taken care of and that we are meeting your needs cost effectively. I want to provide you with a better service and help you get *greater* satisfaction. My intentions are for you to continue allowing us to service you at our best. Does that sound fair enough. (*Assumptive*)

STEP 10   Objections

See Chapter 15.

STEP 11   Close

What time of the day are you and **(partner or spouse)** available, during the morning or afternoon, or is evening better? I have **(day)** or would you prefer **(day)**? How about **(time)** or **(time)**. Which is better for you and **(partner or spouse)**?

STEP 12   Postclose

To save you time and to allow me to *personalize* the information, I need a little more information. (*Ask additional questions to do your preliminary profile. Make sure they jot down the appointments on their calendars. Remind them of who you are. Thank them for their time and tell them you look forward to meeting them personally!*)

Infomercial

STEP 1   Introduction

Good_____, (**your company name**). How may I help you?

STEP 2   Establish Rapport

This is (**your full name**) and who am I speaking with?

What is the correct spelling of your last name?

Mr./s. (**first and last name**)?

How did you hear about us? (Or) How did you learn about (*describe*)?

STEP 3   Purpose of Call

(**Prospect's name**), what information can I help you with?

STEP 4   Approach

I would be happy to offer you information about (*describe*). In order to provide you with the information that you're most interested in, I need ... > to ask you *just* a couple of *quick* questions if you don't mind. (*Assumptive*) (Or) To save you time and provide you with the information you're looking for, I need ... > to ask you *just* a couple of *quick* questions if you don't mind.

STEP 5   Probing (Pick and Choose)

Q: What impressed you most about our (*describe*)?

Q: Describe to me the areas you need more information about.

Q: What (*describe*) have you attempted to use in the past and what were the results?

Q/W: Based on what you have seen on our commercials [or advertisements], who would benefit you the most?

W: What results are you looking for?

W: What motivated you to contact us and learn more about our (*describe*)?

C: How valuable would it be to increase your (*describe*) with very little effort while achieving optimum results in a short period of time?

STEP 6   Restate

Based on what you said (*restate their answers*), is that correct?

STEP 7   Features and Benefits

I recommend **(feature)**. I recommend this because of **(functions)**. This will provide **(implied benefits)** and, more important, ... > you can/will **(stated benefits)**.

STEP 8   Get Reaction

How important is this to you? (Or) How valuable would this be to you?

STEP 9   Trial Close

I suggest you try (*describe*) for 30 days. If you're not *absolutely* satisfied with the results and the *increased* (*describe benefits*) that you're anticipating within that 30-day time frame, simply return the program for a *complete* refund. We simply don't deserve the right to have your *continued* business. Does that sound fair enough. (*Assumptive*)

STEP 10   Objections

See Chapter 15.

STEP 11   Close

Assumptive Close: In addition to the benefits that we've discussed, is there anything else we need to consider before I process your order?

Direct, Contained-Choice Close: I can accept your Visa, MasterCard, Discover, or American Express, which do you prefer?

Contained-Choice Close: Which card do you prefer: Visa, MasterCard, Discover, or American Express?

STEP 12   Postclose

To *ensure* this reaches you quickly, I need a little more information from you. What is your mailing address? What is your card number and expiration date? I will have (*describe*) shipped out to you within (*state when*), and you should expect it within the next (*state when*). Before I finalize your order, is there any other information you need at this time? Thank you for your interest. Should you need any further assistance, please don't hesitate to call, we would be happy to help you. Again, this is **(your name)** and you have a nice day! (*Smile*) (*Whenever you are unable to close the prospect, go into your "Easy Close."*)

Easy Close

I would like to *send* you information regarding (*describe*). In this way you will have the information you need to determine your options. Would that be all right *with* you. (*Assumptive*) Once you have had the opportunity to review the information, we would like to get your feedback. Does that sound fair enough. (*Assumptive*)

Inquiry

STEP 1   Introduction

Good_____, **(your company name)**. How may I help you?

STEP 2   Establish Rapport

This is **(your full name)** and who am I speaking with?

What is the correct spelling of your last name?

Mr./s. **(first and last name)**?

How did you hear about us? (Or) How did you learn about our company?

STEP 3   Purpose of Call

What information can I help you with **(prospect's name)**?

STEP 4   Approach

I would be happy to provide you information about (*describe*). In order to provide you with the information that you're most interested in, I need ... > to ask you *just* a couple of *quick* questions if you don't mind. (*Assumptive*) (Or) To save you time and provide you with the information you're looking for, I need ... > to ask you *just* a couple of *quick* questions if you don't mind. (*Assumptive*)

STEP 5   Probing (Pick and Choose)

Q: What impressed you most about our (*describe*)?

Q: Based on what you have seen and heard about (*describe*), what additional information do you need to have?

Q: Who, other than yourself, would benefit by having this?

Q: Please share with me whether you have used a product similar to ours?

W: What results are you looking for?

W: What motivated you to contact us and learn about our program?

C: If you could gain the benefits described in the (*state where they learned of your product [or service]*), how valuable would this be for you?

Easy Close

Thank you for sharing this information with me. I would like to send you information regarding (*describe*). Would that be all right *with* you. (*Assumptive*) Once you've had the opportunity to review the information, I would like to gain your feedback. Does that sound fair enough. (*Assumptive*)

Inbound Order Supplies

STEP 1   Introduction

Good morning, **(name of company)**. How may I help you?

STEP 2   Establish Rapport

I would be happy to assist/help you. This is **(your first and last name)**, and who am I speaking with? (Or) and your name is? Mr./s. **(first and last name?)** And the correct spelling of your last name is? How did you hear about us? (Or) Who is your representative?

STEP 3   Purpose of Call

How can I help you? (Or) What shall I tell **(name of person)** is the purpose of your call? (Or) What can I do for you today?

STEP 4   Approach

In order to service you more effectively, I need … > to ask you *just* a couple of *quick* questions if you don't mind. (*Assumptive*) (Or) To determine your needs and provide you with the best price, I need … > to ask you *just* a couple of *quick* questions if you don't mind. (Or) To save you time and provide you with the information you're looking for, I need … > to ask you *just* a couple of *quick* questions, if you don't mind. (*Assumptive*)

STEP 5   Probing

Q: How many do you need_____ or_____? (*optional question*)

Q: I noticed you have (*describe*). Who are you ordering (*describe*) from? (*optional question*)

Q/W: How soon do you need it delivered?

W: What other products are you running low on at this time?

W/C: I noticed you haven't ordered (*state*) for some time. What can we do to meet your needs better?

C: What steps have you taken to compare our cost and service to determine ... > if we can meet your needs regarding service and price?

STEP 6   Restate

I want to be sure I have your order correct....Is that correct?

Note: Based on responses with creating a need (C) questions, you may proceed to steps 6 to 12 in your "Cross-Selling Accounts" script. Otherwise, your next step is to close.

STEP 10   Close

Before I finalize your order, is there anything else I can help you with?

To process your order more efficiently, I need to go over the information to make sure I have everything correct. (*Go over your order form.*) What else do we need to consider before I finalize your order? Thank you for your order. You will receive delivery on (**give date**). Your next delivery is (**give date**). I will be calling you on (**give date**) to check your inventory.

Inbound Order Taking

STEP 1   Introduction

Good morning, (**your company and department name**). How may I help you?

STEP 2   Establish Rapport

I would be happy to assist/help you; this is (**your first and last name**), and who am I speaking with? (Or) and your name is?

Mr./s. (***first* and last name**)? And the correct spelling of your last name is? How did you hear about our company? (Or) Who is your parts representative?

STEP 3   Purpose of Call

How can I help you? (Or) What shall I tell (**person's name**) is the purpose of your call? (Or) What can I do for you?

STEP 4   Approach

I would be happy to take your order. To ensure it's processed correctly, I need...> to ask you *just* a couple of *quick* questions, if you don't mind. (*Assumptive*)

STEP 5   Probing

Q: What part do you want to order?

Q: What is the number on the part?

W: When do you need it?

W: What model and year is the (*describe*)?

C: What about the associated areas, what is the condition and if not replaced, how will that effect your (*describe*)?

STEP 6   Restate

I want to be sure I have the information correct.... Is that correct?

STEP 7   Resolve

I'm going to check my stock and see what I have available. Just one moment and I'll get back with you. Yes, I have that available. The functions are (*describe*) and it has a guarantee of (*describe*). I can get it to you at (*describe*) price. With a delivery time of **(date)**.

STEP 8   Get Agreement

How does that sound to you?

STEP 11   Close

I can have it shipped out to you by **(date)** or if you prefer, you can pick it up any time today. What would be best for you?

17
Common Objections and Answers

There are common objections you will hear again and again. You must learn how to overcome them. This chapter answers the common objections that the telemarketing sales representatives (TSRs) and customer service representatives (CSRs) face in their daily activities. Although the 12 steps are designed to overcome resistance before it occurs, some objections will arise. They are inevitable.

Using the techniques taught in Chap. 15, each objection is scripted out with exactly what to say. This will give you greater control of your presentation and make objection handling easier. Keep in mind that these ideas are to help you until you have the opportunity to work the objections out on your own. Be sure to rewrite them to fit your own style and personality. When doing so, try to identify which methods are used in each example. This will help you gain a better understanding of how to use them proficiently.

Remember that during the probing, *Q* stands for qualify, *W*, establish wants, and *C*, create the need.

Outbound

Orphaned Client Doesn't See a Need to Change

I appreciate the fact that you feel *confident* with the products that we have recommended to you. Because of our service and the quality of our products, it's not uncommon that our clients do not need to change. My objective in contacting you was to introduce myself and to ensure *all* our clients are receiving the *best* service and recommendations available. When reviewing your account, this will just give me an *opportunity* to introduce myself, show you what I specialize in, in *comparison* to what you've experienced previously. My intentions are … > that you have peace of mind about the products and services that have been recommended to you. More important, … > that you are getting the most cost-effective rates that you're entitled to. Does that sound fair enough. (*Assumptive*)

"I'm Tired of Getting Calls by Another Salesperson from Your Company!"

I appreciate your concerns and the feeling that you're not getting a stable representative to handle your (*describe*) needs. That is the main reason why I felt *challenged* to take on your account and try to contact you personally.

According to our records, you don't have a representative from our office servicing you and keeping you up to date and *informed* of additional products and services you are entitled to. This is why I have contacted you personally. I *specialize* in working with clients who need someone they can *depend* on to keep them up to date with product and service options.

My objective in contacting you is to introduce myself and share with you my expertise, so in the *future* when you're ready to make changes or *enhance* your current (*describe*), that you can *depend* on my knowledge and the service I provide to ensure that your needs are being met. The benefit to you is peace of mind knowing (*describe*) and that you are receiving the best products at the most competitive rates that you're *entitled* to. How valuable is that service to you? (*Go into trial close, step 9.*)

"I'm Not Interested" During Get Reaction, Step 8

Thank you for letting me know that. What are some of your concerns?

Earlier we discussed that fact that you were (*reflect to step 5 answers*) and that (*reflect to step 5 answers*). One of the other areas we did not discuss is **(features and benefits)**. How important would that be. (*Assumptive*) (*Get a yes response, then close.*)

"I'm Not Interested" During Trial Close, Step 9

Earlier we talked about many important benefits. You mentioned you like the fact that we can (*go back into step 7, features and benefits*) also that we can provide you with (*go back into step 7, features and benefits*). One of the areas we haven't discussed is how we can (*add additional features and benefits*). How *important* is this to you? (Or) What other concerns do you have about allowing us the *opportunity* to validate this further?

"We're Satisfied with What We Have"

I'm sure you have a great product. However, earlier you mentioned that you had not had the opportunity to *compare*. You also felt that it would be beneficial for you to gain a second opinion to *determine* ... > if you could *improve* (*describe*). What other concerns do you have in allowing us the opportunity to conduct a competitive analysis?

Features and Benefits of Comparing

I recommend a second opinion. You will be able to better *compare* what you have with other options available to you. You may be able to *increase* the quality of your *existing* product line while *reducing* the cost factors, thereby generating a *higher* profit margin for your bottom line. How valuable is this information to you? (*Go into your close at this point if you receive a positive reaction. Otherwise, probe or use other methods of objection handling.*)

"I Don't Have Time"

I realize your time is valuable. Other than time, what additional concerns do you have? Allow us to meet with you and offer (*describe*). If you are not *impressed* with our products and you feel what you have is better and more cost-effective, then we won't take up anymore of your time. We simply don't deserve your future business. Does that sound fair enough. (*Assumptive*)

(Or)

I realize your time is valuable. Earlier you mentioned (*explain*) would be beneficial. This gives you the peace of mind of knowing what products you have and how cost-effective they are. You also like the fact that (*explain*) can help to lower your overhead cost and allow more *flexibility* to *maximize* your (*describe*) with other profitable programs. What other concerns do you have about evaluating this information?

(Or)

I understand your time is valuable. If I'm unable to impress you with worthwhile information that will help you to increase your benefits while lowering your costs in the first 15 minutes of our time together, I won't bother to take up anymore of your time. I simply don't deserve your future business. Does that sound fair enough. (*Assumptive*)

"Your Products Cost More"

Thank you for letting me know that. So what you're saying is, if we can be more competitive, and offer you greater value with a superior product, then you would *consider* a time we *could* get together in order to *validate* this further, is that correct? (*Get a positive commitment, then probe.*)

Q: What other products have you looked into, and what are they offering you that we are not?

Q/W: Share with me if you have tried our products and fully compared the difference and if so, what were the results of that comparison?

W: What would you like to see improved in our products?

C: When was the last time you made a *comparison* to determine ... > the value of our products and how they will benefit you and your customers? (*Go through steps 6 to 12.*)

"I'll Think It Over"

I agree that you should review the information. Upon your review, what will you be *considering* and comparing this information with? (*Probe deeper, restate, and add features and benefits, step 7.*)

"I Need to Ask My Partner"

It's *important* that both of you agree. If I'm understanding you correctly, you are *considering* our proposal providing your partner approves, is that correct? (*Wait for a positive reply.*) Since you have expressed an interest in the (*describe*) and you need your partner's approval, I recommend that we set a convenient time to discuss this together. Both of you can examine the features and benefits of (*describe*) with the cost savings. Should your partner have any concerns, we can address them together. Does that sound fair enough. (*Assumptive*)

"I'm Really Happy with My Present Company"

Thank you for letting me know that. It's important you feel *confident* in the products and services you participate in. Our company is very strong in that same belief, and I respect that. Just out of curiosity, what is it about the products, the services, and the cost factors that keep you a satisfied customer? If you could make *any* enhancements regarding any of the products we've discussed, what would they be. (*Assumptive*) When was the *last* time you made a *comparison,* to ensure ... > that you're getting the most value from your products and that you are *still* receiving the kind of excellence in service that you're entitled to? (*Restate, add benefits, get reaction, and close.*)

"I Have Damaged Products"

I apologize that you have been inconvenienced. We will be *more* than happy to credit your account or provide you with product replacement. Which do you prefer? (*Resolve and close.*)

"I Never Received Your Information and/or Brochure"

I'm sorry that you didn't receive it. I requested the brochure packet to be sent to you on **(offer date)**. The information is about our services regarding (*describe*) and a list with our statements of endorsements. I can briefly describe the information to you. Would that be all right *with* you. (*Assumptive*) (*Go into information.*)

"We Already Have Our Budget for This Year"

If I'm understanding you correctly, you have selected and *paid* for the (*describe*) for this year's budget. Is that correct? (*If they have, find out when they would be reconsidering and try to recontact them at that time. Otherwise, continue.*) What budget have you set for this? When selecting a company to service your needs, what will you be considering? (*Request a second opinion.*)

"Call Me Back and Then We Will Set an Appointment"

I would be happy to. However, if you're looking for an appointment around that time frame, now would be the best time to set that up. Since you are positive that you want to get together, I recommend that we set a convenient time and I will contact you the day before to reconfirm. Does that sound fair enough. (*Assumptive*) (Or) I would be happy to. So if I am understanding you correctly, you definitely want to get together, and you are willing to set the appointment providing I call next week. Is that correct? What concerns do you have in taking a look at our calendars now so that we can set up a time that meets both our schedules?

They Like It But They Want Information Sent (before Step 5)

I would be happy to. To *ensure* that I send information that you would have an interest in, I need ... > to ask you *just* a couple of *quick* questions, if you don't mind. (*Go into step 5.*) Thank you for the information, I will send our brochure today. Once you've had the *opportunity* to review the information, I would like to gain your feedback. Does that sound fair enough. (*Assumptive*)

Product Sales

"Send Me Information"

I would be happy to. So if I am understanding you correctly, based on what we've discussed so far, you have an interest in our (*describe*), and you feel it would be *important* for your company. However, you feel you need additional information that I have not provided prior to your investment. Is that correct? (*Wait for a response.*) Other than wanting to receive our information, what other concerns do you have? (*If none, then proceed. Otherwise, keep probing.*)

I recommend that you review (*describe*). You have an *opportunity* to get a hands-on experience with this unique (*describe*) for a 30-day trial. If you are not *absolutely* satisfied with what we have to offer and are *unable* to see the benefits you are *entitled* to, then return the (*describe*) undamaged and we will reimburse your investment in full, *100 percent*! Does that sound fair enough. (*Assumptive*)

Insist on Sending Information

I would be happy to. Once you've had the *opportunity* to review our information and you feel *impressed* with the quality of our company and our clientele, then you want to proceed in taking advantage of our offer, is that correct? (*If yes, proceed, if no, probe,*) I will be sending you some information today and you should receive it by (*state when*). I will contact you back on (*state when*) to answer any of your questions. Does that sound fair enough. (*Assumptive*) Would you prefer me to contact you during the morning or would afternoon be better? I have (*state*) or would you prefer (*state*). I have that on my calendar, do you? In order to *ensure* the information arrives in a timely manner, I need a little more information from you. (*Begin probing.*)

Whose attention shall I send the information to?

What is the correct spelling of your last name?

What is your correct mailing address?

If you were to take advantage of the program, how would you acquire the program: by credit card, check, or our 4-month plan?

Where can you be reached during the day time?

What is your evening number?

I appreciate the additional information. I'll have the information sent to you right away. I'll be contacting you (*state*) to gain your feedback. Is there anything else I can do for you at this time? Thank you for your interest and I look forward to talking with you soon!

"No! I Don't Want You to Call Me Back!"

I respect that. Just out of curiosity, what originally motivated you to call us? What is your *greatest* concern in allowing me the opportunity to see if I can provide you with *additional* information so you can better determine the benefits? (*Probe until you have all the real issues. Overcome and get reaction, close.*)

"I Don't Have a Credit Card"

That's all right. Many families who call in *prefer* to have it sent by COD. The benefit is that it allows time for delivery and (*describe*). By the way, you are still *entitled* to our unconditional 30-day *money back* guarantee. After 30 days, if you're not absolutely *impressed* with the results and (*describe*), simply return the program, and you will get 100 percent of your investment back. It costs you nothing, except for your time. Does that sound fair enough. (*Assumptive*)

"I Can't Afford It Right Now"

Thank you for letting me know that. If I'm understanding you correctly, you like what the program can do, you clearly see the benefits, and if it were financially affordable you would take advantage of the program today. Is that correct? (*If customer says yes, continue. Otherwise, probe.*) Other than the affordability factor, what other concerns do you have at this time? (*If they have no other concerns, continue. Otherwise keep probing until all issues have been uncovered.*) If a credit card is out of the question, you can take advantage of our easy 4-month plan. We will spread out your investment over the next 4 months. (*Describe how the plan operates.*) If you had a credit card, the monthly would be much lower; however, you would have additional cost in the interest charges. Our easy 4-month plan is *completely* interest-free. This saves you money! Does that meet your expectations?

"I Don't Know If I Have Enough on My Credit Card"

I can appreciate that! If I'm understanding you correctly, you have an interest in (*describe*) and the benefit it offers. The only concern you have is that you want to charge it; however, you feel the total amount of the product may not fit on your credit card. Is that correct?

This is not unusual, and we have a solution in these types of circumstances. We can try $40 on the card and providing that goes through, we'll go ahead and send out your product today. In this way, you can start achieving results immediately. Then, each month we'll charge your account only $47.63 for the next 4 months to make it easier for you and to allow you to continue using your card for *other* purposes. This is just another way to service our customers by providing them with the product they want while making it extremely cost-effective. Does that seem reasonable. (*Assumptive*)

"I Have to Talk It Over with My Partner"

Of course we want your **(partner)** to be included. This is an exciting and terrific opportunity for both of you. Understanding the program and all the benefits and the quick results that you will achieve, what concerns would your **(partner)** have regarding this opportunity?

"I Just Need to Discuss Our Finances"

If I'm understanding you correctly, you feel your **(partner)** would share the same excitement as you have; however, she [or he] has never had the opportunity to see the commercials or discuss the program together with you to determine ... > if she [or he] would agree to the investment as you have. Is that correct?

I recommend that you both evaluate the program together in detail. This gives you the opportunity to (*describe*). You will actually experience what the program has to offer and see the results. We are so confident in our product and our ability to meet your expectations that we offer a 30-day money back guarantee. If you're not absolutely satisfied with our product and you are not getting what you expected, simply return the program; we will return your investment 100 percent. How does that sound?

"I Prefer to Talk It Over with My Partner"

I appreciate and respect that. Why don't I send you our information. (*Assumptive*) Also I recommend that your **(partner)** view our 30-minute commercials. This will reinforce the features and the benefits and help validate the information I am about to send to you. Does that seem reasonable to you?

Once you've had the *opportunity* to review the information, we would like to gain your feedback. Does that sound fair enough. (*Assumptive*)

In order to *ensure* the information gets to you in a timely manner, I need a little more information from you.

To whose attention shall I address the information?

What is the correct spelling of your last name?

What is your correct mailing address?

If you were to take advantage of the program, how would you acquire the program: by credit card, check, or our 4-month plan?

Where can you be reached during the day time?

What is your evening number?

I appreciate the additional information. I'll have the information sent to you right away. Please look through your local *TV Guide* for our 30-minute commercial, so both you and your **(partner)** can review the information together. I'll be contacting you back within the next week or so to gain your feedback. In the meantime, is there anything else I can do for you?

Thank you for your interest, and we look forward to talking with you soon!

"Send Me Information"

I would be more than happy to! In order for me to send you information that you are looking for, I need ... > to ask you *just* a couple of *quick* questions, if you don't mind. (*Assumptive*) (*Start asking probing questions to determine needs.*)

"I Will Call Back"

I can help you, and if not I'll find someone who can. What would you prefer?

"How Can I Be Sure You're Going to Handle This?"

I can appreciate your concern Mr./s. (**customer's name**). This is what I can do (*describe*). If you're not satisfied, I'll find someone who *can* assist you further. Does that sound fair enough. (*Assumptive*) (*Start probing to gain additional information. Restate, resolve, get agreement, and close.*)

"I'm Upset"

I apologize Mr./s. (**customer's name**). I want to help. Please share with me what happened? How can *I* help you today? (*Wait for them to open up.*) What would it take to *ensure* you're satisfied with our efforts? (Or) Earlier we talked about many issues. You mentioned the fact that (*describe*), also (*describe*). One of the areas we didn't cover is … (*resolve*). How important is this to you? (Or) What other concerns do you have that I can help you with?

Probing Questions

When was the last time you discussed your concerns with us so we can ensure you're fully knowledgeable of the benefits you're entitled to?

What areas are most important to you?

Based on the previous service we provided you, how confident were you about that service and the results?

(*Restate, resolve, get agreement, and close.*)

Features and Benefits. We are a reputable company, we do our best to offer our customers premium service. We have an excellent track record of servicing many people with (*describe*). What other concerns do you have about our service and how it meets with what you are looking for?

Tried That Before and Didn't Like It

Thank you for sharing that with me. What was it about the service we provided that you were unhappy with? What steps did you take to communicate your concerns to our customer service department so we could try to rectify the situation? Where did you get that information from? What would you like to see improved? (*Restate, resolve, get agreement, and close.*)

"That Is Not Important to Me"

I respect that. Other than (*describe*), what is important to you? Who, other than yourself, takes care of (*describe*), so that I can determine the areas in which you need assistance? (*Probe and request information on key person.*)

"Your Prices Are Too High"

I can appreciate your concern for the cost. I know that price is important to you and that you want the best price possible. Before I can address this further, I need more information (Or) I need ... > to ask you *just* a couple of *quick* questions if you don't mind. (*Assumptive*)

(*The following questions are your probing step:*)

What are you comparing our service and price with?

When did you last make that comparison?

How did you arrive at that figure?

What other options (or) services (or) time frame are involved that would provide (or) validate a more accurate and cost-effective figure?

(*Restate, resolve by overcoming the price issue, get agreement, and close.*)

Rude Customer

Mr./s. (**customer's name**) I want to help and *ensure* that your needs are being taken care of and that you receive the full benefits you're entitled to. In order to accomplish this, I need ... > to ask you *just* a couple of *quick* questions, if you don't mind. Share with me if you had an *opportunity* to (*describe*), and, if so, what other concerns do you have regarding what we have to offer?

Complaints about Ridiculous Requirement

I understand your frustration, and I know your time is valuable. In order for us to ensure ... > that we process this accurately *and* in a timely manner, I need more information such as: (*probe, restate, offer resolution, and close.*)

Screaming Customer

Wait until they're done screaming or until customer asks, "Are you still there?"

CSR: Yes, I'm still here.

CUSTOMER: Well, what do you have to say?

CSR: I understand your concerns, and I want to try and keep your best interest in mind. In order to meet your needs within the guidelines of our servicing procedures, I need ... > to ask you *just* a couple of *quick* questions, if you don't mind. (*Assumptive*) (*Probe, restate, resolve, get agreement, and close.*)

"What Is the Name of Your Boss?"

The name of our general manager is (**name of person**). I understand your concerns, and I want to *ensure* that your needs are met within the parameters of our department procedures. In order to determine how we can try to satisfy your needs better, I need...> to ask you *just* a couple of *quick* questions, if you don't mind. (*Assumptive*) (*Probe, restate, resolve, get agreement, and close.*)

"Is There Someone Else I Can Talk to?"

Certainly. Please share with me what are some of your concerns by not allowing me the *opportunity* to assist you in this matter? What would you recommend that I do to meet your needs better and process this in the time frame you are hoping for? (*Probe if necessary and finalize.*)

"I'd Rather Talk to Someone Else"

I respect that. In order for me to *ensure* that I direct you to the person who can assist you better, I need ... > to ask you *just* a couple of *quick* questions, if you don't mind. (*Assumptive*)

What was it about my efforts you were unhappy with?

Other than (*describe*), what other concerns do you have?

What additional information do you need to ensure your needs are met?

(*Restate and try to offer solution or direct to other party. Be sure to let customers know who you'll be directing them to. Inform other party objectively of the situation.*)

Placed on Hold Too Long

I apologize that you were inconvenienced. This is (**your full name**) and your name is? What can I do to help you?

Cannot Get Through to Certain Office (Runaround)

I apologize that you have been inconvenienced. This is (**full name**) and who am I speaking with? The department you're calling into is (**name of department**). In order for me to *determine* how I can assist you better, I need ... > to ask you *just* a couple of *quick* questions, if you don't mind. (*Assumptive*) (*Probe, restate, resolve, get agreement, and close.*)

Customer Knows It All

(*Let customer talk. When customer has finished talking, proceed to restate.*) If I'm understanding you correctly, you (*restate*). Is that correct? To save you time and to allow me to provide you with the information you're looking for, I need ... > more information. (*Probe, restate, resolve, get agreement, and close.*)

"I Only Want to Work with ..."

I appreciate your interest in wanting to work with (**person's name**). I know service is important to you and that you want the best service possible. That is what I want to provide you with along with (*describe*). I have been given the opportunity to be your representative, and I am prepared to quickly assist you. Would that be all right *with* you. (*Assumptive*)

"I Don't Want to Do It This Way"

What concerns do you have about our procedure? Other than (*describe*), what other concerns do you have? Understanding our position, what would you recommend instead? (*Restate, offer solution, get agreement, and close.*)

"I Heard the Industry Is Doing Terrible Now"

I appreciate your letting me know that. Where did you hear this information and when? Other than (*describe*) what other resource did you use to validate this information? What steps have you taken to take profitable advantage of a soft market that is in your favor? (*Restate*)

(*Resolve:*) Thank you for sharing the information with me. I understand your concern, and that would be a greater concern for me, especially since this is the first I have heard this. However, I can assure you that we are a solid, growing company that is taking advantage of this market, selling more products, *and* at more competitive prices. We are servicing more customers today than ever before. This is *extremely* positive to the growth of our company and to the *security* of our customers. The security of knowing they *can* count on us to *continue* to service their needs. Provided I can *validate* this further, how *important* is working with a reliable, stable, and strong company to you?

"I Just Want a Quote Right Now"

I appreciate your interest, and I know that getting a quote is important to you and you want the best quote possible. In order to *ensure* I give you an exact figure that you will be happy with, I need ... > a little more information from you. (*Start probing, restate, get agreement, and close.*)

"How Come You Didn't State This in the Agreement?"

I'm glad you have read your agreement. Most people I talk with have not. As you can see, the agreement is quite extensive, and it is difficult to list each and every circumstance, since the services are so vast and diversified. We recommend that if there is ever a doubt about what is or is not covered to please contact our claims [or benefits] department. They are prepared to address any questions or concerns our customers have about benefits or coverage. In this way, prior to (*describe*), you will have assurance you're covered and you receive the service you're entitled to. In the future, I recommend you contact our customer service department prior to (*describe*) so we can assist you better. In the meantime is there anything else I can do for you?

"Your Policies Are Senseless"

I understand your concerns and I respect them. What are some of your concerns about our guidelines, and what would you recommend we do instead? Other than (*describe*) what concerns do you have? (*Restate, resolve, get agreement, and close.*)

"Is There a Manager There?" (Not Available)

If I'm understanding you correctly, you would feel more confident discussing the situation with our manager, and you feel she [or he] would be able to offer better assistance. Is that correct? We have a manager on staff who can assist you. However, she [or he] is in a special meeting all day. What I *can* do is have our assistant manager help you and if she [or he] isn't able to, then our manager can contact you tomorrow. What would you prefer. (*Assumptive*)

"Your Service Is Different Than Most"

Thank you for letting me know that. What are you comparing us with? When did you last make a comparison? What steps have you taken to evaluate the benefits to validate the service issues? (*Restate, resolve, get agreement, and close.*)

"I Want to Talk to (*Name of Person*) Now!"

I appreciate that Mr./s. (**customer's name**). Mr./s. (**person's name**) is currently with another customer. However, I will **ensure** that your call will be returned promptly. Would that be all right *with* you. (*Assumptive*)

"Can't You Place Me on Hold?"

I apologize for the inconvenience. Unfortunately, that would tie up all our other incoming lines and (*explain why*). What I *can* do is ensure ... > the person who can assist you, will contact you within the next (*offer time frame*). Would that be all right *with* you. (*Assumptive*)

"Why Hasn't She [or He] Returned My Call?" "Will She [or He] Call Me Back?"

I apologize that you have been inconvenienced, and I appreciate your patience. (**Name of person**) hasn't received their messages yet. As soon as she [or he] returns I will ensure she [or he] gets your message. Would that be all right *with* you. (*Assumptive*). (Or) I apologize that you have been inconvenienced, and I appreciate your patience. I gave (**person's name**) your messages with the dates and times you have called. I would be happy to take another message, or if you like I can try to find someone else to assist you. What would you prefer?

"Where Is He [or She]—I Just Spoke to Him [or Her]?

(**Person's name**) is currently with another customer. I can have him [or her] call you back within the next (*offer time frame*). What number can you be reached at so she [or he] can return your call promptly?

"When Is She [or He] Going to Be in?"

I am not certain of the exact time however, I would expect (**person's name**) to return or at least call in for messages soon. What I *can* do is ensure that she [or he] gets the message as soon as she [or he] returns. Is that agreeable to you. (*Assumptive*)

"I Want You to Take a Message Right Now!"

I apologize for the delay; however, I have other calls coming in before yours. If you will wait just one moment I can assist you next, or if you like I can have someone else assist you. What would you prefer. (*Assumptive*)

Inbound

"I'm Not Interested"—(when prospect says this before step 9)

Thank you for letting me know that. What are some of your concerns? Earlier we discussed that fact that you were (*reflect*) and that (*reflect*). One of the other areas we did not discuss is (*describe*). How important would that be? (*Get a yes response then close.*)

"I'm Not Interested"—(when prospect says this after step 9)

Earlier we talked about many important benefits. You mentioned you like the fact that we can (*reflect*), also that we can provide you with (*reflect*). One of the areas we haven't discussed is that we can (*describe*). How *important* is this to you? (Or) What other concerns do you have about allowing us the *opportunity* to validate this further?

"We're Satisfied with What We Have"

I'm sure you have a great product. However, earlier you mentioned that you had not had the opportunity to compare and that it would be beneficial to have a taste test to determine if you could improve the quality and taste for your customers. What other concerns do you have in allowing us the opportunity to conduct a taste test with our products so you have something to compare?

Features and Benefits of Comparing

I recommend a second opinion. You will be able to better compare with what you have and other options available to you. How this benefits you is that you may be able to increase the quality of your existing product line and reduce the cost factors, thereby generating a higher profit margin on your bottom line. How valuable is this information to you? (*Go into your close at this point if you received positive reactions. If you received negative reaction, probe or use other methods of objection handling.*)

"I Don't Have Time"

I realize your time is valuable. Other than time, what further concerns do you have at this time? Allow us to meet with you and offer a taste test. If you are not impressed with our products and you feel what you have is better and more cost-effective, then we won't take up anymore of your time, we simply don't deserve your future business. Does that sound fair enough. (*Assumptive*)

"Your Products Cost More"

Thank you for letting me know that. So what you're saying is, if we can be more competitive, while offering you greater value and a better-tasting product, then you would consider a time we could get together to validate this further, is that correct? (*Get a positive commitment, then probe.*)

Q: What other products have you looked into and what are they offering you that we are not?

Q/W: Share with me if you have tried our products and fully compared the difference and if so, what were the results of that comparison?

W: What would you like to see improved in our products?

C: When was the last time you made a taste *comparison* to determine … > the value of our products and how they will benefit you and your customers? (*Go through steps 6 to 12.*)

"I'll Think It Over"

I agree that you should review the information. While you are reviewing, what will you be *considering* and comparing this information with? (*Probe deeper. Restate and offer recommendations.*)

"I Want to Discuss This with My Partner"

It's *important* that you both choose the right products together. If I'm understanding you correctly, you are considering what we have to offer providing your partner approves. Is that correct? (*Wait for a positive reply.*)

Since you have expressed an interest in the products we've discussed and would like your partner's approval, I recommend that we set a convenient time to discuss this together. We can examine the features and benefits of our products and the cost savings to your company, and, if your partner has any concerns, we can address them during that time. Does that sound fair enough. (*Assumptive*)

"I'm Happy with My Present Company"

Thank you for letting me know that. It's important you feel confident in the products offered to you. We want all our customers to feel the same way about us.

W: Just out of curiosity, what is it about the products, the services, and the cost that keeps you a satisfied customer?

W: If you could make any enhancements regarding any of the products we've discussed, what would they be. (*Assumptive*)

C: When was the last time you made a *comparison,* to ensure ... > that you're getting the most value from your products and still receiving the kind of excellent service you're entitled to? (*Restate and finish remainder of steps.*)

"I Have Damaged Products"

I apologize that you have been inconvenienced. We will be *more* than happy to credit your account or provide you with product replacement. Which do you prefer? (*Resolve and close.*)

"I Didn't Receive All My Products"

I'm very sorry for the inconvenience. Let me see what I can do to *ensure* you get the products you've ordered.

Probing

1. Who originally did you place your order with?
2. What is your account number?

3. What products are you missing?

Restate

I want to be sure that I have everything correct.... Is that correct?

Resolve

According to my records ... (*Get agreement and close.*)

"You're Never There When I Call You"

I'm very sorry, I can understand your frustration. I'm glad you we're persistent. What can I do for you *today*? (*Listen, probe, restate, and resolve.*)

"I'm Going with Competitor"

I'm very sorry you feel that way.

1. What are some of your concerns about the service we've provided you?

2. Other than (*restate*), what other concerns do you have?

3. What can we do to regain your *faith* in our *ability* to service you better?

(*Restate, resolve, and close.*)

"How Can I Be Sure You're Going to Handle This?"

I can appreciate your concern, Mr./s. **(last name)**. This is what I *can* do (*describe in detail*). If you're not satisfied, I'll find someone who can help you to *ensure* your needs are being taken care of. Does that sound fair enough. (*Assumptive.*) (*Start probing and gain more information, restate and resolve, get reaction, and close.*)

"I Haven't Received My Credit Yet"

I can understand your concern Mr./s. **(last name)**. In order for me to *determine* why, I need ... > to ask you *just* a couple of *quick* questions, if you don't mind. (*Assumptive.*) (*Go on to probe:*)

1. When did you originally request a credit?

2. Who did you speak with?

(*Ask whatever probing questions apply to assist in handling the situation. Restate and resolve and close.*) Mr./s. **(last name)** I will *personally* handle your account. This is **(your name)**, and I will personally see to it that you get the information you're looking for. Later, I will contact you to make sure *everything* is okay. Does that sound fair enough. (*Assumptive.*) (Or) Mr./s. **(last name)** I will *personally* handle your account. This is **(your name)**. I will check our records to see what has happened, and I will *personally* call you back as *soon* as I have any information. Does that sound fair enough. (*Assumptive*)

"I'm Upset"

I apologize for any inconvenience we have caused you. (*Then probe:*)

1. What are some of your concerns?
2. How can I help you today?
3. What would it take to *ensure* you're satisfied with our efforts?

(Or) Earlier we talked about many issues. You mentioned the fact that (*reflect*), also (*reflect*). One of the areas we didn't cover is **(solution)**. How important is this to you? (Or) What other concerns do you have?

1. When was the *last* time you discussed your concerns with us so we could take the steps to correct the situation?
2. We discussed many areas you are unhappy about. What is you primary concern that you would like me to try and resolve first?
3. Based on the previous service/product we provided you, how confident were you about our efforts? (*Restate and offer a solution, get reaction, and close.*)

Tried That before and Didn't Like It

Thank you for sharing that with me. (*Probe:*)

1. What about the service were you unhappy with?
2. What would you like to see improved?
3. What steps did you take to communicate your concerns to our customer service department?
4. Where did you get your information from?

(*Restate, resolve, get reaction, and close.*)

Screaming Customer

(*Wait patiently until customer is done and asks, "Are you still there?"*)
   For example:

   CSR: Yes, I'm still here (*in a calm voice*).

   CUSTOMER: Well, what do you have to say?

   CSR: I understand your frustration and I know you have your best interest in mind. In order to meet both you and your company's needs within the guidelines of our company, I need ... > to ask you *just* a couple of *quick* questions, if you don't mind.

(Probe, restate, resolve, and so on.)

What Is the Name of Your Supervisor?"

The name of my supervisor is_____. I understand your frustrations, and I want to help you to *ensure* your needs are met within the parameters of our company. In order to *determine* how I can accomplish this, I need ... > to ask you *just* a couple of *quick* questions, if you don't mind. *(Assumptive.)* *(Probe, resolve, get reaction, and close.)*

"Why Do You Have to Ask So Many Questions?"

I know it can be frustrating for you and that your time is valuable. In order for me to process this *faster* so you can get your products in a timely manner, I need additional information. Would that be all right *with* you. *(Assumptive)*

"Is There Someone Else I Can Talk to?"

Certainly. *(Then probe:)*

1. What are some of your concerns with allowing me the *opportunity* to assist you in this matter?
2. What can I do to meet your needs better and process this in the time frame you're hoping for? *(Keep probing, if necessary, and finalize.)*

"I Rather Talk to Someone Else"

I respect that. In order for me to *ensure* that I direct you to the person who can assist you *better*, I need ... > to ask you *just* a couple of *quick* questions, if you don't mind. *(Assumptive.)* *(Then probe:)*

1. Other than *(reflect)*, what other concerns do you have?
2. What about my efforts were you unhappy with?
3. What information can I provide you with to *ensure* your needs are being fully met?

(Restate and try to offer solution or facilitate to other party. Be sure to let customers know who you'll be directing them to. Inform other party objectively of the situation.)

Placed on Hold Too Long

I apologize for the inconvenience. This is **(your full name)** and who am I speaking with? What can I do to help you today?

Customer Knows It All

(*Let customer talk; when she [or he] is done, then proceed to restate.*)

If I'm understanding you correctly, you (*restate*). Is that correct? (*Resolve, get reaction, and close.*)

"I Only Want to Work with ..."

I appreciate your interest in wanting to work with (**name of other person**). I know that the service is *important* to you and that you want the *best* service possible. I want to provide you with the information you need along with the service you are expecting. I am your representative, and I'm prepared to *quickly* assist you with the detailed information you need, since I have access to your area. Would that be all right *with* you. (*Assumptive*) (*Probe, restate, and finish the remaining steps.*)

Credit and Collections

Why Did You Deny My Credit?

I appreciate your concern and that you were *counting* on an approval. When this happens, and customers like yourself are disappointed, it's difficult to try and communicate the circumstances. In order for me to *advise* you as to why your application was not approved, I recommend you request *directly* to the credit agency that we obtained a report from. Your report is confidential, and only they can provide you with the status of your credit report and why your credit was not approved. We *only* receive a rating that is based upon your credit report by the reporting agency. Unfortunately ... > the rating we received, was not in the range we could approve. Once you have your report, we *can* be more helpful to you by determining ... > *other* ways to assist you. I can provide you with the information of how to get a copy of your credit report, would that be all right *with* you. (*Assumptive*) The address is (**state address**). In the meantime, are there any other questions or concerns you have that I can help you with?

"Why Do You Have to Ask So Many Questions?"

I know it can be frustrating and your time is valuable. In order for me to process this faster so you can get your approval [or the information], I need this information. Would that be all right *with* you. (*Assumptive*).

"When Can I Expect Authorization?"

How soon did you need this authorized? Our standard procedures of authorization are (*describe*). Many want an authorization sooner, and we do cur best to try and accommodate that request. To speed up the process, I need you to (*explain*). Would that be all right *with* you. (*Assumptive*)

Customer Has to Notify in Writing of Any Address or Phone Change

This is extremely important if you want continued coverage [or service]. We *can* service you *better* provided that we are up to date with our information. In order for me to accomplish this, I need ... > to ask you *just* a couple of *quick* questions, if you don't mind. (*Assumptive*.) (*Probe, restate, and close.*)

Receptionist

"All I Want To Know Is the Price!"

I want to help you (**customer's name**). I'm the receptionist and not aware of our prices. However, I will *ensure* that (**person's full name**) will call you to provide you with all the information you're looking for. Would that be all right *with* you. (*Assumptive*)

"Why Can't I Just Talk with Someone Now?"

I understand (**customer name**). We have a unique program called client coordination. This will save you time and frustration. Will this be too much of an inconvenience for you to have (**person's name**) contact you, in order to have one of our more experienced representatives provide you with all the information you're looking for?

Customers Are Insistent

Understanding that I don't have someone available at this particular moment and that we do care about your interest, how would you like me to handle this? (Or) What would you recommend? (Or) I appreciate your interest; however, I am the client coordinator, my position is to direct the calls to certain people within our company who are more capable of addressing your particular needs. We will ensure a prompt response to you. I will have (**person's name**) contact you back within (*offer time frame*). Would that be all right *with* you. (*Assumptive*)

Why-Was-I-Holding-So-Long Questions from Car Phone and Long-Distance Callers

(**Customer's name**), I apologize you had to wait so long. My incoming phone lines became very busy. (**Person's name**) is in a meeting [or is unavailable] at this time. I will inform him [or her] of your call as soon as I can. Would that be all right *with* you. (*Assumptive*)

"They Have My Phone Number!"

I understand, however **(person's name)** requested ... > I personally get this information on *every* incoming call to *ensure* better customer servicing. This will help your representative to contact you faster, since often **(person's name)** returns calls where phone numbers are not available.

1. What is the correct spelling of your name?
2. What company are you with?
3. What number can you be reached at?

Thank you for calling **(customer's name)**. I'll see that **(person's name)** receives your message the moment she [or he] returns. In the meantime, is there anything else I can do?

"Why Hasn't He Returned My Call?"
"Will She Call Me Back?"

(Customer name). He hasn't received his messages yet. As soon as he returns, I will personally see to it that he gets your message promptly. Does that sound fair enough. (*Assumptive.*) (Or) **(Customer name)**, I gave **(person's name)** your message. I am confident she will get back to you as quickly as she can. I would be more than happy to take another message, or, try to find someone else who may be able to assist you now. Which do you prefer?

"I Thought the Other Person Was Patching Me through to ..."

I apologize for the inconvenience. This is **(your name)** and your name is? Hello, **(customer's name)**, who would you like to speak with? (*Refer to balance of your script.*)

18

For Your Information

For Your Information—on Customer Service

Companies are spending more training dollars today than ever before to teach their employees customer service etiquette. Today, for most companies, it's costly to gain a new customer but even more costly to replace a lost customer. Approximately 60 percent of the attrition rate factor for losing a customer is due to poor customer servicing. It is extremely vital that anyone who has contact with customers, whether face to face or over the telephone, learn customer-servicing techniques.

This chapter includes proper holding techniques that enable the CSR to handle a longer volume of inbound calls while offering extra customer service. Voice exercises are provided to help increase the tonality and word pronunciation of the CSR. Listening evaluations designed for CSRs are also provided to help improve their skills and techniques. The importance of tabulating inbound call activity is discussed. In addition, the methodology to effectively monitor, measure, and track calls and marketing data is included—plus, the means to keep it all simple. Verbiage is very important to anyone who is dealing with people on a day-to-day basis. Using professional language and positive words that encourage interaction and influence others are a vital aspect in today's business communication. A list of different kinds of words and phrases are included in this section for you to review and start using in your vocabulary. Also included is a list of words and phrases to take out of your vocabulary.

Placing Customers on Hold

As we become more computerized and sophisticated with our telecommunications, a lack of good customer servicing is becoming more evident, especially at the receptionist or switchboard operator level. Think about the situations that you have personally experienced. For example, how many times have you called a company and the receptionist or the switchboard operator says, "XYZ company, will you hold?" Before you get to say yes you have already been placed on hold, or when you say that you are in a hurry and can't be placed on hold, then the receptionist responds with, "I have another call, I have to put you on hold." Before you can say who you would like to be directed to, the receptionist/operator has placed you on hold. In the time they took to explain this, your call could have been directed to whomever you wanted to speak with. These are just a few examples and I'm sure you have experienced other more frightening situations. This is why I have included material on placing customers on hold into this chapter. If you are going to learn how to increase your company's customer service etiquette, then it is vitally important to include the one who represents the front cover of your company—your receptionist or your switchboard operator.

Depending on your telecommunications system and the volume of calls your receptionists or switchboard operators receive, their job function greatly depends on which procedure they would use when handling their inbound calls. Keep in mind that every company and department will have different scenarios. The following examples and suggestions are generalized but will help you to gain some ideas.

When you have more than one incoming call, it may be necessary to put one or more of your customers on hold. As an example, examine one call and the typical pattern.

Good morning, 12 Step Productions, where may I direct your call?

When another call comes in, let it ring at least two times, then, depending on where you're at in your steps, the following is an example to tell your first customer:

> **Pardon me, this is Lloyd Hansen and who am I speaking with?** (*Wait for response.*) **Ms. Adams, I have another incoming call I need to direct, just one moment please, and I'll get right back with you. Would that be all right *with* you.** (*Assumptive*)

Wait to get your customer's response—she or he may not be able to hold. Give your customer the time to *object* or *accept* being placed on hold. Once you have asked and he or she has accepted, say **thank you** to show your appreciation. You may now answer the second incoming call.

> **Good morning, 12-Step Productions, where may I direct your call?** (*Find out the nature of the call and whether the customer can be directed quickly. If yes, then do so, otherwise continue.*) **This is Lloyd Hansen, and who am I speaking with?** (*Wait for response.*) **Mr. Lane, I have another customer waiting before you, please wait for *just* one moment, and I'll get right back with you. Would that be all right *with* you.** (*Wait for response.*) **Thank You.**

In most cases, the second customer will agree. However, make sure you get a response first. Don't just put customers on hold without giving them the chance to object or accept. They may not wish to be placed on hold for one reason or another. It may be an emergency, a customer that may previously have been getting the runaround or who has been disconnected or a customer who can be directed quickly without being placed on hold. Waiting for their responses is being sensitive to their needs.

Remember, all your customers are equally important, so give equal time and attention. Once the second caller says yes, a thank you is in order to show your appreciation.

Now go back to the *first call* and address that customer accordingly, such as,

Ms. Adams? Thank you for your patience....

If it sounds like the call may take some time, ask if the customer would mind waiting again, since you still have another customer to get back to. You may also arrange for a call back as soon as you take care of the second customer.

It is not best to let your customers be on hold for more than 1 or 2 minutes at any one time. Your holding customers will become irritated and hang up or may become difficult to deal with. Once you get back to them, apologize for the delay and thank them for being patient. There is no need to explain why they were placed on hold. *This is unprofessional and a waste of time.*

This process will be appreciated by all your customers. Customers will know when they contact your company that they will be treated with value, courtesy, and efficiency. When handled properly, customers don't mind being placed on hold. This increases the development of faith in the customer service department and reflects a positive image of your company!

If you are extremely busy and unable to handle the calls this way, then it is recommended that your company have another customer service representative to assist the high traffic of calls during peak hours. By tabulating you will know when the peak hours are to have extra assistance. A company may feel it's a waste of money to pay for extra assistance, but it's even more expensive when we *lose* customers by not servicing them well! The benefits are rewarding to the customer and to the overall company image you paint in your customer's mind that brings long-lasting results!

Another way to describe this better is to imagine how you would want your customers to be treated if they were walking through your company's door as opposed to contacting you by telephone. If you had a customer walk in and you were assisting her or him, then suddenly someone else walks in and needs assistance, you would not ignore the second customer. The best way to provide that extra customer service is to at least acknowledge his or her existence and let him or her be aware that you will be back in just a moment. You may even want to offer a cup of coffee and a magazine. If the second customer can be directed or serviced quickly, and, providing it would not take away time from the first customer, then you would do so. This is the same scenario with regard to servicing customers over the telephone. Keep a mental picture of servicing your inbound customers the way you would service your face-to-face customers; this will make it easier to bring excellent service across when implementing good telephone etiquette into your company.

Voice Mail

Voice mail is an area that could use a great deal of attention, but to keep it simple, briefly let's go over the most important issues regarding this topic. We are coming into an age of total computerization, and that can be very good and yet also a little frightening, especially if we don't keep the customer as our priority. What you don't want to have happen is to throw customer service out the door and do away with the personable image of customer servicing. Voice mail, if done right, will save a company money and can save the customer time. However, in many situations the exact opposite has happened. Customer complaints are usually on the lines of, "I'm annoyed by voice mail," "I don't have the patience for it," or, "If I continue to have a difficult time getting through, I would rather take my business elsewhere." Companies are losing money due to poorly designed voice-mail systems. Unfortunately, studies have not been made available to determine exactly how much business is lost by voice mail. More emphasis has been in the area of how much more increased business or productivity time is saved by having voice mail. This should not be misunderstood, I am not suggesting that voice mail is ineffective; it can be very useful to many companies providing the function of the system places the customer as its *primary* concern.

To be able to determine this, let's begin by asking some simple questions such as: Why a voice-mail system? What are your objectives? Who is it primarily for? Will the customer benefit by it? How will the system be programmed? Does the benefit outweigh the cost?

Let's take the first question, Why voice mail? If your company is growing and receives volumes of inbound call activity and your switchboard operator has had trouble handling this volume, then voice mail is a cost-effective solution to this problem. What are your objectives? Your primary one is to offer better and faster service to your customers. Your secondary objective is to allow each individual and department to have greater control of their inbound call activity.

Who is it for? The customer! Will customers benefit? Sure they can! It all depends on how the system is programmed. The approach needs to be customer-service oriented and user friendly. The system should be programmed by observing and evaluating the pros and cons of other companies' voice-mail systems. For example, too many options to choose from a list of menu items can be confusing. Customers may be annoyed by fully automated systems as opposed to having an opportunity to choose whether they want to speak with a live operator or leave a computerized message. Another annoyance could be when the operator uses the voice-mail system to avoid personally dealing with or assisting the customers. This is especially true when customers prefer to speak with the operator and yet they are still facilitated to someone's voice mail.

Does the benefit outweigh the cost? Only when the customer benefits by it! Take careful consideration when providing voice mail for your inbound call activities. If you don't have voice mail, research your options, talk with other companies who have it, and, more important, survey your existing customers and get their personal opinions. Doing so will not only help you determine the type of system you should invest in, but the best way to program it to ensure you will continue meeting your customers' needs!

The Post Call

Whenever you have finished servicing your customer, especially when you have been dealing with difficult or unhappy customers, you need to ask yourself some key questions:

Was your customer satisfied?

Did your customer get what he or she wanted: information, an individual, a product, or department?

Was the contact positive?

Did your close end in a positive attitude for your customer?

Was the customer happy?

Did the customer feel the call was worth *her* or *his* time?

Was the course of your conversation smooth?

Did you gracefully go into your close without the customer feeling rushed, unimportant, or like just another telephone line?

Did your customer get a good overall feeling of the entire conversation?

Was your customer connected back and forth?

These are mental notes for before, during, and after each inbound call. This will maintain your current customer base, contribute in a major way to your company's positive public image, and directly affect your company's growth potential.

Customer Service Etiquette

You've heard it, been taught it, and yet many struggle with it—"the customer *always* comes first!" "How can it be when the customer is screaming and directing bad language at me? When I try to be nice and yet the customer doesn't even notice or care. The customer is taking it out on me, and it's not my fault, it was the shipping department's." Yes, it is very difficult to keep the customer number one, and that is why the following information will help you to keep that into focus.

Let's take a moment and pretend you are the customer. Think back and try to remember how you were not treated fairly or as number one. Now that you have come up with some situations, list a few of these instances:

1. _____

2. _____

3. _____

4. _____

5. _____

These are as annoying to you as they are to your customer. Poor customer service etiquette not only increases the risk of losing customers forever but it leaves a negative impression of you in the customer's mind the same as your own perspective toward the customer service representative who poorly serviced you. Below are some instances that are common in poor customer service etiquette. Think about the ones you or others in your company need to avoid.

Situations to Avoid

Arguing

Interrupting

Inattentiveness (ignoring)

Frowning

Rushing

Boring

Phony attitude

Unprofessional behavior

Short answers/statements

Passing the customer to someone else without an explanation

Customer on hold too long without an explanation

CSR not knowledgeable as to company products, services, or procedures

Unprofessional language

Slamming phone down, losing temper

Chewing, eating, drinking over the phone

Having another conversation while you have your customer on line

Being impatient

Speaking in monotones

Using "buzz" words

Mispronouncing or misspelling customer's name

No greeting

Placing Customers First.   Use common courtesy. A few words like, "Please let me know where you'd like it shipped," "Thank you for your order," "We really appreciate your business," "Thank you for your patience," "I want to help," "Thank you for sharing that with me," "I apologize that you've been inconvenienced," can work miracles! In any customer service situation make the customer feel important. Customers really are not interested in you, your problems, or what you want. It's up to *you* to prove your concern for them, their problems, and their needs.

One important study of consumer behavior uncovered the fact that 68 percent of customers stop doing business with a company because they feel *ignored*. Every call you make or receive gives you a golden opportunity to show the customer how much you care. When a CSR doesn't care, a company is really in trouble! Remember, you're not making just a sale or handling another call, you're establishing a potential customer for life.

That's why it's important that you begin by consciously examining and possibly redeveloping your basic telephone skills. A clear voice that is well-paced, friendly, and sincere are manners that are professional and persuasive. A courteous telephone behavior and the ability to listen are crucial for long-lasting customer relationships.

Self-Evaluation.   Ask yourself a few key self-evaluation questions: "Am I a person I'd really want to talk with?" "Would I be pleased?" "Impressed?" "Flattered? "Stimulated?" "Convinced?" When you can honestly answer yes! you're on your way to becoming a successful customer service representative.

Remember, in every inbound call you take, you are projecting the image of your company. As far as the customer is concerned, you are the company you represent. The following are tips to help you be aware of customer service qualities to incorporate:

1. Positive Enthusiastic Attitude.

2. Professional and proper phone etiquette.

3. Efficiency and Responsiveness.

4. Agreeing and being positive with their feelings.

Achieving Successful Customer Service Relationships.   Always do the following:

Use the customer's name periodically.

Give your full name.

Smile at all times.

Apologize when ever necessary.

Be prepared and well organized.

Speak approximately 25 percent louder.

Speak distinctly and articulate clearly.

Speak conversationally, use a good tone, and a natural pitch.

Answer promptly.

Listen continuously.

Be sincere.

Picture customers in your mind.

Paint positive mental pictures in their minds.

Make them feel important.

Give clear and complete information.

Verify the information.

Summarize your conversation by restating.

Ask key open-ended probing questions.

Call back when promised.

End the call with "Thank you for calling" or "Have a nice day."

Be consistent in your professionalism.

Remember the customer's point of view.

Be the person you would like to talk with.

Put a smile in your voice.

Speak slowly, clearly, and convincingly.

Strictly follow the code of good telephone manners.

Be positive, persuasive, and persistent.

Listen effectively.

Always remember: To the person on the telephone you are the company you represent!

A Customer Is ...

- *A customer* is the most important person in any business.

- *A customer* is not dependent on us. We depend on customers.

- *A customer* is not an interruption of our work. Customers are the purpose of it.

- *A customer* does us a favor when she or he comes in. We are not doing customers favors by waiting on them.

- *A customer* is part of our business, not an outsider.

- *A customer* is not just money in the cash register. Customers are human beings with feelings, like our own.

- *A customer* is a person who comes to us with needs and wants. It is our job to fulfill them.

- *A customer* deserves the most courteous attention we can offer. Your customers are the lifeblood of your and every business. They pay our salary. Without our customers we would have to close our doors.

The 3 Ps of Successful Customer Service

Positive. Don't use negative words such as "We don't," or "I can't." Tell them what you do have, not what you don't have. Say, "Here's what I can do for you," rather than, "I can't" or, "Here's what we do have," rather than, "We don't."

Persuasive. Let your own enthusiasm for your product or service be contagious. If you seem indifferent or disinterested, the customer won't feel any better either. Know your product! Describe it accurately and precisely. Use strong, provocative words to get your message across.

Persistent. It isn't a matter of never taking no for an answer. It's a matter of listening to what the customer is saying, overcoming objections, and closing with the customer satisfied with the result!

Excellent versus Poor Customer Service Representatives.   Customer service representatives who are:

Organized. Prepare themselves before they start the day. Versus

Disorganized. Keep you waiting while they look for what they need.

Diligent. Answer inbound calls promptly. Versus

Negligent. Keep customers waiting too long.

Courteous. Identify themselves and always use the customers' names. Versus

Discourteous. Rarely use or frequently forget customers' names.

Attentive. Avoid distracting backgrounds. Versus

Inconsiderate. Chew gum or eat food. Noisy background.

Good Communicators. Use good language skills and speak clearly. Versus

Poor Communicators. Try to impress customers with "buzz" words.

Good Listeners. Listen patiently and effectively. Versus

Poor Listeners. Interrupt or finish customers' sentences.

Honest. Admit to not knowing the answer to a question. Versus

Dishonest. Fake answers or ignore questions entirely.

Friendly. Remain pleasant at all times and put a smile on. Versus

Unfriendly. Take a bad day out on customers and project dissatisfaction in their jobs.

Customer-Focused. Talk about customers and their needs. Versus

Boastful. Talk about themselves.

Respectful. Agreeable, acknowledge customers. Versus

Disrespectful. Argumentative, uncooperative.

Polite. Thank customers for their time and patience. Versus

Rude. Slam the receiver down.

Controlling the Call

It's important that you control your customers. They expect it! Most people are followers and are impressed with a good leader. As a customer service representative, this is *your responsibility.* Controlling the call is challenging and can make a difference in the results you want to achieve with the customer!

Here are some suggestions for controlling your calls:

Be pleasant, confident, and positive.

Ask open-ended questions.

Use active listening.

Restate and paraphrase.

Develop your own style.

Combine correct information with your own personality.

Use customer's name periodically.

Validate any claims.

Use strategic pauses from time to time.

Speak approximately 25 percent louder.

Don't respond to customers answers with your opinions or personal comments.

Other helpful hints include:

Speak directly into the transmitter. Your mouth should be about half an inch from the mouthpiece. Don't jiggle the receiver around or keep moving your head. It's more professional and productive to use a headset. Headsets allow you to freely express yourself, using your hands, and so on.

Enunciate your words clearly. The English language is full of similar sounds such as *t, d, p,* and *b.* Also, never talk with gum, food, a pencil, or anything foreign that doesn't belong in your mouth. This is distracting, rude, and annoying to your customers. Whether you realize it or not, they *can* hear this distraction.

Relax and sound natural. The person at the other end should feel like he or she is talking with another human being, not a "canned" commercial. Be comfortable, relaxed, professional, and personable.

Record yourself. Does your voice convey warmth, sincerity, confidence, and interest? Remember your voice is painting the mental picture the listener is forming of you. You also represent the company image. Keep painting positive mental pictures to impress your customers.

Compare ideas. Listen to some of the national newscasters. Broadcasters and professional speakers are carefully trained in the art of good communicating. They learn the skills to deliver messages that leave unforgettable impressions.

Voice Exercise

Try reading the passage on the following page aloud, incorporating all the things you've just learned. You should be able to get through it in about 90 seconds (1-½ minutes) without stumbling. But it isn't just a matter of getting through it. Your goal is to make it a good story, too, keeping your imaginary listener eager and interested to the very end.

Voice Exercise Story

Once upon a time there lived in the San Francisco Bay area a small boy by the name of Theophilus Thistle, who was a successful thistle sifter. Next door to the thistle sifter, Theophilus, lived another small boy, Peter Piper, the pickled pepper picker. Unfortunately, Theophilus Thistle often thrust three thousand thistles through the thick of his thumb. And Peter, while pickling peppers, often got pickled himself.

One afternoon, after Peter was through pickling a peck of pickled peppers and had become quite pickled, Peter wandered down to the beach of Pescadero to do a little fishing by the seashore of his dreams.

Now, to make your story simple, you shall call the girl "She." She sold seashells by the seashore. Peter the pickled pepper picker saw She selling seashells, by the seashore. While fishing, Peter fell in love with She at first sight! Peter fishing, decided to wed. Peter Piper picked Theophilus Thistle to be his best man. Theophilus Thistle said he gladly would. The day of the wedding, behold! Theophilus Thistle, who was really a very successful thistle sifter, stayed at home thrusting three thousand thistles through the thick of his thumb. But Peter Piper, who wasn't pickled, and She, who wasn't selling seashells, by the seashore, got married anyway, while Theophilus Thistle was thrusting three thousand thistles through the thick of his thumb. And they lived happily ever after, thrusting thistles, pickling pickled peppers, and selling seashells by the seashore.

Tabulating Inbound Call Activities

You need to keep a thorough list of information on inbound calls. This list is a valuable tool that can be used by other people within the organization. When designing these information forms, be sure to consult other department managers to agree on what inbound-call information to collect so it will be beneficial to all concerned.

Depending on the company and department, each will have its own data that need to be collected from the customer. The information can be linked to increase the level of internal communication and better service the customer. For example, some customers may complain to the receptionist about someone or a situation in another department, but the receptionist may not feel comfortable sharing this information directly. The receptionist would be doing the customer and the company a good service by tabulating that information and relaying it to his or her supervisor. This is not meant as a "tattle"; it is primarily geared to ensure that the customer's needs are being fully met and the company can continue to earn the right to rectify the situation and ensure that it won't be repeated. The following are examples of what you should consider.

How Many Inbound Calls Is the CSR Getting Each Hour? This will determine peak hours of call activity. Should the CSR be busier at a certain time of the day and there is a track record of such, then the company can add additional CSRs to help relieve the pressure and offer faster service to the customer.

How Did the Customer Hear about Your Company? A company will learn what is working and what is not. I am surprised how many companies spend many advertising dollars for their telephone directory and yet never measure how many calls they are getting from their investment. How can they possibly justify the cost?

What Department Did the Customer Get Directed to? Should the company find that a particular department is getting more calls than usual, then it can track this activity to that particular department and evaluate its tabulation records to determine why. In this way, you can better control time management and how these calls are being handled.

What Are the Concerns or Complaints of Each Customer? Should the finding prove that particular departments or individuals are not doing their jobs correctly, you can "nip it in the bud" quickly and ensure these habits do not become habitual. This also allows the company to recontact the customer to try and rectify the situation if it was the fault of the company. By doing so, the company will retain customers longer and increase its revenue.

How Many Customers Did You Need to Direct to a Supervisor? This happens when the CSR passes the call or the customer insists on speaking with the supervisor. You can tabulate both separately since both would be handled differently. For example, if the calls were being passed, meaning the CSR could not deal with the customers and decided to pass them on to a supervisor, then retraining the CSR may be necessary.

How Many Customers Did You Successfully Handle and Feel Good about the Results? This offers its own rewards or the company may want to offer recognition for exceptionally successful encounters with unusual customer problems. Tabulating can also be used to share positive encounters from which other CSRs can learn.

Keeping data documentation on a tabulation form will give you, your department, and your company a better idea of the amount of activity for each hour and throughout the day. Documentation also lets you know how effective the other departments are in handling customers. In addition, sharing ideas with others lets them know what steps you and your department need to take to prevent and to correct any problems.

Listening Evaluations for the CSR

It is important to conduct hands-on evaluations of each CSR's live calls. See Fig. 18-1. These evaluations ensure they are using the skills taught at the time

CUSTOMER SERVICE REPRESENTATIVES
LISTENING EVALUATION FORM

Name _____   Date _____

STEPS	RATING	COMMENTS

(0=left out, 1=poor, 2=good, 3=excellent)

A.   PRESENTATION
Step 1/Introduction

Greeting	0	1	2	3 _____
Co/Dept Name	0	1	2	3 _____
Request	0	1	2	3 _____

Step 2/Establish Rapport

Exchange Names	0	1	2	3 _____
First Name Cue	0	1	2	3 _____
Reference	0	1	2	3 _____

Step 3/Purpose of Call

Purpose	0	1	2	3 _____
Open-Ended	0	1	2	3 _____

Step 4/Approach

Benefit Statement	0	1	2	3 _____
I need... >	0	1	2	3 _____
"Just...quick..."	0	1	2	3 _____
"If you don't mind."	0	1	2	3 _____

Step 5/Probing

Open-Ended	0	1	2	3 _____
Responding				
with Questions	0	1	2	3 _____
Create a Need	0	1	2	3 _____

Step 6/Restate

Accurate	0	1	2	3 _____
Dynamic	0	1	2	3 _____
Ask for a				
Positive Response	0	1	2	3 _____

Figure 18-1. CSR listening evaluation form.

of their original training and they are improving as you conduct each new evaluation. It is wise to keep the evaluations for at least 6 months, preferably for 1 year. You can use this form for several areas that will benefit the CSR and the department.

The primary function of the form is to have a tool that you can use to objectively critique all CSRs in the same format. The form has all the features and

STEPS	RATING	COMMENTS

(0=left out, 1=poor, 2=good, 3=excellent)

Step 7/Resolve

Direct the Call	0	1	2	3 _____
Handle Concerns	0	1	2	3 _____
Offer Solution	0	1	2	3 _____
Provide Information	0	1	2	3 _____
Take a Message	0	1	2	3 _____
Pass the Call	0	1	2	3 _____
Overall Performance	0	1	2	3 _____

Step 8/Get Agreement

Ask for a

Positive Response	0	1	2	3 _____
Assumptive	0	1	2	3 _____

Step 9/Objections

Recognize	0	1	2	3 _____
Overcome	0	1	2	3 _____

Step 10/Close

Warm and Friendly	0	1	2	3 _____

Step 11/Inform

Informed	0	1	2	3 _____
Confirmation	0	1	2	3 _____

Step 12/Direct the Call

Connect Customer	0	1	2	3 _____

Get Back

with Customer	0	1	2	3 _____

End the Call?
("Thank you, goodbye, anything else

I can do?")	0	1	2	3 _____

VOICE

Rate of Speech	1	2	3 _____
Tone	1	2	3 _____
Volume	1	2	3 _____

Personality

(attitude/enthusiasm)	1	2	3 _____

Figure 18-1. CSR listening evaluation form (*Continued*)

functions of the CSR's presentation along with evaluating voice, rate of speech, attitude, and so forth. On the far right side you can note your personal comments and recommendations. This evaluation will help to improve your CSRs and ensure they are progressing rather than regressing.

The second function of using this form is in the event you need validation for employees who are insubordinate and refuse to improve. Keeping these forms up to 1 year will enable you to have a solid track record to validate your reasons for termination or a reduction in pay. Be sure to fill out the form in detail and date it; once you have discussed your evaluation with the CSR, you may want the CSR you are evaluating to sign her or his name on the form. This reinforces your time with the CSR and reduces the possibilities of poor communication.

Words and Phrases That Impact Your Presentation

Emotion-Packed Words. When selling the benefits or resolving a problem, it is essential to incorporate emotionally evocative words into your presentation. This will stimulate your prospect or your customers into being more receptive and will allow them to participate more readily in your selling or customer-servicing process. Creating positive images will help hold your prospects' and customers' concentration. The following are just some examples of emotionally charged words you can begin to incorporate into your vocabulary. Select the words that apply to your department and particular situations.

Admired	Fun	Progress
Advise	Genuine	Proven
Affectionate	Growth	Quality
Aggressive	Guaranteed	Recommended
Ambition	Health	Referred
Amusement	Highly	Relief
Appetizing	Home	Reputation
Approval	Hospitality	Respected
Availability	Hunting	Return
Bargain	Increased	Review
Beauty	Independent	Royalty
Capacity	Investment	Safe
Civic pride	Love	Scientific
Confidence	Low-cost	Secure
Consistent	Maximize	Sociable
Cost-effective	Maximum	Status
Courtesy	Modern	Stimulating
Durable	Necessary	Stylish
Earning	Objective	Successful
Economical	Patriotism	Support
Educated	Peace of mind	Sympathy
Elegance	Performance	Tasteful
Enormous	Personality	Tested
Excel	Popular	Thinking
Expandable	Power	Time-saving

| Expressive | Preferred | Up-to-date |
| Friendly | Professional | Value |

In contrast, many words are *neutral* and *nonassertive*. These are some examples of negative-influence words and phrases to avoid:

Possibly	I think	I might
Honestly	To be honest with you	I feel
It could	Probably	I don't know
It should	I was wondering	Perhaps
Buy	I believe	I guess
Sometimes	If, maybe	I'm not sure
Could you	Would you	Tell me
Could I	Can you	Risk
Free	No obligation	May I

The following create *positive* reactions and encourage interaction:

What is your opinion?	I beg your pardon.
What do you think?	Will you help me?
Please illustrate …	It's been a pleasure.
What do you consider … ?	I'm so sorry.
Explain to me …	You were very kind.
What happened then?	It was my fault.
What are the circumstances?	Please …
Describe some of the …	I'm proud of you.
Share with me …	Thank you.
That's terrific!	Congratulations!

The following are irritating words and phrases:

Me, my, mine	Understand?
Okay!!	Old pal!
Ya know	Get the point?
Old friend!	I'll tell you what …
See what I mean?	But honestly now!
You don't say?	Don't you know … ?
No, really?	To be honest with you …
Sorry, what did you say?	Man …
Do you understand?	Are you following me?
What's up?	Yeah?!
Na …	Uhmm …
Excuse me?!	Ahh …

I don't know.	You have to …
Is that right?	I can't …

Phrases That Create Interest.   There are thousands of words and phrases that will help to motivate your prospects and customers. The phrases that follow produce *positive results* particularly in business-to-business marketing. Select the ones you can adapt for your own presentation. The phrases are designed to pique someone's interest. Incorporate them into your probing questions, selling and resolve steps, and trial-close summary. Construct some of your own. Be creative!

- Increase your work output
- Maximize your potential
- Increased production
- Increased efficiency
- Avoid duplication
- Control your cost
- Cost-effective
- Educated choice
- Increased awareness
- Make decisions faster
- Eliminate hidden costs
- Encourage new business
- Expand your market share
- Widen your territory
- Develop new markets
- Increase sales volume
- Get your share of the market
- Improve customer service
- Simplify customer purchase selections
- Stay ahead of your competition
- Receive the best value
- Gain customer loyalty
- Reach (or surpass) your sales objectives
- Keep up with new developments
- Offer the best
- Saves you time
- Offer you peace of mind
- Increase your knowledge/awareness

- Longevity of service
- Provide a competitive analysis
- Secure your financial stability
- Provide convenient and reliable service
- Product diversification

For Your Information—on Telemarketing

"For Your Information" provides enough information to give you an awareness of: how to set goals, implement time management, and self-motivate. Suggestions are made to increase employee motivation using a variety of ideas to maintain the momentum while eliminating the monotony. Listening evaluations are discussed that enable the TSR to understand what the prospect is saying and use the information to effectively close. In addition a trainer will learn techniques on how to conduct effective role playing that is fun, productive, and doesn't take too much time away from the telephone activity. The tabulation process is discussed as a learning tool to compile weekly, monthly, quarterly, and annual statistics. Tabulating can be tedious if not done properly, but it's essential in every telemarketing center, and the rewards are worth it to everyone! The best times for prospecting in the business-to-business market are categorized according to industry, and the residential market call times are categorized according to highest contact ratio.

After you have read through the information provided in this chapter, you have an opportunity to utilize all or a portion of the ideas. The important issue is to be creative and continuously increase your knowledge enabling you to further enhance your telemarketing efforts.

Approach and Hook

An *approach* is when you make a statement to the prospect. A *hook* is when the statement creates an interest that arouses your prospect's curiosity. You want to utilize approaches and hooks throughout your presentation. The following are some approach-and-hook methods and the steps in which they can be used most effectively. Consider which ones you'll use when designing and redefining your presentation scripts.

Benefit Approach.   This approach uses statements that focus directly on the benefits of the product or service (steps 7, 9, and 10):

> **Increase your production ...**
> **Maximize your income ...**
> **Offer peace of mind ...**

Opinion Approach.   Attention is focused on your product, and the customer becomes a part of your presentation (steps 5, 6, 8, and 10):

> What comparisons have been made to determine if you're getting *maximum results?*
> ... and you have not had an *opportunity* to evaluate the cost-effectiveness, is that correct?
> How important is that to you?

News Approach.   Newspaper stories or magazine articles often validate information to the customer (steps 7, 9, and 10):

> According to a recent article in *Business* magazine, telemarketing will be the world's *largest* growth industry in the next decade.

Curiosity Approach.   Use this approach to arouse the prospect's interest and curiosity (steps 2, 4, and 5):

> We specialize in your industry....
> My company requested ... > I contact you personally.
> What steps have you taken to measure the *effectiveness* of your prospecting efforts?

I-Am-Here-to-Help-You Approach.   People cannot resist a confident, direct, and enthusiastic offer of help. This approach works if you can follow up with facts that prove your proposal (steps 6, 7, 9, and 10):

> I would like the *opportunity* to show you the type of service I provide and how this will benefit you directly.
> If I am unable to *impress* you in the first 15 minutes ...
> I want to be sure I have the information correct.... Is that correct?

Factual Approach.   Turn an interesting fact about the service you are offering into an opening "catch." The statement must be true and the sentence brief (steps 5, 7, and 10):

> You see the value in training. What are your plans to reevaluate the *effectiveness* of your training efforts to *ensure* that you're maximizing your productivity?
> Our 12-step training will overcome *most* objections before they surface, thereby increasing ... > your *confidence* and *motivation* when prospecting.

Shock Approach.   Use this in your opening statement. Example: Missing out on a sale or low inventory (steps 2 and 4):

> You requested ... > I contact you as soon as we had the product you're looking for.
> We're contacting our *preferred* customers about an upcoming sale we're having.

Service Approach.   Present something unique about your service to attract customers (steps 2, 4, 5, 7, 9, and 10):

> **We specialize ... > in motivational training.**
> **... In order for us to service you *better*. ...**
> **What sets us *apart* from our competitors ...**

Mail-Piece Approach.   Refer to a marketing item, perhaps a sale announcement or a special offer (steps 2, 4, 7, 9, and 10):

> **I recently sent you some information.**
> **I'm following up on the information you requested.**
> **I recommend ... > you take advantage of the discount coupon you received, and I recommend this because ...**

Premium Approach.   Few customers turn down a complimentary gift or sample. By accepting it, customers usually feel obligated to hear your presentation or to allow you to stop by (steps 7 and 9):

> **I recommend a *complimentary* consultation.**
> **I will provide you with *complimentary* information about your estate planning that will offer ideas to help *protect* you and your family from hefty estate taxes.**

Third-Party Reference Approach.   You and the prospect have a mutual acquaintance. This will help break the ice and arouse curiosity about what you have to offer (steps 2 and 4):

> **Karen Johnson, who is a mutual friend of ours, recommended ... > that I contact *you* personally.**
> **Tim Peters was able to receive valuable information about ...**

Problem-Solving Approach.   Customers are interested in ideas that help solve their problems (steps 7, 9, and 10):

> **I recommend.... I recommend this because of ...**
> **I understand it is important to you and you can achieve that by ...**

Question Approach.   Ask an interesting question about what you are offering. The question should be simple, noncontroversial, and factual (steps 5 and 10):

> **When was the last time you received a consultation to determine ... > what your options are?**
> **How often does your representative follow up and *ensure* that your needs are fully met?**

Controlling Your Prospect

It's important that you control your prospects. They expect it! This is not meant that you should intimidate them and you should not be aggressive.

Instead you are to be assertive and confident, especially with your selection of words and phrases. Most people are followers and are impressed by a good leader. In prospecting, your responsibility is to lead. Controlling the prospect is challenging and will make a difference in your closing ratios!

Some methods of controlling include:

- Be pleasant, confident, and positive.
- Use customer's name.
- Ask open-ended questions.
- Promote active listening.
- Repeat and paraphrase (restate).
- Develop your own style.
- Combine correct information with your own personality.
- Never mention price before presenting features and benefits.
- Validate any claims.
- Use strategic pauses.
- Speak 25 percent louder.
- Don't respond to your prospect's answers to your probing questions.
- Be careful not to use words such as, *Could I, would you, can you, may I, is it all right if.* (See positive and negative words and phrases.)

Know Your Goals and Manage Your Time

Personal Goals.   It is important to set goals for yourself. This will increase your motivation to be more successful. Set realistic short- and long-range goals for your personal and business career. Make your short-term goals achievable. Once you've attained them, strive for new and higher goals. Set goals for yourself that are measured on the following bases:

- Daily
- Weekly
- Monthly
- Quarterly
- Yearly
- Short- and Long-Term
- Realistic

Once you have achieved these personal goals, reward yourself!

Keep a Chart and Measure Yourself.   Keeping a chart will help you find ways to improve yourself. Know your business and strive to be the best you can.

Set time aside each day to learn something new about your trade. Imagine the effect of learning just one new idea a day for a year! This impresses your coworkers, managers, your prospects, your customers, and yourself.

√ Determine and list your long-term goals. Make two lists, one for your personal life and one for your career.

√ List goals for the next 6 months.

√ Prioritize the goals.

√ Prioritize the subgoals as A-1, A-2, and so on.

√ List activities that will help you meet each particular goal.

Design a Daily To-Do List

√ Update your list on a regular basis.

√ Prioritize the daily to-do list. Use the same A, B, C categories as on the goals list. Then, begin work on your A categories. The only time you will do Cs is if they happen to be your boss's As, or if there is time enough and you have completed your As and Bs.

√ Do not touch a piece of paper more than once.

√ Do it now. Do not procrastinate!

√ Question yourself before beginning a new activity. Ask yourself, "What's the best use of my time right now?"

Make a Chart.   To have an effective chart that will be a progressive tool for personal growth in your field, keep in mind the following suggestions:

√ Stick with it.

√ Update continuously.

√ Share and discuss with coworkers, family, and friends.

√ Monitor your progress.

√ Find better solutions.

√ Be creative.

√ Set new, higher goals.

√ Reward your self-improvements.

√ Be competitive with others in your field.

√ Set affordable contests.

√ Be accountable to yourself for results.

Time Management.   Determine the steps you will take to improve your time management. Start with the areas you can affect immediately. Gradually progress to the areas which are more difficult and take greater effort. Fill in the following:

Step 1. _____

Step 2. _____

Step 3. _____

Organizational skills I will possess:

_____

_____

A Parable to Ponder

The following is a story that may seem familiar. Perhaps you know someone that fits this description. The purpose of the story is to compel you to increase your knowledge, to find ways to become creative and more valuable to your company and to yourself.

> A teacher worked in the same school for 20 years. A better, higher-paying position was created in the school, and because of his seniority and experience, the teacher was confident he would be selected to fill this new position. A new teacher, however, was hired instead. Upon hearing the news, the teacher complained, "I've been here for 20 years, have been loyal and have always been dutiful in my job. Why was the position given to a newly hired teacher?" The school board's reply was, "Yes, we know you have been with us for 20 years. What you learned in 1 year, however, was merely repeated 20 times. Loyalty and diligence are fine attributes, but without growth, their value is limited."

The moral? Take an active and aggressive interest in growing professionally. Don't just put in the hours, don't just add up the time. Instead, use the time to become the best, most knowledgeable person you can be. Become committed to the idea that you are going to expand your professional and personal horizons. In doing so, you become more valuable to yourself and to your company.

Steps to Increase Your Knowledge

Through the years I have met many different types of people, from highly motivated and successful achievers to those who have the desire to succeed but lack everything else to make it happen. This was more common than I had thought, and I became troubled with the idea that many people were spending hundreds of dollars trying to buy their success. What they failed to realize is that success is not something you can buy and take home with you and all you have to do is plug it in and there you have it! It requires more drive and dedication than that. I truly believe that we are our own worst enemies. We cause ourselves not to be successful even though all of us can be as successful as we really want to be providing we have what it takes to get success. It's not money nor is it just having a natural talent or ability. It is a three-letter word to achieve success; this three-letter word is called the *DEW* method. What does this translate to?

D = desire to grow

E = eagerness to learn

W = willingness to be taught

These three elements are the very key to being successful. Many people judge success by money or materialism, but these are temporary and don't last. Having a desire to grow, to advance yourself, to expand your capabilities and an eagerness to learn are very important to being successful. But all these are wasted if you do not have the willingness to be taught. To open your mind and learn what it takes to be the best that you can be at what you do, no matter the job you have or the income you make. Just striving to be the very best is success. If you continually worry about being underpaid and only put out what you are getting in, you will never get success because you will be ordinary as opposed to extraordinary. You need to continually set yourself apart from others, and the most successful way to achieve this is, DEW it!

Below are some ideas that will help you to grow and become more successful. Just remember, DEW it!

- *Prepare* your sales presentations and know every aspect of your:
  √ Product
  √ Competitors
  √ Industry
- *Subscribe* to and read professional and trade magazines. Be aware of news, developments, and trends in your industry.
- *Update* your information, know and review your:
  √ Skills
  √ Sales-aid tools
  √ Present marketing campaigns and promotions (radio, television, newspaper, special offers, discount ads)
- *Manage* and make the most of your time:
  √ Listen to instructional and motivational tapes while traveling (in the course of one year, you can get quite an education!).
  √ Invest in developing a professional library of books and tapes to promote your own growth.

By taking steps to increase your knowledge, you will enhance your growth, become better at your job, increase your value to yourself and to others, and, of course, when you are successful you may even be able to increase your income potential in the process! Challenge yourself! There are new ideas and skills to learn. Develop a proactive learning attitude. Remember, there are three types of people: Those who make things happen, those who watch things happen, and those who wonder what happened. Find ways to *make* things happen. Excel in your field! By doing this, you will take the monotony out of your daily activities and see each new day for what it really is—an exciting challenge!

The Biggest Time-Wasters

Whether you work in the office, in the field, or out of your home, your productivity can suffer from these "time bandits":

- *Visual distractions.* Try rearranging your work environment so that you can keep focused on your job and your performance. Set rules for others to stay away while you are prospecting so you will not be distracted.

- *Noise.* Minimize outside noises such as third-party conversations. Place a sign at your workstation, "Do not disturb, I'm prospecting." Your coworkers may be offended at first, but once they see how serious you are and dedicated to being successful they will be envious, and many will follow your lead in doing the same—especially when management encourages it! Some companies have a paging system that can be very distracting. Instead, use voice mail or pagers to eliminate the distraction.

- *Telephone.* This is a difficult one to overcome. This is the primary time-management problem I have seen during the many years I have been a consultant. A company's policy should restrict any incoming and outgoing personal phone call unless it is an emergency. Personal calls should be at designated times only. If companies could accurately monitor this time waster, they would be alarmed at how much revenue is lost due to productive time being spent unproductively by personal telephone calls.

- *Mistakes.* We all make them, and we will continue making them. However, one way to minimize mistakes is to recognize them, evaluate what occurred to cause the mistake, and learn how to correct it. Most mistakes are made due to time-management crisis. Try not to be in a rush and set your priorities. Do your best not to shift your priorities once they have been established.

- *Drop-in visitors.* Again, place your "do not disturb" sign up, set company policies, and enforce them. However when you get outside visitors who are not aware of your deadlines and how busy you may be, then inform them of your situation and that you only have a few minutes to spend with them. Most people will understand and will not feel offended. This is called "healthy communication," and you will be more respected for it than allowing your visitors to unconsciously take advantage of your valuable time.

- *Mechanical breakdown.* In most cases, this is out of your control. One way to help you reduce certain mechanical breakdowns, especially if you are the operator, is to keep equipment maintained. If you are not responsible for this, find someone who is and make them accountable for the maintenance.

- *Unscheduled meetings.* During emergency situations you need to have your meeting. However, you can control the length of the meeting by setting up guidelines or parameters of how long the meeting will be, what the meeting will be about, and how much time will be set aside for questions and answers. Once the meeting is underway, appoint a leader to ensure that the conversation doesn't get off track. This could lengthen the meeting considerably and lose sight of your objectives.

- *Wrong or lost information.* Having an accountability factor built in to your department and to each individual will help minimize this time bandit. Keeping your internal communication flowing on a universal system will enable everyone to have better control of managing information.

- *Self-interruption ("I think I'll get some coffee.").* Set guidelines for yourself to follow. Make yourself accountable to someone else to help you increase your time management. If you are responsible for others' time management, set the rules and set yourself as an example.

- *Crisis.* Prioritize the crises. Some crises seem urgent at the moment, but once your emotions have settled, you can think more clearly and better manage the problem. If a crisis causes you to reshift your priorities, so be it! But don't allow it to be stressful for you, just concentrate on handling the situation. Delegate to others whenever possible to help you meet your priorities.

- *Shifting priorities.* It is appropriate to shift priorities only when you can better manage your time by doing so and during emergency situations. When people ask you to shift your priorities, make them aware of what you need to shift, then ask if they still want you to shift your priorities.

- *Cluttered desk.* Prepare your work space. Keep it organized throughout the day. At the end of each day, organize your work space to meet the next day's activities. It is easier to be organized when you are automated. When you are on a paper system, then you must have your own filing and suspense system set up that will keep you organized. Never touching a piece of paper more than once and filing it immediately when you are finished will make it easier to avoid a cluttered desk. Have an "in and out" box so that others will not clutter your desk. Be sure to establish the guidelines so that your needs will be respected by others.

- *Inability to say no.* Those who tend not to delegate or who feel that they can do it better and faster on their own or who simply cannot say no are continually on a roller coaster trying to do it all and do it all today! You cannot possibly be all things to all people. You must learn to delegate and especially learn to say no. If this feels uncomfortable for you, then try using some psychology behind it. For example, when someone asks you to do something and it is not in your job description, then say, "I would be more than happy to help you, however, I have a list of priorities that I have scheduled for myself to do today, and if I shift them it will cause me to fall behind schedule. If you are not able to get anyone else to help you, let me know and I will schedule it in my calendar on Wednesday. Please be sure to give me at least 24 hours notice, so that I can devote the necessary time to work on it. Does that sound fair enough." (Say this by using an assumptive statement!) If the individual needs it immediately and cannot wait, then you would say, "I would be happy to help you. Here is my list of things I need to do today, what project can you help me with so that I can also dedicate time to work on yours?" When your superior wants you to shift your priorities, then you can say, "I would be happy to do this for you, and I appreciate you thinking of me. Here is a list of projects that I must do today. Please help me to determine what I should shift so that I can spend the time needed to work on this new project for you?"

These suggestions can be reworded to fit your style and personality, but you get the point. The concept behind this is to let people know you are willing to help, but there is a sacrifice. You must help them to help you make a decision of how you are going to shift your priorities so you can meet your daily objectives while still being able to assist them. Knowing you are busy they could consider someone other than yourself for the job. Maybe you were their first pick because they know that they can count on you. It may be time that they try and find others within the company they can also count on during a crunch!

- *Failure to delegate.* This is usually caused by your feeling that you can do it better and faster if you did it yourself. Cross-train others to do a certain job task that is more tedious. Your time may be more valuable in others areas, and it certainly would be more profitable for the company. You could ask in such a way as to make others feel important: "I really need your help and I feel confident that you are the best to do the job the way I would do it myself."

- *Socializing.* This is why companies have designated times for breaks and lunch. However, many do not follow this policy. This is a management problem, a weakness that can develop into a cancer throughout an entire company. Policies are written to be carried out, and they must be enforced only by management. Should others try to socialize while you are working, then you must tell them gently that you cannot be disturbed and that you need to get back to work. If you say it correctly, most will not be offended by your request. However, if you give in to them, you are encouraging this to recur, and it won't stop until you put it to a stop. You can gently communicate this by saying, "I really wish I could spend time to talk with you right now, but I have a deadline to meet, and I am already behind schedule. Can we talk during our break or after work?"

When colleagues make this a daily routine, then you have a few choices to try and resolve this problem. You can take a break and buy them a cup of coffee and say, "I really need your help and I hope you will understand and not take it personally. Recently I have made some very demanding goals for myself and because of this, I had to make some changes regarding my work habits. But I need you and everyone else to be patient with me and to help me. Each day I prioritize my projects, and taking breaks and lunch all into consideration, I lock in the time it will take me to accomplish these projects. This means I cannot shift my priorities and I have to sacrifice my personal time. I can't even take the time out and talk with you or others unless it is related to my projects or when we are on breaks. This is very important to me and I don't want you to take this personally."

These predators of your time are the result of:

√ Illusion of courtesy ("how can I say no?")

√ Image of availability ("my door is always open")

√ Need to socialize

√ Desire to be informed

√ Low value of own time

√ Presumption of the legitimacy of the interruption

Naturally, not all these time bandits are within your power to control. Delays and interruptions will occur despite your best efforts! Don't compound the problem by creating your own diversions, just try to communicate your needs to others and request that they respect you for wanting to improve on your time management.

Tips for Self-Motivation

Studies show that people who are self-motivated enjoy greater job satisfaction and success. If you are looking for a way to become more confident and self-motivated, here are *10 tips* you will want to try. Increasing your *self-confidence* can be acquired one step at a time. Work your way through each tip.

1. *Write out your career goals.* List key steps that will help you reach those goals.

2. *Think positively.* Maintain faith in your abilities. You will be more capable of handling difficult situations that arise if you perceive them as creative challenges!

3. *Make a diary of your accomplishments.* Keep a running list of your accomplishments and periodically review them. Look back at what you have achieved. This will reinforce your sense of self-esteem, which in turn will motivate you to strive for future success.

4. *Seek new responsibilities.* For instance, if you discover an easier way to do something at the office, speak to your boss about it. Your initiative will be appreciated, and you will be able to take pride in the contribution you have made. Your company may want to provide a bonus system for ideas that either increase business, save the company money, or ensure better customer servicing.

5. *Increase your knowledge.* Learn as much as you can about your products and services. Keep up to date on current information and your competitors. If you are well-informed, you will be more self-assured and better equipped to do your job.

6. *Surround yourself with successful people.* Spend time with those who stimulate, inspire, and encourage you to do your best. Avoid absorbing the negative attitudes of complainers and dissatisfied coworkers.

7. *Continue to meet new challenges.* Try new ways to advance your career goals. What you learn from mistakes can make you better prepared for future challenges. Mistakes are learning experiences too.

8. *Be open to new experiences and ideas.* You will be more likely to become spontaneous, creative, and knowledgeable.

9. *Trust your judgment.* If you have weighed all the options and tested the possibilities and you feel confident about your decisions, others will also respect your viewpoint.

10. *Consider your job as an opportunity.* Spend time to develop new skills and gain more experience. By mastering challenges, you will become motivated to reach for higher goals.

Let's Role-Play

When learning new concepts, you need to practice them prior to actual implementation. Role playing is extremely effective for this. Below are some ideas that will motivate role playing, add fun, and offer challenging ways to keep role playing interactive with willing participants. Cooperation is a key factor, and simulating actual calls is essential.

Discuss and review the objections and techniques. Use examples of the objection-handling process that you have customized for your product or service. Ensure that you use the six techniques listed below, individually or in combination.

1. Restate, agree, and probe
2. Keep selling
3. Reflect
4. Feel, felt, found
5. Ask prospect for best solution
6. "If I could ... , would you ... "

Create a positive and nurturing atmosphere to discuss fears and apprehensions. Remind yourself of the benefits of role play, such as the opportunity to:

- Practice new skills.
- Reinforce what is learned.
- Watch and learn from others.
- Discuss weaknesses in skills and knowledge.
- Improve your skills before using them in the workplace.

Provide clear directions and stress techniques you will be looking for based on the skills and the 12 steps. Techniques include voice inflection, variable speeds in pacing, strategic pauses, and so on.

Ask for volunteers or assign people to roles and use these guidelines:

- Encouraging volunteers is best. However, also give roles to those who will not volunteer, especially those who really need it.

- Assign roles. In business-to-business prospecting, be sure to assign someone to role-play the secretary to be screened. When role playing inbound calls, assign the switchboard operator or receptionist. Try to simulate every aspect of the inbound or outbound call activity.

- Use necessary scripts and objections. Be sure those who are role playing will use them. Prevent them from trying to "wing it through," because their natural way of prospecting will take over, and momentum in your role playing is lost.

- Create actual atmosphere with furniture, tabulation sheets, hardware, phones, and so on. This will help staff to get in the mood and simulate their roles more precisely.

The following are rules for role playing:

Clarify the guidelines of the role play in advance so all participants will know what to expect. Ensure that there are no interruptions or comments from the trainer or the group during role playing unless you plan to conduct a stop-and-go method of role playing. For example, whenever individuals being evaluated make a mistake (they are not following the 12 steps or the functions within the steps), stop the role play and ask the individuals what happened. Try to get them to determine where they went wrong and what they should have done differently. Whenever they cannot make this determination, then ask one of your observers (those who are not participating in the role play) to share with the group what went wrong and what should have been done. This is a more advanced method of role playing and is only recommended when you are dealing with well-seasoned TSRs and CSRs or those who have been through extensive training.

Observe and use the Listening Evaluation Form to evaluate the performance of the participant. Have each of those who are observing evaluate the role-play session. Once the role play is completed, give the observers time to complete their evaluations, then ask the individuals being observed to make their comments first before the observers participate.

Record the session on video- or audiotape, then later evaluate the performance of the participants and the observers. Look for how the participants perceived themselves and how the observers communicated their observations. Evaluate the selections of words and phrases to determine whether they were constructive and positive. Plan what you can do to use the video- or audiotape as a training tool to demonstrate what participants could have done differently. You can even create scripts of what should have been done and try the role play again. Allow the observers to hear the difference when they are following the techniques.

Critique the participant by using constructive and positive words that are encouraging. Below is a checklist to help remind you how to critique:

√ *Interact* with the people being evaluated. Ask what they liked about the role play and what they would have done differently.

√ *Observe* and first compliment, then critique the actions of the participant, but avoid critiquing the participant personally.

√ *Supervise* the interaction with suggestions to remedy problems in technique.

√ *Stress* to the group the need to be tactful and to use customer service approaches when critiquing and offering recommendations. Encourage participants to be honest and thorough, while also being constructive. Otherwise, no learning is achieved.

√ *Get final comment* on the group's observation by the TSRs being evaluated. Ask what they would like to see improved in the role playing.

√ *Provide an evaluation form* with a complete listing of strengths and areas to be improved along with the steps to make this improvement. Keep a record of dates when the role plays were evaluated and file them. Later you can bring them out and compare the difference. When there has been improvement, it is encouraging to the participant. When there are areas of repetitive weakness, then you need to spend more attention to strengthen them.

Implement role playing at least once a week to sharpen skills and provide experience with unusual prospecting scenarios. This will make everyone quick to think and respond with confidence!

Listening Evaluations for the TSR

It is important to conduct hands-on evaluations of each TSR's live prospecting calls. This ensure that TSRs are using the skills taught at the time of their original training and they are improving as you conduct each new evaluation of them. It is wise to keep the evaluations for at least 6 months, preferably for one year (see Fig. 18-2). You can use this form for several areas that will benefit the TSR and the department.

The primary function of the form is to have a tool that you can use to objectively critique all TSRs in the same format. The form has all the features and functions of the TSRs' outbound presentations along with evaluation of their voices, rates of speech, attitudes, and so forth. On the far right side you can note your personal comments and recommendations. This evaluation will help to improve your TSRs and ensure they are progressing rather than regressing.

The second function of using this form is in the event you need validation for employees who are insubordinate and refuse to improve. Keeping these forms for up to 1 year will enable you to have a solid track record to validate your reasons for termination or a reduction in pay. Be sure to fill out the form in detail and date it; once you have discussed your evaluation of them, you may want the TSRs you are evaluating to sign their names on the forms. This reinforces your time with them and reduces the possibilities of poor communication.

TELEMARKETING SERVICE REPRESENTATIVES LISTENING EVALUATION FORM

Name _____   Date _____

STEPS	RATING			COMMENTS
	(0=left out, 1=poor, 2=good, 3=excellent)			

A.   PRESENTATION

Step 1/Introduction

Greeting 0	1	2	3	_____
Establish Contact 0	1	2	3	_____
First Name Cue 0	1	2	3	_____
Introduce Self & Co. 0	1	2	3	_____
Location/Landmark 0	1	2	3	_____

Step 2/Reference

Reference 0	1	2	3	_____

Step 3/Request for Time

I hope... >

Strategic Pause 0	1	2	3	_____
Inflection (...*have* 1.) 0	1	2	3	_____
2nd Function				
(...*with* you.) 0	1	2	3	_____

Step 4/Purpose

Benefit Statement 0	1	2	3	_____
I need... >...........................0	1	2	3	_____
"*Just...quick...*"...............0	1	2	3	_____
"If you don't mind." 0	1	2	3	_____

Step 5/Probing

Open-Ended 0	1	2	3	_____
Responding				
with Questions 0	1	2	3	_____
Create a Need 0	1	2	3	_____

Step 6/Restate

Accurate 0	1	2	3	_____
Dynamic 0	1	2	3	_____
Ask for a				
Positive Response 0	1	2	3	_____

Step 7/Features & Benefits

Features................................ 0	1	2	3	_____
Functions 0	1	2	3	_____
Implied Benefits 0	1	2	3	_____
Stated Benefits 0	1	2	3	_____
Customization....................... 0	1	2	3	_____

Figure 18-2. TSR listening evaluation form.

STEPS	RATING			COMMENTS

(0=left out, 1=poor, 2=good, 3=excellent)

Step 8/Get Reaction

Ask for a Positive Response
("How valuable?") 0   1   2   3 _____

Step 9/Trial Close

Summarize 0   1   2   3 _____

Ask for a Positive Response
("Does that sound
   fair enough.") 0   1   2   3 _____

Step 10/Objections

Recognize 0   1   2   3 _____
Overcome 0   1   2   3 _____

Step 11/Close

Type of Close Used? 0   1   2   3 _____

Step 12/Post-Close

Benefit Statement 0   1   2   3 _____
Probing Questions 0   1   2   3 _____
Recap 0   1   2   3 _____
End the call? 0   1   2   3 _____

B.   **VOICE:**

Rate of Speech 1   2   3 _____
Tone 1   2   3 _____
Volume 1   2   3 _____
Personality (attitude/enthusiasm) 1   2   3 _____

C.   **TECHNIQUE:**

Maintain Control 0   1   2   3 _____
Use of Strategic Pauses 0   1   2   3 _____
Follow "12 Steps" 0   1   2   3 _____
"Smile & Dial?" 0   1   2   3 _____
Organize/Prepared 0   1   2   3 _____
Tabulating Results 0   1   2   3 _____

D.   **ADDITIONAL COMMENTS:**

_____

_____

E.   **RECOMMENDATIONS:**

_____

_____

Evaluated By: _____

Figure 18-2. TSR listening evaluation form. (*Continued*)

Call Objective Planning

Planning is vital to help you customize your presentation according to the prospecting calls you know will be made. This will help to organize your presentation so you will be confident at all times during your presentation. This is not meant to clutter your desk with another form, and it is not just another paper for a TSR to fill out. It's to help you plan "measurable and realistic call objectives." This is a *tool* to increase your confidence in prospecting. If you use it, you will be better prepared to deliver your message.

Call Objective Planning Checklist. Once you are skilled in delivering the 12 steps (script writing is easy when using the step method), you will no longer need this precall objective planning worksheet. Unless you are working on projects you may not be accustomed to, then it would be helpful to use the chart.

CALL OBJECTIVE WORKSHEET

Company Name _____

Industry _____

Contact Title/Position _____

Phone Number _____ Fax _____

Address _____

Products/Services _____

My Call Objective _____

_____

My Opening Statement _____

_____

Information Required _____

_____

_____

NEEDS

Points to close on _____

_____

Motivation to buy _____

_____

Features, Functions, Implied & Stated Benefits: _____

_____

_____

OBJECTIONS

Possible _____

Actual _____

Answers _____

_____

_____

_____

Figure 18-3. Call objective worksheet form.

Below is a checklist that will help you begin preparing. Before filling out your call objective worksheet (Fig. 18-3) check the list below to be sure you have done everything you can to prepare yourself in advance.

A. Set specific goals by asking yourself:
　　1. How many telephone dials to make?
　　2. How many telephone presentations to complete?
　　3. What will my daily production be?
　　4. What weekly results do I want to achieve?
B. Gather your information:
　　1. About the product or service you are prospecting or selling
　　2. About the contact person or company you will be approaching
C. Prepare your opening statement (steps 1 to 4):
　　1. Establish rapport.
　　2. Identify yourself, your company, and your landmark, location, or territory.
　　3. State your reference.
　　4. Respect their time.
　　5. State the purpose of your call.
D. Information required from customer (step 5):
　　1. Use open-ended questions.
　　2. Qualify.
　　3. Establish wants.
　　4. Create needs.
E. Prepare your sales presentation (steps 6, 7, and 8):
　　1. Restate information you gained from prospects and get confirmation.
　　2. Stress benefits, not features.
　　3. Use emotion-packed words.
　　4. Overcome possible objections before they surface by validating your claims.
　　5. Get a positive response.
　　6. Prepare trial-closing questions (step 9).
　　7. Summarize the benefits.
　　8. Ask closed-ended, nonthreatening committing questions.
G. Prepare to handle objections (step 10):
　　1. List the type of objections you may receive.
　　2. Determine how you will overcome or outweigh them.
　　3. Write down your prepared answers.
H. Select closes that would best fit your presentation (step 11):
　　1. Assumptive close (assume prospect will set an appointment).
　　2. Contained-choice close (select proposed options).
　　3. Direct close (to the point).
I. Postclose (step 12):
　　1. Offer words of encouragement to reinforce what took place.
　　2. Prepare additional questions to strengthen sale or presentation.
　　3. Reaffirm prospect's commitment.
　　4. End the call graciously.

5. Never hang up first.
J. Prepare a call-back presentation:
   1. Evaluate prospect's information.
   2. Create additional needs to increase prospect's interest.
   3. Determine possible literature to send.
   4. Make an appointment to call back.

Call Objective Planning Tips.   Here are some exercises you can practice to help you prepare your call objective planning. This will help you to sharpen your newly acquired skills and allow you to think quickly on your feet when live prospecting.

√ Gather your facts and set your goals.

√ Go through each step of the telemarketing call in advance, as it is outlined in this manual, from the *introduction,* step 1, to the *Postclose,* step 12.

√ Think about what you will want to ask, how the prospect might respond, and how you will control the conversation.

√ Make notes on what you decide to include in your presentation on the product information worksheet.

√ Keep your notes in front of you in an organized fashion. You will learn to depend on them less frequently the more you prospect.

Now that you have all the tools to be well-prepared, start completing the call objective worksheet for your *next* prospect!

Tabulating Outbound Activities

Whether or not your telemarketing center is automated, tabulation is a very critical part of operating an outbound telemarketing center. Tabulation provides the company, department, supervisor-manager, and the TSR with information to analyze operational cost, determine budgets, and to evaluate TSRs' performance.

Most software provides tabulation functions and you can customize software to meet your particular needs. The most valuable information typically required is how many dials and contacts were made and what were the results of that activity. Some companies need to know the average length of each call made for budgeting and time management purposes. Tabulating on an automation system will provide you with more accurate information but can be limited, since not all over-the-counter software is capable of fully providing information for each and every company's needs. However, if you are running your telemarketing operation on a manual system, or you prefer to manually tabulate certain information, then you can have a form prepared and customized for your particular needs. (Again, the information is only as accurate as the person performing the tabulation.) For example, if you wanted to know the best times for prospecting, you would tabulate each hour, how many dials were made, and, out of those dials, how many decision makers were available to take your call. Realistically you need to know in advance what the percentage of those figures are so you have something to compare the information with.

When residential prospecting, you would ordinarily dial about 30 to 50 phone numbers per hour and contact approximately 20 to 30 decision makers per hour. These figures reflect dialing manually during prime time for prospecting, such as evenings. If you were on an automated system, then these figures would almost double, especially with a predictive dialer.

Out of the 20 to 30 contacts each hour, you would want to know what happened during the presentation. For example, tabulate how many prospects said, "Call me back at another time," or, during a presentation they interrupted the TSR and said "I'm not interested," or "I need to discuss it over with my partner," or tabulate whether you made a sale or an appointment.

In a business-to-business application the dials-contact ratio is quite different. Instead, the dials would be anywhere from 20 to 30 dials per hour and 5 to 15 contacts per hour. This depends greatly on several particulars. For example, if you need to contact a president or vice president of a company, your contact ratio would not be as high when calling someone who is the head of purchasing or marketing. Also, these figures would vary according to the size of company you are calling into. The larger the company (more employees), the more difficult it is to get to the person who makes the final decision. Often times you may need to go through the "influencer" first in order to get to the final decision maker. This is discussed further in your scripts under "Secretarial Screen Script."

The benefit of tabulating this information is to determine the TSR's strengths and weaknesses; when following the 12-step presentation, you can determine exactly where TSRs went wrong in their presentations. Tabulating is essential not only in determining a telemarketing department's bottom line, but also in enhancing the skill level of the TSR.

When tabulating, there are certain areas you need to look for that will help train both you or your TSRs better. For example, if you are tabulating how many decision makers told you to call them back for some reason or another and this occurred more than five to seven times each hour, then this activity was encouraged. The weakness occurred during two possible steps, either during the request for time, step 3, going *high* on the *I* when saying, " ... *have I."* The other area where this may occur is during the trial close, step 9, when you say, **"Does that sound fair enough,"** and your prospect says, "I need you to call me back at another time." This indicates that the prospect was not convinced, and if you agreed to call the prospect back, you did not use your objection technique, keep selling, to properly overcome this objection. Another area you could tabulate is how many prospects said "I'm not interested" in the first 30 seconds (the first four steps) of your presentation. Remember, if you are getting more than 10 percent of this response, it is being encouraged because you are not following the functions within the steps. For example, if this is occurring after mentioning your company name, then you paused too long and did not immediately use your fifth function, landmark or location, by saying, " ... and we're *located* ... > near the airport." Most of the time you will receive resistance during this critical moment.

Tabulating can determine exactly what you are doing wrong and what you can do to correct it. The quicker you can identify this information, the better you will be at developing good prospecting skills while meeting your department and individual goals.

Best Times for Prospecting

The following information is provided to give you an idea of the best times for prospecting residential and business applications. The time frames for calling are not absolute and could vary depending on where you are and whom you are calling. However, the times are standardized enough to help make it more useful in assisting you as a starting point, especially when prospecting in certain industries that you are not accustomed to. Tabulating your activity will give you a more precise method for determining the best times for prospecting.

Residential.   The best times are listed in order of preference. You will notice certain times are not as good as others. This doesn't indicate that you do not prospect during the low peak times, it is telling you that your contact ratio will be lower and you need to take that into consideration when reporting your tabulation figures. However, for those who are only prospecting on a part-time basis, this will help you to determine the high peak hours that you should consider to have them prospect. In this way you will make your TSRs' time more productive and profitable. The best times are:

Saturday: 10:00 a.m. to 12:00 p.m.

Tuesday, Wednesday, and Thursday: 7:00 p.m. to 8:30 p.m.

Tuesday, Wednesday, and Thursday: 8:30 a.m. to 11:30 a.m.

Tuesday, Wednesday, and Thursday: 3:00 p.m. to 5:00 p.m.

As you have noticed, I did not include Sundays, Mondays, and Fridays. On Sundays, most people, if they are not working themselves, are spending their time with family or church; this is their typical day of rest. Mondays seem to be a more difficult day for calling. People tend to not be as receptive on the beginning day of the week, and during football season you may get the "silence and guttural" treatment such as, "I'm in the middle of my football game, I'm not interested!" or the answering machine is on. On Fridays, people tend to go out for dinner, movie, visit friends.... Not everyone goes out on a Friday night, so you will get people home. However, the contact ratio is so low that it may be more cost-effective to have your TSRs work on Saturdays.

The hours of 5:00 p.m. to 7:00 p.m are prime-time dinner hours for most; you will usually get, "We're eating dinner, I'm not interested!" During the hours of 11:30 a.m. to 3:00 p.m. you will find yourself competing with answering machines, since most people are not at home during these times—they are either shopping, running errands, or working. During the evening from 7:00 p.m. to 8:30 p.m. is an acceptable time to call. However, be sensitive to more of the rural areas and the "mature market" (retired folks), since they tend to end their evenings by 8:30 p.m. The best time for calling them is between 6:30 p.m. and 8:00 p.m.

Again, these are not conclusive. Be flexible but be sensitive. For example, when the president of the United States is speaking or there is a special broadcast the majority of people are watching on television, such as a political election or the Oscars, then during that time you will experience greater resistance. Just use your common sense and be respectful. Whenever you have interrupted people, use your easy close and try to recontact them at a time they suggest is more convenient.

Business to Business.   When calling businesses, it seems there is never a better time to call, at least that is what the typical response is when you ask. However, because of the 12 steps and the secretary screen script, you will have a greater opportunity to overcome this situation. Various professional TSRs who are experts at prospecting business-to-business helped to compile the list of business categories below. Again, they are not conclusive, and you need to be flexible with areas and size of the business.

Attorneys	3:00 to 5:30 p.m.
Chemists	4:00 to 5:30 p.m.
Clergy	Monday to Friday, daytime hours
Contractors	Before 9:00 a.m., after 5:00 p.m.
Dentists	Before 9:30 a.m.
Druggists	1:00 to 3:00 p.m.
Engineers	2:00 to 4:00 p.m.
Executives	After 10:30 a.m.
Farmers	3:00 to 5:00 p.m.
Government employees	At home, 7:00 to 8:30 p.m.
Government officials	2:00 to 5:00 p.m.
Grocers	1:00 to 3:00 p.m.
Homemakers	10:00 to 11:00 a.m., 2:00 to 4:00 p.m.
Merchants	After 10:30 a.m.
Morticians	10:00 to 11:00 a.m.
Nurses	7:00 to 8:30 p.m.
Physicians	9:00 to 11:00 a.m., 1:00 to 3:00 p.m.
Printers	3:00 to 5:00 p.m.
Accountants	Avoid January 1 thru April 30
Publishers	After 3:00 p.m.
Salespeople	8:00 to 11:00 a.m., 3:00 to 5:00 p.m.
Schoolteachers	At home, 7:00 to 8:30 p.m., at school, 3:30 to 5:00 p.m.

Secretaries   10:00 to 11:00 a.m., 2:00 to 4:00 p.m.
Stockbrokers   Before 10:00 a.m., after 3:00 p.m.

Glossary of Terms

An important and helpful feature of this book is this glossary—a select group of terms commonly used in the telemarketing and business telecommunications industry.* Each month, *Telemarketing Magazine* will present new terms and acronyms listed under the "Square One Glossary of Terms"; this is provided in order to give the reader a complete telemarketing vocabulary. *Telemarketing Magazine* has contributed their "square one glossary of terms" to ensure this book will be complete. These terms will give you a clearer understanding of the telemarketing industry to assist you in managing a successful telemarketing operation.

1 Service: An inbound long-distance service that is free to the caller, paid for by the recipient. At one time, this type of incoming long-distance service was offered only by AT&T and the Bell Operating Companies (BOCs), but since divestiture, is also offered by some other common carriers.

Abandoned Call: A call that is canceled by the caller after a connection has been made, but before the conversation takes place.

Additive Queuing: Automatic call distributor (ACD) feature that allows the ACD to place a call into a queue for one or more additional agent groups that would not otherwise take the call.

Ad Hoc Video Teleconference: Video teleconference (see teleconference) designed and set up for a special purpose, and not an ongoing electronic network that remains in place from day to day.

Agree and Probe: To arrive at an understanding and then gain additional information.

American Standard Code of Information Interchange (ASCII): A widely used code that assigns an octal sequence to each letter, number, and selected control characters, adopted by the American Standards Association for transmission of information.

*This glossary is reprinted from *Telemarketing*® magazine, published by Technology Marketing Corporation. One Technology Plaza, Norwalk, CT 06854 USA. Copyright © 1994 Technology Marketing Corporation. All rights reserved. Subscriptions: $49.00 domestic, $69.00 Canada, $85.00 foreign. To order, call toll-free 800-243-6002 or 203-852-6800.

Analog Facsimile: Facsimile in which each millimeter of a document is scanned resulting in a slower transmission speed, but with higher quality.

Analog Signals: Transmission of signals, like voltage, reflecting variations in quantity such as loudness of voice. As opposed to digital signals.

Anti-Glare Filter: Device placed over video display terminal (VDT) screen that is designed to reduce glare and improve contrast.

Area Code: The first three digits of a subscriber's telephone number, which identifies a specific area of the country.

Assumptive Statements: To ask a question which assumes the prospect's response. Presenting a question in the form of a statement.

Asynchronous: Corresponds to one of two ways that data transmitting devices resynchronize. Each character or block has a start and stop element which defines its beginning or end—the transmitter and receiver are resynched at the beginning of each character for smooth transmission.

Attendant: A switchboard operator.

Audio Conferencing: The simplest and most available form of teleconferencing in which three or more people communicate simultaneously in conference style, by telephone, in real-time without visual aid.

Autobauding: Automatic baud rate detection.

Automatic Call Distributor (ACD): Equipment that automatically manages and controls incoming calls, evenly sends calls to the telephone rep who has been idle the longest, answers and queues calls during busy periods, and plays recorded messages for delayed callers. Automatically overflows calls to a secondary group if they are delayed too long and provides management reports on the call activity. The ACD can stand alone or be integrated with a PBX (see **PBX**).

Automatic Dialer: A telephone feature or stand-alone device capable of storing phone numbers in memory and allows user to dial these preprogrammed numbers with one command.

Automatic Gain Control (AGC): A feature built into the amplifier system of a telephone headset that ensures that incoming signal levels do not exceed a fixed pressure or amplifies signal levels that are weak.

Automatic Number Identification (ANI): A feature which automatically identifies the directory number or equipment number of a calling station.

Automatic Redial: A telephone feature that permits the last number dialed to be automatically dialed again at the push of a button.

Automatic Route Selection (ARS): A switching system that chooses the least costly path from available owned or leased circuits. It is transparent to callers (see **Least-Cost Routing**).

Band: The range of frequencies on a single transmission channel, or, with WATS, the geographic area from which the customer can call.

Barge Out Device: A machine that announces the same outgoing message to all callers.

Basic Rate Interface (BRI): Classification of ISDN (integrated services digital network) lines that has two "B," or bearer channels, and one "D" channel, which carries control information and interacts with the network. Serves individual users and local Centrex connections (see **Primary Rate Interface**).

Baud: A unit of signaling speed in telegraphic code. The number of bits per second that can be transmitted in a given computer system.

Behavior Modeling: A training technique that ignores attitudes and shows participants exactly how to implement desirable skills in typical on-the-job situations.

Bell Operating Companies (BOCs): The seven regional phone companies which were divested from AT&T as a result of the AT&T antitrust settlement.

Benefits: Advantages gained.

Binary Digit: A numeral in a base 2 number system.

Binaural: Referring to a headset style which is designed with two receivers so that a conversation is heard by the wearer simultaneously in both ears.

Bits: Stands for binary digit, the smallest unit of binary information, either one or zero.

Bits Per Second (BPS): Rate at which binary encoded information is transmitted over a communication channel.

Blocked Calls: Calls that receive busy signals.

Boiler Room: Refers to telephone selling lacking appropriate professionalism, controls, positive atmosphere, telecommunications equipment, etc.

Boom: A semi-rigid, tube-like apparatus which extends from the headset, placing the mike close to the user's mouth.

Burnout: A phenomenon of exhaustion and lack of motivation often experienced by TSRs working long shifts without the proper training or compensation.

Business-to-Business Telemarketing: Telemarketing to industry.

Business-to-Consumer Telemarketing: Telemarketing to individuals at their residences.

Byte: A group of bits that is considered its own unit. Usually 8-bit or 16-bit bytes.

Cable: Assembly of equipment, such as wire, that carries an electric current and, as an assembly, allows transmission of electric currents separately or in groups.

Call Accounting: Refers to equipment that provides a record of calls placed by extension, time, date, number dialed, and length of call.

Call Center: The location or facility where a telemarketing operation is housed.

Call Detail Recording (CDR): A PBX and electronic key system feature that generates a chronological listing of every call leaving the system, including the extension that made the call, duration of the call, etc.

Call Diverter: Transfers calls from one telephone number to another pre-arranged phone number (see **Call Forwarding**).

Call Forcing: A call distribution feature, it automatically directs a waiting call onto an available agent as soon as that person has completed a previous call. The agent receives an audible tone burst that signals the call coming through. A button need not be pressed to receive this call.

Call Forwarding: A telephone feature that programs calls to be directed to an individual at another station or outside location without the caller having to dial the alternative number.

Call Management: Process of selecting and managing optimum mix of equipment, network services, and labor to achieve maximum productivity from a telemarketing center.

Call Management System: Equipment which gives detailed information on telephone activity and cost.

Call Outline: A call outline is a sales dialog designed to guide TSRs through pertinent data they need to obtain or discuss while using their own judgment and choice of wording.

Call Parking: By "placing" a call on hold or an imaginary extension ("parking it"), the call can be retrieved from any other phone within the system.

Call Queuing: Places incoming call in a waiting line for access to an operator station.

Call Restriction: The precise range of calling power given to employees. The system is designed so that, for instance, certain phone users will only be permitted to make internal calls, and only selected personnel will be able to make long-distance calls.

Call Sequencer: Distributes incoming calls by allowing operators to make the decision on longest idle calls. Has basic management information reports. Also makes announcements to callers in overload situations.

Camp-On: Allows an incoming call to wait on a line until it is available, at which time the call goes through automatically.

Carpal Tunnel Syndrome (CTS): Type of repetitive stress injury in which inflammation of the wrist tendons occurs. Often associated with video display terminal use.

Carriers: Transmission facilities suppliers.

Cash On Delivery (C.O.D.): Method of payment where a respondent buys a product over the telephone and pays when it is received.

Cathode Ray Tube (CRT): The viewing screen of a computer terminal.

Cellular Radio Telephony: Technology using radio transmission to access telephone network. Geographical areas are divided into coverage areas called "cells" which contain low-powered antennae that transmit and receive telephone calls which are ultimately connected to a central computerized switch. When a caller moves out of a cell's antenna range, the switch automatically routes the transmission to another cell.

Census Tract: An area within a zip code group that denotes households with uniform social and economic characteristics.

Central Office (CO): Telephone company facility where subscriber's lines are joined to switching equipment for connecting other subscribers to each other, locally and long-distance.

Central Processing Unit (CPU): The part of the computer that interprets and executes commands.

Centrex: A centrally located, multiline business service offered by local exchange carriers that employs those carriers' central office switching and transmission facilities to permit subscribers to intercommunicate within their organization and access the public switched network.

Channel Bank: An interface device that converts telephone signals from analog to digital or digital to analog.

Closed-ended Question: Used to elicit a specific ordered choice answer of *a*, *b*, or *c*, or an unordered choice where the customer can choose more than one specific answer. Also questions that are designed to get only a "yes" or "no" response. Each question begins with a Have, Would, Could, Is, Are, Does, Did, etc.

Closing: The act of consummating a sale or scheduling an appointment over the phone.

Cluster Workstations: A workstation configuration in which stations are "clustered" or grouped together into a unit that radiates from a central core. Designed to make more efficient use of space in facilities such as large telemarketing centers.

Clustering: Grouping names on a telemarketing list according to geographic, demographic or psychographic characteristics.

Coaxial Cable: A wire cable over which voice, data, and video traffic can be transmitted at much higher frequencies than a single-wire pair.

Codec: A device which converts digital signals into analog for transmission over voice-grade analog lines.

Cold Calling: Making sales calls to an audience that is unfamiliar with the caller.

Committee Consultatif International Pour Telegraphic Et Telephonie (CCITT) International Telegraph And Telephone Consultative Committee: An advisory committee to the ITU, a telecommunications agency of the United Nations, that recommends international policies that affect the international telecommunications industries. For instance, this committee specified standards for uniform compatibility of competitive facsimile machines to allow standardized communication.

Common Carriers: Provide transmission for voice, data, video, and facsimile over wholly owned and/or leased facilities. The three largest are AT&T, MCI, and Sprint.

Communications: The exchange of information by means of a system, such as mail or telecommunications, in order to successfully communicate. Message must be sent and received to communicate.

Communicator Call Report (CCR): Identifies, for each telephone sales representative, what calls were handled, the date, the contact name, and all information pertaining to the details of each call made during a shift.

Computer-Telephone Integration (CTI): The merging of computer and telephone technologies to provide users with strategic communications applications.

Consultative Selling: Personalized method of sales that first identifies a customer's needs and then sells a product or service to meet those needs.

Contact Management: The process of organizing and prioritizing account information, such as appointments, call backs, information sent, and customer data. *Note:* Today, computerized contact-management software handles a multitude of simultaneous tasks, and the possibilities for the future are virtually endless.

Consultative Committee for International Telegraph and Telephone (CCITT): Advisory committee to the ITU, a telecommunications agency of the United Nations, that recommends international telecommunications industries. For example, the committee specified standards for uniform compatibility of competitive fax machines to allow standardized communication.

Copy Holder: Computer accessory that holds a computer user's copy or documents. Designed to reduce eye and neck strain.

Cordless Phone: A telephone without wires that utilizes FM frequency for transmission.

Cost Per Thousand (CPM): Common rate for list rentals where fee is based on every 1,000 names rented to the telemarketer.

Creating a Need: A final question is asked during the probing step that the prospect is most likely unable to answer. The typical response would be, "I don't know," "I haven't." This type of question serves to create doubt in the prospect's mind, giving you a better opportunity to create the need for your products or service.

Cross Selling: Selling an additional product or service while servicing a customer.

Customer Cycling: Planned, regular contact to previous customers.

Customer Premises Equipment (CPE): Telephone equipment provided by a customer and connected to telco facilities.

Customer Profile: Pertinent information about a customer, including purchase history, address and phone number, demographic, and psychographic information.

Customer Service Representative (CSR): One who handles client concerns, complaints, and inquiries.

Data Base: A collection of data to support the requirements and requests for information of a specific group of users. The difference between data and information can best be illustrated by imagining all the names and telephone numbers from a phone book written on different pieces of paper and thrown into a barrel. The barrel contains a huge amount of data, but unless it is organized (as in the phone book) its value as information is questionable.

Data Communications Equipment (DCE): Equipment that connects data terminal equipment (DTE), such as modems.

Data over Voice (DOV): A process in which the same wires are used for both telephones and computer terminals for simultaneous voice and data communications.

Data Processing: The manipulation of data for the purpose of producing desired information. It involves functions such as recording, classifying, sorting, summarizing, calculating, dissemination, and storing data. A computer or word processing system merely automates these functions and reduces the amount of human intervention required to perform these tasks.

Data Terminal Equipment (DTE): Includes the computer and terminal equipment.

Dedicated Line: A communications line provided to an organization that is used by that organization only.

Defuse: To cool down an irate prospect or customer.

Demographics: A description of the vital statistics of an audience or population. Includes personal characteristics, name, title, occupation, address, phone number, etc.

Detailed Station Message Accounting (DSMA): Specifies details of numbers of called, listing the most often reached areas, etc. Can highlight system abuses and pinpoint or lead to optimum configurations.

Digital Facsimile: Facsimile in which only portions of a document that contain copy are scanned to transmit at high speeds.

Digital Signals: Transmission signals where information is encoded in binary digits. As opposed to analog signals.

Direct Close: A technique used to conclude a sale over the phone in which the salesperson directly asks the prospect if he or she would like to buy a product or service.

Direct Distance Dialing (DDD): Long-distance calling that does not utilize operators.

Direct-in Lines: If one department or employee receives the bulk of incoming calls, direct-in lines allow regular callers to reach the people they need without going through the central console, thus speeding call handling and giving the attendant more time to extend courtesy to others.

Direct Inward Dialing (DID): A system in which a company buys a package of numbers, usually in lots of 100, and assigns individual users access numbers of their own so they can call into the office and receive an outside trunk connected to the company (see **Direct Inward System Access**).

Direct Inward System Access (DISA): A telephone feature which allows an individual who is away from the office to call into a special number at the office, dial an access code and receive an outside company trunk including WATS, Tie lines, etc. (see **Direct Inward Dialing**).

Direct Mail: Printed matter, usually carrying a sales message or announcement, designed to elicit response from a carefully selected consumer or business market.

Direct Marketing: Use of one or more media to most effectively elicit the transfer of goods and services to the buyer.

Direct Marketing Association (DMA): Organization representing special interests of those in the business of direct mail and direct marketing. Has subgroups, including Telephone Marketing.

Direct Response: Response as a result of receiving an advertised message through any media.

Direct Sales: A sales group that is employed by the manufacturer that sells to the end users.

Dish: Satellite receiving device also known as a downlink.

Display: Viewing device to show the picture at a video teleconference. Television monitors and video projection systems are displays.

Display Telephones: Sometimes called smart phones—provide an English language display of the extensions calls are forwarded to and under what circumstances—no answers, busy signals, etc.

Distributor: Distributors typically stock a manufacturer's product and resell it to end users. Usually the distributor provides some level of customer support and service.

Divestiture: The ruling by U.S. District Judge Harold Green, as part of the AT&T antitrust settlement, whereby AT&T was ordered to sever ties with all seven Regional Bell Operating Companies (RBOCs).

Drop Closing: The process of completing a sale by offering top-of-the-line items or services and moving to lower ranges.

Dual Tone Multi-Frequency (DTMF): Refers to push-button or touch-tone phones.

Earth Stations: The antennae and associated equipment used to receive and/or transmit signals via satellite.

Easy Close: To gracefully back-off from your presentation and attempt to keep the door open for future contact.

Electronic Communication Systems: PBX and key telephone systems (EPBX and EKTS) which have replaced the older electro-mechanical switches and relays with microprocessor "chips."

Electronic Mail: The process of sending messages electronically from a computer terminal to another terminal or printer.

Encryption: The encoding of a message or data for transmission to eliminate understandable reception by unauthorized parties.

End User: The organization that buys and uses the product.

Ergonomics: The study of the problems of people adjusting to their environment; especially the science that seeks to adapt work or working conditions to suit the workers.

Establishing Wants: Asking questions to determine the prospect's needs.

Facsimile (FAX): A method of information transfer of text. Image is scanned by the Fax, transmitted over telephone lines, and reconstructed and duplicated at receiving Fax.

Features: The product or service you are promoting.

Federal Communications Commission (FCC): A federal agency whose duty is to regulate communication by wire and radio—including licensing of the two.

Fiber Optics: Cable made of thin filaments of glass through which light can be transmitted for long distances.

Final Mile or Last Mile: Electronic facilities connecting the downlink to the viewing site for video teleconferencing.

First Mile: A nonliteral term referring to the electronic facilities required to get the television signal from the point of origin to the uplink to facilitate a video teleconference.

Fixed Receiving Dish: A permanently mounted satellite receiving apparatus.

Follow-Up System: An automated or manual telemarketing system that keeps track of calls that should be recycled into the outgoing program and rescheduled at a later time. Its purpose is to trap information and release it back to communicators at the appropriate time.

Foot Rest: Ergonomic device designed to support a computer user's feet, easing leg and back stress.

Foreign Exchange Lines (FX): Provide local telephone service from a central office which is outside (foreign to) the subscriber's switching area.

Frequency: The rate of a transmission current—measured in Hertz.

Fulfillment System: For calls that require sending follow-up materials to the prospect or purchaser, its purpose is to produce the fulfillment package or lists for fulfillment operations. Very often, a word processing system is utilized in meeting this requirement.

Full Duplex: Communications system or equipment capable of simultaneous transmission in two directions.

Functions: The features of the product or service you are promoting. What the product or service does, its size, weight, shape, and performance.

Getting Reaction: Asking an open-ended probing question once you have completed your selling step. This determines if you have fulfilled the prospect's or customer's needs.

Guided Scripting: The use of key words or prompters rather than fully worded scripts to guide TSRs through sales process.

Hardware: Physical equipment excluding functional software properties, i.e., the housing cabinets.

Hertz (Hz): Unit of signal frequency equal to one cycle per second.

Hybrid System: A phone system that combines the attributes of both key and PBX systems. A hybrid operates like a key system, providing direct access to outside line, and like a PBX, with incoming and outgoing calls routed through a central switch.

Implied Benefits: Indicating specifically the particular "good" that someone may gain by accepting your offer.

In-Band: ISDN (integrated services digital network) terms used in connection with ANI (automatic number identification) or Caller ID. The in-band ANI signal is delivered without a "D" channel, either before the first ring or between the first and second ring (see **Out-of-Band, Basic Rate Interface, Primary Rate Interface**).

Inbound: Calls that are received by a telemarketing call center (see **Outbound**).

In-House Telemarketing: Telemarketing done within a corporation as a supplementary or primary method of marketing and selling that company's own products.

Incentive Program: A program designed to motivate employees and optimize their performance through the expectation of a reward. Incentive programs, often implemented through contests, may reward employees with gifts, time off with pay, trips, or cash awards.

Indirect Sales: A small sales group that is employed by the manufacturer that sells to resellers.

Integrated Services Digital Network: Project within CCITT to standardize network digital transmission services worldwide so that voice, data, and pictures can be mixed and transmitted between any equipment with ISDN capabilities.

Integrated Voice/Data Terminal (IVDT): A system that includes a terminal, keyboard/display and a telephone, and may contain some processing power.

Intercom Callback Request: An electronic message left by someone within an organization, for someone who is out of the office or tied up on the phone. The internal caller's station number appears on the digital readout display of the other person's phone automatically.

Interconnect Companies: Companies that supply telephone equipment, other than the serving telephone company.

Integrated Marketing: The synergistic combination of a variety of marketing techniques to achieve superior sales results.

Jack: Device that allows wiring of a circuit to be temporary. Plug can be inserted or removed to connect or disconnect circuit.

Keep Selling: Make prospects accountable for what they previously agreed to during "get reaction" (after the selling step), then offer additional features and benefits that the prospects haven't considered.

Keyboard Drawer: Drawer mounted on or beneath desktop or set below computer monitor, designed to house a computer keyboard. Allows computer operator to position keyboard at comfortable angle, and provides storage and protection when keyboard is not in use.

Key Service Unit (KSU): The housing for the electric or electronic circuits that operate the features in key system telephones.

Key System: Phone system characterized by buttons or "keys" which correspond to outside lines coming into the system and can be pressed to access outside lines. Since outside lines are common to all stations, calls can be answered from any phone eliminating the need for calls to be answered by an operator at a central console or switchboard.

Lead Qualification: Determination, by telemarketing, of customer's level of interest, willingness and ability to buy a product or service.

Leads: Potential clients that have been pre-screened by telemarketing or direct contact.

Leased Telephone Lines: The permanent connection of two transmitting devices to an office. These are economical if used more than a few hours per day.

Least-Cost Routing (LCR): Equipment that automatically makes a decision for the users as to the most economical method of calling telephone numbers; routing outgoing calls via the most cost-effective lines available to the system.

Line: A transmission wire within a telephone system; part of a local loop that connects a subscriber to the central office.

Line Capacity: The total number in-house telephones that a switch can accommodate.

List: A compilation of information that typically provides names, addresses, phone numbers, and possibly other information in greater detail.

List Management System: A database system that manages customer and prospect lists. Its major function is to merge and purge duplicates between in-house lists and those obtained from outside sources. It is also utilized to select names for both direct mail promotions and outgoing telemarketing programs.

Local Access and Transport Area (LATA): Geographic regions served by the Bell Operating Companies (BOCs). Intra-LATA (local) telephone rates are regulated while Inter-LATA (long-distance) rates are now deregulated.

Local Area Network (LAN): A privately owned network (see **Network**) which integrates voice, data, and video technologies and supports this communication within a few miles.

Local Exchange Carriers: Regional Bell Operating Companies (RBOCs) and approximately 1500 other operating companies that provide local services and connections to long-distance carriers.

Look-Up Service: A service organization that adds telephone numbers to lists.

Magnetic Tape: A film for storing electronically recorded data; often in list formats to allow computerized matching with other lists for purposes of appending phone numbers or eliminating duplicates.

Management Information System (MIS): System, automated or manual, that provides sales support information for both the sales representative to enhance sales activity and management to evaluate sales performance.

Manufacturer's Representatives (Rep): A rep acts as an agent of the manufacturer and typically has a defined territory or vertical market.

Market: The total of all individuals or organizations that represent potential buyers.

Marketing Mix: The various marketing elements and strategies that must be used together to achieve maximum effectiveness.

Market Research: A research methodology that obtains information from prospective customers to develop marketing and sales programs.

Market Share: The percentage of customers that a company has based upon the total of potential customers a company markets to.

Merge-Purge: Combining two or more lists for list enhancement, suppression, or duplication elimination by a computerized matching process.

Messages-on-Hold: Professionally produced, prerecorded audio message programs that impart sales, marketing, or informational messages to incoming callers who are waiting on hold.

Micro, Mini, and Mainframe Computer Systems: With the current explosion in capabilities at the low end of computing (micros), even with the computer industry it is almost impossible to present a firm definition differentiating one from the other. Currently, the main differentiating factors are those of cost, processing speeds, storage capabilities, number of terminals supported, and microprocessing capabilities.

Microphone Mute Switch: A device that allows headset wearers to turn off their microphones so as not to be heard by the party to whom they are connected.

Microwave System: Communication of voice, video, and data by transmitting signals between land-based antennae. A broadcast medium which can carry many thousands of voice channels without the use of cable.

Modem: A device that converts computer generated digital signals into analog (voice) signals, or vice versa, to allow transmission over telephone lines.

Monaural: A headset built with one receiver so that sound is transmitted to the user in only one ear.

Monitoring: The ability to listen in on telephone conversations, usually for TSR training. Also known as "service observing."

Multiplexer: Allows one telephone line to be shared by several terminals. (Also spelled "multiplexor.")

Network: A series of communications channels or telephone lines that connect, as in a basic data communications system, a central computer, modems, and a remote terminal.

No-ops: "No-ops" occur when an outbound call made by a power or predictive dialing systems is answered with no operator available to talk to the party the instant the connection is made.

Noise Canceling: A feature of some telephone headsets that drastically reduces or eliminates background noise.

Nonblocking: Within a telephone system, all station instruments can be used simultaneously for either incoming or outgoing calls. Designed to reduce busy conditions.

Objection: When prospect or customer is not in agreement with you. An expression of opposition or disapproval.

Off-Net: Meaning off the network. Commonly used in conjunction with *other common carriers,* referring to geographic areas not accommodated by a long-distance service company.

One-A-2 (1A2) Key System: The earliest key systems. A generic term referring to a low featured, electromechanical key telephone system.

One-Ring Dialer: Single-line telephone instrument that automatically dials a predetermined telephone number when the receiver is lifted off the hook.

Open-Ended Question: Sales technique designed to elicit respondents' replies in their own words, as opposed to giving a "yes" or "no" response. Each question begins with a Who, What, Where, Why, When, How, Explain, Describe, and Share.

Operating Telephone Company (OTC): A user's local telephone company.

Original Equipment Manufacturer (OEM): The manufacturer of equipment that is marketed by another vendor and usually sold under the name of the reseller. Often, the OEM makes only one component of a system that is then configured with other software or hardware.

Other Common Carrier (OCC): Also called specialized or alternative common carriers. Companies offering long-distance telephone service in competition with AT&T, the common carrier.

Out-of-Band: Refers to the ISDN (integrated services digital network) "D" channel. Information, such as ANI (automatic number identification) is delivered separately from the main transmission line (see **In-Band, Basic Rate Interface, Primary Rate Interface**).

Outbound: Calls that are placed by the telemarketing center (see **Inbound**).

Packet Switching: The transmission of multiple data streams over a single common transmission path. Packet switching services are allocated to customers in a fixed amount of transmission or bandwidth on the channel whether the customer is actually transmitting data or not.

Para Sales Force: A side team that works along side of another sales team either on the telephone or in the field as a supplement to the other.

Peg Count: A tally of the number of calls made—or received—over a set period of time.

Phonathon: Conducting a fund-raising effort by phone.

Pilot: Trial program designed to test feasibility of a potential telemarketing program.

Ping-Pong: The prospect and TSR/CSR exchange—combat for control by allowing the prospect to go back and forth with objections.

Pixels: Individual dots of light that make up the characters on a video display terminal.

Plain Old Telephone (POT): A single line telephone.

Polling: A means of controlling and allowing orderly flow of communication lines—data to central location or telephone calls to and from two points.

Port: A point of access into communications switch—a computer, a network, etc.

Port Oriented: A multiterminal voice frequency transmission network of an indeterminate number of terminals. A port may be two-wire or four-wire, and one-way in, one-way out, or two-way.

Postclose: Reaffirm what the prospect agreed to and ask additional questions to gain information prior to sending information or finalizing an appointment or a sale. Also, to reaffirm an appointment or delivery dates.

Precall Planning: Preparation before a sales call to promote maximum effectiveness.

Predictive Dialer: Type of auto-dialing technology that uses a pacing algorithm to determine the rate at which calls are placed by "predicting" information about calls, such as call length or number of calls that will be answered. User-adjustable; often screens out busy and unanswered calls.

Prerecorded Messages: Taped messages, often recorded by celebrities or authority figures, which are played to inbound callers or interjected within an outbound call.

Presentation: A dialog that helps you to organize what to say to the prospect or customer. This is also called a "call guide."

Primary Rate Interface (PRI): Classification of ISDN (integrated services digital network) lines. Based on T-1 service with 24 channels, 23 of which are "B," or bearer channels, and a "D" channel, which carries control information and interacts with the network (see **Basic Rate Interface**).

Private Automatic Branch Exchange (PABX): An automatic telephone switch that serves various telephone sets within a business and also accesses the public network.

Private Branch Exchange (PBX): A private phone switching system allowing communication within a business and between the business and the public network. Calls are received at a centralized console for rerouting or can be designated to individuals. Modern PBXs are automated and called PABXs (Private Automatic Branch Exchanges).

Private Network: A network operated by a private organization or corporation.

Proactive Telemarketing: Seller initiated or outbound calling.

Probing Questions: Questions that explore, investigate, gain information, etc. that will help you to direct your presentation.

Product Mix: A product that complements the reseller's other product lines or fills a void.

Programmable Toll Restrictions: Allows you to restrict various phones from dialing certain or all long-distance areas.

Prospect: A potential client.

Protocol: The established format for sending and receiving messages.

Psychographics: A description of the lifestyle and attitudinal statistics of a target market.

Public Utility Commission (PUC): Regulatory body within a state that regulates intrastate utilities, including telecommunications.

Pulse Amplitude Modulation (PAM): Analog speech signal is sampled at specific short intervals to produce a series of pulses identical in duration but of various patterns, imitating the original speech wave.

Pulse Code Modulation (PCM): The most frequently used method of converting analog signals into digital bits. The process involves transforming an analog wave into quantified steps, assigning the wave a discrete set of values, sampling it periodically, and coding the values of those samples into a digital bit stream. At the receiving end, the digital codes are transformed back into analog value and the original signal is reconstructed.

Qualifying: To ask questions that will identify your specific market. This is used in the probing step and identified with the letter Q.

Queue: A function that holds all inward bound calls in the order in which they arrive until the next available agent takes the first in line, moving the next call into the front position.

Reactive Telemarketing: Customer-initiated buying by telephone (inbound calling).

Real Time: Processing transactions as they occur, instead of, for example, holding all orders and batching them into a group at the end of the day.

Reflect: Making the prospect and customer accountable for the information they previously gave you during the time you were asking probing questions.

Regional Bell Holding Company (RBHC): One of the seven "baby bells" separated from AT&T by divestiture that provide regulated and nonregulated telephone services. The seven Bell Holding Companies are: NYNEX, BellSouth, Pacific Telesis, U.S. West, Southwestern Bell Corporation, Bell Atlantic, and Ameritech.

Rejection: To refuse. Not in agreement.

Remote Diagnostics and Maintenance: Allows a service technician from a remote location to connect into a system processor in order to diagnose and correct problems or test and modify the system program.

Remote Network: Beyond the physical scope of one building (see Network).

Repetitive Stress Injuries (RSI): Upper-limb discomfort or pain resulting from the performance of repetitive tasks, such as computer keyboarding.

Request for Proposal (RFP): A proforma device for outlining specific purchasing requirements that can be responded to in kind by vendors.

Response Rate: Percentage of return. In the case of an advertised 800 number, the percentage rate of call-in responses to that advertisement.

Restate: To summarize prospect's answers from your probing questions and get a confirmation that this summary is correct.

Restate and Probe: To summarize prospect's objection response but say it with a more positive rendition and then get a confirmation that the summary is correct.

Roll-Out: Full-blown telemarketing effort after an initial test.

Routing: The assignment of a communications path for a telephone call to reach its destination.

RS-232-C: The most common interface used between computers and modems.

Sales Conversion Rate: Number of sales in relation to number of calls initiated or received.

Satellite Transmission: Satellites establish a communications link using microwave transmission. The satellite receives microwave signals at a given frequency (the uplink) and transmits them at a given frequency (the downlink). The frequency is changed to avoid interference between the weak signal and the powerful outgoing signal.

Screening: Evaluation of who is calling and why that person is calling by someone other than the decision maker, usually a secretary.

Script: A prepared text presentation that is closely followed by sales personnel as a tool to convey a sales message in its entirety.

Sectional Center Facility (SCF): Geographic area designated by the first three digits of the zip code.

Seeding: Dummy names "planted" in a mailing list to check usage, delivery, or unauthorized reuse.

Segmentation: The process of separating characteristic groups within a list for target marketing.

Shared Tenant Services: The sharing of equipment, facilities, and other resources such as telephone and data transmission, air-conditioning, heating, elevators, etc., by separate establishments residing within a common building or office complex.

Silence of Guttural Utterances: The prospect is not participating, either has hung up, or shows no interest early-on in the presentation.

Site Selection: An organized and systematic process of choosing the best location for your business, taking into account geography, demographics, overhead/cost-of-living, labor supply, and availability of necessary technologies and services.

Software: The intelligent program within a computer that makes the system function.

Source Identification: An audible identification of where the next call an agent is receiving is originating from in terms of geographic location. Part of an ACD system.

Space Segment: Satellite portion of a video teleconference network.

Speed Dial: A telephone feature which allows frequently dialed numbers to be programmed and stored for one-button dialing.

Standard Industrial Classification (SIC): Used to segment telephone calling lists and direct marketing mailing lists; classifies businesses as defined by the U.S. Department of Commerce.

Stated Benefits: Money or time the prospect/client will make or save by your offering.

Station Message Detail Recording (SMDR): Provides a record of telephone system call activity including station (or attendant) numbers, starting time, call duration, and trunk groups. (SMDR does not provide the cost of the call.)

Sub-distributor: A smaller reseller that works primarily for a distributor. It may or may not inventory products or provide technical support.

Success Model: A set of logical steps followed by successful salespeople to sell a product or service. Used as a training example for new salespeople.

Surge Suppressor: Power protection device that is designed to protect electronic equipment and data from potentially damaging high-voltage spikes and surges.

Switch: Equipment that is designed to set up and route communication paths between individual extensions.

Switched Telephone Lines: Identical to those used in the home. Provide dial-up service between devices in which only the time connected is billed.

System Integrator (SI): An SI usually provides a large turnkey system to an end user that includes multiple vendor's products. SIs are especially geared to work with the government.

T-1: A T-1 trunk is a direct digital line to a telephone company's long-distance switch. It is the equivalent of 24 local, analog lines.

Tape Library: Equipment designed to automatically play a variety of outgoing messages to callers.

Target Market: The most likely group—based on any number of criteria—determined to have the highest potential to buy a product or service.

Tariff: The formal process and published rate for communications services, equipment, and facilities to be provided to the user from the communications carrier.

Technical Support: Training and assistance with technical problems.

Telco: A telephone operating company.

Telecollections: The process of utilizing telemarketing skills to contact debtors and collect outstanding debts.

Telecommunications: Any electrical transmission of voice or data from sender to receiver(s), including telegraphy, telephony, data transmission.

Telecommuting: The practice of employees working in their homes while linked to the office by telephone and, in most cases, a computer.

Telemarketing: The discipline that puts advanced telecommunications technology to work as part of a well-organized and well-managed marketing program. It uses sophisticated management information systems and emphasizes the use of personal selling skills to help companies keep in close contact with their customers, increase sales, and enhance business productivity, all while reducing costs.

Telemarketing Service Vendor: One who sells the service of conducting telemarketing calls. Also called telemarketing agencies and telemarketing service bureaus.

Telemedia: Refers to the use of the phone, interactive voice and fax services for marketing, advertising, promotion, entertainment, or information-provision purposes. Combines 900 pay-per-call and 800 access with audio, fax, data, and live operator.

Telephone List Appending: The adding of telephone numbers to mailing lists.

Telephone Preference Service (TPS): A program of the DMA which allows consumers who do not want telemarketing calls to have their names removed from a majority of telemarketers' lists with one request.

Telephone Record Control: A device used to record and/or monitor both sides of a telephone conversation based on on-hook or off-hook condition.

Telephone Sales Representative (TSR): Also referred to as telemarketers or agents—those who market and sell by phone.

Telephone Sales Supervisor (TSS): Position that oversees the performance of TSRs (telephone sales representatives).

Telephony: The electrical transmission of sound. Also the manufacture and technology of telephone equipment.

Teleprinter: Equipment used to "electrically" transmit data from one point to another. Also called a teletypewriter.

Television Receive Only (TVRO): Commonly refers to a dish that can only receive a satellite signal and cannot transmit.

Telex: A public switched communications network which links remote teleprinters that communicate with hard copy output. A connection is established over common carrier transmission lines and the receiving terminal prints out the incoming message. Teleprinters are leased from a common carrier.

Test Market: Trial market for a new product or service or offer.

Tickler File: A reminder system used in a telemarketing operation to track call-backs and leads.

Tie Lines: Two-way transmission voice circuits that directly connect PBXs or LANs.

Time Division Multiplexing (TDM): A process which divides a single communications path into a number of time slots and assigns each signal its own intermittently repeated time slot.

Time Zone Sequencing: Preparation of national telemarketing lists according to time zones so calls can be made at the most productive times.

Transportable Earth Station (TES): A portable uplink which can be transported to an origination site.

Trial Close: Prior to the final "close," you would summarize the benefits one last time then get a commitment by asking a closed-ended question using the assumptive statement technique.

Trunk: A communications channel linking a central office with a PBX or other terminal equipment. A trunk is a local line originating from the telephone company central office to a business telephone system, terminating in a PBX.

Trunk Capacity: The number of outgoing circuits connecting a site to the telephone company.

Trunk Queue: Capability that puts a call into a queue when lines are not available for an outside call. The caller's phone automatically rings as soon as a line becomes available to place a call.

Turnkey System: A complete communications system, fully assembled by one vendor and sold as one package.

Turnover: The ratio of the number of workers employed as compared to those hired to replace those who have left over a given period of time.

Twisted Wire Cable: Twisted wire cable is insulated copper wire twisted in pairs to minimize electromagnetic interference between one pair and another when they are packed into a large cable. These cables are the primary path (the local loop) between a subscriber's premises and the telephone company's local central office.

Uniform Call Distributor (UCD): A telephone device that puts telephone agents in uniform line, and routes calls not to the next available agent, but to the available agent closest to the top of the line.

Uninterruptable Power System (UPS): Power protection device that is designed to prevent breaks or interruptions in a facility's power supply and provides back-up power.

Uplink: Transmitting equipment that sends television signals to satellites.

Valued-Added Reseller (VAR): A VAR provides enhanced product offering by adding value to a vendor's product. This may be accomplished through the use of hardware, software, or service.

Vendor: A company that furnishes telemarketing products or services to clients.

Verbatim Script: A verbatim script is a complete word-for-word sales dialog designed for TSRs to follow through the entire call without deviating from the format, content, or style.

Vertical Market: A group of prospects or businesses that have similar functions.

Video Display Terminal (VDT): A computer terminal screen.

Video Teleconferencing: The use of live, closed-circuit TV, transmitted by microwave and/or satellite to facilitate communications between groups of people at two or more locations.

Videotex: Computer systems which transmit text and graphic information for display on television. The heart of a videotex system is a computer database which stores the pages.

Voice Input: The process of commanding a computer to function with speech, as opposed to using a keyboard.

Voice Mail: Multi-user, disk-based voice response device. Allows voice interaction between caller and device, transferring information from an authorized user to a separate database. Typically a human verbal message is recorded and converted into a recognizable format by the computer to be stored for retrieval.

Voice Output: The ability of a computerized machine to communicate in an audio mode.

Voice Recognition: Ability of a device to recognize the meaning and act upon the words of a human voice, such as voice-to-text computer application without the use of a keyboard.

Voice Response: Type of voice technology in which callers communicate with a computer via telephone. Usually, the keypad on a touch-tone phone is used to enter and retrieve computer data or prerecorded audio information.

Voice Technology: An umbrella term that covers three distinct technologies: voice mail, interactive voice response (IVR), and voice recognition. All three technologies allow callers to use a phone to communicate with another person or with a computer without having to wait to speak to a "live" person.

Wrist Rest: A device designed to prevent repetitive stress injuries in computer keyboard users by supporting the wrists, holding them in the proper keyboarding position.

WATS (Wide Area Telecommunications Service): A discounted long-distance service. Prior to divestiture, it was available from only AT&T and the BOCs; but it is now also provided by many of the OCCs.

Workstations: The area where telephone reps perform their jobs (see also Integrated Voice/Data Terminal).

Zip (Zone Improvement Program) Code: Registered trademark of the U.S. Postal Service. Five- or nine-digit code that identifies regions in the United States.

Index

About the Author

Kathy Sisk is the founder and President of Telemarketing Consulting Services, which provides training and consultation for telemarketing sales and customer services nationwide and internationally. Clients who have used her 12-Step Training Courses include Citicorp, Coca-Cola, Prudential, Century 21 International, MCI, and IBM. You may contact the author or one of her staff by calling 1-800-UROLEPL (876-5375) should you have questions regarding this field.